MEDIA POWER IN POLITICS

MEDIA POWER IN POLITICS

Doris A. Graber, editor
University of Illinois at Chicago

a division of
Congressional Quarterly Inc.
1414 22nd Street, N.W., Washington, D.C. 20037

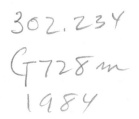

Printed in the United States of America

Library of Congress Cataloging in Publication Data

Graber, Doris A. (Doris Appel), 1923-

    Media power in politics.

    1. Mass media — Political aspects — United States. 2. Mass media — Social aspects — United States. I. Title.
HN90.M3G72   1984   302.2′34   83-23921
ISBN 0-87187-285-4

For triple M, double K, and G plus X.
To put their world into perspective

TABLE OF CONTENTS

PREFACE

Interest in the media's role in American politics has been growing by leaps and bounds. So have the numbers of published studies exploring various aspects of this role. Courses focusing on the media's influence on politics have multiplied, but the supply of texts designed for use in these courses has lagged.

This text solves the perennial problem of finding ways to expose students to the best literature in a growing field without burdening them with an excessive amount of reading and countless trips to the library's reserve room. As described fully in the Introduction, *Media Power in Politics* provides a carefully selected collection of essays that lends itself to use at undergraduate and graduate levels.

The book is intended for courses on mass media and politics, public opinion, political communication, and mass media and society. It is also suitable as supplementary reading in American government courses and in courses focusing on public policy formation. The approach throughout is interdisciplinary, drawing from several social sciences as well as from media and government professionals.

The book is divided into six sections, prefaced by introductions, which signal major areas of media impact. A brief commentary precedes each article highlighting its major contribution and introducing the author(s). The selections reprinted in *Media Power in Politics* follow the originals in all essential matters. Deletions, editorial inserts, and minor changes are clearly marked. Footnotes have been renumbered when necessary to maintain unbroken sequences. Factual errors, such as wrong dates and misspelled names, have been corrected.

The 37 selections in the book represent the work of 62 authors. Many of them are known nationally and internationally; others have just begun careers that promise to earn them distinction. I thank all of them for the contributions they have made to the understanding of media power and for their willingness to allow me to include their work in this collection of readings. Thanks also are due to the many publishers who consented to my use of selections that originally appeared in their books and journals.

The final shape of *Media Power in Politics* owes a great deal to the staff at Congressional Quarterly and to the perceptive, unnamed readers who reviewed the initial proposal. Special thanks are due to Joanne Daniels, director of CQ Press, and Janet Hoffman, project editor. Able research and technical assistance was provided by Sharon O'Donnell and Robert Cohen. I am grateful for their diligence and skill.

Doris A. Graber

MEDIA POWER IN POLITICS

INTRODUCTION

The literature dealing with mass media's impact on politics has been expanding rapidly in recent years, in the wake of evidence that media influence is pervasive and profound. Research efforts have been diverse, including examinations of the news media's influence on the political beliefs of average individuals, studies of the use of the media to advance group interests, and assessments of media impact on domestic and foreign politics. The abundance of the literature makes it difficult for newcomers to the field to gain an overview of its substantive knowledge and research approaches. A book of readings simplifies the task.

Media Power in Politics offers a representative sampling of the best research in the field and serves as a guide to further exploration of selected areas of knowledge. The essays emphasize mass media effects on the political system in general and on political subsystems, such as Congress and the executive branch, political parties, organized lobbies, and the poor and powerless. The changes brought about in the structure and functions of such groups through their interactions with the mass media have profound political consequences for these groups and for American politics. The nature and magnitude of such changes raise exceptionally interesting questions about the roles that a privately controlled profession—journalism—and the private mass media enterprise as a whole play and should play in the political process. While the collection's emphasis is on how the media affect the course of politics, media impact on the thinking of average individuals also is examined.

The book is built around the central theme that the powerful influence of the mass media has been demonstrated in many facets of American politics. Each of the six sections into which the essays have been grouped illustrates one of these facets. Following an introduction that deals with mass media effects in general, the selections explore mass media impact on public opinion, on elections, on participants within and outside the political power structure, and on domestic and foreign public policies. The book ends with a chapter on the politics behind efforts here and abroad to control mass media impact.

The choice of specific selections was guided by several principles, most importantly, the significance and quality of the research, the authors' recognition among scholars, and the attractiveness of the manner of presentation. Essays were chosen to make the book well-rounded yet cohesive and

1

readily comprehensible to students. A few "classics" in the field have been selected to show its intellectual origins. Otherwise, the emphasis has been on including the most recent and thought-provoking scholarship. The book,
therefore, alerts readers to the latest developments in a rapidly growing
interdisciplinary area of study. To stimulate thinking about the processes for
acquiring knowledge, along with thinking about substantive issues and public
policies, several of the selected readings contain information about theories,
research designs, and research methods.

The roster of authors encompasses political scientists, sociologists,
communications researchers, and media and government practitioners. Their
diverse contributions will provide exposure to practitioners' perspectives and
an appreciation of the rich intellectual sources that nourish the field. Each author is represented by only one selection to allow offering as many different
approaches as possible. The footnotes and bibliographies found in most
selections provide ample leads to additional readings.

Readers should keep in mind that the excerpts were chosen with a
specific purpose in mind: to demonstrate the impact of the media on the
political process. In many instances this was not the primary purpose of the
author. One therefore should not judge the thrust of the entire original work
from the thrust of the excerpts presented here. Readers also must consider
that some interesting details and side arguments have been removed from
several selections to hone the main argument and accelerate the pace. These
cuts enhance the essays' succinctness and allow their important conclusions to
emerge with greater clarity.

While the selections highlight the impact of the media on politics, they
can be used to focus on historical trends in media coverage (e.g., Roshco,
Adams, Grossman & Kumar, Muccigrosso), or to examine the media's role in
recent major governmental crises such as the Cuban missile confrontation,
Vietnam, and Watergate (e.g., Small, Halberstam, Lang & Lang, Sandman
& Paden). They also demonstrate the results that flow from a variety of
research techniques. These include content analysis (e.g., Gerbner et al.,
Dominick, Altheide, McCombs & Shaw, Robinson), qualitative content
evaluation (e.g., Paletz & Entman, Tichenor et al., Nimmo & Combs), along
with large- and small-scale surveys and psychological tests using cross-
sectional or panel approaches (e.g., Patterson, Rothman & Lichter, Arterton,
Miller). Other research techniques illustrated in various selections are
participant observation (e.g., Crouse, Ostroff, Goldenberg, Altheide) and
experimental research (Iyengar et al.). The readings also document changing
trends in research approaches (e.g., Klapper, McQuail, Iyengar et al.,
McCombs & Shaw).

The essays can be used to study various aspects of the newsmaking
process. All selections are relevant, but several address the topic explicitly
(e.g., Roshco, Tichenor et al., Goldenberg, Bagdikian). The study of
newsmaking raises questions about the implications of the television age for
the quality of American democracy when public opinion, elections, and the
impact of pressure groups have been altered by the medium. These questions

are touched peripherally in many essays. In a few they are at the heart of the argument (e.g., Lippmann, Manheim, Paletz & Entman, Tichenor et al.).

The boundaries between parts are flexible because many essays illustrate points covered by several sections. For instance, the McCombs and Shaw essay presents newsmaking in the context of a presidential election. But it is set in Section 2, which deals with shaping the political agenda, rather than Section 3, which concerns the impact of media on elections. Selections in Section 4, which report how the media treat specific political actors, can be supplemented with the Pentagon papers case in Section 6, which illustrates aspects of the relationship between the media and the judiciary. Several other selections in Sections 5 and 6 also shed light on the relations between the media and the courts, as well as on the reciprocal influence of the media and the executive branch, Congress, and pressure groups (e.g., Krasnow et al., Schoenfeld, Miller, Russell).

Similarly, discussion of media impact on various public policy areas is not limited to Section 5. In addition to the issues discussed there, several articles in other sections raise policy issues concerning the treatment of deprived and dissident groups (e.g., Goldenberg, Gitlin, Kelly & Mitchell, Schiller), issues of regulation of various economic sectors (e.g., Dominick, Krasnow et al., Schiller, Merrill), and issues of foreign policy (e.g., Small, Schiller, Merrill, the Pentagon papers case). All of these selections broaden the picture sketched out in Section 5.

The flexibility of *Media Power in Politics* springs from its rich content and from the variety of its disciplinary viewpoints. The fascination of the subject has attracted many brilliant scholars. We invite readers to sample their offerings in this collection in ways best suited to each individual's purposes.

Section One

MASS MEDIA EFFECTS: FROM THE PAST TO THE FUTURE

This section puts mass media and mass media effects research into historical perspective. Where have we been? Where are we going? Bernard Roshco traces the development of mass media in the United States and shows how it was shaped by economic, social, and cultural conditions. He demonstrates that media, like all social institutions, are products of their environment. Societal factors determine what is and what is *not* news. In turn, the nature of news determines what its effects are apt to be. When early newspapers presented little news beyond business announcements or strictly partisan diatribes, their narrow appeal precluded the effects made possible by the wide dispersion and mass appeal of modern American media.

Joseph Klapper summarizes the pre-1960 literature and theories on media effects. His book, often misinterpreted, became the bible from which scholars argued that media effects are minimal. These contentions led to the widespread belief that the study of media effects was not rewarding. Accordingly, media effects research dwindled sharply in the 1960s and early 1970s.

Denis McQuail brings the study of media effects research up-to-date. His essay presents a broad overview of current theories, research, and knowledge about mass media impact on politics. In place of the minimal effects theory there are now new hypotheses about the diversity, interaction, and context of media effects.

One of the most difficult aspects of the study of media effects has been to find ways to demonstrate them. The media are just one of many factors that influence individual thinking and play a part in political events. How can one isolate media influence from the totality of influences? Shanto Iyengar, Mark D. Peters, and Donald R. Kinder suggest one way. They conducted a series of ingenious experiments to demonstrate the impact of stories included in news broadcasts. Their work is an example of the adaptation of scientific methodologies to modern mass media effects research. In addition to experimental research, the arsenal of methodologies also includes interviews of various kinds to assess media impact on people's knowledge and opinions and content analysis techniques ranging from impressionistic scanning of stories to sophisticated computer analysis. Many of the studies cited by the authors in this section demonstrate the growing sophistication of research techniques. These emerging trends bode well for the quality of future findings of mass media effects studies.

1. THE EVOLUTION OF NEWS CONTENT IN THE AMERICAN PRESS

Bernard Roshco

Editor's Note. Bernard Roshco traces the development of American newspapers from the early specialized papers in the eighteenth century to modern mass-appeal publications. Vast changes have occurred because of major transformations in the nature of audiences, the nature of technology, and the nature of the social role of journalism.

Roshco highlights also a troublesome dilemma facing a modern press dedicated to the code of impartiality. How can journalists combine objective reporting with enough interpretation to make the meanings and implications of stories clear to the reader? Such clarity is important because shared exposure to mass-produced, mass-oriented news generates public opinion that is a powerful factor in the politics of democratic societies. Roshco shows that the content of news overall is shaped by the dominant values in American society. It is also heavily influenced by the newsgathering strategies of news organizations.

Bernard Roshco holds degrees in journalism and sociology from Columbia University and has worked as a journalist, educator, and public opinion analyst. He is the director of the Office of Opinion Analysis in the State Department's Bureau of Public Affairs. This selection is from *Newsmaking*, Chicago: University of Chicago Press, 1975.

From Reprinting to Reporting

. . . The format of news presentation now accepted as conventional grew out of a succession of innovations, introduced in response to a changing social environment. Until the 1830s, virtually every newspaper in the United States fell into one of two categories: it might be an organ of a political party, therefore most concerned with arguing political and economic issues according to the party's platform; or it was mostly a schedule of business activities, listing ship arrivals and departures, commodity prices, and other commercial information needed by merchants. Local news, besides reports of business transactions, might include reports on trials involving commercial or political issues. Foreign news was likely to get more space than local news, which had been the case since the founding of the first English newspapers in the seventeenth century.

Before a popular press could come into being, a new content that would attract a largely nonpolitical, nonbusiness audience had to be invented. Though such a drastic institutional change was fostered by individuals, it was generated within a social context. From a sociological perspective, the introduction of new procedures of news-gathering and the emphasis on new categories of news content are at least as much the result of changing social conditions as of innovating individuals. Robert E. Park described this adaptive process as "natural history," which he defined as the analytical account of how institutions evolve in response to the changing circumstances encountered within a particular society.[1] . . .

At any particular time, past history and current circumstances interact to create the frame of reference from which those working within an institution perceive their obligations and their opportunities. A basic condition that long inhibited newspaper development was the literal shortage of publishable news. News-gathering was as fitful and precarious as the mails, which meant that editors were never sure they would have enough fresh news to fill their columns. When the first American newspaper, *Publick Occurrences Both Forreign and Domestick,* made its initial appearance in Boston on September 25, 1690, it announced that it would publish "once a month (or if any Glut of Occurrences happen, oftener)." The paper folded after one issue.

By 1800, there were 235 newspapers, 24 of them dailies, but the shortage of news remained a constant concern.[2] The (New) *Orleans Gazette* filled space in its issue of May 28, 1805, with this mock-humorous comment on its news-gathering difficulties:

> No mail yesterday—we hardly know what we shall fill our paper with that will have the appearance of *news.* If we can get no mail—nor any papers by sea—we shall either have to print without, or get it manufactured at home. We therefore propose petitioning for leave to have established in some eligible part of this city a manufactury of news, on such principles as will always afford a sufficiency for current use.

The change from scarcity to plentitude in the production of news began in 1833, with the advent of the first American "penny paper," the *New York Sun.* Hawked daily on the streets by newsboys for a penny per copy, it introduced a new price, a new way to sell papers, and a new content to daily journalism. The *Sun* pretty much ignored the month-old account of foreign events that was a staple of the six-cent businessmen's papers, gave short shrift to political commentary and relatively little space to political reporting. Instead, in a breezy style that was novel for the time, it devoted most of its space to local news, with special emphasis on a feature new to American readers, stories of metropolitan low-life drawn from police-court cases.

The new, popular press was based on two concepts already proven popular in England: low-priced papers and the "human-interest" story. When the *Sun* showed how successful the formula could be in the United States, competitors sprang up in New York and imitators appeared in other cities. Two years after the *Sun* dawned, a Scotch-born, ex-schoolteacher, ex-reporter in New York, James Gordon Bennett, unemployed, forty years old, refused a job on the *Sun* and started the city's third penny paper, the *New York Herald*. He expanded and exploited the new formula in ways that established him as the leading news entrepreneur of his time and the forerunner of Hearst and Pulitzer.

Bennett recognized that every large city already had the news "manufactures" the editor of the *Orleans Gazette* had once thought a fantasy. From his first issue on May 6, 1835, Bennett exploited his insight so prodigiously that one of the earliest analysts of the American press declared seventy-five years later, "James Gordon Bennett invented news as we know it." [3]

Bennett's ruthless prying drastically violated, and subsequently altered, the existing norms of what should be made visible to newsmen. With his genius for vulgarity, Bennett had the imagination to think of more locales than his competitors in which to find news and the consummate bad taste to offer it for sale. By undermining the standards of privacy then current among the "better" classes, the *Herald* became an overnight success. As a consequence, the conventions of news publishing were revolutionized.

Bennett ranged from boardroom to bedroom. He abandoned the facetious tidbits about drunks and petty thieves introduced by the *Sun,* substituting a sweeping view of high-life as well as low-life throughout the city. He was the first editor to sensationalize a murder trial in which the principals were not socially prominent, devoting virtually entire issues to a case in which the murder victim was a prostitute and the accused a clerk. Other members of the press quickly followed on his heels. He created modern business news by offering financial reporting that went far beyond the usual stock-market quotations and shipping reports. Covering Wall Street personally, his probing "money articles" gained enough attention to win him readers among subscribers to the mercantile newspapers.

Bennett not only invaded the sacrosanct precincts of business for the first time, he also created the forerunner of modern "society" news with reports of goings-on at expensive parties. Using initials to intimate the "names" that were involved, he made upper-class scandal a news staple. Where the great editorial writers, such as his contemporary, Horace Greeley, were read for their personal views of public affairs, Bennett introduced a new kind of personal journalism by publicizing his private affairs. There was nothing detached in tone or "objective" in viewpoint about his style of presenting news. He even announced his forthcoming wedding in a signed article printed beneath a headline composed from the *Herald's* largest type.

Bennett's novel emphasis on news was eventually adopted, though reluctantly and far more restrainedly, even by an editor like Greeley, who always preferred commenting on public affairs to reporting them. Bennett thus played a crucial role in altering and enlarging the content of daily journalism. . . .

The new, low-priced press transformed the scale of newspaper sales. Instead of the few thousand names found on the subscription lists of the mercantile papers, these papers built up street sales that reached tens of thousands. When the *Sun* began to publish, the largest circulation in New York was 4,500, and the circulation of the city's eleven daily papers totaled 26,500. Some two years later, and only six weeks after the *Herald* had appeared, the city's three penny papers had a combined circulation of 44,000 and the *Sun* was claiming the largest circulation in the world, 19,000.

In order to exist, let alone grow, the popular press required a dependable network for gathering news, the machinery for large-scale printing, and a sizable audience of readers. These complementary entities, which made the beginning of mass communication possible, could not have been assembled and linked if economic circumstances had not been congenial, the political system had not been amenable, and the technology had not been available. Bennett and his fellow editor-entrepreneurs could not have invented the popular press a quarter-century earlier. By the 1830s, history was on their side in the sense that the social environment made their timing propitious.

Early in the nineteenth century, the productivity of the printing press was still what it had been all through the eighteenth century, approximately 200 hand-made impressions an hour. Newspaper size was therefore limited to four pages, which resulted in the conventional layout of putting advertisements on pages 1 and 4, and news and editorials on pages 2 and 3. Ads were printed first, allowing maximum time for gathering news and setting the stories in type. The inside, news pages were printed in a second run through the press.

In 1814, the *London Times* became the first newspaper to adopt the newly invented "cylinder" press, which supplied ink from a revolving drum and was powered by steam. It delivered 2,000 impressions an hour. In 1822, the first machine for typecasting replaced the hand-manufacture of type. In 1825, the *New York Advertiser* became the first American newspaper to install a steam-powered press. In 1830, a new machine made large-scale papermaking possible. In 1832, the double-cylinder press increased printing speed to 4,000 impressions an hour.

The first edition of the *Sun*, probably comprising 1,000 copies, consisted of four 8½-by-11-inch pages printed on an obsolete press at the rate of some 200 double-page impressions an hour. By 1836, the *Sun* was running off 19,000-copy editions of 14-by-20-inch pages at the rate of about 2,000 copies an hour on its steam-powered press. In 1847, the rotary press provided the next major technical advance in printing. Now the type was also fastened to a revolving cylinder, instead of resting on a flat bed, as it had since Gutenberg. Each such cylinder could print 8,000 impressions an hour, a forty-fold increase in less than forty years.

By 1860, a quarter-century after the founding of the *Herald*, it had the world's largest daily circulation, 77,000. The weekly edition of Greeley's *Tribune* had achieved, in even less time, a nationwide circulation of 200,000. Although the circulation of most dailies was only a few thousand and that of most weeklies only a few hundred, the total number of newspapers in the United States had tripled since the founding of the *Sun*.

Among the factors contributing to this expansion was the national growth in population and even the improvement of home lighting. The transition from candles to oil, and then to gas, made nighttime reading more inviting. At the same time, public education supplied the requisite reading public. Enough readers were sufficiently schooled for Greeley's daily *Tribune* to introduce the first daily book reviews in 1849. Public policy also fostered newspaper circulation by means of special mailing privileges. Publishers had been allowed to mail copies to each other, postage-free, since 1792. From the mid-nineteenth century on, various federal statutes provided either for free delivery or cut-rate postage for newspapers. . . .

Technology altered content by changing the criteria of timeliness. Early in the 1830s, news reports still traveled by horse and boat or, occasionally, even by carrier pigeon. Through the mail, local publishers received newspapers from out of town and, in the case of coastal cities, from abroad. Most of a paper's news content was reprinted from the newspapers it received in the mail. Essentially, each newspaper ran a clipping service for its local readers.

A fundamental change in news-gathering came with the invention of the telegraph and the installation of telegraphic communication between far-flung cities.[4] . . .

News increased in importance as it increased in immediacy. The widespread American populace was becoming a public because it could now share, in common, knowledge of recent events and therefore react, in unison, to current issues.[5] As news reports became more immediate, access to them became a crucial concern for publishers. No longer was it sufficient to wait for the mails to bring in a stock of newspapers. Competitors might be receiving the same news, far more immediately, from the telegraph.

The heightened value and salability of news, resulting from the installation of telegraphic communication, is demonstrated by the formation of the Associated Press in 1848, only four years after the first news story came over the wire. The AP began as a monopolistic cooperative of six New York papers, including the leading "penny" and mercantile papers.[6] The publishers had little in common but their shared interest in cutting the cost of news-gathering and assuring their access to telegraphic facilities. They also feared that the telegraph companies might go into the news business and freeze them out entirely.[7] Under the new arrangement, they had equal access to pooled news telegraphed from other cities, and they sold the news available from their collective output in New York to clients in other cities. Thus, the "wire service" of today was born.

The rising importance of news was accompanied by some expressions of concern with the norms of good reporting, a subject almost as old as the newspaper. Individual editors had promulgated the principles of nonpartisan, detached reporting—what finally came to be known as "objective" journalism—long before these ideals were adopted as the institutional ideology of the American daily press. The reportorial convention of identifying the source and allowing the reader to infer any implicit bias for himself goes back to the handwritten newsletters of the sixteenth and seventeenth centuries that preceded printed newspapers.[8]

From the press's earliest days, the purveyors of news (in contrast to the polemic pamphleteers) had the merchandizing problem of demonstrating they were not personally responsible for any taint of error in their product. Unable to affirm the validity of the news they proffered, the best they could do was vouch for their own lack of deliberate bias. . . .

Even when the party press was superseded by the allegedly nonpartisan "penny" press, the news continued to be slanted in the direction that editors leaned. As one historian of the press has noted: "The Superintendent of the Census of 1860 reflected the prevailing view when he classified eighty percent of the periodicals of the country, including all 373 daily newspapers, as 'political in their character.' " [9]

What the nonparty press offered, instead of outright political allegiance, was its own "independent" judgment. Thus, the norm of good reporting was defined not as opinionless detachment but as opinion reached after an impartial weighing of the facts. Although nonpolitical news, especially crime and scandal, was the spur to mass circulation, most editors, including Bennett, had strong, and strongly expressed, political preferences. The period before the Civil War was the age of the great advocate-editors, most notably Horace Greeley, who wielded his influence not only through the daily *Tribune* but also through its nationally circulated weekly edition. The balance between news and commentary was gradually shifting toward news. But, outright advocacy and reports heavily interlarded with opinion filled a good deal of most newspapers. . . .

Balanced presentation of opposing viewpoints became, in time, the identifying mark of objective reporting. In the meantime, outright editorials were increasingly segregated from news because more space was being accorded the latter. The first paper in the United States to print a separate "editorial page" as it is recognized today was Greeley's *Tribune*.[10]

The strongest influence promoting unadorned factuality in reporting came from the Associated Press, which soon after its founding began to employ its own reporters instead of relying entirely on stories culled from member papers. Since AP stories were sold impartially to papers of all political persuasions, AP reporters tended increasingly to leave out opinion, which could always be inserted by the client. Even as the early days of the Civil War evoked flights of fustian from many of the correspondents who covered the conflict for individual papers, the veteran head of the AP Washington bureau, who had worked for the press association since 1848, described his assignment in a clipped, straightforward style that evokes the newspaper prose of a later day:

> My business is to communicate facts; my instructions do not allow me to make any comment upon the facts which I communicate. My dispatches are sent to papers of all manner of politics, and the editors say they are able to make their own comments upon the facts which are sent them. I therefore

confine myself to what I consider legitimate news. I do not act as a politician belonging to any school, but try to be truthful and impartial. My dispatches are merely dry matters of fact and detail. Some special correspondents may write to suit the temper of their organs. Although I try to write without regard to men or politics, I do not always escape censure.[11] . . .

. . . Once the Civil War began, reporters swarmed to the battlefields. They went where, for that time, they were unexpected and often unwanted, pried where they were resented, and increasingly gained acceptance, although often grudgingly, in bivouacs as well as barracks.[12] As the war dragged on, news permanently displaced advertisements on almost all of the front pages in New York, already the press capital of the country and the only city with eight-page newspapers. This new prominence of display set the capstone on news, rather than commentary, as the preeminent commodity of daily journalism.

The press emerged from the Civil War with greatly extended acceptance of its right to report on public affairs to the limit of its new initiative. Since the advent of the penny press, the question of what sort of truths should be reported had sometimes inspired more public controversy than the truthfulness of the reports. Because of the titillating subject-matter that Bennett, especially, had made a news staple, the propriety of news content sometimes became as much of an issue as its factual accuracy. In the *Herald* of May 11, 1835, Bennett had set forth the penny papers' broadened approach to reporting by describing the "beats" he intended to cover:

We shall give a correct picture of the world—in Wall Street—in the Exchange—in the Police Office—at the Theatres—in the Opera—in short, wherever human nature or real life best displays its freaks and vagaries.

Most of the realms of news that Bennett mapped were eventually claimed by all of the press. . . .

Next to James Gordon Bennett, the most significant innovator of news content was Joseph Pulitzer, who combined sensationalism and crusading in a mixture never previously offered to newspaper readers. As publisher of the New York morning, evening, and Sunday *Worlds,* Pulitzer had a dual personality. On the one hand, he was willing to vie in vividness with William Randolph Hearst, who became his archcompetitor after taking over the *New York Journal* in 1895. Together, they have been deemed the co-creators of "yellow journalism," best remembered as a melange of illustrations, comics, oversized headlines, and overblown trivia—overlaid in the colors made possible by new developments in printing technology. On the other hand, Hearst as well as Pulitzer repeatedly focused attention on the machinations of robber barons and political bosses, utilizing the same "yellow" attention-getting devices for their exposés.

Pulitzer, especially, was instrumental in shaping the tradition of newsmaking initiative, which has been rewarded in subsequent generations of newspapermen through his endowment of the Pulitzer Prizes. . . . In 1878, at the age of thirty-one, he put together the *St. Louis Post-Dispatch* by buying the moribund *Dispatch* for $2,500 at a sheriff's sale and joining it to the moderately successful *Post,* of which he became co-owner. The new publication quickly became the city's best-selling evening newspaper and provided Pulitzer with the wherewithal to make a downpayment on the *New York World* in 1883. . . .

Pulitzer's morning *World,* his key paper, was no paragon of what was to become known as "objective" reporting. The *World* was unique, however, in the extent to which it made a virtue of its biases. Pulitzer went beyond his predecessors by not only reporting news but actually making it, through active intervention in public affairs. A statement in the first Pulitzer-owned issue of the *World,* published May 11, 1883, announced in part:

> There is room in this great and growing city for a journal that is not only cheap but bright, not only bright but large, not only large but truly democratic—dedicated to the cause of the people rather than to that of the purse potentates—devoted more to the news of the New than the Old World—that will expose all fraud and sham, fight all public evils and abuses—that will battle for the people with earnest sincerity.

Pulitzer's willingness to use the full resources of his paper in campaigning for his beliefs might seem a throwback to wholly partisan journalism, except for three significant differences: he was interested in winning and holding a truly *mass* audience, not merely the adherents of a particular political viewpoint; his approach to advocacy increased the importance of reporting, since he depended on the revelations in his news columns to buttress policies advocated on his editorial page; he was more interested in promoting social-welfare objectives than in garnering votes for a particular party, so that the news was far less likely to be slanted in the interests of political partisanship. Pulitzer was thus a forerunner of the "muckraking" magazine journalism of the early twentieth century, which exposed the corruption of big-city political machines and big-business monopolies, irrespective of political party.

Pulitzer gave reader-winning prominence to a spate of campaigns and crusades, all presented as news. "What Pulitzer discovered," the muckraking reporter, Will Irwin, wrote in *Collier's* magazine in 1911, "was the means of fighting popular causes by the news." Irwin described Pulitzer's innovation:

> The process was not wholly original with him; the New York "Times" had smashed the Tweed Ring by publishing plain accounts of their corrupt transactions. . . . Pulitzer was first to go out systematically and find evil before evil obtruded itself on public notice.[13]

. . . The *World* took over and exploited the device of sending reporters on extended adventures, which Bennett's son and successor had introduced by sending Stanley to find Livingstone. (For the *World,* a woman reporter went around the world in less than eighty days, in headlined competition with Verne's fictional hero.) More significantly and with more novel initiative, the *World* exposed the abuse of power by vested interests, attacking practices by the New York Central, Standard Oil, the Bell system, a roster of local aldermen who took bribes for a streetcar franchise, and others. It won reform of the treatment given immigrants at Ellis Island, and it also combined some of the services of ward boss and settlement house with its free Christmas dinners and summer excursions for the poor. Always aware of the self-publicizing value of public service, it introduced the fund-raising drive sponsored by a newspaper, soliciting enough contributions to finance the pedestal of the Statue of Liberty. . . .

Though Pulitzer developed and popularized the role of the reporter as investigator, the more prevalent roles were the reporter as eyewitness and, increasingly, as interviewer. . . . Formal interviewing of public figures who consented to be questioned did not become a standard procedure for news-gathering until decades later. Possibly the first such interview was Horace Greeley's story of his conversation with the Mormon leader, Brigham Young, which appeared in the *Tribune* in 1859.[14] During the Civil War, eyewitness reporting from the battlefields was the focus of expanding news coverage, although correspondents in Washington occasionally reported interviews. The first newspaper interview with a president did not occur until after the Civil War, when a reporter for the *St. Louis Globe-Democrat* interviewed Andrew Johnson.

Not infrequently, the reporters of the nineteenth century resembled the contemporary candid photographers who haunt celebrities, their lenses aimed to capture any absent-minded indiscretion. In 1886, newsmen intruded on President Grover Cleveland by camping out on the lawn of his honeymoon hideaway during his wedding night.[15] The reporter as eyewitness undoubt-edly helped win acceptance for the reporter as interviewer. Inviting him in the door at an agreed-upon time made him less likely to peek through the keyhole at other times.

By granting the press the privilege of institutionalized access by such formal means as interviews and press conferences, American society's higher strata came to terms with the intrusion upon their privacy pioneered by Bennett. Interviewing became a device for both permitting and controlling the public visibility of elite members of "society," government, and private organizations.

As the press increasingly divorced itself from overt partisan allegiances in its news columns, the interview also became a standard technique for reporting public controversies, especially politics. However, the new reporting device had no lack of early critics. A writer for the *Nation* declared in 1869: "The 'interview' as at present managed is generally the joint product of some humbug of a hack politician and another humbug of a reporter." Over time, the pairing of conflicting opinions solicited in interviews became the routine way newspapers demonstrated their nonpartisanship. . . .

Press Releases and Pulitzer Prizes: The Diverse Meanings of "Objective" News

. . . The publisher who is the exemplar of what came to be known as ob-jective reporting was Adolph S. Ochs of the *New York Times*. Diligently, he sought to distill out of his newspaper's columns any signs of the biases held by his reporters, his editors, or himself. . . . In 1896, at the age of thirty-eight, he took over the languishing *New York Times,* whose circulation was down to 9,000. In a city where Pulitzer's *World,* selling 370,000 copies daily, and Hearst's *Journal,* selling 385,000, competed in stridency, Ochs found his audience by presenting an ample roundup of news in an even-tempered voice.

In the first issue under his control, dated August 19, 1896, Ochs announced that he intended to publish a "high-standard newspaper, clean, dignified, and trustworthy." The *Times* set itself the task not only of printing the news more voluminously than its competitors but also of avoiding the deliberate slanting by omission about which Greeley had once complained and which remained a characteristic of most of the press through the nineteenth century. The *Times* carried its emphasis on reporting opposing views even into its columns of "letters to the editor." [16] . . .

. . . As news became more plentiful, selling it became more competitive. The daily paper became a multiple-edition paper. With the resultant need for speedier processing of news to enhance immediacy, the exigencies and pressures of newspaper editing and production were intensified.[17] Under these circumstances, editors were more interested in sources who offered a dependable supply of stories than in assigning reporters to spend valuable time probing beneath the surface of events.

The reporter as interviewer became the salient role of the daily journalist, as statements on matters of complex, controversial policy were routinely issued by various "authorities." . . . Even when he was an eyewitness to events, the reporter increasingly relied on institutional sources for authoritative confirmation of the data he reported. If he covered a parade, he quoted the highest-ranking police official who was present as to the size of the onlooking crowd. In 1950, a commentator described how reporters were usually instructed to perform: "Somewhere a city editor is always saying: 'You can't write that unless you can quote somebody.' " [18]

The injunction to "quote somebody" illustrates the routine role-performance that came to be expected of most reporters most of the time. The reporter as crusading investigator was a deviant who might win a Pulitzer Prize; the reporter as "objective" interviewer, recording all authoritative opinions impartially, conformed to the unwritten, but increasingly stringent, rules governing reporter-source interaction.

The act of interviewing had developed into a complex mode of behavior. Knowing who might be quoted, and under what circumstances, became an essential part of reportorial expertise. These rules often allowed sources to reduce their public visibility by selecting the mode of self-disclosure most advantageous to themselves. Increasingly, the public-relations man in business and the press officer in government became buffers for executives and public officials. Making themselves readily available, these specialists in dealing with reporters became substitute sources.[19]

Although the relationship between sources and reporters was developing unanticipated complexities, it was useful to the press that objective reporting should be its occupational ideology.[20] For example:

1. Easily employed guidelines for selecting and evaluating news content facilitated rapid processing and publication of a wide variety of news stories.

2. Giving sources the responsibility for supplying content freed reporters from the need for extensive knowledge about subject-matter.

3. Making technique rather than substance the basis of judging role-performance helped insulate reporters—and their media—from charges of error, bias, and other forms of unprofessional performance.[21]

4. Because reporters were usually interchangeable, an editor could assign the same reporter to cover many kinds of news. The easily recruited and trained general-assignment reporter, rather than the specialist in a particular field, became the backbone of the news-gathering operation.

As the twentieth century wore on, however, editors and reporters became increasingly aware that standards of role-performance promulgated in the eighteenth and nineteenth centuries were increasingly inadequate for enabling their audience to comprehend twentieth-century events. As the historian of American journalism, Frank Luther Mott, noted, "The bald and exact fact was no longer enough to make the world understandable." [22] . . .

Not only was the world changing in drastic ways that could not be explained within the restrictions of time-honored reportorial methods, the structure of the press was also changing in ways that altered the press's—and the public's—conception of adequate reportorial performance. With the arrival of radio broadcasting and the newsmagazine in the 1920s, newspapers had lost their monopoly over news. . . .

Gradually, the need for presenting more "background"—the context of which the reported event was a part—was increasingly accepted as a necessary adjunct to daily reporting. In 1933, the American Society of Newspaper Editors passed a resolution at its annual convention that urged editors to "devote a larger amount of attention and space to explanatory and interpretive news and to presenting a background of information which will enable the average reader more adequately to understand the movement and the significance of events." [23] . . . Nevertheless, in most daily reporting—particularly by the wire services—digging "below the surface" was a matter solely of preachment. It remained standard practice to demonstrate objectivity by sticking to surface factuality. Subsurface reporting was largely left to a privileged few—syndicated columnists, correspondents in Washington and foreign capitals, and sports writers. By and large, interpretation remained the prerogative of editorial writers. . . .

In the early twenties, Walter Lippmann took note of the subjectivity of news judgment, a theme that has consistently reappeared in discussions of what constitutes journalistic objectivity. Lippmann put it this way:

> Take two newspapers published in the same city on the same morning. The headline of one reads: "Britain pledges aid to Berlin against French aggression; France openly backs Poles." The headline of the second is: "Mrs. Stillman's Other Love." Which you prefer is a matter of taste, but not entirely a matter of the editor's taste. It is a matter of his judgment as to

what will absorb the half hour's attention a certain set of readers will give to his newspaper.[24]

Each editor's decision regarding which story to headline is as subjective as his readers' preference in newspapers. But the content of either news story can be verified objectively. Lippmann was further concerned with the limited range of news that could be reported objectively. In the reporting of opinion, for example, objectivity usually lay in reporting the expressed opinions accurately, rather than in assessing their truthfulness. There was not likely to be an objective way of determining whether the opinion was itself truthful: "Between Judge Gary's assertion that the unions will destroy American institutions, and Mr. Gompers' assertion that they are agencies of the rights of man, the choice has, in large measure, to be governed by the will to believe." [25] Lippmann highlighted the difficulty of reporting objectively at low levels of factual visibility, which was to become a basic concern regarding what was to become known as "interpretive" reporting. . . .

Two phenomena of the years following World War II, one technological and the other political, did most to stimulate reappraisal of standard reportial methods and the news content they usually generated. Television and McCarthyism, which together produced some of the most striking journalism of the fifties, separately demonstrated that the print media, especially, needed new ways of responding to the growing complexity of the world and increased diversity of news media. Like radio before it, television exploited the incontestable immediacy of its reportage to compete with newspapers. Using wire-service news for the most part, it relied on wire-service news judgment and adopted wire-service news values. In content, televised news became largely a "headline service." Now that television regularly scooped newspapers in reporting the "hard"—that is, most visible—news of the day, the printed media increasingly began to report undercurrents not visible to television's cameras.

Even the *New York Times* began to revise its stolid approach to the news. By 1953, an assistant managing editor of the *New York Times* was explaining that "All the News . . ." might now include not only accounts of what happened but also explanations of why they happened:

> We have found in many cases, and now accept the idea as a sound method of operation, that it is not the event itself that is of major importance but what caused it—or, at any rate, the cause is of equal importance. Too much of past reporting has dealt only with the surface facts—the spot news—and too rarely has dug into the reasons for them.
>
> A race riot, a prison outbreak, a bad slum condition—even a murder—has a social background, deeply rooted perhaps in the customs, traditions, and economic condition of a region or community, but it is there and discoverable. It's the newspaper's job, it seems to us, to discover it.[26]

The obituaries for old-fashioned objectivity did not indicate where, how, or from whom reporters were to derive their interpretations. The implication seemed to be that reporters would be assigned the additionl role of independent investigators, analyzing the causes and consequences of complex social events by means of their own research and expertise.

In practice, two principal developments in news content have followed from the growing concern with "interpretive reporting." For one, the press has simply extended its old practice of editorial comment. But, instead of confining this prerogative to the editor or to editorial writers, space or time has been allotted to a growing roster of "analysts." Radio and television have commentators; the newsmagazines, once written anonymously, have by-lined columns and articles; newspapers not only have syndicated columnists but increasingly allow their own senior reporters to write by-lined analyses. A second, more prevalent means of embodying interpretation in news coverage has been to make it part of "objective" news coverage in the older manner. Reporters remain interviewers but now seek the views of new categories of sources, whose opinions are quotable within the constraints of objective reporting. Thus, a growing roster of "experts," whether physicists, psychiatrists, economists, or specialists on any problem newly arrived in the public spotlight—slums, race, drugs, youth, population control, ecology, consumerism, women's rights, energy resources, and the latest issue that will arise tomorrow—have joined public officials and institutional spokesmen as authoritative interpreters of events and definers of situations. Just as the press learned to report political opinion within the objective format, it has extended the same format in order to report an ever-broadening range of "interpretive" opinions.

The problem of including interpretive content in an "objective" news report was thus solved easily—if the interpretation could be attributed to a source. In that case, the interpretation took the form of a recent assertion about a current issue, which made it timely information, hence news. Unattributed information that had interpretive value as context for a news event could be included in a story without raising the issue of the reporter's objectivity under one condition—if it did not take issue with the attributed information for which it provided background. . . .

. . . Eventually, in the course of the press's "natural history," many thoughtful members of the press arrived at a time when they felt impelled to examine the consequences, for the press as an institution and also for the society it served, of confining news content within the ideological definition of objectivity that governed the role-performance of newsmen.

By the early 1950s, Senator Joseph McCarthy's escalating accusations about the presence of Communists in the federal government, reported under a ceaseless stream of large headlines and in the glare of television, had made at least some newsmen dissatisfied with what Elmer Davis dubbed "dead-pan objectivity." [27] Davis had gone on from the *New York Times* of the 1920s to become, during the early days of World War II, one of the country's best-known radio commentators. . . . Davis described two modes of falsification between which conscientious reporters should steer:

> The good newspaper, the good news broadcaster, must walk a
> tightrope between two great gulfs—on one side the false objectivity that

takes everything at face value and lets the public be imposed on by the charlatan with the most brazen front; on the other, the "interpretive" reporting which fails to draw the line between objective and subjective, between a reasonably well established fact and what the reporter or editor wishes were the fact. To say that is easy; to do it is hard. No wonder that too many fall back on the incontrovertible objective fact that the Honorable John P. Hoozis said, colon quote—and never mind whether he was lying or not.[28] . . .

The debate over the nature of reportorial objectivity raised the question of what constituted adequate role-performance. In seeking an answer, at least some newsmen were led to an enlarged definition of reportorial responsibility, one that allowed reporters to exercise a larger measure of the news judgment usually reserved for editors. Many news sources had learned how to exploit the media's bureaucratized standards of news judgment and its norms for ensuring the appearance of impartiality. As a consequence, reporters were editorializing, not deliberately as in the days of the party press, but by default. In order to enable the audience to grasp the implications of events, news increasingly needed to be supplemented by untimely information that might not be available from quotable sources. . . .

A redefinition of objectivity was needed, so that validity would be valued equally with impartiality. To that end, "interpretation" was given a definition specific to news reporting, just as "objectivity" had earlier been defined in a way unique to journalistic practice. Objective "interpretation" was distinguished from subjective "editorializing," the term long given to expressions of personal or medium opinion. In contrast, interpretive reporting was defined to mean that reporters should have role-obligations comparable to those of scientific researchers. A newsman would therefore become responsible for indicating the validity of the data he reported as well as for assuring the accuracy of the attribution. He would do this by comparing a source's assertions to other available data; if he deemed it necessary, he could then include in his reporting verifiable material—not necessarily directly quoted or attributed—that might reflect on the validity of quoted assertions attributed to news sources. Thus defined, interpretive reporting would be far closer to objective research as conducted by scientists than was old-fashioned "objective" reporting as long practiced in news reporting. . . .

As Elmer Davis and other journalistic proponents of interpretation have acknowledged, the reporter's opportunity to slant news increases with his freedom to interpret. Yet there is no reason for assuming that the freedom to interpret may not serve to free the reporter from the biases of sources, editors, and publishers at least as much as they permit him to give freer play to his own. . . .

Just as institutional dilemmas opened the door to interpretive reporting, institutional requirements cause most reporting still to be conducted within the restrictions imposed by the traditional definition of reportorial objectivity. Herbert Gans, who has studied various news-gathering organizations, has pointed out that the traditional definition accommodates news-gathering procedures to the prevailing institutional needs of the mass media:

> Viable substitutes for objectivity [that is, objective acquaintance-with] can be formulated, but they require reporters and editors far more knowledgable—able to generalize about and evaluate the data they gather—and fewer generalists—with more time to gather and report the news—which will raise the cost of the news considerably. Until the audience or someone else (e.g., the government) is willing to provide the necessary funds, however, we will have to rely on relatively low-cost news, and for this reason alone objectivity is likely to remain an important guiding principle of journalistic method.[29] . . .

NOTES

1. Robert E. Park, "The Natural History of the Newspaper," *American Journal of Sociology* 29 (November 1923): 273-89. Collected in Turner, ed., *Robert E. Park on Social Control and Collective Behavior,* p. 97.

2. Alfred McClung Lee, *The Daily Newspaper in America* (New York: Macmillan, 1937), p. 718.

3. Will Irwin, "The Dim Beginning," article 2 of "The American Newspaper: A Study of Journalism in its Relations to the Public," *Collier's,* February 11, 1911, p. 15. This fifteen-article series was reprinted in facsimile as *The American Newspaper* (Ames, Iowa: The Iowa State University Press, 1969), edited and with comments by Clifford F. Weigle and David G. Clark. Will Irwin was a newspaper reporter turned investigative magazine reporter. His articles constitute one of the earliest critical examinations of the American press. Further references cite the reprint.

4. For a summary discussion of the effect of more than a century of technological innovations on news coverage, see Boorstin, *The Image; A Guide to Pseudo-Events in America* (New York: Atheneum, 1962), pp. 12ff.

5. "The leading citizens living in an aristocratic country can see each other from afar, and if they want to unite their forces they go to meet one another, bringing a crowd in their train. But in democratic countries it often happens that a great many men who both want and need to get together cannot do so, for all being very small and lost in the crowd, they do not see one another at all and do not know where to find one another. Then a newspaper gives publicity to the feeling or idea that had occurred to them all simultaneously but separately. They all at once aim toward that light, and these wandering spirits, long seeking each other in the dark, at last meet and unite." (Alexis De Tocqueville, *Democracy in America* [New York: Doubleday Anchor Books, 1969], p. 518; translation based on 1850 edition).

6. The *Herald* raised its price to two cents during its second year of publication, as did the *Tribune* and *Times* after coming out initially at one cent.

7. Oliver Gramling, *AP: The Story of News* (New York: Farrar and Rinehart, 1940), p. 20.

8. Joseph Frank, *The Beginnings of the English Newspaper: 1620-1660* (Cambridge, Mass.: Harvard University Press, 1961), p. 3.

9. Louis M. Starr, *Bohemian Brigade: Civil War Newsmen in Action* (New York:. Alfred A. Knopf, 1954), p. 6, citing the *Preliminary Report on the Eighth Census* (Washington: 1862), 103.

10. Frank Luther Mott, *The News in America* (Cambridge, Mass.: Harvard University Press, 1952), p. 72.

11. Starr, *Bohemian Brigade,* p. 9.

12. Starr, *Bohemian Brigade,* passim.

13. Irwin, in *The American Newspaper,* p. 14.
14. For a brief history of the interview, and a discussion of its increasing utilization as a "newsmaking" device, see Boorstin, *The Image,* pp. 14 ff.
15. Don R. Pember, *Privacy and the Press: The Law, the Mass Media, and the First Amendment* (Seattle: University of Washington Press, 1972), p. 16.
16. Elmer Davis, *History of the New York Times, 1851-1921* (New York: The New York Times, 1921), p. 217.
17. For a discussion of some consequences of speeded-up publishing, see Boorstin, *The Image,* esp. p. 14.
18. "Reporting 'Background': You Can Interpret and Still Retain Objectivity," *Nieman Reports* 4 (April 1950): 29.
19. "The net effect of the press conference, the background interview, the rules governing anonymous disclosure and attribution to sources, and particularly the growing use of the public information officer within government, is to routinize the reporter's function and to grant to the source exceptional control over news dissemination" (James W. Carey, "The Communications Revolution and the Professional Communicator," in Paul Halmos, ed., *The Sociology of Mass-Media Communicators. The Sociological Review,* Monograph no. 13 [Keele University, Keele, England, January 1969], p. 33).
20. "There may at first seem little justification in employing the term 'ideology' in connection with the set of beliefs and rationales which editors and other media practitioners employ, not only to explain and defend themselves in their contacts with others outside their own sphere of work, but also to guide themselves and their colleagues in the day-to-day exercise of their particular craft. However, there are reasons for applying the label, the most obvious one being that one is dealing with *beliefs,* and not with empty formulae" (Roger L. Brown, "Some Aspects of Mass Media Ideologies," in *The Sociology of Mass-Media Communicators,* p. 156).
21. ". . . newsmen need some working notion of objectivity to minimize the risks imposed by deadlines, libel suits, and superiors' reprimands" (Gaye Tuchman, "Objectivity as Strategic Ritual," *American Journal of Sociology* 77 (January 1972): 662.
22. Mott, *The News in America,* p. 70.
23. *Proceedings,* Eleventh Annual Convention, American Society of Newspaper Editors (1933), p. 74.
24. Walter Lippmann, *Public Opinion* (New York: The Free Press, 1965), p. 223.
25. Ibid., pp. 227-28.
26. Robert E. Garst, "The News Behind the Facts," *Neiman Reports,* 7 (July 1953): 7.
27. Elmer Davis, "News and the Whole Truth," *The Atlantic Monthly,* August 1952, p. 35.
28. Ibid., p. 38.
29. Herbert J. Gans, "The Famine in American Mass-Communications Research," *American Journal of Sociology* 77 (January 1972): 703.

2. THE EFFECTIVENESS OF MASS COMMUNICATION

Joseph T. Klapper

Editor's Note. What effect does published news have on society? Joseph Klapper addresses this question through a comprehensive examination of the findings of modern communications research during its formative years between 1940 and 1960. More than 1,000 studies were evaluated to produce *The Effects of Mass Communication*.

Although Klapper warned that many important media effects might have escaped attention in the early studies, his findings were interpreted as demonstrating that media effects are minimal. While the minimal-effects phenomenon has turned out to be an outgrowth of the research approaches used in the 1960s, Klapper's work remains a sound analysis of the implications of this early research. His findings are essential for understanding the directions of subsequent research on the effects of mass communication.

Joseph T. Klapper is a Columbia University-trained sociologist who has served on the faculties of the University of Washington, Stanford University, City College of New York, and Brooklyn Polytechnic Institute. He has held various research positions in government and the private sector. Currently, he is the director of social research for the Columbia Broadcasting System (CBS). This selection is from *The Effects of Mass Communication*, New York: Free Press, 1960.

Twenty years ago, writers who undertook to discuss mass communications typically felt obliged to define that then unfamiliar term. In the intervening years, conjecture and research upon the topic, particularly in reference to the *effects* of mass communication, have burgeoned. The literature has reached that stage of profusion and disarray, characteristic of all proliferating disciplines, at which researchers and research administrators speak wistfully of establishing centers where the accumulating data might be sifted and stored. The field has grown to the point at which its practitioners are periodically asked by other researchers to attempt to assess the cascade, to determine whither we are tumbling, to attempt to assess, in short "what we know about the effects of mass communication."

Reprinted with the permission of Macmillan Publishing Company from *The Effects of Mass Communication* by Joseph T. Klapper. Copyright © 1960 by The Free Press, a Corporation.

What we know of course varies, depending on whether we are discussing one type of effect or another. In regard to some points, the evidence is remarkably consistent. In regard to others, the data contain apparent anomalies or apparent outright contradictions. These characteristics of the data are by now well known, and they have given rise to a widespread pessimism about the possibility of ever bringing any order to the field.

The author acknowledges and will here briefly document the pessimism, but he neither condones or shares it. He will rather propose that we have arrived at the brink of hope. More specifically, he will here propose that we have reached the point at which certain empirical generalizations may be tentatively formulated. A few such generalizations will be presented, and it will be further proposed that they are capable of ordering a good deal of the data, of resolving certain apparent anomalies, and of indicating avenues for new and logically relevant research.

The Bases of Pessimism

The pessimism, at present, is widespread, and it exists both among the interested lay public and within the research fraternity.

Some degree of pessimism, or even cynicism, is surely to be expected from the lay public, whose questions we have failed to answer. Teachers, preachers, parents, and legislators have asked us a thousand times over these past fifteen years whether violence in the media produces delinquency, whether the escapist nature of much of the fare does not blind people to reality, and just what the media can do to the political persuasions of their audiences. To these questions we have not only failed to provide definitive answers, but we have done something worse: we have provided evidence in partial support of every hue of every view. We have claimed, on the one hand, and on empirical grounds, that escapist material provides its audience with blinders and with an unrealistic view of life,[1] and, on the other hand, that it helps them meet life's real problems.[2] We have hedged on the crime and violence question, typically saying, "Well, probably there is no causative relationship, but there just might be a triggering effect." [3] In reference to persuasion, we have maintained that the media are after all not so terribly powerful,[4] and yet we have reported their impressive successes in promoting such varied phenomena as religious intolerance,[5] the sale of war bonds,[6] belief in the American Way,[7] and disenchantment with Boy Scout activities.[8] It is surely no wonder that a bewildered public should regard with cynicism a research tradition which supplies, instead of definitive answers, a plethora of relevant but inconclusive and at times seemingly contradictory findings.

Considerable pessimism, of a different order, is also to be expected within the research fraternity itself. Such anomalous findings as have been cited above seemed to us at first to betoken merely the need of more penetrating and rigorous research. We shaped insights into hypotheses and eagerly set up research designs in quest of the additional variables which we were sure would bring order out of chaos and enable us to describe the process of effect with sufficient precision to diagnose and predict. But the variables emerged in such a cataract that we almost drowned. The relatively placid waters of "who says what to whom" [9] were early seen to be muddied by audience predispositions, "self-selection," and selective perception. More recent studies, both in the laboratory and the social world, documented the influence of a host of other variables including various aspects of contextual organization;[10] the audiences' image of the sources;[11] the simple passage of time;[12] the group orientation of the audience member and the degree to which he values group membership;[13] the activity of opinion leaders;[14] the social aspects of the situation during and after exposure to the media,[15] and the degree to which the audience member is forced to play a role;[16] the personality pattern of the audience member,[17] his social class, and the level of his frustrations;[18] the nature of the media in a free enterprise system;[19] and the availability of "social mechanism[s] for implementing action drives." [20] The list, if not endless, is at least overwhelming, and it continues to grow. Almost every aspect of the life of the audience member and the culture in which the communication occurs seems susceptible of relation to the process of communication effect. As early as 1948, Berelson, cogitating on what was then known, came to the accurate if perhaps moody conclusion that "some kinds of *communication* on some kinds of *issues,* brought to the attention of some kinds of *people* under some kinds of *conditions,* have some kinds of *effects.*" [21] It is surely no wonder that today, after another decade at the inexhaustible fount of variables, some researchers should feel that the formulation of any systematic description of what effects are how effected, and the predictive application of such principles, are goals which become the more distant as they are the more vigorously pursued.

But, as has been said, the present author takes no such pessimistic view. He rather proposes that we already know a good deal more about communication than we thought we did, and that we are on the verge of being able to proceed toward more abundant and more fruitful knowledge.

The Bases of Hope

This optimism is based on two phenomena. The first of these is a new orientation toward the study of communication effects which has recently become conspicuous in the literature. And the second phenomenon is the emergence, from this new approach, of a few tentative generalizations.

In describing the new approach, and in presenting the generalizations, the author submits rather than asserts. He hopes to be extremely suggestive, but he cannot yet be conclusive. And if these pages bespeak optimism, they also bespeak the tentativeness of exploratory rather than exhaustive thought. Explicit note will in fact be taken ... of wide areas to which the generalizations do not seem to apply, and warnings will be sounded against the pitfalls of regarding them as all-inclusive or axiomatic.

The "Phenomenistic" Approach

The new orientation, which has of course been hitherto and variously formulated, can perhaps be described, in a confessedly oversimplified way, as a shift away from the concept of "hypodermic effect" toward an approach which might be called "situational" or "functional." [22] Because of the specific, and for our purposes sometimes irrelevant, connotations attached to these two terms, we will here use a word coined by the present author in an earlier publication and refer to the approach as "phenomenistic." [23] Whatever it be called, it is in essence a shift *away* from the tendency to regard mass communication as a necessary and sufficient cause of audience effects, toward a view of the media as influences, working amid other influences, in a total situation. The old quest of specific effects stemming from the communication has given way to the observation of existing conditions or changes, followed by an inquiry into the factors, *including* mass communication, which produced those conditions and changes, and the roles which these factors played relative to each other. In short, attempts to assess a stimulus which was presumed to work alone have given way to an assessment of the role of that stimulus in a total observed phenomenon.

Examples of the new approach are becoming fairly numerous. The so-called Elmira[24] and Decatur[25] studies, for example, set out to determine the critical factors in various types of observed decisions, rather than to focus exclusively on whether media did or did not have effects. The Rileys and Maccoby focus on the varying functions which media serve for different sorts of children, rather than inquiring whether media do or do not affect them.[26] Some of the more laboratory-oriented researchers, in particular the Hovland school, have been conducting ingeniously designed controlled experiments in which the communication stimulus is a constant, and various extra-communication factors are the variables.[27]

This new approach, which views mass media as one among a series of factors working in patterned ways their wonders to perform, seems to the author already to have been extremely useful, and to have made possible a series of generalizations which will very shortly be advanced.

Before the generalizations are advanced, however, a few words of preliminary warning about the phenomenistic approach seem highly in order. For that approach, despite its usefulness, may, if relied upon too exclusively, tend to obscure the very issues it is intended to elucidate.

It is possible that the phenomenistic approach may so divert our attention to the factors with which mass communication is in interplay, or to the fact that interplay exists, that we forget our original goal of determining the effects of mass communication itself. For example ... the effects of mass communication are likely to differ, depending upon whether the communication is or is not in accord with the norms of groups to which the audience members belong. ... [T]he effects of fantasy and of media depictions of crime and violence are likely to have different effects among children who are primarily oriented toward different types of groups. This is valuable information which contributes greatly to our knowledge of the processes and types of mass communication effect. But if research is to provide socially meaningful answers to questions about the effects of mass communication, it must inquire into the relative prevalence of these different conditions under which mass communications has different effects. Unfortunately, communication research has not often addressed itself to such questions.... It may, however, be noted that if the phenomenistic approach thus tends to delay the provision of definitive answers, it does so in the interests of the eventual answers being the more meaningful.

It must be remembered that though mass communication seems usually to be a *contributory* cause of effects, it is often a major or necessary cause and in some instances a sufficient cause. The fact that its effect is often mediated, or that it often works among other influences, must not blind us to the fact that mass communication possesses qualities which distinguish it from other influences, and that by virtue of these qualities, it is likely to have characteristic effects. Neither the phenomenistic approach nor the proposed generalizations deny these possibilities; they are, in fact, explicitly stated in the third and fourth generalizations below. But there seems some danger that attention may at times become too exclusively focused on the other factors to which the phenomenistic approach points, and the dangers of such neglect must be kept in mind.

Precautions can, of course, be taken against such dangers as have here been outlined, and given such precautions, the phenomenistic approach seems to the present author to offer good hope that the disarray of communications research findings may to some degree be ordered. He feels, as has already been noted, that the approach has in fact made possible a series of generalizations which will now be advanced. They are submitted very gingerly. They seem to the author at once extremely generic and quite immature; they seem on the one hand to involve little that has not been said, and on the other hand to be frightfully daring. They do seem, however, to be capable of relating a good deal of data about the processes, factors, and directions of communication effects, and of doing this in such a way that findings which hitherto appeared to be at best anomalous if not actually contradictory, begin to look like orderly variations on a few basic themes.

Emerging Generalizations

The generalizations will first be presented in their bare bones and without intervening comment.... Without further ado, then, it is tentatively proposed that:

1. Mass communication *ordinarily* does not serve as a necessary and sufficient cause of audience effects,[28] but rather functions among and through a nexus of mediating factors and influences.

2. These mediating factors are such that they typically render mass communication a contributory agent, but not the sole cause, in a process of reinforcing the existing conditions. (Regardless of the condition in question—be it the vote intentions of audience members, their tendency toward or away from delinquent behavior, or their general orientation toward life and its problems—and regardless of whether the effect in question be social or individual, the media are more likely to reinforce than to change.)

3. On such occasions as mass communication does function in the service of change, one of two conditions is likely to exist. Either:

    a. the mediating factors will be found to be inoperative and the effect of the media will be found to be direct; *or*

    b. the mediating factors, which normally favor reinforcement, will be found to be themselves impelling toward change.

4. There are certain residual situations in which mass communication seems to produce direct effects, or directly and of itself to serve certain psychophysical functions.

5. The efficacy of mass communication, either as a contributory agent or as an agent of direct effect, is affected by various aspects of the media and communications themselves or of the communication situation (including, for example, aspects of textual organization, the nature of the source and medium, the existing climate of public opinion, and the like). . . .

Conclusions

It would seem desirable to conclude . . . with an evaluative note on the five generalizations. . . . What follows is . . . a purely subjective and personal offering. As in all previous such contexts, the author here submits rather than asserts.

On the positive side, the generalizations appear to have served three major functions.

First . . . the generalizations have permitted us in some measure to organize, or to "account for," a considerable number of communications research findings which have previously seemed discrete and anomalous. The author submits, tentatively, that the set of generalizations has in fact made possible organization of several different orders:

> It has enabled us to relate the *processes* of effect and the *directions* of effect. Put another way, it has provided us with a concept of the process of effect in which both reinforcement and change are seen as related and understandable outcomes of the same general dynamics. This concept enabled us to account for the relative incidence of reinforcement and change in reference to attitudes on specific issues, and provided an orientation which was found to be applicable in one or another degree to reinforcement and change in regard to a wide variety of audience orientations.

> It has enabled us to view such diverse phenomena as audience predispositions, group membership and group norms, opinion leadership, personality patterns, and the nature of the media in this society, as serving similar functions in the process of effect—as being, so to speak, all of a certain order, and distinct from such other factors as the characteristics of media content.

> It has enabled us to view other seemingly unrelated phenomena, such as the efficacy of the media in creating opinions on new issues and the effect of role-playing, as manifestations of the same general process—as specific combinations of known variables, the outcomes of which were predictable.

So much for the organizational capabilities of the generalizations. But note that this organization of existing data, even within so sketchy a framework as these generalizations provide, permitted us to see gaps—to discover, for example, that certain presumed outcomes have to date been neither documented nor shown not to occur. This points to a second contribution: the generalizations seem capable of indicating avenues of needed research which are logically related to existing knowledge. But virtually *any* set of generalizations, or any theoretical framework, will point to gaps and needed research. The fact that these generalizations do so thus in no way gainsays the fact that future thought and research must inevitably change the generalizations themselves. As presently formulated, they constitute only a single tentative step forward, and it may reasonably be hoped that their refinement or emendation would enlarage rather than reduce the area of their applicability.

Finally, it is in the extent of the applicability of the generalizations, coupled with their present primitive nature, that the author finds particular basis for hope. Sketchy and imperfect as they are, these propositions regarding the process and direction of effect seem applicable to the effects of persuasive communications and to the effects of various kinds of non-persuasive media content upon a wide range of audience orientations and behavior patterns. Furthermore, the mediating variables to which the generalizations point— variables such as predispositions, group membership, personality patterns, and the like—seem to play essentially similar roles in all these various kinds of effects. Even if the generalizations turn out to be wholly in error, they seem nevertheless sufficiently useful and sufficiently applicable to justify the faith that *some* generalizations can in due time be made. And the author has indicated, from the ouset, that he is "less concerned with insuring the viability of these generalizations than he is with indicating that the time for generalization is at hand."

For certainly these particular generalizations do not usher in the millennium. They are imperfect and underdeveloped, they are inadequate in scope, and in some senses they are dangerous.

They do not, for example, cover the residuum of direct effects, such as the creation of moods, except to note that such effects exist. They recognize, but in no way illuminate, the dynamism of the variety of effects stemming from such contextual and presentational variables as order, timing, camera angles, and the like. They are less easy to apply, and are conceivably inapplicable, to certain other broad areas of effect, such as the effect of the media upon each other, upon patterns of daily life, and upon cultural values as a whole. To be sure, we have spoken of cultural values as a mediating factor which in part determines media content, but certainly some sort of circular relationship must exist, and media content must in turn affect cultural values.

Such concepts suggest what is perhaps the greatest danger inherent both in these generalizations and in the approach to communications research from which they derive. And that danger ... is the tendency to go overboard in blindly minimizing the effects and potentialities of mass communications. In reaping the fruits of the discovery that mass media function amid a nexus of other influences, we must not forget that the influences nevertheless differ. Mass media of communication possess various characteristics and capabilities distinct from those of peer groups or opinion leaders. They are, after all, media of *mass* communication, which daily addresss tremendous cross-sections of the population with a single voice. It is neither sociologically unimportant nor insignificant that the media have rendered it possible, as Wiebe (1952) has put it, for Americans from all social strata to laugh at the same joke, nor is it insignificant that total strangers, upon the first meeting, may share valid social expectations that small talk about Lucy and Desi, or about Betty Furness, will be mutually comprehensible. We must not lose sight of the peculiar characteristics of the media nor of the likelihood that of this peculiar character there may be engendered peculiar effects.

We must remember also that under conditions and in situations other than those described in this volume, the media of mass communication may well have effects which are quite different and possibly more dramatic or extensive than those which have here been documented.

For example, the research here cited which bears upon mass communication as an instrument of persuasion has typically dealt with non-crucial issues and has been pursued either in laboratories or in naturalistic situations within a relatively stable society. Little attention has here been given to the potentialities of persuasive mass communication at times of massive political upheaval or in situations of actual or imminent social unrest. Given the rumblings of serious social malcontent—or, in terms of our current orientation, given individuals with predispositions toward change, unstructured as the envisaged change may be—mass communication would appear to be capable of molding or "canalizing" the predispositions into specific channels and so producing an active revolutionary movement. Some such process, in miniature, appears to have occurred in the . . . cases of Nazi and North Korean soldiers who, upon the dissolution of their primary groups, became susceptible to Allied propaganda. A similar process of greater social width may well have occurred in under-developed countries in which the Communist party has recently become a major political force. Mass communication in such areas has of course been deliberately and carefully abetted by personal influence and by the formation and manipulation of reinforcing primary and secondary groups. Although it cannot therefore be said to have been a sufficient cause of the observed social changes; it may well have been an extremely important or even a crucial cause. Its effects may have been largely restricted to the activation and focusing of amorphous unrest, but these effects appear to have had consequences far beyond those normally associated with the reinforcement of pre-existing and specific attitudes. The fear that a similar activation process may occur, or that the media might actually create new attitudes, presumably lies behind the totalitarian practice of denying media access to voices of the political opposition.[29]

Even within a relatively stable social situation, the media of mass communication may well exercise extensive social effects upon the masses by the indirect road of affecting the elite. Particular vehicles of mass communication (e.g., *The New York Times*) and other vehicles directed toward a more specialized audience (e.g., *The Wall Street Journal* or *U.S. News and World Report*) may reasonably be supposed to affect the decisions and behavior of policy-making elites. Individual business and political leaders may or may not be "opinion leaders" in the sense in which the term is used in communications research—i.e., they may or may not critically influence a handful of their peers. But their decisions and their consequent behavior in themselves affect society at large, and the mere fact of their taking a particular stand frequently serves to make that stand and the issue to which it pertains a topic of media reporting and debate, and a topic in regard to which personal influence, in the more restricted sense of the term, is exercised. The media may, in short, stimulate the elite to actions which affect the masses and which incidentally restimulate and so affect both the media and channels of interpersonal influence.

It has also been suggested that the classic studies of how voters make up their minds—e.g., Lazarsfeld, Berelson, and Gaudet (1948) and Berelson, Lazarsfeld, and McPhee (1954)—provide an incomplete picture of the total effects of mass communication because they concentrate only on effects which occur *during* the campaign itself. Lang and Lang (1959), for example, point out that although most of the voters observed in such studies apparently kept to a decision made before the campaign began, shifts in voting behavior sufficient to produce changes of administration do occur. They suggest that such changes take place slowly *between* the campaigns, as new issues arise and as images of the parties change or fail to change. Mass communication, they propose, makes these issues salient and builds the party images, and may thus exercise a much more extensive effect than is revealed in the classic voting studies. The Langs call for research designed to investigate the possiblity of such effects and of various other types of effect which they believe mass communication may exercise upon political opinion.

Some elections, furthermore, may be more "critical" than others. Key (1955), for example, notes that there is "a category of elections," including those of 1896 and 1928, in which

> ... voters are, at least from impressionistic evidence, unusually deeply concerned, in which the extent of electoral involvement is relatively quite high, and in which the decisive results of the voting reveal a sharp alteration of the pre-existing cleavage within the electorate. Moreover, and perhaps this is the truly differentiating characteristic of this sort of election, the realignment made manifest in the voting in such elections seems to persist for several succeeding elections.[30]

The elections on which the classic voting studies focus are not "critical" by these criteria, but are rather occasions on which previously manifested alignments held more or less stable. What role mass communication may play in determining voters' decisions before a "critical" election is not yet known.

Mass media may also have extensive but as yet undocumented effects of various non-political sorts. We have already alluded, for example, to the probable but unmapped interplay between the mass media and cultural values. To look more closely into one aspect of this matter, one might postulate that the media play a particularly important role in the socialization and acculturation of children. . . . But to what degree do the media structure, even for younger children, the society and the culture which they are entering? The influence of the media in these respects is no doubt modified by the influence of the family, of the school, and of peer groups; but the question of ultimate media effect is complicated, perhaps beyond the possibility of simplification, by the fact that the persons comprising these very sources of extra-media influence are themselves exposed to and affected by the media. The role and the effects of the media in the socialization of the child can perhaps no longer be accurately assessed, but some concept of its possible scope may be obtained by performing the mental experiment of imagining the process of socialization occurring in a society in which mass media did not exist. Our knowledge of primitive cultures and of pre-media years suggests that the present social system and the present culture are at least in part a product of the existence of mass communication, and may be dependent upon such communication for their continued existence.

One may also speculate on the possibility that some of the functions served by mass communication may, perhaps indirectly and perhaps only after a long period, have certain effects both upon the audience as individuals and upon integral elements of the social structure. We have noted, for example, that certain light media material, such as comic strips, serves certain audience members by providing a common ground for social discourse. It is interesting to speculate on what alternative systems of serving the same function may be thereby replaced, may be reduced in importance, or may simply fail to develop for lack of being needed. If no comic strips or other mass media material existed to serve the conversational needs of the adult males observed by Bogart (1955), might they and others like them perhaps be more actively interested in each other's real life goals and problems? Do mass media, by providing an easily available and common ground for chit-chat, perhaps reduce or retard the development of interest in one's fellow men? And to what degree, if any, has the serving of such functions by mass media affected the functions previously served by such institutions as the neighborhood bar and barber shop? . . .

The phenomenistic approach, which our generalizations suggest, also has its dangers and limitations. As we have noted, the identification of conditions under which mass communication has different effects is only a step in the direction of answering the basic questions about the incidence of such effects. If the influence of mass communication is to be described in socially meaningful terms, research must also inquire into the relative prevalence of the conditions under which the several effects occur.

The need of recognizing such limitations and of taking precautions against such dangers does not seem to the author, however, to compromise the usefulness of either the generalizations or the phenomenistic approach. The most fruitful path for communications research appears to him to be neither the path of abstract theorizing nor the path, which so many researchers have deserted, of seeking simple and direct effects of which mass communication is the sole and sufficient cause. The author sees far greater hope in the new approach which begins with the existing phenomenon—an observed change of opinions, for example—and which attempts to assess the roles of the several influences which produced it. He sees similar hope in the pursuit of logically related controlled experiments in which the multifarious extramedia factors being investigated are built into the research design. These are the paths which seem to him to have brought us to the point of tentative generalization and which seem likely to lead further toward the still distant goal of empirically-documented theory.

NOTES

1. e.g., Arnheim, Rudolf (1944). "The World of the Daytime Serial," and Herzog, Herta (1944). "What Do We Really Know about Daytime Serial Listeners," in Lazarsfeld, Paul F. and Stanton, Frank N., eds., *Radio Research 1942-1943,* New York: Duell, Sloan and Pearce.
2. e.g., Warner, W. Lloyd and Henry, William E. (1948). "The Radio Day Time Serial: A Symbolic Analysis," *Genetic Psychology Monographs,* XXXVII, 3-71.
3. This is a typical conclusion of surveys of pertinent literature and comment, e.g., Bogart, Leo (1956). *The Age of Television.* New York: Frederick Ungar Publishing Company, pp. 258-74.
4. e.g., Lazarsfeld, Paul F. and Merton, Robert K. (1948). "Mass Communication, Popular Taste and Organized Social Action," in Bryson, Lyman, ed., *The Communication of Ideas,* New York: Harper and Brothers; Klapper, Joseph T. (1948). "Mass Media and the Engineering of Consent." *American Scholar,* XVII, 419-29.
5. Klapper, Joseph T. (1949). *The Effects of Mass Media.* New York: Bureau of Applied Social Research, Columbia University, pp. II-25, IV-52.
6. Merton, Robert K. (1946). *Mass Persuasion.* New York: Harper and Brothers.
7. The efficacy as well as the limitations of media in this regard are perhaps most exhaustively documented in the various unclassified evaluation reports of the United States Information Agency.
8. Kelley, Harold H. and Volkart, Edmund H. (1952). "The Resistance to Change of Group Anchored Attitudes," *American Sociological Review,* XVII, 453-65.
9. Lasswell proposed in 1946 (Smith, Bruce L.; Lasswell, Harold D.; and Casey, Ralph D. (1946). *Propaganda, Communication and Public Opinion.* Princeton: Princeton University Press, p. 121) that communications research might be described as an inquiry into, "*Who* says *what,* through what *channels* (media) of communication, *to whom,* (with) what ... results." This now classic formulation was widely adopted as an organizational framework for courses and books of reading in communication research and greatly influenced research orientations as well.
10. Hovland, Carl I. (1954). "Effects of the Mass Media of Communication," in Lindzey, Gardiner ed., *Handbook of Social Psychology.* Cambridge, Mass.: Addison-Wesley Publishing Company, Inc., II, 1062-103; Hovland, Carl I., et al. (1957) *The Order of Presentation in Persuasion.* New Haven: Yale University Press.
11. e.g., Merton (1946), p. 61 ff; Freeman, Howard E.; Weeks, H. Ashley; and Wertheimer, Walter I. (1955). "News Commentator Effect: A Study in Knowledge and Opinion Change," *Public Opinion Quarterly,* XIX, 209-15; Hovland, Carl I.; Janis, Irving L.: and Kelley, Harold H. (1953). *Communication and Persuasion.* New Haven: Yale University Press, Chapter ii, which summarizes a series of studies by Hovland, Weiss, and Kelman.

12. Hovland, Carl I.; Lumsdaine, Arthur A.; and Sheffield, Fred D. (1949) *Experiments on Mass Communication,* "Studies in Social Psychology in World War II." Vol. III. Princeton: Princeton University Press, in re "sleeper effects" and "temporal effects."

13. e.g., Kelley and Volkart (1952); Riley, John W. and Riley, Mathilda White (1959). "Mass Communication and the Social System," in Merton, Robert K.: Broom, Leonard; and Cottrell, Leonard S. Jr., eds.; *Sociology Today: Problems and Prospects.* New York: Basic Books; Ford, Joseph B. (1954). "The Primary Group in Mass Communication," *Sociology and Social Research,* XXXVIII, 3; Katz, Elihu and Lazarsfeld, Paul F. (1955). *Personal Influence: The Part Played by People in the Flow of Mass Communication.* Glencoe, Ill.: The Free Press, reviews a vast literature on the subject (pp. 15-133).

14. Katz, Elihu (1957). "The Two-Step Flow of Communication: An Up-to-Date Report on an Hypothesis," *Public Opinion Quarterly,* XXI, 61-78, provides an exhaustive review of the topic.

15. Freidson, Eliot (1953). "The Relation of the Social Situation of Contact to the Media of Mass Communication," *Public Opinion Quarterly,* XVII, 230-38. For an earlier insight, see Cooper, Eunice and Johoda, Marie (1947). "The Evasion of Propaganda," *Journal of Psychology,* XXIII, 15-25.

16. Janis, Irving L. and King, B. T. (1954). "The Influencing of Role-Playing on Opinion Change," *Journal of Abnormal and Social Psychology,* XLIX, 211-18; King, B. T. and Janis, Irving L. (1953). "Comparison of the Effectiveness of Improvised Versus Non-Improvised Role-Playing in Producing Opinion Change," Paper presented before the Eastern Psychological Association; Kelman, Herbert C. (1953). "Attitude Change as a Function of Response Restrictions," *Human Relations,* VI, 185-214, all of which is summarized and evaluated in Hovland, Janis and Kelley (1953), also Michael, Donald N. and Maccoby, Nathan (1953). "Factors Influencing Verbal Learning from Films under Varying Conditions of Audience Participation," *Journal of Experimental Psychology,* XLVI, 411-18.

17. Janis, Irving L. (1954). "Personality Correlates of Susceptibility to Persuasion," *Journal of Personality,* XXII, 504-18; Hovland, Janis and Kelley (1953) chap. vi; Janis, et al. (1959). *Personality and Persuasibility.* New Haven: Yale University Press.

18. Maccoby, Eleanor E. (1954). "Why Do Children Watch TV?" *Public Opinion Quarterly,* XVIII, 239-44.

19. e.g., Klapper (1948); Klapper (1949); pp. IV-20-27; Wiebe, Gerhart D. (1952). "Responses to the Televised Kefauver Hearings," *Public Opinion Quarterly,* XVI, 179-200.

20. Wiebe, Herbert D. (1951). "Merchandising Commodities and Citizenship on Television," *Public Opinion Quarterly,* XV, 679-91.

21. Berelson, Bernard (1948). "Communication and Public Opinion," in Schramm, Wilbur, *Communications in Modern Society.* Urbana, Ill.: University of Illinois Press, p. 172.

22. Berelson, Bernard; Lazarsfeld, Paul F. and McPhee, William N. (1954). *Voting: A Study of Opinion Formation in a Presidential Campaign.* Chicago: University of Chicago Press, p. 234 for "hypodermic effect."

23. Klapper, Joseph T. (1957-58). "What We Know About the Effects of Mass Communication: The Brink of Hope," *Public Opinion Quarterly,* XXI, 4.

24. Berelson, Lazarsfeld, and McPhee (1954), p. 234.

25. Katz and Lazarsfeld (1955).

26. Riley and Riley (1951) and Maccoby (1954).

27. e.g., The experimental program described in Hovland, Janis and Kelley (1953), Hovland et al. (1957) and Janis et al. (1959).

28. Occasions on which it does so serve are noted in generalizations 3, 4, and 5.

29. Monopoly propaganda, as practiced by totalitarian governments, and a kind of unwitting monopoly propaganda practiced in democracies in favor of certain cultural values, are believed by some authors to be in themselves very effective persuasive procedures. See, for example, Lazarsfeld, Paul F. (1942). "The Effects of Radio on Public Opinion," in Waples, Douglas, ed., *Print, Radio and Film in a Democracy,* Chicago: University of Chicago Press, Lazarsfeld and Merton (1948), and Klapper (1948) and (1949, IV-20-27). In general, these writers suggest that the monopoly propaganda continually reinforces the attitudes it espouses, while simultaneously handicapping the birth and preventing the spread of opposing views. The argument is logically appealing and has been advanced as a conjectural explanation of various attitude and opinion phenomena, but it has been neither substantiated nor refuted by empirical research.
30. Key, V. O. (1955). "A Theory of Critical Elections," *Journal of Politics,* XVII, p. 4.

3. THE INFLUENCE AND EFFECTS OF MASS MEDIA

Denis McQuail

Editor's Note. It is clear from recent research that questions about the effects of the mass media cannot be answered in broad generalities. Scholars have learned to ask about various types of effects, on various types of people and institutions, at various levels of society, and under a variety of conditions. Denis McQuail provides an overview of these contingencies in a diverse array of important media situations. In addition to discussing the general nature of mass media effects, McQuail traces the history of effects research in Europe and the United States. He follows this with examples of research findings produced by several kinds of investigations. His bibliography is an excellent starting point for review of the English language literature on media effects through 1976.

Denis McQuail is a professor of sociology and mass communication at the University of Amsterdam in the Netherlands. In the past, he has taught at the University of Southampton, England, and at the University of Leeds. He has written several books on the sociology of mass communication. The selection is from *Mass Communication and Society,* edited by James Curran, Michael Gurevitch, and Janet Woolacott, Beverly Hills, Calif.: Sage Publications, 1979.

The questions most insistently asked of social research on mass communication, and perhaps least clearly answered, have to do with the effects and social influence of the different mass media. The reasons for asking are understandable enough, given the amount of time spent attending to the mass media in many countries and the amount of resources invested in mass media production and distribution. Although much has been written by way of answer and a good deal of research carried out, it has to be admitted that the issue remains a disputed one—both in general about the significance of mass media and in particular about the likely effect of given instances of mass communication. Inevitably, this discussion has to begin with some clarification of terms, since one of the perennial difficulties in the case has been the lack of communication between those who have investigated the question of media influence on the one hand and, on the other, the public, media producers and those concerned with public policy for the media.

The "Influence and Effects of Mass Media" by Denis McQuail is reprinted by permission of the publisher from *Mass Communication and Society,* edited by James Curran, Michael Gurevitch, and Janet Woolacott, pp. 70-93. Copyright © 1977 by The Open University. Copyright © 1979 by Sage Publications Inc. Sage edition published by arrangement with Edward Arnold (Publishers) Ltd.

Perhaps it should first be claimed that the question of effects is a somewhat unfair one, one rarely asked of comparable institutions like religion, education or the law which all in their way communicate to the public or to particular publics and where questions about effects as well as aims could well be asked. The mass media are highly diverse in content and in forms of organization and include a very wide range of activities which could have effects on society. To make the question not only more fair, but also more meaningful, we need to introduce a number of qualifications and specifications. First, we can distinguish between effects and effectiveness, the former referring to any of the consequences of mass media operation, whether intended or not, the latter to the capacity to achieve given objectives, whether this be attracting large audiences or influencing opinions and behaviour. Both matters are important, but a different set of considerations relates to each. A second, though perhaps minor, point on which to be clear concerns the reference in time. Are we concerned with the past, or with predictions about the future? If the former, we need to be precise. If the latter, and often it is a prediction about what is going on now and its results which is a main concern, then some uncertainty is inevitable.

Third, we need to be clear about the level on which effects occur, whether this is at the level of the individual, the group, the institution, the whole society or the culture. Each or all may be affected in some way by mass communication. To specify the level meaningfully also requires us to name the kinds of phenomena on which influence may be exerted. We can investigate some phenomena at several levels—especially opinion and belief which can be a matter of individual opinion as well as the collective expression of institutions and societies. On the other hand to study the effect of the media on the way institutions operate requires us to look at the relationships between people occupying different roles and at the structure and content of these roles. Politics provides a good example, where the mass media have probably affected not only individual political opinions but also the way politics is conducted and its main activities organized. Political roles may have been changed, as well as our expectations of politicians, the relationships of followers to leaders, and even perhaps some of the values of political life. All this is a matter of historical change, much slower and less reversible than any influence on opinion, attitude or voting behaviour. Again it is clear that difference of level of effect is also related to different time spans. Changes in culture and in society are slowest to occur, least easy to know of with certainty, least easy to trace to their origins, most likely to persist. Changes affecting individuals are quick to occur, relatively easy to demonstrate and to attribute to a source, less easy to assess in terms of significance and performance. Hence we tend to find a situation in which the larger and more significant questions of media effect are most subject to conflicting interpretation and the most certain knowledge we have is most open to the charge of triviality and least useful as a basis for generalization. Perhaps one could usefully add a further set of distinctions which have to be made early on, whatever the level of analysis. This relates to the direction of effect. Are the media changing something, preventing something, facilitating something or reinforcing and reaffirming something? The importance of the question is obvious, but it is worth stressing early in the discussion that a 'no change' effect can be as significant as its reverse and there is little doubt that in some respects the media do inhibit as well as promote change.

The History of Research Into the Effects of Mass Communication

. . . [W]e can characterize the 50 years or more of interest in media effects in terms of three main stages. In the first phase, which lasts from the turn of the century to the late nineteen thirties the media, where they were developed in Europe and North America, were attributed considerable power to shape opinion and belief, change habits of life, actively mould behaviour and impose political systems even against resistance. Such views were not based on scientific investigation but were based on empirical observation of the sudden extension of the audience to large majorities and on the great attraction of the popular press, cinema and radio. The assumption of media power was also acted upon, as it were, by advertisers, government propagandists in the First World War, newspaper proprietors, the rulers of totalitarian states, and accepted defensively by nearly all as the best guess in the circumstances. It is not irrelevant that this stage of thinking coincided with a very early stage of social science when the methods and concepts for investigating these phenomena were only developing.

The second stage extends from about 1940 to the early 1960s and it is strongly shaped by growth of mass communication research in the United States and the application of empirical method to specific questions about the effects and effectiveness of mass communication. The influence of this phase of research is surprisingly great, given the rather narrow range of the questions tackled and relatively small quantity of substantial studies. Most influential, perhaps, were the studies of Presidential elections in 1940 and 1948 by Lazarsfeld (1944), Berelson [et al.] (1954) and the programme of research into the use of films for training and indoctrination of American servicemen undertaken by Hovland et al. (1950). An earlier and longer tradition of social-psychological inquiry into the effects of film and other media on crime, aggression and racial and other attitudes should also be mentioned (e.g. Blumer, 1933). In practice, a small number of much cited studies provided the substance for the general view of media effects and effectiveness which was generally being disseminated in social and political science by the end of the 1960s. Where there was research outside the United States (e.g. Trenaman and McQuail, 1961), it was in the same mould and tended to confirm rather than challenge the agreed version of media effects. Basically, this version affirmed the ineffectiveness and impotency of mass media and their subservience to other more fundamental components in any potential situation of influence. The mass media—primarily radio, film or print at the time most research was conducted—emerged as unlikely to be major contributors to direct change of individual opinions, attitudes or behaviour or to be a direct cause of crime, aggression or other disapproved social phenomena. Too many separate investigations reached similar negative conclusions for this to be doubted. The comment by Klapper (1960) in an influential view of research, that 'mass communication does not ordinarily serve as a necessary and sufficient cause of audience effects, but rather functions through a nexus of mediating factors' well sums up the outcome of the second phase. Of course, research had not shown the different media to be without effects, but it had established the primacy of other social facts and showed the power of the media to be located within the existing structures of social relationships and systems of culture and belief. The reversal of a prior assumption by scientific investigation was striking and seemed the more complete because the myth of media power was so strong and occasionally uncritical and naive. At the same time, it should be admitted that neither public anxiety about the new medium of television nor professional opinion in the field of advertising and mass communication was much changed by the verdict of science. In fact, hardly had the 'no effect' conclusion become generally accepted than it became subject to re-examination by social scientists who doubted that the whole story had yet been written.

The third phase, which still persists, is one where new thinking and new evidence is accumulating on the influence of mass communication, especially television, and the long neglected newspaper press. As early signs of doubts we could cite Lang and Lang (1959) or Key (1961) or Blumler (1964) or Halloran (1964). The case for re-opening the question of mass media effects rests on several bases. First of all, the lesson of 'no-effects' has been learned and accepted and more modest expectations have taken the place of early belief. Where small effects are expected, methods have to be more precise. In addition, the intervening variables of social position and prior audience disposition, once identified as important, could now be more adequately measured. A second basis for revision however, rested on a critique of the methods and research models which had been used. These were mainly experiments or surveys designed to measure short-term changes occurring in individuals, and concentrating especially on the key concept of attitude. Alternative research approaches might take a longer time span, pay more attention to people in their social context, look at what people know (in the widest sense) rather than at their attitudes and opinions, take account of the uses and motives of the audience member as mediating any effect, look at structures of belief and opinion and social behaviour rather than individual cases, take more notice of the *content* whose effects are being studied. In brief, it can be argued that we are only at the start of the task and have as yet examined very few of the questions about the effects of mass media, especially those which reveal themselves in *collective* phenomena. Some of these matters are returned to later, and at this point it is sufficient to conclude that we are now in a phase where the social power of the media is once more at the centre of attention for some social scientists, a circumstance which is not the result of a mere change of fashion but of a genuine advance of knowledge based on secure foundations. This advance has been uneven and buffeted by external pressure, but it is real enough. . . .

The Evidence of Effects

In order to discuss the results of research into mass media effects in a meaningful way, it may be helpful to divide up the problem under a set of headings which in a composite way reflects the various distinctions which have already been mentioned: of level; of kind of effect and of process; of research strategy and method. Although the headings which follow do not divide up the field in a mutually exclusive way, they do separate out the main topics which have been discussed and provide a basis for evaluating research evidence. Basically what is being indicated is a set of media situations or processes which have distinctive features and require separate evaluation. The most important media situations are: (1) the campaign; (2) the definition of social reality and social norms; (3) the immediate response or reaction; (4) institutional change; (5) changes in culture and society.

The Campaign. Much of what has been written about the effects or effectiveness of the media either derives from research on campaigns or involves predictions about hypothetical campaign situations. In fact, the campaign is not the most common form of media provision nor its reception the most usual audience experience. Nevertheless, because the campaign is often treated as the paradigm case it is useful to pick it out, try and define what it means and what kinds of media experience are illustrated by campaign-based evidence. The kinds of media provision which might fall under this heading include: political and election campaigns, attempts at public information; commercial and public service advertising, some forms of education; the use of mass media in developing countries or generally for the diffusion of innovations. We recognize the similarity of these different activities. The campaign shares, in varying degrees, the following characteristics: it has specific aims and is planned to achieve these; it has a definite time-span, usually short; it is intensive and aims at wide coverage; its effectiveness is, in principle, open to assessment; it usually has authoritative sponsorship; it is not necessarily popular with its audience and has to be 'sold' to them; it is usually based on a framework of shared values. The campaign generally works to achieve objectives which in themselves are not controversial—voting, giving to charity, buying goods, education, health, safety, and so on. We can recall many variants and daily examples and readily see the distinctive features of this form of media content. There are fringe areas where the relevance of the campaign concept is unclear, for instance the case of news which has presumably an informative intention and may be given the features of a campaign by a particular newspaper or regarded in this light by part of an audience.

The main aim in singling out this special kind of media situation is to bring together, in summary form, the accumulated evidence bearing on campaign effects and in doing so to reduce the risk of transferring these conclusions to situations where they may not be appropriate. We can also say more with certainty about the conditions affecting the success of campaigns than about any other kind of media situation. Rather than discuss evidence in detail, which space would not allow, a brief assertion of a general condition of effect is made, with some reference to a source or summarizing work which justifies the assertion. One set of relevant factors has to do with the audience, another with the message and a third with the source or the system of distribution. Amongst audience factors, an obvious primary condition is that a large audience should be reached. Second, the appropriate members of the audience should be reached, since size alone does not guarantee the inclusion of those for whom the campaign is relevant. The classic example of an information and orientation campaign reaching an already informed and well oriented public is described by Star and Hughes (1951). Third, the dispositions of the audience should at least be not antipathetic or resistant. Political campaigning is most subject to this constraint and there is evidence that the lack of strong disposition either way and a condition of casual attention may be most favourable to the success of mass propaganda. (Blumler and McQuail, 1968.) A part of this condition relates to the need for consistency with the norms of locality and sub-culture as well as the presence of broad societal consensus. Fourth, success is likely to be greater when, within the audience, the flow of personal communication and structure of relevant interpersonal status is supportive of the mass media campaign and its aims. (Lazarsfeld, [*et al.*] 1944; Katz and Lazarsfeld, 1956; Rogers and Shoemaker, 1971.) Fifth, it is important that the audience understands or perceives the message as intended by its originators (Cooper and Jahoda, 1947; Belson, 1967) and does not selectively distort it.

Factors to do with the message or content are also important. First, the message should be unambiguous and relevant to its audience. The factor of relevance and a parallel self-selection by the audience makes it likely that campaigns are most successful at reinforcing existing tendencies or channelling them into only slightly different pathways. Second, the informative campaign seems more likely to be successful than the campaign to change attitudes or opinions. (Howland *et al.*, 195[0]; Trenaman and McQuail, 1961.) Third, in general, subject matter which is more distant and more novel, least subject to prior definitions and outside immediate experience responds best to treatment by the campaign. The essential point is that the receiver has no competing sources of information and no personal stake in resisting an appeal or disbelieving information. It is easier to form opinions and attitudes about events abroad than events at home, about unfamiliar than about familiar matters. Fourth, the campaign which allows some immediate response in action is most likely to be effective, since behaviour generally confirms intention and attitude, whether in voting or buying, or donating to a charity. Fifth, repetition can be mentioned as a probable contributor to effect, although this is a common-sense assumption rather than well demonstrated. As far as the source is concerned, we should mention first the condition of monopoly. The more channels carrying the same campaign messages, the greater the probability of acceptance. This is not easy to demonstrate and there are circumstances where an imposed monopoly invites distrust and disbelief. (e.g. Inkeles and Bauer, 1959.) But, in general, this condition is presupposed in several of the conditions already stated. Second, there is evidence that the status or authority of the source contributes to successful campaigning and the principle is applied in most campaigns whether commercial or not. The source of attributed status can of course vary, including the strongly institutionalized prestige of the political or legal system or the personal attractiveness of a star or other 'hero' of society or the claim to expert knowledge. Endorsement by an individual or institution embodying strong claims to trust and attachment can be crucial in a campaign. Third, there is a variable condition of affective attachment to a media source. There is evidence that loyalty and affective ties exist in relation to some media rather than others which may affect their ability to influence. (Butler and Stokes, 1969; Blumler *et al.*, 1975.)

These factors are all important in the process of intentional influence. While our knowledge of them is variable and incomplete they provide, even in this summarily listed form, some guide to the complex matter of determining or predicting the short-term effects of the media. We need to be careful in translating their lessons to other non-campaign circumstances, but, as we will see, they often do have a wide range of application even in adapted forms. If we accept the validity of these points we are already very far from thinking the mass media to be ineffective, [n]or can it be said that we have no certain knowledge of the effects of mass media.

The Definition of Social Reality and the Formation of Social Norms. The topics we should look at under this heading are diverse and the processes involved equally so. Here we mainly consider the process of learning through the media, a process which is often incidental, unplanned and unconscious for the receiver and almost always unintentional on the part of the sender. Hence the concept of 'effectiveness' is usually inappropriate, except in societies where the media take a planned and deliberate role in social development. This may be true of some aspects of socialist media (see Hopkins, 1970) or of some media in applications in developing countries. (Pye, 1963; Frey, 1973.) There are two main aspects to what occurs. On the one hand, there is the provision of a consistent picture of the social world which may lead the audience to adopt this version of reality, a reality of 'facts' and of norms values and expectations. On the other hand, there is a continuing and selective interaction between self and the media which plays a part in shaping the individual's own behaviour and self-concept. We learn what our social environment is and respond to the knowledge that we acquire. In more detail, we can expect the mass media to tell us about different kinds of social roles and the accompanying expectations, in the sphere of work, family life, political behaviour and so on. We can expect certain values to be selectively reinforced in these and other areas of social experience. We can expect a form of dialogue between persons and fictional characters or real media personalities and also in some cases an identification with the values and perspectives of these 'significant others.' We can also expect the mass media to give an order of importance and structure to the world they portray, whether fictionally or as actuality. There are several reasons for these expectations. One is the fact that there is a good deal of patterning and consistency in the media version of the world. Another is the wide range of experience which is open to view and to vicarious involvement compared to the narrow range of real experience available to most people at most points in their lives. Third there is the trust with which media are often held as a source of impressions about the world outside direct experience. Inevitably, the evidence for this process of learning from the media is thin and what there is does little more than reaffirm the plausibility of these theoretical propositions. The shortage of evidence stems in part from a failure to look for it, until quite recently, and in part from the long-term nature of the processes which make them less amenable to investigations by conventional techniques of social research than are the effects of campaigns. That the media tend to be both consistent amongst themselves over time and also rather given to patterning and stereotyping has been demonstrated often enough in studies of content. We can cite Galtung and Ruge (1965) on foreign countries, Berelson and Steiner (19[63]) on American ethnic minorities, Baker and Ball (1969) on the portrayal of violence, De Fleur (1964) on occupations, Franzwa (1974) on the representation of women's roles, Hartmann and Husband (1974) on immigrants in Britain, Halloran *et al.* (1970) on the newspaper portrayal of a militant demonstration, Hartmann (1976) on reporting of industrial relations. A long list of studies can be cited showing the media to have certain inbuilt tendencies to present a limited and recurring range of images and ideas which form rather special versions of reality. In some areas, as with news reporting, the pattern is fairly inescapable, in others the diversity of media allows some choice and some healthy contradiction. What we lack is much evidence of the impact of these selective versions of the world. In many cases discount by the audience or the availability of alternative information must make acceptance of media portrayals at face value extremely unlikely or unusual. We should certainly not take evidence of content as evidence of effect. There is no close correspondence between the two and some studies show this. For example Roshier (1973) found public views about crime to be closer to the 'true' statistical picture than the somewhat distorted version one might extract from the content of local newspapers. Similarly Halloran's study of audience reaction to television reports of the 1968 demonstration shows this to have been rather little affected by the 'one-sided' version presented on the screen. Even so, there is enough evidence as well as good theory for taking the proposition as a whole quite seriously. The case of the portrayal of an immigrant, especially coloured, minority provides a good test, since we may expect the media to be a prominent source of impressions for those in Britain who have little or very limited personal contact with 'immigrants.' Hartmann and Husband (1974), in an investigation of school children, show that, while degree of media exposure and degree of 'prejudice' are not directly correlated, the media are a more important source of knowledge and ideas than are personal contacts in areas where immigrant populations are small. They also show that the media are associated with a view of immigrants as likely to be a cause of trouble or be associated with conflict. It also seems that impressions attributed to the media as source show a rather higher degree of internal similarity and to be in general less evaluative than those derived from personal contact. The main contribution of the mass media is not, according to this study, to encourage prejudice (often the reverse) but in defining the presence of immigrants as an 'objective' problem for the society.

Another case of a somewhat different kind can be found in the portrayal of certain out-groups and in defining the degree and nature of their deviance. Again the media stand in for experience. Cohen's (1973) study of the media portrayal of Mods and Rockers has no evidence of effect, but here the direction of public response, guided by a near-fictional media presentation of events seems predictable. The view taken by Cohen is that 'the mass media provide a major source of knowledge in a segregated society of what the consensus actually is and what the nature of deviation is.' In his view the media are responsible for promoting 'moral panics,' identifying scapegoats, and acting as a guide to social control. The terms 'amplification' and 'sensitization' and 'polarization' have been used to describe the tendency of the media to exaggerate the incidence of a phenomenon, to increase the likelihood of it being noticed and to mobilize society against a supposed threat. In recent times, it has been argued that this treatment has been allotted to drug-taking (by Young, 1973), to mugging and to left-wing militants. It is notable that the groups receiving this form of polarizing treatment tend to be small, rather powerless and already subject to broad social disapproval. They are relatively 'safe' targets, but the process of hitting them tends to reaffirm the boundaries around what is acceptable in a free society.

When the question of media effects on violence is discussed, a rather opposite conclusion is often drawn. It seems as if general public opinion still holds the media responsible for a good deal of the increasing lawlessness in society (Halloran, 1970), a view based probably on the frequency with which crime and violence is portrayed, even if it rarely seems to be 'rewarded.' It is relevant to this section of the discussion to explore this view. American evidence obtained for the Kerner Commission on Violence and reported by Baker and Ball (1969) shows there certainly to be much violence portrayed on the most used medium, television. It also shows that most people have rather little contact with real violence in personal experience. The authors chart the public expression of norms in relation to violence and also television norms as they appear in content and find a gap between the two. Thus, while public norms cannot yet have been much affected directly, the gap suggests that the direction of effects is to extend the boundaries of acceptable violence beyond current norms. In brief then, the authors of this study lend support to one of the more plausible hypotheses connecting crime and violence with the media—that the tolerance of aggression is increased by its frequent portrayal and it becomes a more acceptable means of solving problems whether for the 'goodies' or the criminals. It should not be lost sight of, even so, that most dependable research so far available has not supported the thesis of a general association between any form of media use and crime, delinquency or violence. (Halloran, 1970.) The discussion linking social norms with violence takes place on the level of belief systems, opinions, social myths. It would require a long-term historical and cultural analysis to establish the propositions which are involved. Nor should we forget that there are counter-propositions, pointing for instance to the selectivity of public norms about violence and aggression. It is not disapproved of in general in many societies, only in its uncontrolled and non-institutionalized forms. Violence, aggression and competition are often held up for admiration when used with 'correct' aims. Whatever the strength and direction of effects, it seems justifiable to conclude that the mass media remain, for most of us, our most persuasive source of representations of violence, crime and socially disapproved behaviour and provide the materials for shaping personal and collective impressions. There is also a strong pattern in the representations put before us, shaped in the one hand by the 'demands' of the audience, and on the other by forces of social control seeking to make rules and draw boundaries. (Gerbner and Gross, 1976.)

Under this heading we can shift ground somewhat to return to a clearer and perhaps better established example of the process of defining reality and influencing norms. It has already been suggested that the media help to establish an order of priorities in a society about its problems and objectives. They do this, not by initiating or determining, but by publicizing according to an agreed scale of values what is determined elsewhere, usually in the political system. Political scientists have been most alert to the process and the term 'agenda-setting' has been given to it by McCombs and Shaw (1972). They found the mass media to present a very uniform set of issues before the American public in the 1968 presidential election and found public opinion to accord in content and order rather closely to this pattern. The phenomenon had been noted earlier in election campaign studies, where order of space given to issues in media content was found to be predictive of changes in order of importance attributed to issues over the course of the campaign. (Trenaman and McQuail, 1961; Blumler and McQuail, 1968.) In one sense the media only record the past and reflect a version of the present but, in doing so, they can affect the future, hence the significance of the 'agenda' analogy. A rather more specific case of this kind of influence from the media is indicated by Seymour-Ure (197[3]) who correlates exceptional publicity given to Enoch Powell in the media with a marked increase in public importance attaching to the issue of immigration and a polarization of views on the question. The likelihood of this occurring is accentuated by the tendency for agreement on news values between different newspapers and different mass media. (Halloran, 1970).

Given the sparseness of evidence, it is not surprising that we cannot so adequately state the conditions for the occurrence or otherwise of effects from the media in the sphere of forming impressions of reality and defining social norms. In particular, we are dealing with society-wide and historically located phenomena which are subject to forces not captured by normal data-collecting techniques in the social sciences. However, if we re-inspect the list of conditions associated with media campaign success or failure, a number will again seem relevant. In particular, we should look first at the monopoly condition. Here what matters is less the monopoly of ownership and control than the monopoly of attention and the homogeneity of content. Uniformity and repetition establish the important result of monopoly without the necessity for the structural causes to be present. The more consistent the picture presented and the more exclusively this picture gains wide attention then the more likely is the predicted effect to occur. (cf. Noelle-Ne[u]mann, 1972.) We can suppose, too, that matters outside immediate experience and on which there are not strongly formed alternative views will also be most susceptible to the level of influence spoken of. Further, we can think that here, as with media campaigns, a trust in the source and an attribution of authority will be an important factor in the greater extension of media-derived opinions and values. Other conditions of social organization must also be taken into account. It is arguable, but untestable, that circumstances of greater individuation and lower ties of attachment to intermediary groups and associations will favour an influence from the media. Finally, we might hypothesize that conditions of social crisis or danger might also be associated with strong short-term effects from the media on the definition of problems and solutions.

Immediate Response and Reaction Effects. To discuss this, we return to questions relating largely to individuals and to direct and immediate effects. We are concerned exclusively with unintended, generally 'undesirable,' effects which fall into two main categories. One relates again to the problem of crime and violence, another to cases of panic response to news or information, where collective responses develop out of individual reception of the media. . . .

. . . One school of thought is now convinced that media portrayals of aggression can provoke aggression in child audiences. (e.g. Berkovitz, 1964.) Another favours the view that the effect of fictional evidence is more likely to be a cathartic or aggression-releasing tendency. (Feshbach [and Singer], 1971) Many experiments have been inconclusive and majority opinion seems inclined to the cautious conclusion that direct effects involving disapproved behaviour are rare or likely to occur only where there is a strong disposition in that direction amongst a small minority of the already disturbed. . . .

The possibility that information received from the mass media will 'trigger' widespread and collective panic responses has often been canvassed, but rarely demonstrated. The 1938 radio broadcast of Wells' *War of the Worlds* which involved simulated news bulletins reporting an invasion from Mars is the case most often cited in this connection mainly because of [research by Cantril *et al.* (1940)] after the event. An event with some similarities in Sweden in 1973 was investigated by Rosengren *et al.* (1975) and the results cast doubt on the thesis as a whole. It seems that in neither case was there much behavioural response, and what there was was later exaggerated by other media. Investigations of news transmission in times of crisis, for instance the studies by Greenberg of the dissemination of news of the assassination of Kennedy (Greenberg [and Parker], 1965) tells us a good deal more of the processes which begin to operate in such circumstances. Essentially, what happens is that people take over as transmitters of information and those who receive news seek independent confirmation from other media or trusted personal sources. The circumstance of solitary, unmediated, reception and response is unusual and short-lived. Shibutani (1966) reminds us that rumour and panic response are the outcome of situations of ambiguity and lack of information and, on the whole the mass media operate to modify rather than magnify these conditions.

In dealing with this aspect of potential media effects, more attention should perhaps be paid to various kinds of 'contagion' or spontaneous diffusion of activities. The situations most often mentioned relate to the spreading of unrest or violence. For instance at times during the late 1960s when urban violence and rioting was not uncommon in American cities it was suggested that television coverage of one event might lead to occurrences elsewhere. Research into the possibility (e.g. Pal[e]tz and Dunn, 1967) does not settle the matter and it remains a reasonable expectation that given the right preconditions, media coverage could spread collective disturbance by publicity alone. Political authorities which have the power to do so certainly act on the supposition that unrest can be transmitted in this way and seek to delay or conceal news which might encourage imitators. The imitation of acts of terrorism or criminality, such as hijacking, seems also likely to have occurred, although the proof is lacking and the phenomenon is different because of its individual rather than collective character. In many areas where there is no institutionalized prohibition there is little doubt that spontaneous imitation and transmission do occur on a large scale by way of the mass media. In the sphere of music, dress, and other stylistic forms, the phenomenon is occurring all the time. It is this which has led to the expectation that the media on their own are a powerful force for change in developing countries (Lerner, 1958), through their stimulation of the desire first to consume and then to change the ways of life which stand in the way of earning and buying. Research evidence (e.g. Rogers and Shoemaker, 1971) and more considered thought (e.g. Golding, 1974) have led to the realization, however, that facts of social structure and of social institutions intervene powerfully in the process of imitation and diffusion. Even so, we should beware of dismissing the process as a misconception or, where it occurs, always as trivial. It is at least plausible that the movement for greater female emancipation owes a good deal to widely disseminated publicity by way of mass media.

Consequences for Other Social Institutions. It was emphasized at the outset that the 'effects' of mass media have to be considered at a level beyond that of the individual audience member and the aggregate of individual behaviours. The path by which collective effects are produced is, in general, simple enough to grasp, but the extent to which effects have occurred resists simple or certain assessment and has rarely been the subject of sustained investigation or thought. As the mass media have developed they have, incontrovertibly, achieved two things. They have, between them, diverted time and attention from other activities and they have become a channel for reaching more people with more information than was available under 'pre-mass media' conditions. These facts have implications for any other institution which requires allocation of time, attention and the communication of information, especially to large numbers and in large quantities. The media compete with other institutions and they offer ways of reaching continuing institutional objectives. It is this which underlies the process of institutional effect. Other social institutions are under pressure to adapt or respond in some way, or to make their own use of the mass media. In doing so, they are likely to alter. Because this is a slow process, occurring along with other kinds of social change, the specific contribution of the media cannot be accounted for with any certainty.

If this argument is accepted, it seems unlikely that any institution will be unaffected, but most open to change will be those concerned with 'knowledge' in the broadest sense and which are most universal and unselective in their reach. In most societies, this will suggest politics and education as the most likely candidates, religion in some cases and to a lesser degree, legal institution[s]. In general we would expect work, social services, science, [and] the military to be only tangentially affected by the availability of mass media. Insofar as we can regard leisure and sport as an institution in modern society this should perhaps be added to politics and education as the most directly in-terrelated with the mass media. The case of education is an interesting one where we can see at first sight a set of circumstances favourable to the application of mass media, or the technologies of mass media, to existing purposes, yet in practice rather little use [is] made of them. Developed educational institutions have resisted any extensive change of customary ways or adaptation of content to take advantage of new ways of communicating to large numbers. (McQuail, 1970.) The mass media have often been regarded as a threat to the values of the institution, but also accepted in those spheres where innovation is taking place, for instance for the extension of education to adults or for more general educational purposes in developing countries. This conflict and correlated resistance is partly a consequence of the early definition of mass media as belonging to the sphere of entertainment and leisure and partly due to normal institutional conservatism.

The case of politics, as conducted in those societies with a broadly liberal-democratic basis, provides more evidence of adaptation and change to the circumstances of a society where the mass media are the main source of public information. In this case, the modern mass media inherited from the press, and retained, an established political function as the voice of the public and of interest groups and as the source of information on which choices and decisions could be made by a mass electorate and by politicians. The case presented for analysis involves an interaction between a profound change in the media institution as a result of broadcasting and a response by political systems which were not generally subject to profound changes. In these circumstances, it is easier to trace a plausible line of connection, although even here the process is interactive. The challenge to politics from media institutions has taken several forms, but has been particularly strong just because the press was already involved in political processes and because the introduction of broadcasting was a political act. The diversion of time from political activity was less important than the diversion of attention from partisan sources of information and ideology to sources which were more accessible and efficient, often more attractive as well as authoritative, and which embodied the rather novel political values of objectivity and independent 'expert' adjudication. As we have seen, it has increasingly seemed as if it is the mass media which set the 'agenda' and define the problems on a continuous, day to day, basis while political parties and politicians increasingly respond to a consensus view of what should be done. The communication network controlled by the modern mass party cannot easily compete with the mass media network and access to the national platform has to be competed for on terms which are partly determined by the media institutions themselves. . . .

Changes of Culture and Society. If we follow a similar line of analysis for other institutions, it is not difficult to appreciate that we can arrive at one or more versions of ways in which culture and social structure can be influenced by the path of development of media institutions. If the content of what we know, our way of doing things and spending time and the organization of central activities for the society are in part dependent on the media, then the fact of interdependence is evident. Again, the problem is to prove connections and quantify the links. The 'facts' are so scarce, open to dispute and often puny in stature that the question is often answered by reference to alternative theories. For some, the answer may still be provided by a theory of mass society of the kind advanced by Mills (1956) or Kornhauser (1959) and criticized by Shil[s] (1975). Such a theory suggests that the mass media encourage and make viable a rootless, alienated, form of social organization in which we are increasingly within the control of powerful and distant institutions. For others, a Marxist account of the mass media as a powerful ideological weapon for holding the mass of people in voluntary submission to capitalism (Marcuse, 1964; Miliband, 1969) provides the answer to the most important effects of the rise of the mass media. A more complex answer is offered by Carey (1969), in his suggestion that the mass media are both a force for integration and for dispersion and individuation in society. Gerbner [and Gross (1976) see] the key to the effects of mass media in their capacity to take over the 'cultivation' of images ideas and consciousness in an industrial society. He refers to the main process of mass media as that of 'publication' in the literal sense of making public: 'The truly revolutionary significance of modern mass communication is ... the ability to form historically new bases for collective thought and action quickly, continuously and pervasively across the previous boundaries of time, space and status.' The ideas of McLuhan (1962 and 1964), despite a loss of vogue, remain plausible for some (e.g. Noble, 1975), especially in their particular reference to the establishment of a 'global village' which will be established through direct and common experience from television. The various theories are not all so far apart. A common theme is the observation that experience, or what we take for experience, is increasingly indirect and 'mediated' and that, whether by chance or design, more people receive a similar 'version' of the world. The consequences for culture and society depend, however, on factors about which the theories are not agreed, especially on the character and likely tendency of this version of reality. Similarly, the available theories are not agreed on the basis of the extraordinary appeal of the mass media, taken in general. Do they meet some underlying human needs? If so, what is the nature of these needs? Alternatively, is the apparent 'necessity' of the media merely the result of some imposed and artificial want? Certainly, the question of what most wide-ranging consequences follow from the media must also raise the question of motivation and use.

The Social Power of Mass Media—A Concluding Note

It has been the intention of this whole discussion to make very clear that the mass media do have important consequences for individuals, for institutions and for society and culture. That we cannot trace very precise causal connections or make reliable predictions about the future does not nullify this conclusion. The question of the power of the mass media is a different one. In essence, it involves asking how effectively the mass media can and do achieve objectives over others at the will of those who direct, own or control them or who use them as channels for messages. The history of mass media shows clearly enough that such control is regarded as a valued form of property for those seeking political or economic power. The basis for such a view has already been made clear in the evidence which has been discussed. Control over the mass media offers several important possibilities. First, the media can attract and direct attention to problems, solutions or people in ways which can favour those with power and correlatively divert attention from rival individuals or groups. Second, the mass media can confer status and confirm legitimacy. Third, in some circumstances, the media can be a channel for persuasion and mobilization. Fourth, the mass media can help to bring certain kinds of publics into being and maintain them. Fifth, the media are a vehicle for offering psychic rewards and gratifications. They can divert and amuse and they can flatter. In general, mass media are very cost-effective as a means of communication in society; they are also fast, flexible and relatively easy to plan and control. If we accept Etzioni's (1967) view that 'to some degree power and communication may be substituted for each other,' then mass communication is particularly well-suited to the 'stretching' of power in a society.

The general case which can be made out along these lines for treating the mass media as an instrument of social power is sufficiently strong for many commentators to regard it as settled. In this view, all that remains is to discover not *whether* the media have power and how it works, but *who* has access to the use of this power. Generally this means asking questions about ownership and other forms of control, whether political, legal or economic. It is arguable, however, that we need to take the case somewhat further and to probe rather more carefully the initial general assumption. That is, we cannot assume that ownership and control of the means of mass communication does necessarily confer power over others in any straightforward or predictable way. The question of how power works may be the critical one. There are likely to be important structural variations in the power relationship established between 'sender' and 'receiver' in mass communication, which need also to be clarified. Compared to other forms of compliance, the case of mass communication is somewhat unusual, since it is generally entered into voluntarily and on apparently equal terms. Given such a situation, it is not so obvious how a position of dominance can usefully be attained by the 'communicators.' To analyse the process of influence in either structural or social-psychological terms is beyond the scope of this paper, but it is important to place the matter on the agenda for further study. In particular, more attention should be given to the various structures of legitimation which attract and retain audiences and which also govern their attitudes to different media sources. There are critical differences between alternative forms of control from above and between alternative types of orientation to the media, both within and between societies. This is, as yet, a relatively unexplored area but meanwhile we should be as wary of trying to answer questions of power solely in terms of ownership as we should be of doing so in terms of 'effects.'

REFERENCES

Baker, R. K. and Ball, S. J., 1969: *Mass Media and Violence.* Report to the National Commisison on the Causes and Prevention of Violence.

Belson, W., 1967: *The Impact of Television.* Crosby Lockwood.

Berelson, B., Lazarsfeld, P. F. and McPhee, W., 1954: *Voting.* University of Chicago Press.

Berelson, B., and Steiner, G., 1963: *Human Behaviour.* Harcourt Brace.

Berkovitz, 1964: 'The effects of observing violence.' *Scientific American,* vol. 210.

Blumler, H., 1933: *Movies and Conduct.* Macmillan.

Blumler, J. G., 1964: British Television: the Outlines of a Research Strategy, *British Journal of Sociology* 15 (3).

Blumler, J. G. and McQuail, D., 1968: *Television in Politics: its uses and influence.* Faber.

Blumler, J. G., Nossiter, T. and McQuail, D., 1975: *Political Communication and Young Voters.* Report to SSRC.

Blumler, J. G. and Katz, E. (eds.), 1975: 'The Uses and Gratifications approach to Communications Research.' *Sage Annual Review of Communication,* vol. 3.

Butler, D. and Stokes, D., 1969: *Political Change in Britain.* Macmillan.

Cantril, H., Gaudet, H. and Herzog, H., 1940: *The Invasion from Mars.* Princeton University Press.

Carey, J. W., 1969: 'The Communications Revolution and the Professional Communicator.' In Halmos, P., (ed.), *The Sociology of Mass Media Communicators.* Sociological Review Monograph 13. University of Keele.

Cohen, S., 1973: *Folk Devils and Moral Panics*. Paladin.
Cooper, E. and Jahoda, M., 1947: 'The evasion of propaganda.' *Journal of Psychology* 15, pp. 15-25.
De Fleur, M., 1964: 'Occupational roles as portrayed on television.' *Public Opinion Quarterly* 28, pp. 57-74.
Etzioni, A., 1967: *The Active Society*. Free Press.
Feshbach, S. and Singer, R., 1971: *Television Aggression*. Jossey-Bass.
Franzwa, H., 1974: 'Working women in fact and fiction.' *Journal of Communication*, 24 (2), pp. 104-9.
Frey, F. W., 1973: 'Communication and Development.' In de Sola Pool, I. and Schramm, W. (eds.) *Handbook of Communication*, Rand McNally.
Galtung, J., and Ruge, M., 1965: 'The structure of foreign news.' *Journal of Peace Research*, vol. 1.
Gerbner, G. and Gross, L., 1976: 'The scary world of TV's heavy viewer.' *Psychology Today*, April.
Golding, P., 1974: 'Mass communication and theories of development.' *Journal of Communication*, Summer.
Greenberg, B. and Parker, E. B. (eds.), 1965: *The Kennedy Assassination and the American Public*. Stanford University Press.
Halloran, J. D., 1964: *The Effects of Mass Communication*. Leicester University Press.
Halloran, J. D. (ed.), 1970: *The Effects of Television*, Paladin.
Halloran, J. D., Brown R. and Chaney, D. C., 1970: *Television and Delinquency*. Leicester University Press.
Halloran, J. D., Elliott, P. and Murdock, G., 1970: *Demonstrations and Communication*. Penguin.
Hartmann, P., 1976: 'Industrial relations in the news media.' *Journal of Industrial Relations*. 6(4) pp. 4-18.
Hartmann, P. and Husband, C., 1974: *Racism and the Mass Media*. Davis-Poynter.
Hopkins, M. W., 1970: *Mass Media in the Soviet Union*. Pegasus.
Hovland, C. I., Lumsdaine, A. and Sheffield, F., 1950: *Experiments in Mass Communication*. Princeton University Press.
Inkeles, A. and Bauer, R., 1959: *The Soviet Citizen*. Harvard University Press.
Katz, E. and Lazarsfeld, P. F., 1956: *Personal Influence*. Free Press.
Key, V. O., 1961: *Public Opinion and American Democracy*. Knopf.
Klapper, Joseph T., 1960: *The Effects of Mass Communication*. The Free Press.
Kornhauser, F. W., 1959: *The Politics of Mass Society*. Routledge.
Lang, K. and Lang, G., 1959: 'The Mass Media and Voting.' In Burdick, E. J. and Brodbeck, A. J. (eds.), *American Voting Behaviour*, Free Press.
Lazarsfeld, P. F., Berelson, B. and Gaudet, H., 1944: *The People's Choice*. Columbia University Press.
Lerner, D., 1958: *The Passing of Traditional Society*. Free Press.
McCombs, M. and Shaw, D. L., 1972: 'The agenda-setting function of mass media.' *Public Opinion Quarterly* 36.
McLuhan, M., 1962: *The Gutenberg Galaxy*. Routledge.
1964: *Understanding Media*. Routledge.
McQuail, D., 1970: 'Television and Education.' In Halloran, J. D. (ed.) *The Effects of Television*. Panther.
Marcuse, H., 1964: *One-Dimensional Man*. Routledge.
Mills, C. W., 1956: *The Power Elite*. Free Press.
Miliband, R., 1969: *The State in Capitalist Society*. Weidenfeld and Nicolson.
Noble, G., 1975: *Children in Front of the Small Screen*. Constable.
Noelle-Neumann, E., 1974: 'The spiral of silence.' *Journal of Communication*, Spring.

Paletz, D. H. and Dunn, R., 1967: 'Press coverage of civil disorders.' *Public Opinion Quarterly* 33, pp. 328-45.

Pye, Lucian (ed.), 1963. *Communication and Political Development.* Princeton University Press.

Roberts, D. F., 1971: 'The nature of communication effects.' In Schramm W. and Roberts, D. F., *Process and Effects of Mass Communication,* University of Illinois Press, pp. 347-87.

Rogers, E. and Shoemaker, F., 1971: *Communication and Innovations.* Free Press.

Rosengren, K. E., 1976: *The Bäxby Incident.* Lund University.

Roshier, B., 1973: 'The selection of crime news by the press.' In Cohen, S. and Young, J. (eds.), *The Manufacture of News,* Constable.

Seymour-Urc, C., 1973: *The Political Impact of Mass Media.* Constable.

Shibutani, T., 1966: *Improvised News.* Bobbs-Merril.

Shils, E., 1975: 'The Theory of Mass Society.' In *Centre and Periphery,* Chicago University Press.

Star, S. A. and Hughes, H. M., 1951: 'Report on an educational campaign.' *American Journal of Sociology* 55 (4), pp. 389-400.

Trenaman J. and McQuail, D., 1961: *Television and the Political Image.* Methuen.

Weiss, W., 1969: 'Effects of the Mass Media of Communication.' In Lindzey, G. and Aronson, E. (eds.) *Handbook of Social Psychology,* 2d edn., vol. V.

Young, J., 1973: 'The amplification of drug use.' In Cohen, S. and Young, J. (eds.) *The Manufacture of News,* Constable.

4. EXPERIMENTAL DEMONSTRATIONS OF THE "NOT-SO-MINIMAL" CONSEQUENCES OF TELEVISION NEWS PROGRAMS

Shanto Iyengar, Mark D. Peters, Donald R. Kinder

Editor's Note. Among significant possible effects of the mass media is "agenda-setting." This refers to the media's ability to establish the importance of certain issues simply by giving them prominent attention. Media audiences, including political elites, take these cues and frequently adopt the media's priorities. These priorities then move into the realm of political action and become part of the public agenda.

The existence, nature, and scope of agenda-setting effects have been investigated by a number of scholars. Most of their studies have involved a combination of content analysis of news media and interviews of media audiences that assess the extent of shared priorities. The findings have been mixed. Shanto Iyengar, Mark D. Peters, and Donald R. Kinder argue that problems with the usual research methodology have obscured agenda-setting effects. Researchers have assumed that audiences were exposed to news without testing what news they had actually selected for attention. Research has been static, measuring agenda-setting effects at a single time rather than dynamic, assessing effects over time in tune with changing media emphases. Most methodologies did not include control groups because it was difficult to find groups that had not been exposed to the media. To overcome some of these problems and measure agenda-setting more accurately, the authors designed the experiments reported here.

The three authors are political scientists who have done extensive research and writing in political psychology and political socialization. Shanto Iyengar and Mark D. Peters are currently at Yale University. Donald R. Kinder is at the University of Michigan. The selection is from *American Political Science Review,* 76 (1982): 848-858. All tables have been omitted.

... Although politically reassuring, the steady stream of minimal effects eventually proved dispiriting to behavioral scientists. Research eventually turned elsewhere, away from persuasion, to the equally sinister possibility, noted first by Lippmann (1922), that media might determine what the public takes to be important. In contemporary parlance, this is known as agenda setting. Cohen put it this way:

> the mass media may not be successful much of the time in telling people what to think, but the media are stunningly successful in telling their audience what to think about (1962, p. 16).

Do journalists in fact exert this kind of influence? Are they "stunningly successful" in instructing us what to think about? So far the evidence is mixed. . . .

. . . [W]e have undertaken a pair of experimental investigations of media agenda setting. Experiments . . . are well equipped to monitor processes like agenda setting, which take place over time. Experiments also possess important advantages. Most notably, they enable authoritative conclusions about cause (Cook and Campbell 1978). In our experiments in particular, we systematically manipulated the attention that network news programs devoted to various national problems. We did this by unobtrusively inserting into news broadcasts stories provided by the Vanderbilt Television News Archive. Participants in our experiments were led to believe that they were simply watching the evening news. In fact, some participants viewed news programs dotted with stories about energy shortages; other participants saw nothing about energy at all. (Details about the procedure are given below in the Methods section.) By experimentally manipulating the media's agenda, we can decisively test Lippmann's assertion that the problems that media decide are important become so in the minds of the public.

Our experimental approach also permits us to examine a different though equally consequential version of agenda setting. By attending to some problems and ignoring others, media may also alter the standards by which people evaluate government. We call this "priming." Consider, for example, that early in a presidential primary season, the national press becomes fascinated by a dramatic international crisis, at the expense of covering worsening economic problems at home. One consequence may be that the public will worry more about the foreign crisis and less about economic woes: classical agenda setting. But in addition, the public's evaluation of the president may now be dominated by his apparent success in the handling of the crisis; his management (or mismanagement) of the economy may now count for rather little. Our point here is simply that fluctuations in the importance of evaluational standards may well depend on fluctuations in the attention each receives in the press. . . .

Method

Overview

Residents of the New Haven, Connecticut area participated in one of two experiments, each of which spanned six consecutive days. The first experiment was designed to assess the feasibility of our approach and took place in November 1980, shortly after the presidential election. Experiment 2, a more elaborate and expanded replication of Experiment 1, took place in late February 1981.

In both experiments, participants came to two converted Yale University offices to take part in a study of television newscasts. On the first day, participants completed a questionnaire that covered a wide range of political topics, including the importance of various national problems. Over the next four days participants viewed what were represented to be videotape recordings of the preceding evening's network newscast. Unknown to the participants, portions of the newscasts had been altered to provide sustained coverage of a certain national problem. On the final day of the experiment (24 hours after the last broadcast), participants completed a second questionnaire that again included the measures of problem importance.

Experiment 1 focused on alleged weaknesses in U.S. defense capability and employed two conditions. One group of participants (N=13) saw several stories about inadequacies in American defense preparedness (four stories totalling eighteen minutes over four days). Participants in the control group saw newscasts with no defense-related stories (N=15). In Experiment 2, we expanded the test of agenda setting and examined three problems, requiring three conditions. In one group (N=15), participants viewed newscasts emphasizing (as in Experiment 1) inadequacies in U.S. defense preparedness (five stories, seventeen minutes). The second group (N=14) saw newscasts emphasizing pollution of the environment (five stories, fifteen minutes). The third group (N=15) saw newscasts with steady coverage of inflation (eight stories, twenty-one minutes). Each condition in Experiment 2 was characterized not only by a concentration of stories on the appropriate target problem, but also by deliberate omission of stories dealing with the two other problems under examination.

Participants

Participants in both experiments responded by telephone to classified advertisements promising payment ($20) in return for taking part in research on television. As hoped, this procedure produced a heterogeneous pool of participants, roughly representative of the New Haven population. . . .

We . . . tried to minimize the participants' sense that they were being tested. We never implied that they should pay special attention to the broadcasts. Indeed, we deliberately arranged a setting that was casual and informal and encouraged participants to watch the news just as they did at home. They viewed the broadcasts in small groups, occasionally chatted with their neighbors, and seemed to pay only sporadic attention to each day's broadcast. Although we cannot be certain, our experimental setting appeared to recreate the natural context quite faithfully.

Results

Setting the Public Agenda

We measured problem importance with four questions that appeared in both the pretreatment and posttreatment questionnaires. For each of eight national problems, participants rated the problem's importance, the need for more government action, their personal concern, and the extent to which they discussed each with friends. Because responses were strongly intercorrelated across the four items, we formed simple additive indices for each problem. In principle, each ranges from four (low importance) to twenty (high importance). . . .

. . . In keeping with the agenda-setting hypothesis, for defense preparedness *but for no other problem,* the experimental treatment exerted a statistically significant effect ($p < .05$). Participants whose news programs were dotted with stories alleging the vulnerability of U.S. defense capability grew more concerned about defense over the experiment's six days. The effect is significant substantively as well as statistically. On the first day of the experiment, viewers in the experimental group ranked defense sixth out of eight problems, behind inflation, pollution, unemployment, energy, and civil rights. After exposure to the newscasts, however, defense ranked second, trailing only inflation. (Among viewers in the control group, meanwhile, the relative position of defense remained stable.)

Experiment 2 contributes further support to classical agenda setting. As in Experiment 1, participants were randomly assigned to a condition—this time to one of three conditions, corresponding to an emphasis upon defense preparedness, pollution, or inflation. . . .

. . . [T]he classical agenda setting hypothesis is supported in two of three comparisons. Participants exposed to a steady stream of news about defense or about pollution came to believe that defense or pollution were more consequential problems. In each case, the shifts surpassed statistical significance. No agenda setting effects were found for inflation, however. With the special clarity of hindsight, we attribute this single failure to the very great importance participants assigned to inflation before the experiment. Where twenty represents the maximum score, participants began Experiment 2 with an average importance score for inflation of 18.5!

As in Experiment 1, the impact of the media agenda could also be discerned in changes in the rank ordering of problems. Among participants in the defense condition, defense moved from sixth to fourth, whereas pollution rose from fifth to second among viewers in that treatment group. Within the pooled control groups, in the meantime, the importance ranks of the two problems did not budge.

Taken together, the evidence from the two experiments strongly supports the classical agenda setting hypothesis. With a single and, we think, forgivable exception, viewers exposed to news devoted to a particular problem become more convinced of its importance. Network news programs seem to possess a powerful capacity to shape the public's agenda.

Priming and Presidential Evaluations

Next we take up the question of whether the media's agenda also alters the standards people use in evaluating their president. This requires measures of ratings of presidential performance in the designated problem areas—national defense in Experiment 1, defense, pollution, and inflation in Experiment 2—as well as measures of overall appraisal of the president. For the first, participants rated Carter's performance from "very good" to "very poor" on each of eight problems including "maintaining a strong military," "protecting the environment from pollution," and "managing the economy." We measured overall evaluation of President Carter in three ways: a single five-point rating of Carter's "*overall performance* as president"; an additive index based on three separate ratings of Carter's *competence;* and an additive index based on three separate ratings of Carter's *integrity.*

In both Experiments 1 and 2, within each condition, we then correlated judgments of President Carter's performance on a particular problem with rating of his overall performance, his competence, and his integrity. . . .

Experiments 1 and 2 furnish considerable, if imperfect, evidence for priming. The media's agenda does seem to alter the standards people use in evaluating the president. Although the patterns are not as regular as we would like, priming also appears to follow the anticipated pattern. A president's overall reputation, and, to a lesser extent, his apparent competence, both depend on the presentations of network news programs. . . .

Conclusion

Fifty years and much inconclusive empirical fussing later, our experiments decisively sustain Lippmann's suspicion that media provide compelling descriptions of a public world that people cannot directly experience. We have shown that by ignoring some problems and attending to others, television news programs profoundly affect which problems viewers take seriously. This is so especially among the politically naive, who seem unable to challenge the pictures and narrations that appear on their television sets. We have also discovered another pathway of media influence: priming. Problems prominently positioned in television broadcasts loom large in evaluations of presidential performance. . . .

Political Implications

We do not mean our results to be taken as an indication of political mischief at the networks. In deciding what to cover, editors and journalists are influenced most by organizational routines, internal power struggles, and commercial imperatives (Epstein 1973; Hirsch 1975). This leaves little room for political motives.

Unintentional though they are, the political consequences of the media's priorities seem enormous. Policy makers may never notice, may choose to ignore, or may postpone indefinitely consideration of problems that have little standing among the public. In a parallel way, candidates for political office not taken seriously by news organizations quickly discover that neither are they taken seriously by anybody else. And the ramifications of priming, finally, are most unlikely to be politically evenhanded. Some presidents, at some moments, will be advantaged; others will be undone.

Psychological Foundations

On the psychological side, the classical agenda setting effect may be a particular manifestation of a general inclination in human inference—an inclination to overvalue "salient" evidence. Extensive experimental research indicates that under diverse settings, the judgments people make are swayed inordinately by evidence that is incidentally salient. Conspicuous evidence is generally accorded importance exceeding its inferential value; logically consequential but perceptually innocuous evidence is accorded less (for reviews of this research, see Taylor and Fiske 1978; Nisbett and Ross 1980).

The analogy with agenda setting is very close. As in experimental investigations of salience, television newscasts direct viewers to consider some features of public life and to ignore others. As in research on salience, viewers' recall of information seems to have little to do with shifts in their beliefs (Fiske, Kenny, and Taylor 1982). Although this analogy provides reassurance that classic agenda setting is not psychologically peculiar, it also suggests an account of agenda setting that is unsettling in its particulars. Taylor and Fiske (1978) characterize the process underlying salience effects as "automatic." Perceptually prominent information captures attention; greater attention, in turn, leads automatically to greater influence.

Judgments are not always reached so casually, however; according to their retrospective accounts, our participants occasionally quarreled with the newscasts and occasionally actively agreed with them. Counterarguing was especially common among the politically informed. Expertise seems to provide viewers with an internal means for competing with the networks. Agenda setting may reflect a mix of processes therefore: automatic imprinting among the politically naive; critical deliberation among the politically alert.

Alterations in the standards by which presidents are evaluated, our second major finding, may also reflect an automatic process, but of a different kind. Several recent psychological experiments have shown that the criteria by which complex stimuli are judged can be profoundly altered by their prior (and seemingly incidental) activation. (For an excellent summary, see Higgins and King 1981.) As do these results, our findings support Collins's and Loftus's (1975) "spreading-activation" hypothesis. According to Collins and Loftus, when a concept is activated—as by extended media coverage—other linked concepts are made automatically accessible. Hence when participants were asked to evaluate President Carter after a week's worth of stories exposing weaknesses in American defense capability, defense performance as a general category was automatically accessible and therefore relatively powerful in determining ratings of President Carter. . . .

REFERENCES

Collins, A. M., and Loftus, E. F. 1975. A spreading-activation theory of semantic processing. *Psychological Review* 82:407-28.

Cook, T. D., and Campbell, D. T. 1978. *Quasi-experimentation*. Chicago: Rand-McNally.

Epstein, E. J. 1973. *News from nowhere*. New York: Random House.

Fiske, S. T., Kenny, D. A., and Taylor, S. E. 1982. Structural models of the mediation of salience effects on attribution. *Journal of Experimental Social Psychology* 18:105-27.

Higgins, E. T., and King, G. 1981. Category accessibility and information-processing: consequences of individual and contextual variability. In *Personality, cognition, and social interaction*, ed. N. Cantor and J. Kihlstrom. Hillsdale: Lawrence Erlbaum.

Hirsch, P. M. 1975. Occupational, organizational and institutional models in mass media research. In *Strategies for communication research*. ed. P. Hirsch et al., Beverly Hills: Sage.

Lippmann, W. 1922. *Public opinion*. New York: Harcourt, Brace.

Nisbett, R. E., and Ross L. 1980. *Human inference: strategies and short-comings of social judgment*. Englewood Cliffs, N.J.: Prentice-Hall.

Taylor, S. E., and Fiske, S. T. 1978. Salience, attention and attribution: top of the head phenomena. In *Advances in experimental social psychology, Vol. 11*. ed. L. Berkowitz, New York: Academic Press.

SHAPING THE POLITICAL AGENDA

Because the media are the main sources of political information in American society, they influence what people learn about society. In this section we focus on the role played by the media in supplying needed information to the general public and to political elites for forming political opinions and making political decisions. We also look at the slant of this information. Does it reflect general American political values? What clues, if any, does a look at the political orientations of newspeople offer for understanding the general political orientation of the news?

Will Rogers, the American humorist, said long ago that "All I know is just what I read in the papers." It seems that there is a good bit of truth in this aphorism. What Americans know about ongoing political events comes primarily from their news media. Maxwell E. McCombs and Donald L. Shaw describe to what extent the topics selected by newspeople for presentation by the mass media become the issues that the public regards as important.

A selection by Walter Lippmann follows in which he comments on the role played by the media in informing citizens. No study of the impact of news on public thinking would be complete without including at least a small portion of the wisdom of this modern political philosopher. His trenchant writings about public affairs spanned more than fifty years and continue to provide important insights into the media's impact on politics.

The kind of news that receives media attention, and the manner in which it is presented, have important consequences for political regimes. Sensitive to the power of the news media to influence the political agenda, governments throughout the world try to control media output either formally or informally. Two selections in this section explore how media provide support for the established political regime. David L. Paletz and Robert M. Entman describe ways in which myths about the dignity and efficiency of governmental performance are generated and sustained. Phillip J. Tichenor, George A. Donohue, and Clarice N. Olien explain the roles played by news stories in creating and solving political and economic controversies about public policies in various types of communities. They also point to the problem of the knowledge gap—the fact that people who enjoy higher social, educational, and economic status usually know and learn more than their less privileged counterparts. Knowledge means power. But in a system where the initiative to pay attention to the news comes from the individual, it is difficult to bridge this worrisome gap.

Aside from covering political issues, the media also create politically relevant images of nonpolitical people and institutions throughout society. Joseph R. Dominick describes the types of images of one very important sector of American society—the business community. According to political folklore, some parts of society are the darlings of the media while others, including business, are the whipping boys. Stanley Rothman and S. Robert Lichter have compared the political and social beliefs of newspeople and business elites in search of possible explanations. Their investigation leaves open the question of the relationship between the world views of newspeople and the orientations reflected in their writings.

The last two essays in this section answer some questions, and raise several more, about the ultimate effects of television news and entertainment programs on public thinking and the democratic process. George Gerbner, Larry Gross, Michael Morgan and Nancy Signorielli describe the nature and impact of typical distortions of reality by television entertainment programs. Jarol B. Manheim, in a broader philosophic vein, projects the consequences of political socialization via television. He does not like what he sees.

5. THE AGENDA-SETTING FUNCTION OF THE PRESS

Maxwell E. McCombs and Donald L. Shaw

Editor's Note. A major factor in reviving the pace of media effects research, after it had been throttled by the minimal effects findings of the 1960s, was a seminal article by Maxwell E. McCombs and Donald L. Shaw. It appeared in 1972 in *Public Opinion Quarterly* and focused on the agenda-setting capacity of the news media in the 1968 presidential election. McCombs and Shaw concentrated on information transmission—what people actually learn from news stories, rather than attitude change—the subject of earlier research. Their study started a stream of empirical research that demonstrated the media's importance as transmitters of political information.

Agenda-setting research continues to be productive in demonstrating and defining the relation between media coverage and the public's thinking. Like much political communication research, it first was used to study the media's influence on public perceptions of presidential candidates but it has moved beyond that narrow realm. In recent years researchers have looked at a wider array of elections as well as at the impact of agenda-setting in other political domains such as public policy formation and perceptions about foreign affairs.

Maxwell E. McCombs is John Ben Snow professor of newspaper research and director of the Communication Research Center at Syracuse University. Donald L. Shaw is a professor in the School of Journalism at the University of North Carolina. The authors are the intellectual godfathers of the "agenda-setting" research approach. The selection is from Donald L. Shaw and Maxwell E. McCombs, *The Emergence of American Political Issues: The Agenda-Setting Function of the Press.* St. Paul: West Publishing, 1977.

We Americans cherish the notion that America is a land firmly based upon laws, not men, and that political choices are made within the arena of competing ideas and issues. Voters carefully weigh both candidates and issues in making political choices. Few of us, however, have direct access to candidates.

We learn from our friends and from the press, newspapers, television, magazines, radio. In a nation in which the average person spends nearly three hours a day viewing television and another half hour reading a newspaper—to mention only two media—it is not surprising that we sometimes ask if the press, or "mass media," to use the term of many, does not do more than merely relay news between candidates and voters.

Does the press not actually create political and social issues by news choices made day after day? Publicity is at least potential power. Historian Daniel Boorstin has pointed out that it has become possible to achieve widespread (if not always longlasting) fame merely by appearing in the national press, particularly television. You can become famous, so to speak, by becoming well known! Can this be true of political candidates or issues?

We are quite aware the press daily brings us news information. We may be less conscious of the way this news over time may add up to shape our ideas about important issues or personalities. Political leaders certainly are aware of the role of the press in campaigns. They usually adapt to the practices and prejudices of the press.

In 1968 Richard Nixon did what many would have regarded as impossible only a few years earlier. He returned from the politically dead to become President in an election squeaker. It was, some said, a "new" Nixon, or as political reporter Joe McGinness put it more simply, a Nixon more able to understand, or use, the press. Mr. Nixon was more approachable. On occasion he even smiled at reporters. He was seen in a bathrobe. Mr. Nixon was—the reporters themselves had to admit it—human. By a close vote he won over Senator Hubert Humphrey.

By 1972, President Nixon won re-election over Democratic Senator George McGovern with one of the largest majorities in history. When it came to voting, those whom President Nixon from time to time had loosely referred to as the silent majority were noisy enough. In that campaign, President Nixon spent only a small amount of time on the campaign trail. Instead he used a carefully constructed media campaign which emphasized selected issues and urged voters to re-elect the president.

Through press news, comment, and advertising, information about issues and personalities spreads throughout the land. But our suspicion remains: does the press merely relay information? Is it only a transmission belt? Or, by exercising conscious and unconscious choice, does the press not have the ability to spotlight certain issues for a short while, hammer away at others over time, and simply ignore still others? This book examines that agenda-setting power of the press, the hypothesis that the press itself has some power to establish an agenda of political issues which both candidates and voters come to regard as important.

The Popular View

Certainly in the popular view mass communication exerts tremendous influence over human affairs. The ability of television, newspapers, magazines, movies, radio, and a whole host of new communications technologies to mold the public mind and significantly influence the flow of history is a widely ascribed power. In the political arena, candidates spend substantial sums for the services of image-makers—a new kind of mass communication artist and technocrat who presumably works magic on the voters via the mass media.

Early social scientists shared with historians, politicians, and the general public a belief in the ability of mass communication to achieve significant, perhaps staggering, social and political effects. But beginning with the benchmark Erie County survey conducted during the 1940 presidential campaign,[1] precise, quantitative research on the effects of mass communication in election campaigns, public information campaigns, and on numerous public attitudes soon gave the academic world a jaundiced view of the power of mass communication. . . .

We moved from an all-powerful *1984* view to the *law of minimal consequences,* a notion that the media had almost no effect, in two decades! But despite the "law," interest in mass communication has proliferated during the past 15 years. Political practitioners, especially, continue to emphasize the use of mass communication in election campaigns.[2] Surely all this is not due simply to cultural lag in spreading the word about the law of minimal consequences. Rather it is because *mass communication does in fact play a significant political role.* This is not to say that the early research was wrong. It simply was limited. To gain precision, science must probe carefully circumscribed areas. Unfortunately, the early research on mass communication concentrated on attitude change. Given the popular assumption of mass media effects, it was not a surprising choice. But the chain of effects that result from exposure to mass communication has a number of links preceding attitude and opinion change. In sequence, the effects of exposure to communication are generally catalogued as:

Awareness —> Information —> Attitudes —> Behavior

Early research chose as its strategy a broad flanking movement striking far along this chain of events. But as the evidence showed, the direct effects of mass communication on attitudes and behavior are minimal. . . . So in recent years scholars interested in mass communication have concentrated on earlier points in the communication process: awareness and information. Here the research has been most fruitful in documenting significant social effects resulting from exposure to mass communication. People do learn from mass communication.

Not only do they learn factual information about public affairs and what is happening in the world, they also learn how much importance to attach to an issue or topic from the emphasis placed on it by the mass media. Considerable evidence has accumulated that editors and broadcasters play an important part in shaping our social reality as they go about their day-to-day task of choosing and displaying news. In reports both prior to and during political campaigns, the news media to a considerable degree determine the important issues. In other words, the media set the "agenda" for the campaign.

This impact of the mass media—the ability to effect cognitive change among individuals, to structure their thinking—has been labeled the *agenda-setting function of mass communication.* Here may lie the most important effect of mass communication, its ability to mentally order and organize our world for us. In short, the mass media may not be successful in telling us what to think, but they are stunningly successful in telling us what to think *about.*[3]

Assertions of Agenda-Setting

The general notion of agenda-setting—the ability of the media to influence the salience of events in the public mind—has been part of our political culture for at least half a century. Recall that the opening chapter of Walter Lippmann's 1922 book *Public Opinion* is titled: "The World Outside and the Pictures in Our Heads." As Lippmann pointed out, it is, of course, the mass media which dominate in the creation of these pictures of public affairs.[4]

More recently this assumption of media power has been asserted by presidential observer Theodore White in *The Making of the President, 1972.*

> The power of the press in America is a primordial one. It sets the agenda of public discussion; and this sweeping political power is unrestrained by any law. It determines what people will talk and think about—an authority that in other nations is reserved for tyrants, priests, parties and mandarins.[5]

The press does more than bring these issues to a level of political awareness among the public. The idea of agenda-setting asserts that the priorities of the press to some degree become the priorities of the public. What the press emphasizes is in turn emphasized privately and publicly by the audiences of the press. . . .

Cognitive Effects of Mass Communication

This concept of an agenda-setting function of the press redirects our attention to the cognitive aspects of mass communication, to attention, awareness, and information. . . . [T]he history of mass communication research from the 1940 Erie County study to the present decade can be viewed as a movement away from short-range effects on attitudes and toward long-range effects on cognitions.[6]

Attitudes concern our feelings of being for or against a political position or figure. *Cognition* concerns our knowledge and beliefs about political objects. The agenda-setting function of mass communication clearly falls in this new tradition of cognitive outcomes of mass communication. Perhaps more than any other aspect of our environment, the political arena—all those issues and persons about whom we hold opinions and knowledge—is a secondhand reality. Especially in national politics, we have little personal or direct contact. Our knowledge comes primarily from the mass media. For the most part, we know only those aspects of national politics considered newsworthy enough for transmission through the mass media.

Even television's technological ability to make us spectators for significant political events does not eliminate the secondhand nature of our political cognitions. Television news is edited reality just as print news is an edited version of reality. And even on those rare occasions when events are presented in their entirety, the television experience is not the same as the eyewitness experience.[7]

Our knowledge of political affairs is based on a tiny sample of the real political world. That real world shrinks as the news media decide what to cover and which aspects to transmit in their reports, and as audiences decide to which news messages they will attend.

Yet, as Lippmann pointed out, our political responses are made to that tiny replica of the real world, the *pseudoenvironment,* which we have fabricated and assembled almost wholly from mass media materials. The concept of agenda-setting emphasizes one very important aspect of this pseudoenvironment, the *salience* or amount of emphasis accorded to various political elements and issues vying for public attention.

Many commentators have observed that there is an agenda-setting function of the press and Lippmann long ago eloquently described the necessary connection between mass communication and individual political cognitions. But like much of our folk wisdom about politics and human behavior, it was not put to empirical test by researchers for over half a century.

Empirical Evidence of Agenda-Setting

The first empirical attempt at verification of the agenda-setting function of the mass media was carried out by McCombs and Shaw during the 1968 U.S. presidential election.[8] Among undecided voters in Chapel Hill, North Carolina there were substantial correlations between the political issues emphasized in the news media and what the voters regarded as the key issues in that election. The voters' beliefs about what were the major issues facing the country reflected the composite of the press coverage, even though the three presidential contenders in 1968 placed widely divergent emphasis on the issues. This suggests that voters—at least undecided voters—pay some attention to all the political news in the press regardless of whether it is about or originated with a favored candidate. This contradicts the concepts of selective exposure and selective perception, ideas which are central to the law of minimal consequences. Selective exposure and selective perception suggest that persons attend most closely to information which they find congenial and supportive.

In fact, further analysis of the 1968 Chapel Hill survey showed that among those undecided voters with leanings toward one of the three candidates, there was less agreement with the news agenda based on their preferred candidate's statements than with the news agenda based on all three candidates.

While the 1968 Chapel Hill study was the first empirical investigation based specifically on agenda-setting, there is other scholarly evidence in the mass communication/political behavior literature which can be interpreted in agenda-setting terms. Let's briefly consider several examples.

The first example comes from the 1948 Elmira study.... For an optimum view of the agenda-setting influence of the press, one should examine those Elmira voters with minimal interpersonal contact.... [F]or those voters the political agenda suggested by the media is not mediated, interpreted, or confronted by interpersonal sources of influence. These voters would seem especially open to the agenda-setting influence of the press.

And the influence was there. These Elmira voters moved with the trend of the times more than did the other voters. Like the national Democratic trend that mounted during the 1948 campaign, these Elmira voters moved rapidly into the Democratic column. The cues were there in the media for all. But persons without the conservative brake of interpersonal contacts moved most rapidly with the national trend reported in the media.

The second example of agenda-setting comes from a study of county voting patterns in an Iowa referendum.[9] In this example it is easy to see the agenda-setting effects of both mass media and interpersonal news sources.

The question before the voters was calling a constitutional convention to reapportion legislative districts. Since large counties stood to gain and small counties to lose from reapportionment, the study anticipated a strong correlation between county population and proportion of votes in favor of the convention. In short, it was hypothesized that counties would vote their self-interest. And, overall, this was strikingly the case. Across all counties, the correlation is +.87 between county population and vote.

But now let us consider whether this pattern is facilitated by the presence of agenda-setting institutions. Two sources of heightened awareness were considered: a citizens' committee in favor of the convention and a daily newspaper in the county.

In the 41 counties where the citizens' committee was active, the correlation was +.92 between vote and population. In the 58 counties without such a group, the correlation was only +.59. Similar findings are reported for the presence or absence of a local daily newspaper. In the 38 counties with a local daily, the correlation was +.92. In the 61 counties without a daily, the correlation was only +.56.

Each agenda-setting source made a considerable difference in the outcome. What about their combined impact? In 28 countries with both a local daily and a citizens' committee the correlation was +.92. Where only one of these sources was present, the correlation declined to +.40; and when neither agenda-setter was present, the correlation declined to +.21.

Self-interest may have motivated many voters. But unless the issue was high on the agenda—placed there via the newspaper and local citizens' committee—this motivation simply did not come into play.

A similar "necessary condition" role for agenda-setting is found in a study of the distribution of knowledge among populations.[10] Generally, there is a knowledge gap between social classes concerning topics of public affairs, typically documented by a rather substantial correlation between level of education and knowledge of public affairs. That is to say, as level of education increases, so does the amount of knowledge about public affairs. But as communication scientist Phillip Tichenor and his colleagues discovered, the strength of this correlation, at least for some topics, is a direct function of the amount of media coverage. They found a monotonic relationship between media coverage and the strength of the education/knowledge correlation. The more the press covers a topic, the more an audience—especially audience members with more education—learn.

The Concept of Agenda-Setting

Agenda-setting not only asserts a positive relationship between what various communication media emphasize and what voters come to regard as important, it also considers this influence as an inevitable by-product of the normal flow of news.

Each day editors and news directors—the gate-keepers in news media systems—must decide which items to pass and which to reject. Furthermore, the items passed through the gate are not treated equally when presented to the audience. Some are used at length, others severely cut. Some are lead-off items on a newscast. Others follow much later. Newspapers clearly state the value they place on the salience of an item through headline size and placement within the newspaper—anywhere from the lead item on page one to placement at the bottom of a column on page 66.

Agenda-setting asserts that audiences learn these saliences from the news media, incorporating a similar set of weights into their personal agendas. Even though these saliences are largely a by-product of journalism practice and tradition, they nevertheless are attributes of the messages transmitted to the audience. And as the idea of agenda-setting asserts, they are among the most important message attributes transmitted to the audience.

This notion of the agenda-setting function of the mass media is a relational concept specifying a strong positive relationship between the emphases of mass communication and the salience of these topics to the individuals in the audience. This concept is stated in causal terms: increased salience of a topic or issue in the mass media influences (causes) the salience of that topic or issue among the public.

Agenda-setting as a concept is not limited to the correspondence between salience of topics for the media and the audience. We can also consider the saliency of various attributes of these objects (topics, issues, persons, or whatever) reported in the media. To what extent is our view of an object shaped or influenced by the picture sketched in the media, especially by those attributes which the media deem newsworthy? Some have argued, for example, that our views of city councils as institutions are directly influenced by press reporting with the result that these local governing groups are perceived to have more expertise and authority than they actually possess.[11]

Consideration of agenda-setting in terms of the salience of both topics and their attributes allows the concept of agenda-setting to subsume many similar ideas presented in the past. The concepts of status-conferral, stereotyping, and image-making all deal with the salience of objects or attributes. And research on all three have linked these manipulations of salience to the mass media.

Status-conferral, the basic notion of press agentry in the Hollywood sense, describes the ability of the media to influence the prominence of an individual (object) in the public eye.

On the other hand, the concept of stereotyping concerns the prominence of attributes: All Scots are thrifty! All Frenchmen are romantic! Stereotyping has been criticized as invalid characterization of objects because of its overemphasis on a few selected traits. And the media repeatedly have been criticized for their perpetuation of stereotypes, most recently of female roles in our society.

The concept of image-making, now part of our political campaign jargon, covers the manipulation of the salience of both objects and attributes. A political image-maker is concerned with increasing public familiarity with his candidate (status-conferral) and/or increasing the perceived prominence of certain candidate attributes.

In all cases, we are dealing with the basic question of agenda-setting research: How does press coverage influence our perception of objects and their attributes?

Issue Salience and Voting

Political issues have become salient as a factor in voter behavior in recent years. The importance of party identification, long the dominant variable in analysis of voter decisions, has been reduced. This stems both from a conceptual rethinking of voter behavior and from an empirical trend.

The role of party identification as the major predictor of how a voter would cast his presidential ballot now appears to be an empirical generalization limited to the 1940s and 1950s. By the 1960s whatever underlying conditions that gave rise to this dominance appear to have shifted and significant declines in the predictive and explanatory power of party identification begin to appear on the empirical record.[12]

Conceptually, issues also began to play a greater role in the analysis of voter decision-making. In 1960 the Michigan Survey Research Center, whose earlier work has provided much of the evidence for the key role of party identification, added a new set of open-ended questions to its interview schedule seeking information about the voter's own issue concerns—that is, those issues which were salient to the individual voter—and the perceived link between those issues and the parties.

Analysis of these questions reveals a major role for issue salience in the presidential vote decision. For example, in predicting voting choice in 1964 the weights were .39 for candidate image, .27 for party identification, and .23 for issues. (Each weight controls for the influence of the two other factors.) . . .

The 1968 Comparative State Election Project (CSEP), conducted by the Institute for Research in Social Science at the University of North Carolina, also gave issues a major conceptual role in the analysis.[13] CSEP examined the "distance" between each voter's attitude and the position of each presidential candidate. Both for the state voter cohorts and nationally, issue proximity was a more powerful predictor of presidential vote than party identification. . . .

In 1972 issues took center stage. Summing up its analysis of that election, the Survey Research Center concluded: "Ideology and issue voting in that election provide a means for better explaining the unique elements of the contest than do social characteristics, the candidates, the events of the campaign, political alienation, cultural orientations, or partisan identification." [14]

Voters do respond to the issues. The new evidence on the impact of issues appearing in the late 1960s and early 1970s provided empirical vindication for V. O. Key, Jr.'s view that "voters are not fools." Key had long contended that voters in fact responded to the issues and to the events creating and surrounding those issues.[15] Again, anticipating the concept of an agenda-setting function of the press operating across time to define political reality, Key argued that the "impact of events from the inauguration of an administration to the onset of the next presidential campaign may affect far more voters than the fireworks of the campaign itself." [16] Even the benchmark Erie County survey found that events between 1936 and 1940 changed more than twice as many votes as did the 1940 presidential campaign itself.

It is, of course, the press that largely structures voters' perceptions of political reality. As we shall see, the press can exert considerable influence on which issues make up the agenda for any particular election. Not only can the press influence the nature of the political arena in which a campaign is conducted but, on occasion, it can define (albeit inadvertently) an agenda which accrues to the benefit of one party. To a considerable degree the art of politics in a democracy is the art of determining which issue dimensions are of major interest to the public or can be made salient in order to win public support.

In 1952 the Republicans, led by Dwight Eisenhower, successfully exploited the three "K's"—Korea, Corruption, and Communism—in order to regain the White House after a hiatus of twenty years. The prominence of those three issues, cultivated by press reports extending over many months and accented by partisan campaign advertising, worked against the incumbent Democratic party. Nor is 1952 an isolated example. One of the major campaign techniques discussed by political analyst Stanley Kelley in *Professional Public Relations and Political Power* is nothing more than increasing the salience of an issue that works to an incumbent's disadvantage.[17]

These are what social scientist Angus Campbell and his colleagues[18] call *valence issues* in contrast to our usual consideration of *position issues* on which voters take various pro or con stances. A valence issue is simply a proposition, condition, or belief that is positively or negatively valued by all the voters. At least two, if not all three, of the 1952 K's were valence issues. . . . To the extent that the press (via its agenda-setting function) has a direct impact on the outcome of a particular election, it is likely to be through the medium of valence issues which directly accrue to the advantage or disadvantage of one political party. . . .

NOTES

1. Paul Lazarsfeld, Bernard Berelson, and Hazel Gaudet, *The People's Choice* (New York: Columbia University Press, 1948).
2. Ray Hiebert, Robert Jones, John Lorenz, and Ernest Lotito (eds.), *The Political Image Merchants: Strategies in the New Politics* (Washington: Acropolis Books, 1971).
3. See Bernard C. Cohen, *The Press and Foreign Policy* (Princeton: Princeton University Press, 1963) p. 13; also Lee Becker, Maxwell McCombs, and Jack McLeod, "The Development of Political Cognitions," in Steven H. Chaffee (ed.), *Political Communication*, Vol. 4, Sage Annual Reviews of Communication Research (Beverly Hills: Sage Publications, 1975), pp. 21-63.
4. Walter Lippmann, *Public Opinion* (New York: Macmillan, 1922).
5. Theodore White, *The Making of the President, 1972* (New York: Bantam, 1973), p. 327.
6. Maxwell McCombs, "Mass Communication in Political Campaigns: Information, Gratification, and Persuasion," in F. Gerald Kline and Phillip J. Tichenor (eds.). *Current Perspectives in Mass Communication Research,* Vol. 1, Sage Annual Reviews of Communication Research (Beverly Hills: Sage Publications, 1972).
7. Kurt Lang and Glady Engel Lang, *Politics and Television* (Chicago: Quadrangle, 1968).
8. Maxwell E. McCombs and Donald L. Shaw, "The Agenda-Setting Function of Mass Media," *Public Opinion Quarterly,* 36:176-87 (Summer 1972).
9. David Arnold and David Gold, "The Facilitation Effect of Social Environment," *Public Opinion Quarterly,* 28:513-16 (Fall 1964).
10. G. A. Donohue, Phillip J. Tichenor and C. N. Olien, "Mass Media and the Knowledge Gap: A Hypothesis Reconsidered," *Communication Research,* 2:3-23 (January 1975).
11. David L. Paletz, Peggy Reichert, and Barbara McIntyre, "How the Media Support Local Governmental Authority," *Public Opinion Quarterly,* 35:80-92 (Spring 1971).
12. Edward C. Dreyer, "Media Use and Electoral Choices: Some Political Consequences of Information Exposure," *Public Opinion Quarterly,* 35:544-53 (Winter 1971-72); also Walter D. Burnham, "The End of American Party Politics," *Transaction,* 7:12-22 (December 1969).
13. David M. Kovenock, James W. Prothro, and Associates (eds.), *Explaining the Vote* (Chapel Hill: Institute for Research in Social Science, 1973).
14. A. H. Miller, W. E. Miller, A. S. Raine, and T. A. Brown, "A Majority Party in Disarray: Policy Polarization in the 1972 Election," Mimeographed report, University of Michigan.
15. V. O. Key, Jr., *The Responsible Electorate* (New York: Vintage Books, 1966).
16. Ibid., p. 9.
17. Stanley Kelley, *Professional Public Relations and Political Power* (Baltimore: Johns Hopkins Press, 1956).
18. Angus Campbell, Philip E. Converse, Warren E. Miller, and Donald E. Stokes, *Elections and the Political Order* (New York: John Wiley and Sons, 1966), p. 170.

6. NEWSPAPERS

Walter Lippmann

Editor's Note. In this classic study, Lippmann shows how journalists point a flashlight rather than a mirror at the world. Accordingly, the audience does not receive a complete image of the political scene; it gets a highly selective series of glimpses instead. Lippmann explains why the media cannot possibly perform the functions of public enlightenment that democratic theory requires. They cannot tell the truth objectively because the truth is subjective and entails more probing and explanation than the hectic pace of news production allows.

Lippmann's analysis raises profound questions about the purity and adequacy of mass media sources of information. Can there be democracy when information is invariably tainted? Are there any antidotes? The answers remain elusive.

Walter Lippmann, who died in 1974, was a renowned American journalist and political analyst whose carefully reasoned, lucid writings influenced American politics for more than half a century. He was the winner of two Pulitzer Prizes, the Medal of Freedom, and three Overseas Press Club awards. In addition to books, he also wrote articles for the *New Republic,* the New York *World,* and the New York *Herald Tribune.* This selection is from *Public Opinion,* New York: Free Press, 1965. It was published originally in 1922.

The Nature of News

. . . In the first instance . . . the news is not a mirror of social conditions, but the report of an aspect that has obtruded itself. The news does not tell you how the seed is germinating in the ground, but it may tell you when the first sprout breaks through the surface. It may even tell you what somebody says is happening to the seed under ground. It may tell you that the sprout did not come up at the time it was expected. The more points, then, at which any happening can be fixed, objectified, measured, named, the more points there are at which news can occur. . . .

Wherever there is a good machinery of record, the modern news service works with great precision. There is one on the stock exchange, and the news of price movements is flashed over tickers with dependable accuracy. There is a machinery for election returns, and when the counting and tabulating are well done, the result of a national election is usually known on the night of the election. In civilized communities deaths, births, marriages and divorces are recorded, and are known accurately except where there is concealment or neglect. The machinery exists for some, and only some, aspects of industry and government, in varying degrees of precision for securities, money and staples, bank clearances, realty transactions, wage scales. It exists for imports and exports because they pass through a custom house and can be directly recorded. It exists in nothing like the same degree for internal trade, and especially for trade over the counter.

It will be found, I think, that there is a very direct relation between the certainty of news and the system of record. If you call to mind the topics which form the principal indictment by reformers against the press, you find they are subjects in which the newspaper occupies the position of the umpire in the unscored baseball game. All news about states of mind is of this character: so are all descriptions of personalities, of sincerity, aspiration, motive, intention, of mass feeling, of national feeling, of public opinion, the policies of foreign governments. So is much news about what is going to happen. So are questions turning on private profit, private income, wages, working conditions, the efficiency of labor, educational opportunity, unemployment,[1] monotony, health, discrimination, unfairness, restraint of trade, waste, "backward peoples," conservatism, imperialism, radicalism, liberty, honor, righteousness. All involve data that are at best spasmodically recorded. The data may be hidden because of a censorship or a tradition of privacy, they may not exist because nobody thinks record important, because he thinks it red tape, or because nobody has yet invented an objective system of measurement. Then the news on these subjects is bound to be debatable, when it is not wholly neglected. The events which are not scored are reported either as personal and conventional opinions, or they are not news. They do not take shape until somebody protests, or somebody investigates, or somebody publicly, in the etymological meaning of the word, makes an *issue* of them. . . .

Let us suppose the conditions leading up to a strike are bad. What is the measure of evil? A certain conception of a proper standard of living, hygiene, economic security, and human dignity. The industry may be far below the theoretical standard of the community, and the workers may be too wretched to protest. Conditions may be above the standard, and the workers may protest violently. The standard is at best a vague measure. However, we shall assume that the conditions are below par, as par is understood by the editor. Occasionally without waiting for the workers to threaten, but prompted say by a social worker, he will send reporters to investigate, and will call attention to bad conditions. Necessarily he cannot do that often. For these investigations cost time, money, special talent, and a lot of space. To make plausible a report that conditions are bad, you need a good many columns of print. In order to tell the truth about the steel worker in the Pittsburgh district, there was needed a staff of investigators, a great deal of time, and several fat volumes of print. It is impossible to suppose that any daily newspaper could normally regard the making of Pittsburgh Surveys, or even Interchurch Steel Reports, as one of its tasks. News which requires so much trouble as that to obtain is beyond the resources of a daily press. . . .

. . . [I]n the reporting of strikes, the easiest way is to let the news be uncovered by the overt act, and to describe the event as the story of interference with the reader's life. That is where his attention is first aroused, and his interest most easily enlisted. A great deal, I think myself the crucial part, of what looks to the workers and the reformer as deliberate misrepresentation on the part of newspapers, is the direct outcome of a practical difficulty in uncovering the news, and the emotional difficulty of making distant facts interesting unless, as Emerson says, we can "perceive (them) to be only a new version of our familiar experience" and can "set about translating (them) at once into our parallel facts." [2]

If you study the way many a strike is reported in the press, you will find, very often, that the issues are rarely in the headlines, barely in the leading paragraphs, and sometimes not even mentioned anywhere. A labor dispute in another city has to be very important before the news account contains any definite information as to what is in dispute. The routine of the news works that way, with modifications it works that way in regard to political issues and international news as well. The news is an account of the overt phases that are interesting, and the pressure on the newspaper to adhere to this routine comes from many sides. It comes from the economy of noting only the stereotyped phase of a situation. It comes from the difficulty of finding journalists who can see what they have not learned to see. It comes from the almost unavoidable difficulty of finding sufficient space in which even the best journalist can make plausible an unconventional view. It comes from the economic necessity of interesting the reader quickly, and the economic risk involved in not interesting him at all, or of offending him by unexpected news insufficiently or clumsily described. All these difficulties combined make for uncertainty in the editor when there are dangerous issues at stake, and cause him naturally to prefer the indisputable fact and a treatment more readily adapted to the reader's interest. The indisputable fact and the easy interest, are the strike itself and the reader's inconvenience.

All the subtler and deeper truths are in the present organization of industry very unreliable truths. They involve judgments about standards of living, productivity, human rights that are endlessly debatable in the absence of exact record and quantitative analysis. And as long as these do not exist in industry, the run of news about it will tend, as Emerson said, quoting from Isocrates, "to make of moles mountains, and of mountains moles." [3] Where there is no constitutional procedure in industry, and no expert sifting of evidence and the claims, the fact that is sensational to the reader is the fact that almost every journalist will seek. Given the industrial relations that so largely prevail, even where there is conference or arbitration, but no independent filtering of the facts for decision, the issue for the newspaper public will tend not to be the issue for the industry. And so to try disputes by an appeal through the newspapers puts a burden upon newspapers and readers which they cannot and ought not to carry. As long as real law and order do not exist, the bulk of the news will, unless consciously and courageously corrected, work against those who have no lawful and orderly method of asserting themselves. The bulletins from the scene of action will note the trouble that arose from the assertion, rather than the reasons which led to it. The reasons are intangible. . . .

Every newspaper when it reaches the reader is the result of a whole series of selections as to what items shall be printed, in what position they shall be printed, how much space each shall occupy, what emphasis each shall have. There are no objective standards here. There are conventions. Take two newspapers published in the same city on the same morning. The headline of one reads: "Britain pledges aid to Berlin against French aggression; France openly backs Poles." The headline of the second is "Mrs. Stillman's Other Love." Which you prefer is a matter of taste, but not entirely a matter of the editor's taste. It is a matter of his judgement as to what will absorb the half hour's attention a certain set of readers will give to his newspaper. Now the problem of securing attention is by no means equivalent to displaying the news in the perspective laid down by religious teaching or by some form of ethical culture. It is a problem of provoking feeling in the reader, of inducing him to feel a sense of personal identification with the stories he is reading. News which does not offer this opportunity to introduce oneself into the struggle which it depicts cannot appeal to a wide audience. The audience must participate in the news, much as it participates in the drama, by personal identification. Just as everyone holds his breath when the heroine is in danger, as he helps Babe Ruth swing his bat, so in subtler form the reader enters into the news. In order that he shall enter he must find a familiar foothold in the story, and this is supplied to him by the use of stereotypes. They tell him that if an association of plumbers is called a "combine" it is appropriate to develop his hostility; if it is called a "group of leading businessmen" the cue is for a favorable reaction.

It is in a combination of these elements that the power to create opinion resides. . . . This is the plight of the reader of the general news. If he is to read it at all he must be interested, that is to say, he must enter into the situation and care about the outcome. But if he does that he cannot rest in a negative, and unless independent means of checking the lead given him by his newspaper exists, the very fact that he is interested may make it difficult to arrive at that balance of opinions which may most nearly approximate the truth. The more passionately involved he becomes, the more he will tend to resent not only a different view, but a disturbing bit of news. That is why many a newspaper finds that, having honestly evoked the partisanship of its readers, it can not easily, supposing the editor believes the facts warrant it, change position. If a change is necessary, the transition has to be managed with the utmost skill and delicacy. Usually a newspaper will not attempt so hazardous a performance. It is easier and safer to have the news of that subject taper off and disappear, thus putting out the fire by starving it.

News, Truth, and a Conclusion

The hypothesis, which seems to be the most fertile, is that news and truth are not the same thing, and must be clearly distinguished.[4] The function of news is to signalize an event, the function of truth is to bring to light the hidden facts, to set them into relation with each other, and make a picture of reality on which men can act. Only at these points, where social conditions take recognizable and measurable shape, do the body of truth and the body of news coincide. That is a comparatively small part of the whole field of human interest. In this sector, and only in this sector, the tests of the news are sufficiently exact to make the charges of perversion or suppression more than a partisan judgment. There is no defense, no extenuation, no excuse whatever, for stating six times that Lenin is dead, when the only information the paper possesses is a report that he is dead from a source repeatedly shown to be unreliable. The news, in that instance, is not "Lenin Dead" but "Helsingfors Says Lenin is Dead." And a newspaper can be asked to take the responsibility of not making Lenin more dead than the source of the news is reliable; if there is one subject on which editors are most responsible it is in their judgment of the reliability of the source. But when it comes to dealing, for example, with stories of what the Russian people want, no such test exists.

The absence of these exact tests accounts, I think, for the character of the profession, as no other explanation does. There is a very small body of exact knowledge, which it requires no outstanding ability or training to deal with. The rest is in the journalist's own discretion. Once he departs from the region where it is definitely recorded at the County Clerk's office that John Smith has gone into bankruptcy, all fixed standards disappear. The story of why John Smith failed, his human frailties, the analysis of the economic conditions on which he was shipwrecked, all of this can be told in a hundred different ways. There is no discipline in applied psychology, as there is a discipline in medicine, engineering, or even law, which has authority to direct the journalist's mind when he passes from the news to the vague realm of truth. There are no canons to direct his own mind, and no canons that coerce the reader's judgment or the publisher's. His version of the truth is only his version. How can he demonstrate the truth as he sees it? He cannot demonstrate it, any more than Mr. Sinclair Lewis can demonstrate that he has told the whole truth about Main Street. And the more he understands his own weaknesses, the more ready he is to admit that where there is no objective test, his own opinion is in some vital measure constructed out of his own stereotypes, according to his own code, and by the urgency of his own interest. He knows that he is seeing the world through subjective lenses. He cannot deny that he too is, as Shelley remarked, a dome of many-colored glass which stains the white radiance of eternity.

And by this knowledge his assurance is tempered. He may have all kinds of moral courage, and sometimes has, but he lacks that sustaining conviction of a certain technic which finally freed the physical sciences from theological control. It was the gradual development of an irrefragable method that gave the physicist his intellectual freedom as against all the powers of the world. His proofs were so clear, his evidence so sharply superior to tradition, that he broke away finally from all control. But the journalist has no such support in his own conscience or in fact. The control exercised over him by the opinions of his employers and his readers, is not the control of truth by prejudice, but of one opinion by another opinion that is not demonstrably less true. . . .

. . . It is possible and necessary for journalists to bring home to people the uncertain character of the truth on which their opinions are founded, and by criticism and agitation to prod social science into making more usable formulations of social facts, and to prod statesmen into establishing more visible institutions. The press, in other words, can fight for the extension of reportable truth. But as social truth is organized today, the press is not constituted to furnish from one edition to the next the amount of knowledge which the democratic theory of public opinion demands. This is not due to the Brass Check, as the quality of news in radical newspapers shows, but to the fact that the press deals with a society in which the governing forces are so imperfectly recorded. The theory that the press can itself record those forces is false. It can normally record only what has been recorded for it by the working of institutions. Everything else is argument and opinion, and fluctuates with the vicissitudes, the self-consciousness, and the courage of the human mind.

If the press is not so universally wicked, nor so deeply conspiring . . . it is very much more frail than the democratic theory has as yet admitted. It is too frail to carry the whole burden of popular sovereignty, to supply spontaneously the truth which democrats hoped was inborn. And when we expect it to supply such a body of truth we employ a misleading standard of judgment. We misunderstand the limited nature of news, the illimitable complexity of society; we overestimate our own endurance, public spirit, and all-round competence. We suppose an appetite for uninteresting truths which is not discovered by any honest analysis of our own tastes.

If the newspapers, then, are to be charged with the duty of translating the whole public life of mankind, so that every adult can arrive at an opinon on every moot topic, they fail, they are bound to fail, in any future one can conceive they will continue to fail. It is not possible to assume that a world, carried on by division of labor and distribution of authority, can be governed by universal opinions in the whole population. Unconsciously the theory sets up the single reader as theoretically omnicompetent, and puts upon the press the burden of accomplishing whatever representative government, industrial organization, and diplomacy have failed to accomplish. Acting upon everybody for thirty minutes in twenty-four hours, the press is asked to create a mystical force called Public Opinion that will take up the slack in public institutions. The press has often mistakenly pretended that it could do just that. It has at great moral cost to itself, encouraged a democracy, still bound to its original premises, to expect newspapers to supply spontaneously for every organ of government, for every social problem, the machinery of information which these do not normally supply themselves. Institutions, having failed to furnish themselves with instruments of knowledge, have become a bundle of "problems," which the population as a whole, reading the press as a whole, is supposed to solve.

The press, in other words, has come to be regarded as an organ of direct democracy, charged on a much wider scale, and from day to day, with the function often attributed to the initiative, referendum, and recall. The Court of Public Opinion, open day and night, is to lay down the law for everything all the time. It is not workable. And when you consider the nature of news, it is not even thinkable. For the news, as we have seen, is precise in proportion to the precision with which the event is recorded. Unless the event is capable of being named, measured, given shape, made specific, it either fails to take on the character of news, or it is subject to the accidents and prejudices of observation.

Therefore, on the whole, the quality of the news about modern society is an index of its social organization. The better the institutions, the more all interests concerned are formally represented, the more issues are disentangled, the more objective criteria are introduced, the more perfectly an affair can be presented as news. At its best the press is a servant and guardian of institutions; at its worst it is a means by which a few exploit social disorganization to their own ends. In the degree to which institutions fail to function, the unscrupulous journalist can fish in troubled waters, and the conscientious one must gamble with uncertainties.

The press is no substitute for institutions. It is like the beam of a searchlight that moves restlessly about, bringing one episode and then another out of darkness into vision. Men cannot do the work of the world by this light alone. They cannot govern society by episodes, incidents, and eruptions. It is only when they work by a steady light of their own, that the press, when it is turned upon them, reveals a situation intelligible enough for a popular decision. The trouble lies deeper than the press, and so does the remedy. It lies in social organization based on a system of analysis and record, and in all the corollaries of that principle; in the abandonment of the theory of the omnicompetent citizen, in the decentralization of decision, in the coordination of decision by comparable record and analysis. If at the centers of management there is a running audit, which makes work intelligible to those who do it, and those who superintend it, issues when they arise are not the mere collisions of the blind. Then, too, the news is uncovered for the press by a system of intelligence that is also a check upon the press.

That is the radical way. For the troubles of the press, like the troubles of representative government, be it territorial or functional, like the troubles of industry, be it capitalist, cooperative, or communist, go back to a common source: to the failure of self-governing people to transcend their casual experience and their prejudice, by inventing, creating, and organizing a machinery of knowledge. It is because they are compelled to act without a reliable picture of the world, that governments, schools, newspapers and churches make such small headway against the more obvious failings of democracy, against violent prejudice, apathy, preference for the curious trivial as against the dull important, and the hunger for sideshows and three legged calves. This is the primary defect of popular government, a defect inherent in its traditions, and all its other defects can, I believe, be traced to this one.

NOTES

1. Think of what guess work went into the Reports of Unemployment in 1921.
2. From his essay entitled *Art and Criticism*. The quotation occurs in a passage cited on page 87 of Professor R. W. Brown's, *The Writer's Art.*
3. Id., supra.
4. When I wrote *Liberty and the News,* I did not understand this distinction clearly enough to state it, but *cf.* p. 89 ff.

7. ACCEPTING THE SYSTEM

David L. Paletz and Robert M. Entman

Editor's Note. Besides keeping Americans in all walks of life informed about political happenings, the media also create support for established authorities. They do this by treating political symbols and rituals with deference and by not questioning the legitimacy of existing institutions. A team of researchers from Duke University, struck by the respectful news coverage given to city council meetings, systematically investigated the relationship between actual conduct and media coverage of the meetings. They found sharp discrepancies between the raw reality and the polished media version. There has been a greater trend toward realism since their investigation, which took place in 1969. But the basic patterns of deferential treatment of public institutions by journalists still hold. When the tone of most news stories suggests that public officials deserve respect, media audiences are apt to absorb this perennial political lesson.

The authors are members of the small group of political science specialists in public policy who have assessed the major roles played by the media in American politics. David L. Paletz was trained at the University of California, Los Angeles; Robert M. Entman was trained at Yale. Both teach at Duke University. The selection is from *Media Power Politics*, New York: Free Press, 1981.

... [T]he general impact of the mass media is to socialize people into accepting the legitimacy of their country's political system; ... lead them to acquiesce in America's prevailing social values; ... direct their opinions in ways which do not undermine and often support the domestic and foreign objectives of elites; ... and deter them from active, meaningful participation in politics—rendering them quiescent before the powerful. ...

Legitimacy

We begin with two concepts: legitimacy and political socialization. Legitimacy is the widely shared public belief that the political system is right for the society, and that governing institutions and officials rightly hold and exercise power. Political socialization is the process by which members of the society acquire political norms, attitudes, values, and beliefs.

From the perspective of elites, political socialization should encourage and sustain legitimacy. For children, it usually does so. Such agents of political socialization as parents, schools, religious institutions, and government, sometimes deliberately, sometimes without conscious intent, help imbue young Americans with an idealized image of their political system, its founders, functions, and purposes.

But political socialization is a continuous process. Adult experiences can shatter childhood illusions. The activities of most local governments possess the potential to destroy faith in their representatives and responsiveness. Watergate possessed the potential to undermine faith in the legitimacy of the entire American political system. Vietnam possessed the potential to challenge long-cherished myths about the innocence and nobility of America's aims as implemented by ruling elites.

The mass media are crucial in all this. Although other socializing agents remain operative, it is the media that bring Watergate and Vietnam and local government—or do not bring them—into American homes. What they communicate, how they frame and present it, influences Americans' beliefs about the legitimacy of their polity. In contrast to the situation in many other countries, the American media are not the playthings of government. And yet, the overall effect of their coverage of activities and events which might undermine legitimacy is to sustain it.

. . .[S]ocialization effects are potent though usually unintentional. We illustrate our argument with case studies of local newspaper reporting of a city council and of national media coverage of Watergate. . . . [The Watergate case study has been omitted.—ed.]

Legitimizing a City Council

In Durham, North Carolina, the city council passes most of the legally binding ordinances and resolutions for the city and therefore occupies a central position of political authority in that community. The *Durham Morning Herald* is the only newspaper in the city which regularly covers council meetings. A comparison of what actually transpired at city·council meetings with the way these events were portrayed in the *Herald* reveals that the coverage consistently reinforced the council's legitimacy. The main explanation: the reporters' concept of professionalism.

By professionalism we mean a set of internalized norms that guide and structure the local reporters' stories. These canons of conventional journalism include condensing and summarizing; investing events with rationality and coherence (even though the events may be confusing to the participants, and the reporters themselves may not fully comprehend what has occurred and its meaning); emphasizing the council's decisions at the expense of its other activities; accurately conveying the specifics of these decisions; and treating the council and its members with respect. The implementation of these norms supports the council's authority in three general ways: by creating a sense of psychological distance between the authority and the reader; by rationalizing time and thereby reducing the reader's anxiety; and by providing symbolic reassurance.

Creating Psychological Distance

Psychological distance heightens the legitimacy of power holders. The *Herald's* coverage of city council meetings creates psychological distance by using official language, referring to collective institutional decisions, using a respectful tone, depersonalizing, and giving minimum coverage to jurisdictional and procedural disputes. Some examples follow.

To achieve accuracy in reporting ordinances passed by the council, reporters sometimes quote directly from official language:

> Whereas there is a spirit of unrest and uneasiness now in evidence . . . be it ordained by the City Council . . . if any group of 25 or more persons desires to use any park, public street, or vacant lot facing a public street in the city for an assembly or group meeting, that written notification be given to the Durham Police Department at least 24 hours prior to the meeting.[1]

Quoting the actual law lends impact to the statements and may impress the reader with the substance of the ordinance. It may appear, however, to have been a decision made not by people but by an authoritative collectivity which sits in a hallowed chamber and hands down laws to protect the people of the city. Legal language adds a tone of legitimacy to the setting of council meetings and to council decisions.

In fact, the *Herald* almost always speaks of decisions as being made by "the council" [2] when in fact they are usually made by two or three of the twelve council members who have particular knowledge of the question at hand. Although an article sometimes mentions who made the determining motion, this council member may or may not be the same person who explained the details of the problem to the other members and thus influenced their decisions.

Reporters further convey distance by writing stories in a tone of respect. They infrequently mention personal jokes made by the council members or describe individual idiosyncracies. The articles are often simple accounts of motions and countermotions with only cursory mention of the names involved. A typical opening paragraph reads:

> The Durham City Council continued to hold a second demonstration control ordinance in abeyance Tuesday night by deferring action on the measure until the next regularly scheduled meeting. Two city laws aimed at controlling demonstrations were presented to the Council March 17. . . . A week later, the council by a nine-to-three vote approved an ordinance regulating use of Five Points Park "in promotion of public safety and welfare." [3]

To hold a decision "in abeyance" is formal and official in connotation, and the image of the council presented here is highly impersonal.

When attending a council meeting, however, one was struck by the distinctive personalities of the members exposed in revealing episodes. It was not rare to find one member dozing off to sleep just as a vote was being taken on a crucial issue, or to see another smacking on a large wad of gum while the intricacies of a public housing dispute were discussed. The mayor, who wore a red carnation at all times, was inclined to add humor to the situation whenever possible. After some elderly citizens requested that their bus rates be reduced during certain slack ridership periods, including 7:00 p.m. to midnight, the mayor commented, "All I have to say is that if you plan to use the bus until midnight, you sure must have a bunch of swingers in your group." That the senior citizens made such a request was fully reported in the *Herald* the following day, but the mayor's comment was not.[4]

Finally, the *Herald* reports the substantial amount of council time devoted to jurisdictional disputes and bickering over procedures so briefly that those arguments do not diminish the council's distance from the citizenry. One example will show this and also illustrate the respectful tone and depersonalization just mentioned.

A large group of people went to the council meeting to protest a proposed public housing project. At this point in the design of the housing plan, the housing authority had control and it was doubtful that the council had any jurisdiction. The group of citizens, however, did not feel that they would be given the proper response to their protest if they took it to the housing authority, and thus came directly to the council. A long discussion over jurisdiction resulted among the council members, and when one suggested that it was not proper for the council to take any action at all, the audience booed and yelled. A motion was made to set up an investigation discussion committee. This resulted in another long discussion of who would comprise the committee. After this had been resolved, another question of procedure was raised as to whether the group should report to the housing authority or to the council. A suggestion by one councilman that it should be left up to the housing authority to consider the merits of the investigation findings resulted in more outcries from the audience, until it was finally decided that the group could report back to the council. The *Herald* report summarized this entire controversy quite neatly: "After much discussion of proper procedure, the offering of a motion, a substitute motion and a substitute for that, the council voted overwhelmingly to look into the matter further." [5]

On the second page inside the paper, the account of the controversy over procedure is expanded, although still concisely and with no reference at all to the effect that the audience participation might have had in deciding the proper procedure in the case. The account of the controversy is at the end of the article, where it is susceptible to deletion.

This kind of coverage occurs because reporters have only a limited space in which to describe council activities. The most important of these activities, they believe (probably rightly), are the decisions reached and ordinances passed. Consequently, little space is devoted to the actions of individual council members, let alone their personal foibles and eccentricities. Moreover, the article cannot be filled with details of procedural and jurisdictional disputes. And to render complex ordinances accurately, it is useful simply to quote the formal legal language. The respectful tone which characterizes coverage of the council stems from the journalistic belief (still widely shared) that those in authority should be written about with respect (often whether they are worthy of such treatment or not). Reporters are therefore simply observing common journalistic norms as practiced particularly in small and medium-sized newspapers.

As a result, the city council is depicted as an authority-wielding body which is organized to deal with problems efficiently; which is responsive to the needs of the people without succumbing to pressure; and which reaches its collective decisions in an impersonal, depersonalized way. Consequently, psychological distance is maintained between the council and its members, on the one hand, and the public on the other; and the council's legitimacy is reinforced.

Reducing Anxiety by Rationalizing Time

One of people's greatest fears is that life may have no ultimate meaning or purpose. To overcome or at least to live and function within the overriding context of this fear, people order life around a concept of time as a progression of moments related to one another through some sort of continuum. Usually this sense of a time continuum is developed to harmonize with society's traditional sense of time. Meerloo observes that the "assimilation of self-time and tradition means the acceptance of authority" [6] and the reduction of anxiety.

The *Herald's* articles on the council appear at regular intervals, invest the council's activity with meaning and coherence, and assert a temporary rationality. Consequently, they probably reduce the reader's potential or actual anxiety by complementing and facilitating his or her own attempts to develop a concept of time and to express it through verbal language. If Meerloo is right, this leads to a greater willingness to accept the council's legitimacy.

It is not, however, simply the regularity of council stories which reinforces the public's collective sense of time. To the *Herald's* reporters the logical ordering of events is the demand of professionalism. One, who did not wish to be identified, commented that "often articles do not follow the order of the meeting itself. The reporter structures and orders the events artificially to try to make sense out of them. Often I join unrelated statements with things like, 'and X responded' when actually the statements are half an hour apart." In this way, the reader does not experience the council members' frustration. Furthermore, the council appears capable of sifting through the complexity of issues to their very crux in order to reconcile difficulties quickly, easily, and gracefully.

Reporters sometimes reinforce this sense of rationality and temporal coherence by adding related material to the article when the story is unclear without it. In this way, no one moment is reported as being isolated from the mainstream. Life is depicted as essentially causal. That the final decision may not have been made for the reasons cited in the article but is rather a hasty "let's just settle this now and get it over with" action is rarely suggested.

Reporters further order time for the reader by summarizing the events of the meeting into a neat package. They find some incidents more important than others, highlight them in their articles, speed up time by omitting other events, and give readers the impression that, for the council, life is a continuous stream of important related moments. Since the existence of boredom and routine moments is not legitimized by recognition in the paper, it is as if they do not exist. The council, consequently, takes on an exceptionally vibrant and appealing image. Such is the result of professional reporting.

Symbolic Reassurance

Much governmental activity is essentially symbolic.[7] Myths, rites, and incantations reassure the public, leading to political quiescence and support of the prevailing institutions of authority. Often this works through what Lassell calls the cathartic function of politics: the formulation of a resolution or law in no way specifically solves the substantive problem but somehow relieves the tension associated with the situation and directs the public's attention elsewhere.[8]

An example appeared in the *Herald* when the Chamber of Commerce concluded a study of housing in Durham and ceremoniously presented it to the city council. The *Herald* accurately reported the event, including the Chamber's recommendations and resolutions. But information extraneous to the specific ceremony was not adduced. For example, it was not mentioned that some of the people who made the study were allegedly the very individuals who build and maintain inadequate housing in the city. Thus the reader was probably left with the feeling of satisfaction that something would be done. Anxiety was diminished because plans for the solution of the problem had been presented in a neat package to the city council. Whether or not action was taken may have been irrelevant as far as the image of the city council is concerned because "people tend to judge a man by his goals, by what he is trying to do, and not necessarily by what he accomplishes or by how well he succeeds." [9]

The flow of symbolically reassuring actions from council to public is unwittingly facilitated not only by what is included in the *Herald's* stories but by what is omitted. A survey of *Herald* articles revealed that the reporters rarely chose to write a story about an individual whose request was denied at a council meeting. Certainly it was news if a large group was denied its request, but the case of the isolated individual, often confused by administrative complexity, was not depicted.

An example: in one council meeting, well over an hour was spent deliberating over a sewage assessment that one man and his next-door neighbor had come to question. After much discussion, the council voted to keep the original assessment. The basic reason that the man had to pay a high fee was that he did not understand the procedure for petitioning the city to extend such service. He told the council that he had come to City Hall to find out the proper procedure, which he then followed, but that he had been given the wrong information. Nevertheless, he would have to pay because everyone else on the block suffered from misinformation and the council decided it would be too difficult to reimburse everyone. This decision came only after much discussion of laws which were not really applicable but served to confuse the petitioner, who was not very well educated. No mention of this discussion, which took one-third of the meeting to resolve, was made in the *Herald* article the next day.[10]

By adhering to the criterion of "interest to the most people," however, the reporter emphasized instead the actions of a senior citizens group. The headline read, "Group at Council Session Seeks Reduced Bus Rates for Elderly." [11] Thus the public is gratified that the city is considering helping its senior citizens rather than frustrated by the treatment the individual man received. The reporter simply chose to report the story which common sense decided had the most appeal. Because of his decision, the council's image as a highly authoritative, responsive governing body was undisturbed.

The newspaper's coverage would not be symbolically reassuring if the council granted requests from individuals and rejected them from groups. In practice, of course, the council is generally responsive to groups, or at least rarely explicitly negative (it tries to obfuscate when necessary). And some rejections of requests from groups (for example, of requests by blacks) are symbolically reassuring to substantial elements of the majority white population.

Caveats

Since the *Herald* study was conducted, cynicism about politics has increased substantially. As a result of the unsavory ambience that now envelops politicians, public attitudes toward council members as a class have no doubt soared. In addition, coverage in cities with a less politically inert populace and a more aggressive newspaper may differ.[12] Even in Durham, more controversies and demands have intruded upon the council, lessening its ability to appear as benevolently responsive to a consensual public interest. But the legitimacy of the city council as an institution endures; it is still thought the proper form of local governance.

There are two major reasons. First, the professional norms of journalists persist. They still inject legal and official language into stories, treat individual members respectfully (at least in print and to their faces), invest their depictions of meetings with rationality and coherence, and omit procedural disputes and small but potentially revealing council contacts with the idiosyncratic demands of individuals.

Second, perhaps more important, local government is not the source of most of the problems that have caused citizen disaffection—assassinations, Vietnam, recession, inflation. Nor is it perceived as the fount of solutions. Public expectations are low.

NOTES

1. "City Council Defers Action on Demonstration Ordinance," *Durham Morning Herald,* April 9, 1969, p. A-1. Henceforth all dates refer to *Herald* stories. This section is based on Paletz, David L., Peggy Reichert, and Barbara McIntyre. "How the Media Support Local Government Authority," *Public Opinion Quarterly* 35 (1971): 80-92.
2. For example, "Council Passes New Sunday 'Blue Law' Effective Oct. 1," September 2, 1969, p. A-1; and "Committee of the Whole to Consider Changing Eno Park Plans Today," February 12, 1970, p. C-1.
3. "City Council Defers Action on Demonstration Ordinance," April 9, 1969, p. A-1, 2.
4. "Group at Council Session Seeks Reduced Bus Rates for Elderly," March 17, 1970, p. B-1.
5. "Housing Project Site to Get Further Study," April 7, 1970, p. A-1.
6. Meerloo, Joost A. M. *The Two Faces of Man.* New York: International Universities Press, 1954, p. 108.
7. Edelman, Murray. *The Symbolic Uses of Politics.* Urbana, Illinois: University of Illinois Press, 1964.
8. Lasswell, Harold D. *Psychopathology and Politics.* Chicago: University of Chicago Press, 1930, pp. 195-198.
9. Edelman (1964), p. 78.
10. "Group at Council Session Seeks Reduced Bus Rates for Elderly," March 17, 1970, p. B-1.
11. Ibid.
12. A once notorious California city hall reporter took umbrage at our analysis. In a personal letter (June 1971), he responded: "I always treasured any sign of life at a meeting, whether an angry crowd—whose epithets and arguments I would quote at length—or a character on the council. (We had one veteran with a real knack for quotes: at one budget session, he snarled, 'My platform is to get everybody at City Hall an electric typewriter and an assistant.' We made a box out of that.)" Michael Kernan is right. Not all reporters are as hidebound as the ones whose reporting we have described. Some relish the cut and thrust of council meetings—when it occurs. As he puts it: the *Durham Morning Herald* may well not be "in the mainstream of local journalism." But it is. As in most cities, the newspaper has a morning monopoly; the evening paper is owned by the same company; the readers are relatively unsophisticated (at least they were when the research was completed); and there is a strong sense of civic pride or boosterism which the newspapers perpetuate. Besides, this disagreement does not vitiate our main argument.

8. COMMUNICATION AND COMMUNITY CONFLICT

Phillip J. Tichenor, George A. Donohue, and Clarice N. Olien

Editor's Note. The authors explain the roles played by the media when conflicts erupt in various types of communities. Tichenor, Donohue, and Olien approach the media from a neglected perspective showing them embedded in their social setting and interacting with their environment. Viewed in this way, the media are an integral part of the political power structure; they serve some contenders in the power struggle and injure others.

The findings reported here are based on surveys of general populations, on interviews with political elites, and on content analysis data drawn from 19 Minnesota communities. These ranged from hamlets of less than 2,000 people to urban and suburban communities of 100,000 people. The conflict situations for which the role of the media was examined include safety concerns about the location of a nuclear power plant and a high voltage power line, environmental issues raised by sewage and industrial waste disposal, protection of wilderness areas from mining and logging operations, and massive job losses through closure of an obsolete steel plant.

The authors have worked as an interdisciplinary team at the University of Minnesota to study links between community structures and roles of the press. Phillip Tichenor is a professor of journalism and mass communication; George A. Donohue is a professor of sociology; and Clarice N. Olien is a professor of rural sociology. The selection is from *Community Conflict and the Press,* Beverly Hills, Calif.: Sage Publications, 1980.

Where Does Information Come From?

While the need for greater citizen understanding of issues may be generally agreed upon, ways of creating that understanding are not. There is, on the one hand, the traditional belief that responsible concerned citizens will inform themselves (Hennessy, 1975). Parallel with that view is the belief that information media such as newspapers, broadcast stations, and educational institutions have a responsibility and should provide the needed knowledge.

The view that individual citizens should bear the *sole* responsibility for finding out about issues is not viable, especially when the information and the system for dissemination within the community may be inadequate or nonexistent. As society becomes more diverse and complex, there is a growing expectation that the information agencies, particularly the mass media, will deliver information and interpretations through the use of experts and news analysis.

Growing diversity in society has been mirrored in the information delivery system, with increased use of such techniques as specialized sections of modern newspapers which appeal singly and in combination to different groups. Rapid growth of specialized magazines and publications targeted to limited and specific audiences also reflects this diversity. The rising importance of the "purposive communicator," (Westley and MacLean, 1957) or advocate for a special interest group which seeks the attention of wider audiences through mass media channels, further suggests a system of social organization based on pluralistic special interest groups. The increasing number of purposive communicators (such as educators, public information and public relations specialists, and advertisers) illustrates not only the increased number of special interest groups but also the interdependence of groups attempting to control both generation and dissemination of knowledge.

A large portion of the information available, then, depends on an information delivery system which reflects the pluralistic organization and vested interests of the society in which it exists. Information appears to be generated and disseminated as a result of joint activity of professionals within the mass media channels and professionals who have advocacy functions for interdependent special interest groups. These professionals represent a form of system linkage and act as an interface among the groups. . . .

Newspapers and Community Controversy

The role of newspapers and other mass media in community conflict is often recognized, and frequently the media are charged with creating the conflicts. They may be accused of "sensationalizing" and "blowing things out of proportion" or of "covering up" and "not paying attention to all sides" of a controversy (Gerald, 1963; Rivers and Schramm, 1969). Members of the media profession often answer the first accusation by saying that bringing things into the open is a necessary contribution to democratic processes (Small, 1970); the second criticism may be answered by the argument that newspapers are not simply conduits but must themselves make judgments about selection and presentation of news if they are to meet their professional obligations to the community in a responsible manner (Hulteng, 1976). In doing so, media professionals may argue, they must decide how much and what kind of play to give each side, risking the possibility that both sides may believe that their views have been underrepresented in the press. . . .

Newspapers regularly engage in message transactions involving major institutions and central values of the community and larger society. One of the newspaper's primary functions is social control, which it performs through persistently drawing attention to the oughts and naughts that generally prevail as a condition of the existing systems. The newspaper performs these functions not by outright moralizing alone, although that may occur, but through a pattern of news selection in topic and source that often reinforces values by implication (Broder, 1977). Neither the newspaper nor the broadcast station is organized to create new ideas or proposals for community consideration. They are only rarely equipped or motivated to examine proposals from different sectors of the community in an evaluative or critical way, let alone create new proposals of their own. Fundamentally, the newspaper and community broadcast station deal with the ideas and initiatives of their sources.

A fundamental hypothesis, then, is that newspapers tend to serve ancillary rather than initiating roles in the development of community conflicts. Concerted social action requires a degree of planning, coordination, and organized activity beyond the staff and capabilities of the newspaper. The organizational processes of governmental agencies, city councils, and legislatures may be neither understood nor appreciated by the individual journalists who report them. It is not unusual to find editors and reporters highly critical, if not hostile, toward committee activity and organizational procedure which are at the core of social action in both public and private sectors.

But if newspapers and other media do not initiate action, from whence comes the belief that community projects may be impossible without the media? The answer in theory is that newspapers like most mass media draw attention to organized activity that is already under way. The power or lack of power of the press stems in large measure from its ability and need to be selective (within limits) in choosing what to accelerate and what to leave languishing. For every urban renewal or environmental project given newspaper publicity in a community, informed citizens can usually name scores of other projects that never gained attention in print or were ignored in broadcast reports. A big question is, "who had the power to be selected for attention by the mass media?"

It may seem contradictory to argue that newspapers deal regularly in conflict while hardly ever initiating it. But the contradiction fades when one realizes that newspapers are regular recipients of ideas and information from a myriad of organized sources. There is very real competition from parties in a conflict for media space and time; even so-called investigative reporting is often a matter of deciding which overtures from news sources to accept (Bethell, 1977). The ordinary front page of a newspaper contains few items that resulted from journalistic initiative alone. A large portion of material is published because someone with a vested interest in the subject brought it to the newspaper's attention. Sigal (1973) found, for example, that nearly 74% of the information channels for foreign and national news in a sample of New York *Times* and Washington *Post* editors were *other* than reporter "enterprise." Press conferences and press releases alone accounted for 42% of the news channels.

If it is true that newspapers choose and select under varying degrees of pressure from items brought in by others, it is equally true that newspapers live with the most intense conflicts of their communities. But by living with these conflicts, newspapers do not necessarily turn the conflicts into public issues. They may play these conflicts down or avoid them entirely as often occurs in small communities or they may give the conflicts sustained front page play as often happens in the metropolitan press. Part of the nature of the newspaper's decision or judgment is a result of the social structure in which the newspaper operates. The characteristic differences between the rural and urban press result from the differences in the newspaper's environment; the environment does not differ because of the newspaper. The content decisions, dependent as they are on community structure, constitute a pattern of information control that has far-reaching implications for what the community will hear about, think about, and talk about.

To say that media are engaged in information control is not to say that diabolical forces are necessarily at work. The potential for such forces is there, however, and may be exploited in certain instances. Information control is one aspect of all information activities, including the conduct of social conflict. Decisions about information are made daily, and growing social and political complexity of the milieu in which communities thrive or falter creates a potential for a wealth of information on diverse topics. It is never possible to transmit or reproduce all of the information available; some decision about what to publish will be made. What is called "news judgment," "censorship," or "publicity" is, in each case, a decision about information and therefore an act of control. There may well be thousands of journalists, officials, functionaries, and citizens who make information judgments without thinking about the consequences, but those decisions are control acts despite this lack of deliberate consciousness.

Newspapers, Conflict, and Knowledge Gaps

There is the traditional viewpoint that resolution of social problems is related to inputs of information. Accordingly, if a system is sufficiently saturated with information, a general understanding of the topic will develop within the system. Once understanding is at hand, resolution is assumed to be at hand.

Behind that viewpoint are at least three assumptions. One is that information itself contributes to resolution of social problems. That assumption is not challenged here. Open for study and examination, however, are two additional assumptions. The first, based on the educational principle of repetition, is that a medium of communication, such as a newspaper, can through sheer redundancy raise the overall level of understanding in the community. The second is that higher levels of information input will lead to a general equalization of knowledge throughout the system. Hence, more effective decision making is assumed to occur.

Both of these assumptions have been brought into question by systematic studies. The first, that redundancy of newspaper reporting can increase levels of understanding, has been difficult to demonstrate in some studies of publicity campaigns (Hyman and Sheatsley, 1947; Star and Hughes, 1950), in which levels of understanding of issues changed little or not at all following media campaigns. The second assumption, that more information inputs lead to equalization of knowledge, is even more strongly questioned. Selective self-exposure to information has frequently been found to be related to level of education. Furthermore, data in recent years indicate that the problem is not so much one of increasing knowledge but, frequently, one of relative deprivation of knowledge. A gap in knowledge between segments within a total system is entirely possible, and since social power is in part based on knowledge, relative deprivation of knowledge may lead to relative deprivation of power (Tichenor, Donohue, and Olien, 1970; Rogers, 1974; Katzman, 1973).

Specifically, several studies have supported the hypothesis that as the flow of information into a social system increases, groups with higher levels of education often tend to acquire this information at a faster rate than those with lower levels of education. This higher rate of acquisition results from the different roles and positions of more highly educated segments in the social system. Groups with higher education have higher verbal skills and more media resources available to them. Educational training creates habits that include a higher rate of attention to certain kinds of media content, including public affairs, and a trained capacity for understanding and retaining that information. Similarly, more highly educated groups are trained to recognize the relevance of information for their particular position in the social structure and for maintenance of that position.

As a result of the differential rates of acquisition, gaps in knowledge between segments with different levels of education tend to increase rather than decrease. Knowledge of space research is an example; after several years of heavy media attention to space rocketry and satellites, the gap in knowledge about that research across educational levels was greater than it had been before the space research program began. Similarly, knowledge gaps widened over time for the smoking and cancer issue.

Many of the findings on knowledge of national issues support the knowledge gap hypothesis. But these findings raise a question of major theoretical and social significance: Under what conditions does it increase and under what conditions, if any, might this knowledge gap be reduced or eliminated? If such gaps widen as the flow of information to specialized groups is increased, then that tendency should be reduced as a public issue is made relevant to the plurality of the groups involved. There may be basic concerns in communities, but the key question may be the extent to which groups singly or in interaction succeed in *defining* the issue as one of basic concern.

Newspaper coverage may be more likely to equalize levels of understanding to the extent that it contributes to the intensity of conflict in a neighborhood. This stimulation may overcome—at least partially—some of the selective dissemination and selective self-exposure patterns that contribute to the widening of the knowledge gap on topics of specialized interest.

If indeed research data indicate that newspaper coverage may lead to increased controversy, which in turn increases equalization of knowledge, the implications may be disturbing. Among dominant community values, frequently, is a belief that calls for quick resolution of conflict, if not elimination of it in the first place. There is also the popular belief that "nobody learns anything in a controversy." The general proposition for study here holds quite the opposite, that controversy draws attention to information which (1) has a bearing on competition between interest groups and (2) potentially puts one group in a better power position as a result of having the information. Underlying this reasoning is the assumption that redistribution of social power among constituent groups is one of the most basic concerns in society generally. This is not to say that all or most groups are necessarily *seeking* a redistribution of power, but that any question of changing power relationships is of general concern and that conflict tends to raise precisely that question. A group seeking to maintain the status quo will be as concerned about redistribution as a group that considers itself deprived and therefore seeks a power realignment. As a result of these concerns, there is an increased likelihood in a conflict that citizens of all status levels will acquire information relevant to that conflict. While there may be limits, the implication would be that intense controversies may lead to greater realization of a general democratic ideal: the sharing of an equalized quantity of information about a situation by nearly everyone. . . .

[Role of the Press in Conflict]

The analysis of conflict situations provides abundant evidence that newspapers and other media of communication are not the independent, self-styled social agents that either they or members of the public may imagine them to be. The efficacy of viewing the press, or any other mass medium, as constituting a separate "fourth estate" is doubtful at best. The press is an integral subsystem within the total system, and its strong linkages with other system components impinge upon it as much as it impinges upon them, if not more. . . .

As an integral part of the community, the newspaper reflects the concerns of the dominant power groupings. The term *reflects* is appropriate in the sense that it is neither a total nor an undistorted reproduction of current events and institutions. Newspapers reflect selectively, in ways determined not by editorial idiosyncrasy but by the structure and distribution of social power in the community. A newspaper in a one-industry town is unlikely to report that industry in a critical way. It will reflect community consensus about that industry through reporting socially noncontroversial aspects of that industry and generally avoid reports that would question it. . . .

While the press does serve as a mirror, however contorted its reflective curvature, it is part of a reciprocal process, being affected *by* that system and affecting it in turn. Rather than being an initiator of basic positions, the press is normally pushed into reporting events by organized forces in the system and its reports become an integral part of the social process which bear on the nature of future events. Community groups may use the press and journalists as sources of intelligence, as indications of reaction of the public to events, and as a device for creating awareness and defining problems. The performance of the press or other medium typically becomes part of the controversy.

... Just as "no man is an island," subsystems are integrated into larger systems. The press is no exception, and the generalizations presented below are illustrative of this perspective.

Newspapers and Information Control

One generalization is that information is part of a general process of social control which includes media participation within different social structures. Information is a prime resource in the creation and maintenance of social power, a point which may become increasingly visible as social conflicts progress. Importance of information control is illustrated by the increasing development of specialized communication centers in business, government, education, and other agencies and interest groups. It is a rare collective action group that does not develop an organizational role or set of roles in communications, carrying titles such as public relations, publicity, outreach, or even "communication specialist.". . .

Community Structure, Media and Media Use

A second generalization is that since communication subsystems are themselves creations of the larger structures in which they operate, both media personnel performance and media use patterns of citizens will differ according to structural characteristics.

In a more highly specialized and diverse urban structure, the reporter is more likely to have a relationship with sources that are limited to the news gathering function, compared with a reporter in the more homogeneous small-town structure. As a consequence, the urban reporter is more autonomous within the system as a whole, vis-à-vis the sources, since the more pluralistic structure tends to reinforce separation of roles according to professional specialization and relationships. . . .

Similarly, media use patterns differ according to community structure. In a small, more tradition-oriented rural community, the local weekly newspaper tends to be dominated by local news, and citizens are less likely to read daily newspapers than are citizens of larger urban centers served by dailies. . . .

These differential media uses lead to different combinations of use patterns that organized groups must take into account if they are to reach the larger public through the various channels that exist. The question of how interest groups develop strategies for different community and media structures is a fruitful area for further study. These strategies require far more than analyzing the audience, finding the media that achieve high audience attention, and placing messages in those media. The "media event" techniques, such as demonstrations or whatever form they take, often involve the media personnel in such a way that they lead to quite different content than might occur if a press release were simply "placed" through routine editorial handling of purposive communications. Reporter involvement in reporting a media event does not necessarily mean the reporter thereby will be sympathetic to the organization staging the event, even though the possibility exists for such sympathy to develop. What is crucial for the strategy of countervailing groups, typically, is that the event be covered and given prominent display by the media. Reports of demonstrations, confrontations, and other media events in a newspaper may gain a level of public awareness and salience which a press release from one side alone is unlikely to have. . . .

System Reinforcement of the Media Role

A third generalization is that since they are dependent upon other parts of the system, newspapers and other media participate in social conflict in circumscribed ways which are reinforced within the system. Media will tend to reflect the perspectives of organizational power centers, which is apparent not only in small, homogeneous communities but is also illuminated in communities or regions where values and outlooks on major issues are highly diverse. Where there is diversity in social power, media tend to reflect the orientations of those segments that are higher on the power scale. In the American experience, this means having the general outlook of the business community, as a number of observers have pointed out (Hennessy, 1976; Davis, Bredemeier, and Levy, 1949; Breed, 1958). This tendency to reflect the outlook of business and other dominant power groups can have consequences in conflict situations. . . .

Structurally, it is predictable that media reports will tend to "back the winner," that is, to reflect the locus of social power and to be reinforced within the system for doing so. . . . It would be structurally unreasonable to expect any mass medium serving a community as a whole to continue backing, through editorials or portrayals, what has come to be known as a lost cause. . . . Within the local community, it is the power elite that ultimately shapes the media outlook and which therefore receives reciprocal reinforcement *from* those media.

Information and Conflict

A fourth generalization considers knowledge as a power resource and conflict as an aspect of the process that coalesces the generation, distribution, and acquisition of knowledge. This generalization runs counter to the view that conflict produces mostly confusion, rumor, and social disorder, a view based on the belief that "emotional" issues lead to "irrationality" with "nobody listening to reason." While it is true that a wide range of intense emotions on the individual level may be aroused and expressed in a conflict, and while break-offs in communication may occur among individuals and groups, the conflict process generally creates greater need for communication at various levels and tends to increase the distribution and acquisition of knowledge among different interest groups....The type of information generated and distributed tends to vary according to the needs of different groups within the structure at different stages of the conflict....

A perspective in general education holds that in reporting ... confrontations, reporters and editors "aren't doing their job" unless they devote large amounts of space to "background" reports based on evidence from scientists and technologists. Such a perspective, however, fails to take into account the nature of the conflict process and the structural principle that editors and reporters at all stages are dependent upon the acts and statements of the various interest groups. From a structural standpoint, it is very understandable why reporters *do* become immersed in the day-to-day chronology of conflict events rather than in background analyses when the conflict reaches a phase of organized confrontations and demonstrations....

Conflict and the Knowledge Gap

A fifth generalization ... is that through being an integral part of a conflict process within a social structure, mass media in performing their particular roles may contribute to either the widening or narrowing of disparities in knowledge within the system. Whether the consequence is to widen knowledge gaps or not depends at least partially upon the nature of conflict itself. Conflict is rooted in social differentiation, and newspapers and other media may contribute to increasing intensity and broadening of the scope of these conflicts while performing according to their traditional roles. This participation may serve to reinforce the differences in orientations and outlooks between different interest groups and sectors of society....

The finding of increasing knowledge gaps in a variety of situations does not mean, however, that the gaps will *always* increase. There are conditions that may lead to a decrease in gaps and to greater equalization of knowledge within a social system. One of these conditions is the existence of increasingly intense levels of social conflict, particularly that associated with community issues that touch basic concerns of different groups among the population. Conflict not only results in generation and dissemination of new knowledge but it is also an intervening variable in coalescing the concern of participating groups to acquire that knowledge. Conflict increases the amount of interaction at various points within the system and leads to a sharpening of the definition of group interests and to greater clarification in the definition of social problems. In this process, conflict leads to clarification of values of groups vis-à-vis other groups in the system and to a sharpening of each group's position. Effective group positions in social controversies include articulation of the relevance of the issue to the interests of other groups. A basic conflict strategy is to engage groups in the larger public which may have previously seen the issue as a distant fray over "somebody else's problem." A small group of employees in a container factory may conduct a strike which is not recognized by any union and may receive the "wildcat" label in newspaper headlines and broadcast news reports. The strikers' organization might then set up a media event, such as a demonstration or press conference, in which they argue that if the companies and "big unions" can join forces to squelch the protest of one small group of workers, they can also do so for other groups in the community. The strikers may also argue that the issue shows how local people are being overrun by external interests, through suggesting that the companies, unions, and perhaps the National Labor Relations Board are creatures of Washington or New York which are not responsive to local concerns.

Rhetoric and other strategies used in these situations are not always as consistent, well documented, or timely as a dispassionate observer might expect them to be. The protest group may lack organizational effectiveness, particularly in the early stages, and it will ordinarily seek to organize more effectively and perhaps recruit new talent as the conflict progresses. . . .

Knowledge Gaps and Organizational Strategy

The occurrence of knowledge gaps in the social system is a phenomenon not of individual behavior but of the group process, and is therefore highly relevant to the question of strategies which groups may employ to advance their collective interests. Familiarity with arguments in controversies, and identification of the use of arguments by different groups, is a vital aspect of knowledge on public affair topics. Even with the most esoteric public questions, the knowledge held and gained by specialists in that area will often center around potential points of debate. To illustrate: A member of the cosmopolitan elite in a community may, as part of that elite role, follow reports of the state legislature closely and be familiar with a wide range of state statutes regarding, say, elementary and high school education. That person might readily comprehend a brief report about a new development on that topic, such as a report about a change in the equalization formula of the state school-aid law. This cosmopolite may anticipate arguments for or against that law from educators and school board members in different kinds of districts, quickly perceiving potential losses to some areas and gains in others. Such perceptions of facts and insights constitute knowledge which further enhances the power of that role within a local elite group, and strengthening such roles translates into increased power for the group in which the role exists. . . .

Existence of knowledge gaps is not necessarily dysfunctional for attainment of such social goals as community development. . . . During times of conflict, elite groups may serve as vital community resources if the school-aid question does become a local issue. In fact, existence of knowledge elites may serve to alert the rest of the community to the relevance of the legislation to local interests and thereby create initial awareness. . . .

Another question about the knowledge gap phenomenon is whether new and more specialized forms of information technology will also tend to widen gaps. A hypothesis which may be offered for future study is that technologies which are organized so as to increase the degree of differential selection of information among groups will increase the disparity in information between the have and have not groups in society. One would also expect such employment of technologies to lead to knowledge gaps on more topics, since these technologies typically are structured to provide information to specialized groups. . . . Cable television has been promoted in some communities as a means for informing a wide range of citizens about community topics, in others as a means of providing highly specialized information to special interest groups. The latter outcome is more likely to occur, however, considering the nature of broadcast systems. In radio broadcasting, for example, the increased number of stations with specialized programming would be expected to contribute to increasing differentials in knowledge particularly in the entertainment area, among different groups, to which the stations direct their differential appeals.

Information, Education, and Attitudes

A final generalization is that opinions and knowledge may be related, but not in the simple and direct way that many observers suggest. Again, the existence of conflict appears to be a central variable. There is little evidence to support the contention that the more people know about a particular course of action being advocated by some group, the more they will support it. Any time there is a dispute within the system, the dispute is a result of vested interests, and the groups use information and knowledge as a source of support for their interests. . . . The intensity of a community conflict appears to reduce the likelihood that individual points of view can be predicted from their educational status or from their levels of knowledge. As a conflict develops, the highly educated individuals become more likely to turn to their vested interests and to the question of whose ox is being gored as a basis for action. . . .

REFERENCES

Bethell, T. (1977) "The myth of an adversary press." Harpers Magazine (January): 33-40.

Breed, W. (1958) "Mass communication and social integration." Social Forces 37:109-116.

Broder, D. S. (1977) "William T. Evjue memorial lecture." Presented at the meeting of the Association for Education in Journalism, Madison, Wisconsin, August.

Davis, K., H. C. Bredemeier, and M. J. Levy, Jr. (1949) Modern American Society: Readings in the Problems of Order and Change. New York: Holt, Rinehart & Winston.

Gerald, E. J. (1963) The Social Responsibility of the Press. Minneapolis: University of Minnesota Press.

Hennessy, B. (1975) Public Opinion. Belmont, Calif.: Wadsworth.

Hulteng, J. (1976) The Messenger's Motives: Ethical Problems of the News Media. Englewood Cliffs, N.J.: Prentice-Hall.

Hyman, H. and P. Sheatsley (1947) "Some reasons why information campaigns fail." Public Opinion Quarterly 11:413-423.

Katzman, N. (1973) "The impact of communication technology: some theoretical premises and their implications." NIH Information Science Training Program Colloquium. Palo Alto, Calif.: Stanford University Press.

Rivers, W. and W. Schramm (1969) Responsibility in Mass Communication. New York: Harper & Row.

Rogers, E. M. (1974) "Social structure and communication strategies in rural development: the communications effect gap and the second dimension of development." Presented at Cornell-CIAT International Symposium on Communication Strategies for Rural Development, Cali, Colombia.

Sigal, L. V. (1973) Reporters and Officials: The Organization and Politics of Newsmaking, Lexington, Mass.: D. C. Heath.

Small, W. (1970) To Kill a Messenger: Television News and the Real World, New York: Hastings House.

Star, S. and H. Hughes (1950) "Report of an educational campaign: the Cincinnati Plan for the United Nations." American Journal of Sociology 55: 389-400.

Tichenor, P. J., G. A. Donohue, and C. N. Olien (1970) "Mass media and differential growth in knowledge." Public Opinion Quarterly 34: 158-170.

Westley, B. H. and M. MacLean (1957) "A conceptual model for communication research." Journalism Quarterly 34: 31-38.

9. BUSINESS COVERAGE IN NETWORK NEWSCASTS

Joseph R. Dominick

Editor's Note. Newspeople try to keep their biases under wraps, at least most of the time. They seem to succeed well for election coverage, but they falter in foreign news coverage and in the way they cover various groups. Their failures on the left side of the political spectrum are pointed out by Todd Gitlin in Section Four. Here the failures on the establishment side are documented. Joseph R. Dominick ponders the likely impact of unduly negative portrayals of business. His article raises questions about the degree to which media images become the political reality reflected in public opinion and governmental policies.

The issue of bias in news coverage, raised by this and other selections, is tricky. If bias means intentional distortion designed to hurt or aid specific groups, it is fairly rare. If bias means slanting stories to make them exciting or to make them conform to the visions of truth held by particular newspeople, it abounds. Exciting news, in American culture, focuses on the exceptional and sensational, seeks out personalities, and stresses the negative side of life. Dominick's essay also illustrates how news carried by different sources is amazingly similiar over time. This similarity reflects the culturally shared news values of American newspeople who exhibit a broad consensus about what is and what is not worth publishing.

Joseph R. Dominick is a professor in the Grady School of Journalism and Mass Communication at the University of Georgia. The research for this selection was supported by a grant from the National Association of Broadcasters. The selection is from *Journalism Quarterly* 58 (1981): 179-185, 191. One table has been omitted.

. . . Business representatives have been highly vocal in their criticisms of broadcast news. Writing in the *Wall Street Journal,* James Ring Adams claimed, "Three of the most profitable companies in America, the commercial networks, produce a steady stream of news reports and documentaries . . . in which businessmen play the heavies." [1] William C. Cates of the Argyle Research Corporation has said, "There's always a subliminal anti-business tone. That's because every cub newscaster knows that business is evil and must be taxed more and more." [2] The chairman of the American Association

Reprinted from the Summer 1981 issue of *Journalism Quarterly* by permission.

of Advertising Agencies recently echoed this same theme, "There seems to be an unwritten rule among some of the TV newscasters that no week should go by without some denunciation of business." [3]

Representatives from the print media have made similar charges. Robert Blieberg of *Barron's* has said, "There is no doubt in my mind that there is antibusiness bias in a good deal of reporting. Television, notably network news programs and documentaries, goes out of its way to exaggerate the flaws of business and minimize the achievements." [4] Kevin Phillips, writing in *TV Guide,* has expressed the problem even more forcefully. If you watch TV news, he writes,

> . . . You're going to get a distorted picture of American business. You're going to wind up thinking that the average U.S. corporation a) makes outrageous profits; b) wallows in illegal payments to foreign governments; c) spends most of its working hours producing pollution and/or trying to slip cancer causing ingredients past Ralph Nader and the FDA.[5]

Other business representatives have made more specific criticisms of broadcast news organizations. Frederick West of Bethlehem Steel, for example, recently argued that reporters were "in over their heads" when it came to reporting business news.[6] Part of this lack of expertise may be due to the fact that the networks do not assign the "business beat" to a few specialized reporters but instead use large numbers of correspondents to report business news thus making it difficult for an individual reporter to gain a depth of knowledge in that area.[7]

Not surprisingly, spokespersons for the broadcast media have not agreed with the criticisms voiced by the business community. William Sheehan, former president of ABC news, has said that the networks handle things with fairness and balance.[8] The networks have also dismissed the complaints about lack of expertise on the part of their correspondents by arguing that business is not a monolith. The garment business is not the oil business, and they both differ from the broadcasting business. Thus, it has been argued, one cannot be an expert in "business." [9]

In short, many individuals connected with the business community have levelled several criticisms at the reporting of business news by broadcast journalism. Since news, especially television news, can influence our sense of what to do next, it seems important to gather information concerning this growing discontent between commercial enterprise and broadcast journalism. Accordingly, the purpose of this study was to test the accuracy of the above criticisms by conducting a systematic content analysis of the amount, type and tone of business news coverage as presented in the three networks' nightly newscasts.

Methods

A composite week of each network's newscasts was assembled for a two-year period, April 1977, to March 1979. For each of the 24 months, one

Monday was drawn at random and the three network newscasts for that day were analyzed using the *Television News Index* published by Vanderbilt University. Next, a Tuesday was randomly selected and the process repeated. The same procedure was followed for Wednesday, Thursday and Friday until all five weekdays were represented. This procedure resulted in a sample of 120 newscasts per network and a total of 360 programs.

Units of Analysis and Variables. Within each newscast, each individual story dealing with business was identified. In order to be included in the analysis, the story had to mention a specific business, industry or trade (auto, chemical, petroleum, primary metals, etc.). General economic stories (movement of the stock market, growth of the money supply, economic indicators, general business forecasts, etc.) were not included unless, of course, the story mentioned a specific business. Also excluded were stories dealing with municipal, state or federal employees, farmers and professionals (teachers, doctors, lawyers).

For each story, the following items were recorded: 1) duration of the story in minutes and seconds; 2) prominence of the story as evidenced by where the item appeared in the newscast (first ten minutes, second ten minutes, third ten minutes); 3) content of the story; 4) industry or business mentioned; 5) if the story was an exclusive (covered by only one network); 6) tone of the story (positive, neutral or negative); and, 7) if the story was covered by an out-of-studio correspondent, the name of the reporter.

Reliability. Only three variables (identifying a story that dealt with business, tone of the story, and topic of the story) required coder judgment. In order to determine the reliability of coding of these items, a random subsample of 25% of the newscasts that were chosen in the original sample were independently coded by two trained coders. The reliability estimates obtained were (1) identifying a story dealing with business or industry, percentage of perfect agreement: 92%; (2) tone of story: .90 (Scott's coefficient); and, (3) topic of story: .92 (Scott's coefficient).[10] The other relevant information was obtained by reference to the *Television News Index* summaries.

Results

Extent of coverage. Assuming that network newscasts are approximately 22 minutes long, the results indicated that the three networks spent almost identical amounts of time covering business news. NBC and ABC devoted 9% of their total time to business news while CBS devoted slightly more (10%). NBC carried 239 minutes and 157 different items while CBS led with 275 minutes devoted to 183 items. On the average, this meant that each network carried about two minutes of business news per newscast. How does this coverage compare with network emphasis of other areas? Lowry found that 10% of all news items in a sample of 44 days of network news were devoted to armed conflict and war stories while roughly 9% consisted of crime news.[11] Thus, it appears that business news was covered to about the same extent as other major news categories.

Topics. Table 9-1 contains a list of the major content categories and the percentages of time devoted to each. These 12 categories accounted for appoximately 91% of all time given over to business coverage. Rank order correlations among the three networks were all significant, indicating that coverage across the three was similar. News concerning strikes was the number one topic across all networks. In second place were stories about kickbacks, illegal payoffs, overcharges, slush funds and illegal contributions. Third in rank were stories about government regulations and business reaction to government regulations. This category was followed by stories concerning environmental problems caused by business activities. The fifth most popular topic consisted of stories about business practices or products that posed health hazards to the individual. These top five categories

Table 9-1   Time Devoted by Network to Topics Dealing with Business[1]

Content Category	ABC Min-utes	%	CBS Min-utes	%	NBC Min-utes	%	Total Minutes
Strikes and strike-related news	45	18	59	22	45	19	149
Kickbacks, payoffs, fraud, overcharges, etc.	26	11	46	17	49	21	121
Government regulations and reactions to regulations	41	17	51	19	27	11	119
Environmental problems	21	9	20	7	12	5	53
Health hazards	17	7	8	3	21	9	46
Sales figures, gains and losses	15	6	15	5	10	4	40
New products and services	5	2	12	4	22	9	39
Price increases	10	4	12	4	12	5	34
Industrial safety	15	6	12	4	5	2	32
Recalls and product failures	15	6	6	2	11	5	32
General union news and routine nego-tiations	6	2	8	3	6	3	20
International dealings	6	2	6	2	3	1	15
Other categories contain-ing less than 2% each	25	10	20	7	16	7	61
Totals	247	100%	275	99%[2]	239	101%[2]	761

Spearman rho ABC-CBS = .66 (p.<.05)
Spearman rho ABC-NBC = .63 (p.<.05)
Spearman rho CBS-NBC = .69 (p.<.05)

[1] Rounded to nearest minute.
[2] Rounding error.

Table 9-2 Time Devoted by Network to Exclusive Stories[1]

Content Category	ABC Min-utes	%	CBS Min-utes	%	NBC Min-utes	%	Total Minutes
Kickbacks, payoffs fraud, overcharges	6	7	27	24	33	29	66
Government regulations and reactions to regulations	21	24	23	20	9	8	53
New products and services	1	1	7	6	19	17	27
Strikes and strike-related news	7	8	14	12	4	4	25
Price increases	10	11	4	4	8	7	22
Sales figures, gains and losses	6	7	11	10	5	4	22
Environmental problems	7	8	10	9	4	4	21
Health hazards	6	7	1	1	9	8	16
International dealings	4	5	4	4	2	2	10
Recalls and product failures	1	1	1	1	7	6	9
Industrial safety	5	6	2	2	—	—	7
General union news and routine nego-tiations	—	—	2	2	—	—	2
Other categories containing less than 2% each	14	16	8	7	13	11	35
Totals	88	101[2]	114	102[2]	113	100	315

Spearman rho ABC-CBS = .62 (p.<.05)
Spearman rho CBS-NBC = .37 (n.s.)
Spearman rho ABC-NBC = .31 (n.s.)

[1] Rounded to nearest minute.
[2] Rounding error.

accounted for 65% of all network news about business, and their content cannot be interpreted as reflecting positively on the business community.

Of course, some stories were almost obligatory for all the nets to cover. A major coal strike, layoffs in the auto industry or an increase in oil prices were stories that had a high probability of being covered by all networks. Thus, it is not surprising to find the similarity across networks in coverage patterns seen in Table 9-1. But what of those stories that are not unanimously judged to be of major importance? These stories might represent exclusives or "enterprisers" that one network thought to be important enough for inclusion or they may be commonly known stories that two networks decided to pass over but were considered important enough by a third to merit coverage. In any event, there was an element of editorial judgment inherent in the selection of these items. Table 9-2 contains a listing of these exclusive stories (items carried by only one network). ABC devoted 88 minutes to exclusive stories, 36% of its total time. CBS reported 114 minutes (41%), and NBC led the three networks in relative time devoted to exclusive items 47% (113 minutes). The total percentage of nonduplicated business coverage across networks (41%) was remarkably similar to the amount of nonduplicated network stories pertaining to all topics as computed by Lemert (42%).[12]

Table 9-2 reveals that news about kickbacks, payoffs and illegal contributions was the number one content category across networks for exclusive stories. It appears that when editorial judgment was exercised, this category of news was thought to be important enough to merit exclusive coverage. Table 9-2 also discloses inter-network differences. ABC and CBS's rank orderings of time spent on story type were significantly correlated while NBC's rankings were unrelated to the other two. The difference appeared to be NBC's tendency to include items about illegal payoffs and kickbacks that the other networks chose to pass over. Twenty-nine percent of NBC's time devoted to nonduplicated stories fell into this category.

Tone of coverage. Table 9-3 presents the results of the analysis of tone of coverage. To arrive at these data, we assigned each item to one of three categories, positive, neutral or negative. An item was placed in the positive category if it reflected positively on business organizations, products or services or if it generally placed business in a favorable light. In short, it was "good" news about business. Into this category were placed stories about lower prices, more jobs, new services, ending or preventing strikes, energy saving programs, new minority training programs, excellent safety records, etc. An item was placed in the negative category if it was judged to report information that was derogatory to business organizations, products or practices or if it generally portrayed business in a negative light. Into this category were placed stories about price hikes, bloated profits, product recalls, industrial pollution, fraud, price fixing, exploitative advertising, mishandling of funds,

Table 9-3   Number of Business Items Judged to be Positive, Neutral or Negative

Tone of Item:	ABC	CBS	NBC	Total
Positive	16	21	13	50
Neutral	61	64	54	179
Negative	80	98	92	270
Total	157	183	159	499
Chi Square = n.s.				

etc. All items that did not fit into either of these categories were placed in the neutral column. As is evident from Table 9-3, most news (54%) about business was negative. There were no inter-network differences, although NBC had slightly fewer positive items and slightly more negative stories. Conducting the same analysis using time per story rather than the item as the unit of analysis produced essentially the same pattern. Thus, it appears that negative news outweighed other business news by a 54% to 46% margin. This ratio was greater than that computed by Lowry who found that across all network news items the ratio of bad news to other news was one-third to two-thirds.[13] . . .

Discussion

These data indicate that, on the whole, many of the complaints voiced by representatives from business may have at least face validity. Bad news about business outweighed neutral and positive news. Stories about strikes, environmental threats, health hazards, product recalls, industrial accidents and illegal financial dealings accounted for almost 60% of the coverage devoted to business. Thus, upon first examination, these data appear to support some of the criticisms of an anti-business bias mentioned in the beginning of this article. Of course it is also true that business people have been at the focal point of several recent scandals which does not reflect positively on business as a whole. Further, many media representatives would argue that the pattern of findings in this study simply reflects the nature of news. A newscast contains information about the unusual, the departure from the norm. No news program, it may be argued, would ever report the thousands of businesses that did *not* make an illegal contribution on any particular day. While this argument has some validity, the current data suggest that the coverage of business is even more negative than the general coverage of all news topics. It might also be noted that news consists of reporting departures from the norm in a positive as well as a negative direction. In this regard, perhaps Robert Blieberg's claim that the network newscasts exaggerate the flaws of business while minimizing its achievements may be partially correct. While it is difficult to assess exaggeration and minimization from a single study, the data do indicate that network news programs in the sample reported few of the positive achievements of business. Some positive activities evidently took place since included in the sample were reports of the discovery of a drug to treat kepone poisoning; Lockheed developing a method to restore damaged antique books; a successful training program for minorities; and, General Motors spending money to improve the plight of blacks in South Africa. These achievements were covered but were overshadowed by the preponderance of negative news.

It was also apparent from the data that the three networks were more similar than different in their patterns of coverage. The amount, content and tone of coverage differed little among the networks, although NBC showed a tendency to emphasize different types of coverage in its exclusive stories. Moreover, it was apparent that certain businesses were covered to a greater degree than others. Networks news paid a good deal of attention to those industries with high sales volume and to those that had a large impact on the audience. Highly centralized and visible businesses (auto and petroleum industries) received the greatest media attention. More decentralized and less visible enterprises (machinery manufacturing, construction, service industries and retail establishments) received less media attention. . . .

NOTES

1. James Ring Adams, quoted in Marvin Barrett, *Rich News, Poor News* (New York: Thomas Crowell, 1978), p. 11.
2. William C. Cates, quoted in Lee Smith, "Business and the Media," *Duns Review*, March 1976, p. 31.
3. Leonard Matthews (Chairman. American Association of Advertising Agencies), quoted in "TV Takes a Beating at AAAA Meeting," *Broadcasting*, November 19, 1979, p. 57.
4. Robert Blieberg, quoted in S. Prakash Sethi, "The Schism between Business and American News Media," *Journalism Quarterly*, 54:240-7 (Summer 1977).
5. Kevin Phillips, "Why Coverage of Business News is Sensationalized," *TV Guide*, February 7, 1976, pp. 6-8.
6. Frederick West, quoted in Deidre Carmody, "Reporters Chided on Business News," *New York Times*, May 5, 1976, p. 38.
7. In response to this criticism, all three networks have recently added an economics reporter to their stable of correspondents.
8. Quoted in Sethi, op. cit.
9. Ibid.
10. William Scott, "Reliability of Content Analysis: The Case of Nominal Scale Coding," Public Opinion Quarterly, 17:321-25.
11. Dennis Lowry, "Gresham's Law and Network TV News Selection," *Journal of Broadcasting*, 15:397-408 (Fall 1971).
12. James Lemert, "Content Duplication by Networks in Competing Evening Newscasts," *Journalism Quarterly*, 51:238-44 (Summer 1974).
13. Lowry, op. cit.

10. MEDIA AND BUSINESS ELITES: TWO CLASSES IN CONFLICT?

Stanley Rothman and S. Robert Lichter

Editor's Note. The media's power to shape political situations rests on the ability of newspeople to select many of the events that will become news and to bury others in the cloak of oblivion. It also depends on their ability to choose the perspectives from which news will be portrayed. What kinds of intellectual predispositions do newspeople bring to the task? To what extent do their world views influence their news choices? This selection by Stanley Rothman and S. Robert Lichter provides answers, but answers that must be appraised in the context of the total news production situation.

Newspeople are not only individuals. They are also organizational creatures. Their individual stances are moderated by organizational philosophy, which generally attempts to stay in tune with the middle-of-the-road philosophy of media audiences. Moreover, it must be kept in mind that Rothman and Lichter compare a very liberal elite to a very conservative elite, making the contrasts sharper than would be true if the media elite had been compared to the views of most Americans. When looking at their comparisons between elites it would help, therefore, to insert an imaginary middle column labeled "Jane and Joe Average American."

Stanley Rothman is Mary Huggins Gamble professor of government at Smith College. S. Robert Lichter, a Harvard-trained political scientist, teaches at George Washington University and is a senior research fellow at Columbia University. The selection is from *The Public Interest* 69 (1982): 111-125.

For some time we have been engaged in a large-scale study of two "elite" groups in American life: business executives and journalists. Businessmen have played a leading role in American history, though today the significance of their role may be diminishing compared with that of elected officials, government bureaucrats, and intellectuals who shape ideas, and the journalists who spread them. In recent years we have seen more and more attention given to competition between what has been called the "new class," and the "old ruling class" of businessmen. The "new class" is variously defined, but

Reprinted with permission of the authors from: *The Public Interest*, No. 69 (Fall, 1982), pp. 117-125. Copyright © 1982 by National Affairs, Inc.

usually refers to those whose base is in government, the universities, and the media. Thus a key question in American politics is whether the elites of government, the universities, and the media are really different in their ideas and outlooks from the business elite.

As part of our larger study of elites, we have been successful in interviewing 240 journalists at what are widely regarded as America's most influential media institutions: *The New York Times, The Washington Post, The Wall Street Journal, Time, Newsweek, U.S. News and World Report,* the three commercial television networks, and public television.[1] Within each organization we randomly selected individuals from news department executives, editorial or production staffs, and working reporters. We also interviewed top and middle level executives of firms drawn from various *Fortune* magazine lists of leading companies in various sectors of the economy. The interviews were conducted during 1979-1980, and the response rate among journalists was 76 percent, while among businessmen it reached 95 percent.

These interviews were compared in order to answer four questions: Do leading journalists differ significantly from business leaders in their political and social outlook? Are they skeptical of traditional American institutions and especially of business? Do the social backgrounds of elite journalists differ significantly from those of the business elite? And, most importantly, do journalists' social and political views affect the way in which they report the news?

We found that the media elite does have a more liberal and cosmopolitan social outlook than either business leaders or the general public. On economic issues they are well to the left of businessmen.[2] Although most are not socialists, they strongly sympathize with the economic and social policies developed by the left wing of the Democratic Party during the 1960s and 1970s. They are also suspicious of and hostile toward business, are far more critical of American institutions than businessmen, and are much more sympathetic to the "new morality" that developed in the 1960s.

For example, 45 percent of the media leaders strongly agree that the American legal system favors the wealthy, double the proportion of businessmen who think so. Conversely, media leaders are three times as likely as businessmen to reject the notion that American private enterprise is basically fair to workers. And 68 percent of the journalists, as against only 29 percent of the businessmen, believe that government should substantially reduce the income gap between the rich and the poor.

Differences on questions related to the "new morality" are even more striking. Businessmen support traditional moral standards by margins of three- and four-to-one over journalists. Only 15 percent of the journalists feel strongly that adultery is wrong, compared to 48 percent of the businessmen. Even fewer journalists, 9 percent, strongly agree that homosexual relations are wrong, compared to 37 percent of the businessmen.

These media and business leaders view each other with mutual suspicion, if not outright hostility. We asked all of them to rate the influence of various groups in our society and to express their preference for the power that each group should have. *Each group rates the other as the most influential group in America; moreover each wants to reduce substantially the power of the other and to take its place as the most influential group.* Leading journalists see themselves as already quite influential, but they want relatively more power in American society than they now have—and certainly more than they perceive businessmen as having.

In order to appraise the differences between these elites more systematically, we used the statistical technique called "factor analysis." The results showed that the social and political attitudes of the two groups form three separate ideological "clusters." The first cluster consists of attitudes favoring the "new morality" (e.g., the belief that adultery is not immoral). The second grouping consists of "antisystem" or "alienated" responses, which involve the view that American society is unjust (e.g., the belief that the American legal system favors the wealthy). Finally, the third cluster involves positive attitudes on liberal economic reforms—those associated with the welfare state—such as income redistribution and guaranteed employment. We compared the scores of media and business leaders on each cluster of attitudes. The scores were "normalized" so that 50 represents an average score. As Table 10-1 shows, journalists outscore businessmen on all three scales by margins of seven to ten points. All of the differences are statistically significant.

We have also found that these attitudes differ within the media from institution to institution (Table 10-2). Journalists at *The New York Times, The Washington Post,* and its sister publication *Newsweek* are well ahead of the other print media in all three measures. Television personnel are much more sympathetic to the "new morality" than are print journalists, and those in public television lead every other group in economic liberalism, alienation, and support for the "new morality."

These differences among media personnel are fairly substantial, and are statistically significant. On our "new morality" scale, for example, the television network personnel score about six points higher than those at *U.S. News and World Report.* On our economic liberalism scale, scores range from 50.7 for *Time* personnel to 58.1 for those at *The New York Times,* and almost 60 for those in public television. Even journalists at the most conservative publications are more liberal than the business elite.

Table 10-1 Scores of Media and Business Elites on New Morality, Alienation, and Economic Liberalism Scales

	Media Elite	*Business Elite*
New Morality	54.8	44.7
Alienation	53.6	46.6
Economic Liberalism	54.7	45.5

Source: Authors' calculations. The scores are normalized, with 50 being an average score.

Table 10-2   Average Scores on New Morality, Alienation and Economic Liberalism at Ten National Media Outlets

	New Morality	Alienation	Economic Liberalism
U.S. News	50.0	49.6	51.3
Wall Street Journal	52.3	51.6	51.7
Time	53.6	48.5	50.7
Newsweek	55.0	55.0	53.9
Washington Post	53.5	53.2	56.2
N.Y. Times	54.4	52.7	58.1
CBS	56.2	52.5	52.8
ABC	56.2	55.2	53.5
NBC	55.1	53.1	52.8
PBS	58.3	59.4	59.5

Source: Authors' calculations. The scores are normalized, with 50 being an average score.

Critics of the "new class" have argued that these differing attitudes are linked to divergent social backgrounds. If this is true, we should find that the media elite is drawn more heavily from urban, secular, highly educated, and affluent upper middle-class professional backgrounds. In general we have found that these assertions are accurate, although the differences are not always large. For instance, 36 percent of the journalists, as against 26 percent of the businessmen, grew up in large cities. The journalists also come from much more highly educated families than the businessmen: 25 percent of journalists' fathers held graduate degrees, twice the proportion among businessmen. And almost one in ten journalists report that their mothers held graduate degrees, compared to only 2 percent among businessmen.

Journalists' parents also tend to come from higher-status occupations. Among journalists' fathers, two in five were professionals and an equal number were businessmen; only 12 percent had fathers who were blue collar workers. Among businessmen, by contrast, only one in five came from professional homes, and the largest proportion, 28 percent, came from blue collar families. Not surprisingly, journalists are more likely than businessmen to say that when they were growing up their parents' income was "above average" (45 percent against 31 percent).

More surprisingly, business leaders are currently only slightly better off economically than the media elite. Only 57 percent of businessmen report family income of at least $50,000 a year, as against 48 percent of media leaders. And 23 percent of the media elite report income of over $75,000 a year, as against 25 percent of business leaders. At the very top of the scale, 3.4 percent of the journalists and only 2.1 percent of the businessmen report family income exceeding $200,000 a year. As one might expect, television salaries bring overall media salaries up. A comparison of businessmen with print media personnel would have produced much greater differences. In addition, a larger number of media personnel than businessmen are either married to working professionals or rely upon inherited wealth. So differences in salary between journalists and businessmen are much larger than differences in family income. (And family income is a better measure of current economic status.)

There are equally interesting differences in education. While a slightly larger percentage of journalists than businessmen completed college (93 percent as against 87 percent), the proportions who have received graduate degrees are about the same (a little over one-third of both groups). However, the journalists are more likely to have attended prestigious schools. We ranked schools on a scale from 1 (lowest) to 7 (highest), based on such factors as size of endowment and student SAT scores. The average rating of undergraduate institutions attended by journalists was 5.56 as against 4.77 for businessmen. The differences between the graduate schools they attended is almost as large (6.34 as against 5.73). Both differences are statistically significant.

Finally, 13 percent of media personnel report that they were raised with no particular religious orientation, as against only two percent of businessmen. Today 50 percent of the journalists we studied regard themselves as agnostics or atheists, compared to only 12 percent of the businessmen. Only one out of seven media leaders attend church at least once a month, while a majority of the businessmen are regular churchgoers.

Do journalists' attitudes really account for the shape and substance of the news? Our interviews contained two tests which examine the way journalists make the "reality estimates" that underlie all news judgments. First, in an effort to understand the perspectives of businessmen and journalists on some aspects of the news, we handed members of both groups cards containing "news stories" we had written. Each story presented conflicting views on a controversial public issue. After returning the cards, subjects were asked to summarize the stories in a sentence or two. (Their summaries were coded by scorers who knew nothing about either the study's purposes or the identities of participants, and each summary was examined separately by two coders. The two scores were in agreement more than 90 percent of the time, suggesting that these classifications are very reliable.)

As it turns out, the interpretations of both journalists and businessmen are indeed related to the manner in which they perceive and describe the world. For example, one story dealt with affirmative action and the charge that it produces "reverse discrimination":

> In the wake of the Bakke decision, a growing number of white males are fighting back against affirmative action programs that favor women and minorities in employment and university admissions. Steelworkers in Louisiana, firemen in Pittsburgh, and teachers in Detroit are all raising their voices in protest.
>
> The chairman of the Equal Employment Opportunities Commission says that this backlash places affirmative action programs in "severe

jeopardy." Conservative forces, he warns, are trying to exploit this reaction against "reverse discrimination" and throttle all efforts to bring women and racial minorities into the economic mainstream.

A white male teacher recently rejected for tenure in favor of a female colleague disputed this, saying, "It's all right to talk about eliminating discrimination, until your ox is gored. Then it brings the issue into focus."

Many people summarized this story in very straightforward or neutral terms: "[It's about] the effect of the Supreme Court's decision on the Bakke case." Others were careful to mention both sides in the conflict: "White males are increasingly resisting affirmative action programs, but the EEOC is defending the concept." About one person in four, however, remembered only one side of the story, and half these responses were sympathetic toward the cause of affirmative action: "Many feel that the Bakke decision will cause a reactionary approach to employment with minorities no longer being given favorable opportunities." Another summary read, "The decision in the Bakke case appears to be resulting in further discrimination of minorities." Other "one-sided" responses stressed the evils of "reverse discrimination": "A lot of people think there is reverse discrimination and affirmative action programs are discriminating" or, "What's good for the goose is good for the gander. The black minority wants equal rights but does not want [them] for the whites."

Overall, members of the media elite chose "positive" summaries over "negative" ones by a margin of 17 percent to 9 percent, almost a two-to-one ratio. By contrast, the business leaders favored the "negative" over the positive summaries by exactly the same margin. Businessmen were also more likely to frame their summaries in quite neutral terms, while journalists tended to portray a conflict between two sides. Differences emerged again when these groups summarized stories dealing with the income gap between blacks and whites, and with the conflict between environmental protection and energy development.

The implication of these findings is clear. Media and business elites interpret the same information quite differently, in ways that correspond to their very different views of the world. This may be especially troubling with regard to journalists, since they control the dissemination of news. It suggests that avoiding conscious bias is not enough, that one must still deal with unconscious bias.

Interpreting news stories is only one facet of the larger question of how elites interpret social reality. To examine this larger question systematically, we administered Thematic Apperception Tests (TATs), a series of ambiguous pictures about which respondents write stories, to both the media and business elites. We also devised a system to score the TATs for social and political imagery. For example, one TAT picture showed a black adult and child talking in a child's room. In the imaginative stories they created about the picture, journalists were over twice as likely as businessmen to mention discrimination encountered by blacks or the poverty that they endure. Another picture showed a young man and an older man talking in an office. Most subjects identified both as businessmen, but some portrayed the characters as involved in illegal, unethical, or corrupt behavior in the pursuit of business interests. Others found a positive message, describing helpful behavior or the social benefits of business.

A typical "positive story" pictures the older man as trying to assist the younger:

> Mr. Jones, son of the founder of the family company, is trying to persuade his own son that there are no new problems being faced by young Jones. Mr. Jones is explaining to his son his own learning experiences a generation before, and offering old-fashioned homilies about continuing to try in the face of difficulties. Young Jones . . . has faced his first major error with the company. . . . His father is trying to explain that such errors are normal, if avoidable. . . . Neither is comfortable doing what he is doing, yet each realizes that he is playing a useful role to each other. . . .

A standard "negative" story, by contrast, focuses on greed and corruption in the boardroom:

> The setting could be McDonnell-Douglas, the aircraft corporation, on the verge of deciding to go into production of the DC-10 transport. The older man has learned that the new design tests show a serious, systematic flaw that will almost certainly cause crashes. The younger man is weighing his own high ambition against the production decision on grounds of safety. The younger executive is deciding that the arguments of his associate are not sufficiently compelling to risk the loss of status and prospects of advancement. He is on the verge of selling out.

Business leaders produced slightly more positive stories about the picture than negative stories. Among the media elite, negative tales outnumberd positive ones by better than a four-to-one margin. Once again, differences were found for all five pictures.

To a much greater degree than businessmen, journalists wrote stories that criticized or lampooned "establishment" or authority figures and portrayed minority or low-status figures as victims of social oppression. In other words, political differences between media and business leaders are reflected in their interpretation of ambiguous social situations. This finding supports the argument that "new class" and traditional elites represent different cultural milieus or symbolic environments. Their divergent political outlooks are only one element of fundamental differences in the ways they perceive and interpret social reality.

A further question is whether the divergent political attitudes of journalists and their perceptions of society are systematically related to one another. For instance, consider a journalist who is economically liberal, and politically alienated. Do these traits make him more likely to interpret an ambiguous TAT picture as a case of business corruption, or to react to a news story about the Bakke decision only in terms of its possible negative effects on minorities?

We first determined that our two measures of social perspective—the "news story" summaries and TAT social imagery—were themselves related.

Someone who gave a liberal slant to the news stories also tended to write TAT stories that had liberal or anti-establishment themes, so we combined these tests into a single scale of "liberal" social perceptions. We found that 98 percent of the journalists produced at least one liberal response, and a majority attained scores of 3 or better. By contrast, fewer than three in ten businessmen gave as many as three liberal interpretations to the news stories and TAT pictures. Overall, the journalists produced a mean score of 2.8 liberal responses, which significantly exceeded the average of 1.7 among the businessmen. Moreover, these social perceptions were significantly correlated with the political attitudes we measured. All three sets of political attitudes—economic liberalism, alienation, and "new morality"—helped to explain social perceptions.

Our results suggest that journalists' perceptions of social reality are influenced by their political attitudes, so it is not unreasonable to infer that their news judgments may reflect both the "progressive" values they hold and the "new sensibility" they represent. But we must urge some caution in interpreting these findings. The press has a longstanding tradition of fairness and nonpartisanship; the ability to overcome one's biases is the hallmark of journalistic professionalism. Among the media leaders we surveyed, two out of three rejected the statement, "Journalists can't be impartial in reporting on issues they feel strongly about." On the other hand, one may strive for impartiality without always attaining it. As a former managing editor told us, "Even though these people are professionals, there's bound to be some slippage. The real problem is, when they're so politically homogenous, the slippage will be mostly in one direction."

The press upholds two conflicting ideals that cannot always be reconciled. The reformer's social commitment coexists uneasily alongside the cool nonpartisanship of the objective observer. This is a dilemma that even the best journalists rarely face head-on. For example, Walter Cronkite was once asked whether journalists were "liberals," biased against established institutions. He replied that this was not the case; they merely tended "to side with humanity rather than with authority." This cuts to the heart of the issue. It is not a matter of conscious bias, but rather of the necessarily partial perspective through which social reality is filtered. If the world is divided into authority and humanity, then naturally one sides with humanity. But how the world is indeed divided, who is assigned to each side and the circumstances in which one takes a stand for one side and against the other—such judgments are anything but self-evident. We all reconstruct reality for ourselves, but journalists are especially important because they help depict reality for the rest of society. They do so through the everyday decisions of their craft: What story is worth covering? How much play should it get? What "angle" should it be given? What sources are trustworthy and informative? The preconceptions journalists bring to such decisions help determine what images of society are available to their audience.

So the reason that the differences in political orientation between journalists and businessmen are important is that journalists are a new strategic elite, responsible for creating and transmitting the information that most Americans depend upon for their understanding of social reality. Whether or not they constitute a "new class," their distinctive mindset does influence the way they—and the rest of us—perceive social reality.

NOTES

1. For evidence that these are our most influential media outlets, see Carol H. Weiss, "What America's Leaders Read," *Public Opinion Quarterly,* no. 38 (Spring 1974): 1-22.
2. For a fuller discussion of these findings see: S. Robert Lichter and Stanley Rothman, "Media and Business Elites," *Public Opinion* (October/November, 1981): 42 ff; and S. Robert Lichter and Stanley Rothman, "The Media and Business: A Question of Bias?" *Journal of Contemporary Studies* (in press); the first article is summarized in "Current Reading," *The Public Interest* no. 67 (Spring 1982): 140-142.

11. CHARTING THE MAINSTREAM: TELEVISION'S CONTRIBUTIONS TO POLITICAL ORIENTATIONS

George Gerbner, Larry Gross, Michael Morgan, and Nancy Signorielli

Editor's Note. The authors of this selection contend that television entertainment programs mold the perceptions of reality held by heavy viewers (four or more hours a day) in socially undesirable ways. Television buffs become hard-line conservatives on civil rights issues and put their personal economic well-being ahead of the public's economic welfare.

The selection is a report on part of the ongoing Cultural Indicators project, conducted since 1967 at the Annenberg School of Communications at the University of Pennsylvania. Investigators associated with the project have examined the impact of television on people's perceptions of reality. They have recorded and analyzed week-long samples of network television dramas each year to establish the kind of world pictured there. They call this "message system analysis." Then, in their "cultivation analysis," they have questioned viewers to assess to what degree their views mirror either the television world or the world of reality, as measured by official records.

Viewers' perceptions are reported and compared using three demographically matched categories: light viewers (25 percent) who report watching less than two hours of television daily, medium viewers (45 percent) who report watching two to three hours daily, and heavy viewers (30 percent) who claim an average daily television diet of four or more hours. The differences in views among these groups constitute the "cultivation differential."

Cultivation analysis findings have been challenged on methodological and philosophical grounds. Specifically, critics have alleged that the research team has made errors in research design and data analysis by collapsing viewing groups improperly. Critics also claim that the research team has misjudged the ways in which media audiences relate the media world to the real world. Still, the major point made by cultivation analysis remains intact: media images are noticeably reflected in public thinking.

The authors are members of the Cultural Indicators research team at the Annenberg School of Communications at the University of Pennsylvania. George Gerbner, the senior author, is the dean of the school. The project has been conducted under the sponsorship of various governmental offices and private organizations. The selection is from *Journal of Communication* 32 (1982): 100-127. Several tables have been omitted.

... Television is a centralized system of storytelling. Its drama, commercials, news, and other programs bring a relatively coherent world of common images and messages into every viewing home. People are now born into the symbolic environment of television and live with its repetitive lessons throughout life. Television cultivates from the outset the very predispositions that affect future cultural selections and uses. Transcending historic barriers of literacy and mobility, television has become the primary common source of everyday culture of an otherwise heterogeneous population.

Many of those now dependent upon television have never before been part of a shared national political culture. Television provides, perhaps for the first time since preindustrial religion, a strong cultural link, a shared daily ritual of highly compelling and informative content, between the elites and all other publics. What is the role of this common experience in the general socialization and political orientation of Americans? ...

... Despite the fact that nearly half of the national income goes to the top fifth of the real population, the myth of [the] middle class as the all-American norm dominates the world of television. Nearly 7 out of 10 television characters appear in the "middle-middle" of a five-way classification system. Most of them are professionals and managers. Blue-collar and service work occupies 67 percent of all Americans but only 10 percent of television characters. These features of the world of prime-time television should cultivate a middle-class or "average" income self-designation among viewers.

Men outnumber women at least three to one. Most women attend to men or home (and appliances) and are younger (but age faster) than the men they meet. Underrepresentation in the world of television suggests the cultivation of viewers' acceptance of more limited life chances, a more limited range of activities, and more rigidly stereotyped images than for the dominant and more fully represented social and dramatic types.

Young people (under 18) comprise one-third and older people (over 65) one-fifth of their true proportion in the population. Blacks on television represent three-fourths and Hispanics one-third of their share of the U.S. population, and a disproportionate number are minor rather than major characters. A single program like "Hawaii Five-O" can result in the overrepresentation of Orientals, but again mostly as minor characters. A study by Wiegel and others (11) shows that while blacks appear in many programs and commercials, they seldom appear with whites, and actually interact with whites in only about two percent of total human appearance time. The prominent and stable overrepresentation of well-to-do white males in the prime of life dominates prime time. Television's general demography bears greater resemblance to the facts of consumer spending than to the U.S.

Census (5, 6). These facts and dynamics of life suggest the cultivation of a relatively restrictive view of women's and minority rights among viewers.

The state in the world of prime time acts mostly to fend off threats to law and order in a mean and dangerous world. Enforcing the law of that world takes nearly three times as many characters as the number of all blue-collar and service worker characters. The typical viewer of an average week's prime-time programs sees realistic and often intimate (but usually not true-to-life) representations of the life and work of 30 police officers, 7 lawyers, and 3 judges, but only one engineer or scientist and very few blue-collar workers. Nearly everybody appears to be comfortably managing on an "average" income or as a member of a "middle class."

But threats abound. Crime in prime time is at least 10 times as rampant as in the real world. An average of five to six acts of overt physical violence per hour involves over half of all major characters. Yet, pain, suffering, and medical help rarely follow this mayhem. Symbolic violence demonstrates power; it shows victimization, not just aggression, hurt but not therapy; it shows who can get away with what against whom. The dominant white males in the prime of life score highest on the "safety scale": they are the most likely to be the victimizers rather than the victims. Conversely, old, young, and minority women, and young boys, are the most likely to be the victims rather than the victimizers in violent conflicts. . . .

The warped demography of the television world cultivates some iniquitous concepts of the norms of social life. Except among the most traditional or biased, television viewing tends to go with stronger prejudices about women and old people (5, 6, 7, 9). Children know more about uncommon occupations frequently portrayed on television than about common jobs rarely seen on the screen (1). Viewing boosts the confidence rating given to doctors (10) but depresses that given to scientists, especially in groups that otherwise support them most (4).

Cultivation studies continue to confirm the findings that viewing tends to heighten perceptions of danger and risk and maintain an exaggerated sense of mistrust, vulnerability, and insecurity. We have also found that the prime-time power hierarchy of relative levels of victimization cultivates similar hierarchies of fears of real-world victimization among viewers. Those minority group viewers who see themselves more often on the losing end of violent encounters on television are more apprehensive of their own victimization than are the light viewers in the same groups (8). Television's mean and dangerous world can thus be expected to contribute to receptivity to repressive measures and to apparently simple, tough, hard-line posturing and "solutions." At the same time, however, the overall context of conventional values and consumer gratifications, with their requirements of happy endings and material satisfaction, may suggest a sense of entitlement to goods and services, setting up a conflict of perspectives.

Thus we can expect the cultivation of preference for "middle-of-the-road" political orientations alongside different and at times contradictory assumptions. These assumptions are likely to include demographically skewed, socially rigid and mistrustful, and often excessively anxious or repressive notions, but expansive expectations for economic services and material progress even among those who traditionally do not share such views. . . .

. . . [T]elevision alters the social significance and political meaning of . . . conventional labels. An example of this transformation is the blurring of class lines and the self-styled "averaging" of income differences. . . . Figure 11-1 shows that low socioeconomic status (SES) respondents are most likely to call themselves "working class"—but only when they are light viewers. Heavy-viewing respondents of the same low-status group are significantly less likely than their light-viewing counterparts to think of themselves as "working class" and more likely to say they are "middle class." The television experience seems to counter other circumstances in thinking of one's class. It is an especially powerful deterrent to working-class consciousness.

Middle SES viewers show the least sense of class distinction at different viewing levels. They are already "in" the mainstream. The high SES group, however, like the low SES group, exhibits a response pattern that is strongly associated with amount of television viewing. More high SES heavy viewers consider themselves to be "working class" than do high SES light viewers.[1]

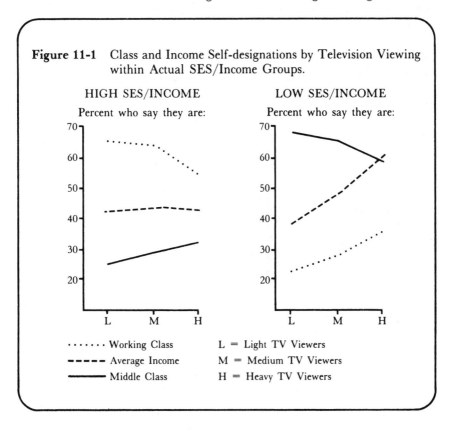

Figure 11-1 Class and Income Self-designations by Television Viewing within Actual SES/Income Groups.

HIGH SES/INCOME

Percent who say they are:

LOW SES/INCOME

Percent who say they are:

L   M   H

L   M   H

· · · · · · · Working Class

- - - - - Average Income

———— Middle Class

L = Light TV Viewers

M = Medium TV Viewers

H = Heavy TV Viewers

Television viewing tends to blur class distinctions and make more affluent heavy viewers think of themselves as just working people of average income.

These processes show up clearly when we relate television viewing to labels of direct political relevance. We used a relatively general and presumably stable designation of political tendency, most likely to structure a range of political attitudes and positions: the self-designations "liberal," "moderate," and "conservative." We are assuming that . . . most of us locate political positions on a continuum ranging from liberal to conservative (if not farther in either direction), owing in part to the generally accepted and commonplace use of these terms in interpersonal and mass media discourse. Consequently, unlike many things respondents might be asked about, we believe that these self-designations have a prior existence and are not created in response to the interview situation.

. . . The most general relationship between television viewing and political tendency is that significantly more heavy than light viewers in all subgroups call themselves moderates and significantly fewer call themselves conservatives. The number of liberals also declines slightly among heavy viewers, except where there are fewest liberals (e.g., among Republicans). Figure 11-2 illustrates the absorption of divergent tendencies and the blending of political distinctions into the "television mainstream." [2]

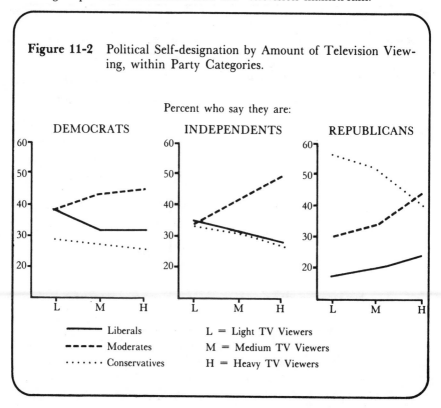

Figure 11-2   Political Self-designation by Amount of Television Viewing, within Party Categories.

Percent who say they are:

DEMOCRATS   INDEPENDENTS   REPUBLICANS

——— Liberals   L = Light TV Viewers
– – – – Moderates   M = Medium TV Viewers
· · · · · · · Conservatives   H = Heavy TV Viewers

On the surface, mainstreaming appears to be a "centering"—even a "liberalizing"—of political and other tendencies. After all, as viewing increases, the percent of conservatives drops significantly within every group (except Democrats), and the relationships of amount of television viewing with the percent of liberals are generally weaker. However, a closer look at the actual positions taken in response to questions about political issues such as minorities, civil and personal rights, free speech, the economy, etc., shows that the mainstream does not always mean "middle of the road." ...

... Light-viewing liberals are always least likely to endorse segregationist statements. Light-viewing moderates and conservatives are, interestingly, often very close; in more than one instance, light-viewing moderates are slightly *more* likely to support racial segregation than are light-viewing conservatives.

More importantly, associations between amount of viewing and these attitudes are sharply different for liberals, moderates, and conservatives. Liberals, who are least likely to hold segregationist views, show some dramatic (and always significant) associations between amount of viewing and the desire to keep blacks and whites separate. Among moderates and conservatives, in contrast, the relationships between viewing and these attitudes are smaller and inconsistent. ... On busing, moderates and conservatives even show a significant negative association, indicating *less* segregationist attitudes among these heavy viewers; this is an instance of viewing bringing divergent groups closer together from both directions.

In general, these patterns vividly illustrate mainstreaming. There are, to be sure, some across-the-board relationships, but even these are markedly weaker for moderates and conservatives. Overall, these data show a convergence and homogenization of heavy viewers across political groups.

The differences between liberals and conservatives—i.e., the effects of political tendency on attitudes toward blacks—decrease among heavy viewers. Among light viewers, liberals and conservatives show an average difference of 15.4 percentage points; yet, among heavy viewers, liberals and conservatives differ by an average of only 4.6 percentage points (t=4.54, p<.01).

Figure 11-3 shows the mainstreaming pattern for three of these items. In the first, opposition to busing, we can see that heavy-viewing conservatives are more "liberal" and heavy-viewing liberals more "conservative" than their respective light-viewing counterparts. In the second instance, opposition to open housing laws, viewing is not associated with any differences in the attitudes expressed by conservatives, but among liberals we see that heavy viewing goes with a greater likelihood of such opposition. Finally, in response to a question about laws against marriages between blacks and whites, we find that heavy viewers in all groups are more likely to favor these laws than are light viewers in the same categories, but this is significantly more pronounced for liberals.

In sum, the responses of heavy-viewing liberals are quite comparable to those of all moderates and conservatives, and there is not much difference

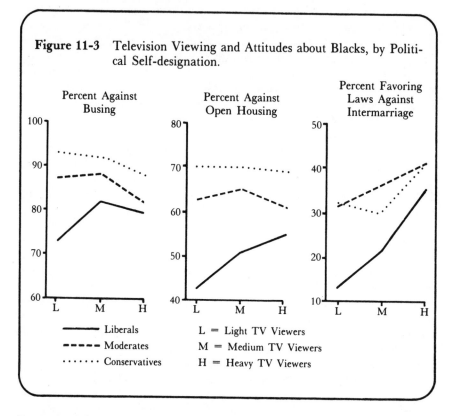

Figure 11-3 Television Viewing and Attitudes about Blacks, by Political Self-designation.

Liberals
Moderates
Conservatives

L = Light TV Viewers
M = Medium TV Viewers
H = Heavy TV Viewers

between moderates and conservatives. The television mainstream, in terms of attitudes toward blacks, clearly runs to the right.

Many of the fiercest political battles of the past decade have been fought on the nation's "home front"—around a group of so-called moral issues which have sharply divided liberal and conservative forces. We find liberals confronting conservatives over the propriety, morality, and even legality of personal behavior. The fights involving reproductive freedom, the rights of sexual minorities, and the Equal Rights Amendment have become a focus of that confrontation.

Our view of television as a stabilizing force, seeking to attract the largest possible audience by celebrating the "moderation" of the mainstream, leads us to expect that heavy viewers, once again, will show a convergence of attitudes on issues of personal morality. We expect to find that self-designated moderates and conservatives are generally close together regardless of television viewing, and that heavy-viewing liberals take up positions alongside moderates and conservatives.

Figure 11-4 supports our predictions. In the case of attitudes on homosexuality, abortion, and marijuana, there is considerable spread between light-viewing liberals and light-viewing conservatives (an average of 28 percentage points); the latter are always much more likely to be opposed.

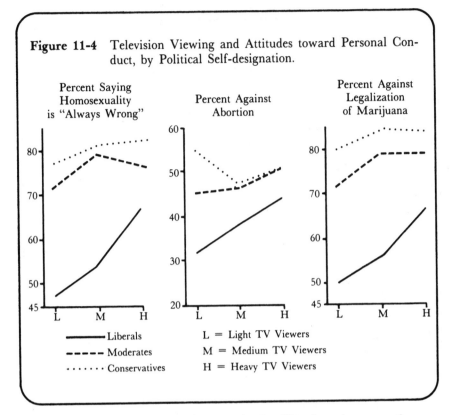

Figure 11-4 Television Viewing and Attitudes toward Personal Conduct, by Political Self-designation.

Percent Saying Homosexuality is "Always Wrong"

Percent Against Abortion

Percent Against Legalization of Marijuana

——— Liberals
– – – – Moderates
· · · · · · · Conservatives

L = Light TV Viewers
M = Medium TV Viewers
H = Heavy TV Viewers

And, once again, the attitudes of heavy-viewing liberals and conservatives are far closer together (an average of 13 percentage points; t=16.6, p<.01), due primarily to the difference between light- and heavy-viewing liberals. ... In all instances, the self-designated moderates are much closer to the conservatives than they are to the liberals. ...

... [T]elevision's relationship to anti-Communist sentiments and to the tendency to restrict free speech ... shows the familiar pattern (illustrated in Figure 11-5). Five out of ten light-viewing moderates and six out of ten light-viewing conservatives consider communism "the worst form [of government] of all." Heavy-viewing moderates and conservatives nearly unite in condemning communism as "worst" by even larger margins (64 and 67 percent, respectively). But viewing makes the biggest difference among liberals: only one-third of light-viewing but half of heavy-viewing liberals agree that communism is "the worst form" of government. ...

Responses on restricting free speech show similar patterns. Heavy viewers of all three political persuasions are more likely to agree to restrict, in various ways, the speech of "left" and "right" nonconformists than are their light-viewing counterparts. There is little difference between conservatives and moderates. But, again, the most striking difference is between light- and heavy-viewing liberals.

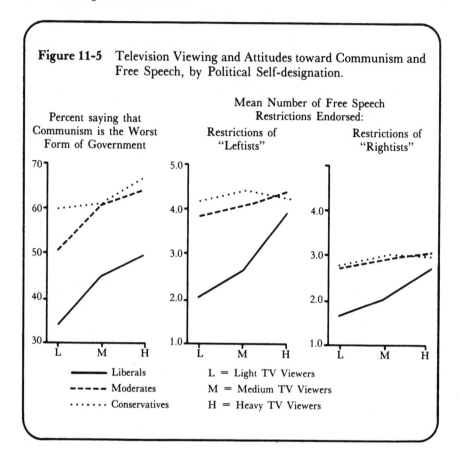

Figure 11-5   Television Viewing and Attitudes toward Communism and Free Speech, by Political Self-designation.

In general, with respect to anti-communism and restrictions on political speech of the left and right, those who call themselves conservatives are in the "television mainstream." Those who consider themselves moderates join the conservatives—or exceed them—as heavy viewers. Liberals perform their traditional role of defending political plurality and freedom of speech only when they are light viewers. Mainstreaming means not only a narrowing of political differences but also a significant tilt in the political balance.

But political drift to the right is not the full story. As we noted before, television has a business clientele which, while it may be politically conservative, also has a mission to perform that requires the cultivation of consumer values and gratifications pulling in a different direction.

A number of surveys have documented the tendency of respondents to support government services that benefit them while taking increasingly hard-line positions on taxes, equality, crime, and other issues that touch deeply felt anxieties and insecurities. The media interpreted (and election results seemed to confirm, at least in the early 1980s) these inherently contradictory positions as a "conservative trend" (2). Television may have contributed to that trend in

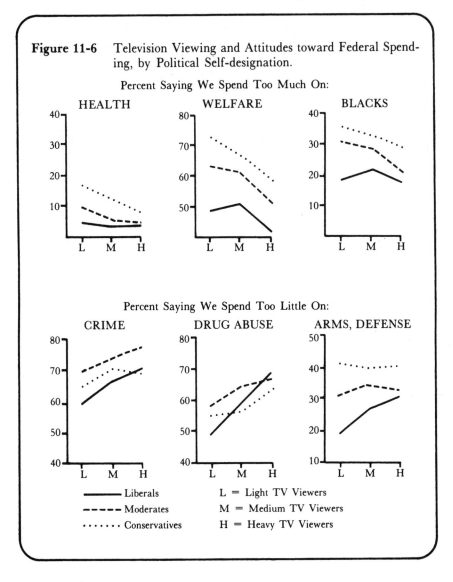

Figure 11-6 Television Viewing and Attitudes toward Federal Spending, by Political Self-designation.

Percent Saying We Spend Too Much On:

HEALTH   WELFARE   BLACKS

Percent Saying We Spend Too Little On:

CRIME   DRUG ABUSE   ARMS, DEFENSE

——— Liberals   L = Light TV Viewers
- - - - Moderates   M = Medium TV Viewers
· · · · · · Conservatives   H = Heavy TV Viewers

two ways. First . . . , heavy viewers have a keener sense of living in a "mean world" with greater hazards and insecurities than do comparable groups of light viewers (3, 8). Second, while television does not directly sway viewers to be conservative (in fact, heavy viewers tend to shun that label), its mainstream of apparent moderation shifts political attitudes toward conservative positions.

When positions on economic issues are examined, however, a different if perhaps complementary pattern emerges. . . . We examined patterns of responses to questions about government spending on 11 programs. . . . Seven are traditional "liberal" issues: health, environment, cities, education, foreign aid, welfare, and blacks. The percents of light, medium, and heavy viewers in the three political categories who say the U.S. spends "too much' on health, welfare, and blacks are shown on the top of Figure 11-6.

Here, instead of heavy-viewing liberals taking positions closer to conservatives, the opposite happens: heavy-viewing conservatives, as well as moderates, converge toward the liberal position on six of the seven issues. The more they watch, the less they say the U.S. spends "too much." On these six issues, the average distance of 16 percentage points between liberal and conservative light viewers is only 9 percentage points for heavy viewers, with conservatives accounting for most of the convergence ($t=8.2$, $p<.001$). The exception is the relatively distant issue of foreign aid.

The remaining four issues are crime, drugs, defense, and space exploration. Percents of respondents who say the U.S. is spending "too little" on the first three issues can be seen on the bottom of Figure 11-6. Here again, with the exception of space, heavy viewers generally want to spend more. As these are somewhat more "conservative" issues, it is the moderates and conservatives who are in the "television mainstream," taking a position toward greater spending, and heavy-viewing liberals stand close to them. On these four issues an average liberal-conservative spread of nearly 10 percentage points for light viewers compares with a gap of 4 percentage points among heavy viewers ($t=2.2$, $p<.12$).

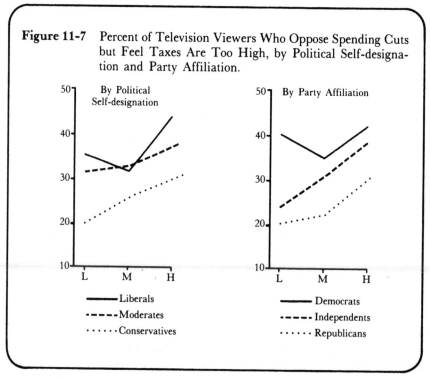

Figure 11-7   Percent of Television Viewers Who Oppose Spending Cuts but Feel Taxes Are Too High, by Political Self-designation and Party Affiliation.

To investigate further the populist streak in the otherwise restrictive political mix of the typology of the heavy viewer, we looked for ... respondents who oppose reductions in government spending and yet feel their taxes are too high. ... [H]eavy viewers are more likely to express this contradictory position in every subgroup (although the relationship remains significant at p<.05 only overall and within six of these groups). Figure 11-7 illustrates the political lineup.

As on the other economic issues, liberals and moderates are close together while heavy-viewing conservatives join the liberal-moderate mainstream; the tilt is in the liberal (if conflicted) direction. Heavy-viewing Republicans and Independents also express attitudes closer to the Democratic position than do their light-viewing political counterparts. But all heavy viewers are more likely to want a combination of more social spending *and* lower taxes. ...

Our analysis shows that although television viewing brings conservatives, moderates, and liberals closer together, it is the liberal position that is weakest among heavy viewers. Viewing blurs traditional differences, blends them into a more homogeneous mainstream, and bends the mainstream toward a "hard line" position on issues dealing with minorities and personal rights. Hard-nosed commercial populism, with its mix of restrictive conservatism and pork-chop liberalism, is the paradoxical—and potentially volatile—contribution of television to political orientations.

The "television mainstream" may be the true twentieth-century melting pot of the American people. The mix it creates is of central significance for the theory as well as the practice of popular self-government. If our charting of the mainstream is generally valid, basic assumptions about political orientations, the media, and the democratic process need to be reviewed and revised to fit the age of television.

NOTES

[1] This result holds even when controlling for residual variation in actual SES within each of the actual SES groups.

[2] ... [T]his moderating effect seems to be a specific correlate of television viewing, and not a general media exposure phenomenon: neither radio listening nor newspaper reading are associated with similar results. ...

REFERENCES

1. DeFleur, Melvin L. and Lois B. DeFleur. "The Relative Contribution of Television as a Learning Source for Children's Occupational Knowledge." *American Sociological Review* 32, 1967, pp. 777-789.
2. Entman, Robert M. and David L. Paletz. "Media and the Conservative Myth." *Journal of Communication* 30(4), Autumn 1980, pp. 154-165.
3. Gerbner, George, Larry Gross, Michael Morgan, and Nancy Signorielli. "The 'Mainstreaming' of America: Violence Profile No. 11." *Journal of Communication* 30(3), Summer 1980, pp. 10-29.
4. Gerbner, George, Larry Gross, Michael Morgan, and Nancy Signorielli. "Scientists on the TV Screen." *Society* 18(4), May/June 1981, pp. 41-44.

5. Gerbner, George, Larry Gross, Nancy Signorielli, and Michael Morgan. "Aging with Television: Images on Television Drama and Conceptions of Social Reality." *Journal of Communication* 30(1), Winter 1980, pp. 37-47.
6. Gerbner, George and Nancy Signorielli. "Women and Minorities in Television Drama 1969-1978." The Annenberg School of Communications, University of Pennsylvania, 1979.
7. Morgan, Michael. "Longitudinal Patterns of Television Viewing and Adolescent Role Socialization." Unpublished Ph.D dissertation, University of Pennsylvania, 1980.
8. Morgan, Michael. "Symbolic Victimization and Real-World Fear." Paper presented at the Symposium on Cultural Indicators for the Comparative Study of Culture, Vienna, Austria, February 1982.
9. Signorielli, Nancy. "Television's Contribution to Sex Role Socialization." Paper presented at the Seventh Annual Telecommunications Policy Research Conference, Skytop, Pennsylvania, April 1979.
10. Volgy, Thomas J. and John E. Schwarz. "TV Entertainment Programming and Sociopolitical Attitudes." *Journalism Quarterly* 57(1), 1980, pp. 150-155.
11. Weigel, Russel H., James W. Loomis, and Matthew J. Soja. "Race Relations on Prime Time Television." *Journal of Personality and Social Psychology* 39(5), 1980, pp. 884-893.

12. CAN DEMOCRACY SURVIVE TELEVISION?

Jarol B. Manheim

Editor's Note. The previous selection by George Gerbner and his associates warns that "basic assumptions about political orientations, the media, and the democratic process need to be reviewed and revised to fit the age of television." This view is based on the belief that television is a permanent fixture on the cultural scene and that it will continue to mold public thinking significantly. Jarol Manheim would like to change this scenario. He presents evidence to show that political thinking is becoming more shallow and that the American public is becoming less interested in public affairs because of television. He then proposes ways to improve news offerings. Regardless of whether one agrees with his views about the decline in the quality of political thinking produced by "the tube," one still can benefit from his suggestions for bettering the quality of information about politics.

Jarol B. Manheim is a political scientist who has done extensive research and writing in political psychology and political socialization. He is a professor at Virginia Polytechnic Institute and State University. The selection is from *Journal of Communication* 26 (1976): 84-90.

For some time now, scholars, educators, and others have been worried about a diminution of the conceptual and operational foundations upon which rests the American culture. One need look no further than the morning newspaper for evidences and expressions of this concern, as in the recent controversies over declining scores on Scholastic Aptitude Tests, the decline noted in the writing skills of young Americans, the inability of a substantial proportion of the American population to perform even the rudimentary mathematical tasks required for comparison shopping or maintaining a checkbook, or the overvaluing of contemporaneity at the expense of history recently noted by the Association of American Historians. And while there may be disagreement over the validity of the instruments used to measure these various skills and attributes, there can be little disagreement that, *whatever* it might be that social scientists are in fact measuring with these tests, that capability is somehow lower for the present cohort than it was for earlier cohorts.

One is thus led to the conclusion that some systematic difference may exist between the experiences (learning environments) of today's adolescents and young adults and those of earlier generations. Indeed, a number of obvious possibilities suggest themselves including, among others, nuclear proliferation, space age technology, unparalleled economic growth, or even the Vietnam War. More compelling than these, however, principally because it relates much more directly to the learning process itself, is television. For the generation of which we speak, the generation which, it is widely claimed, cannot write, cannot read, and cannot add and subtract with the rest of us, is, in effect, the first television generation, the first cohort which cannot recall that day that mom and dad brought home their first TV set.

This observation is of interest in the present context because it is my contention here that, largely as a result of its more general cultural effects, television is diluting the experiential and informational base of the American *political* culture and that as a consequence it is altering the nature and effectiveness of American democracy. Indeed, I believe that numerous findings from such diverse disciplines as psychology, sociology, communication, and political science, when juxtaposed with one another, make such a conclusion virtually inevitable, for these findings strongly suggest that as the reliance on television as a teaching/learning device (in the largest sense) increases, many interpretive and interactive skills may fall into disuse and decay. And since human interaction is the very heart and soul of the political process, a general decline in the analytical and expressive skills which characterize that interaction in the society as a whole cannot help but be reflected in the polity as well.

I hope to suggest the outlines of these findings in such a way as to make apparent their implications for the political culture and to suggest a set of policy responses which might alter the flow of events in what I personally would regard as desirable ways. Toward the first of these ends, I offer the following five propositions.

Proposition 1. *The learning of political information under conditions of low psychological involvement facilitates the manipulation of behavior and reduces the individual's cognitive understanding of his behavior.*

Two elements are apparent in this argument. First, as argued by the proponents of the so-called social judgment-involvement approach to attitude change and, to a lesser extent, by the proponents of cognitive dissonance theory, the less an individual cares about, is interested in, and/or views as central to his personal well-being the holding of a particular attitude, the more easily he may be persuaded to change that attitude and its attendant behavioral tendencies (9, 18). In such instances, the perceptual screen may be easily circumvented, and new information may enter the individual's cognitive space having undergone little or no interpretation or even recognition by the person in question. Second, and directly related to this, further evidence developed in the context of advertising research indicates that information which has arrived in this manner has the potential under certain supportive circumstances to induce behavior or behavior change prior to the development of attitudes supportive of that behavior. Attitude change then follows behavior as cognitive consistency is restored (10).

Proposition 2. *Though they accept the norm of participation, a substantial majority of Americans are relatively disinterested and uninvolved in day-to-day political events (other than elections), and regard the political process in general as distant from their own lives.*

This assertion is consistent with the thrust of much of the research on political participation in recent years (20) and is of significance here in that it suggests that to a great extent the learning of political information is in fact quite likely to be of the type noted in Proposition 1, which is to say uninvolving but nevertheless both internally and externally supported. Moreover, even with regard to voting in presidential elections, which is the *only* regular political activity undertaken by more than half of the American adult population, recent evidence suggests that as many as one-third of those who actually cast their votes, and many more who ultimately do not, also operate under similar conditions of low psychological involvement (15). For most Americans, it seems, politics is little more than a set of images which pass through their livingrooms and out into the netherworld of history. It is something to be watched and perhaps mistrusted, but seldom to be considered in depth.

Proposition 3. *A plurality of Americans, and a consistently increasing number, rely upon the public affairs content of television (including news) for their political information and, indirectly, for cues regarding political behavior.*

This is, of course, the clear result of the numerous studies which have been done by Roper (16, for example) and others for some two decades or more, studies which in general reflect not only an increasing reliance on television, but an increasing trust in its product as well. It is no joke that Walter Cronkite may be the most trusted man in America, but rather a commentary on the credibility of the medium itself. Still, this fact is of importance in the present context only if, in considering the nature of the content of television news and public affairs programming, one finds in that content indications that the intellectual quality of the information communicated is either (a) declining over time, or (b) consistently lower than that from other media which have been displaced by television. Both possibilities have a certain intuitive appeal. (Referring to a recent trend toward increasing the entertainment content of television news, *Newsweek's* Joseph Morgenstern once commented, "If no news is good news, then *Eyewitness News* is the best show on the air.") Both are also supported by a comparison of the decision-making criteria of editors and reporters in the various media and by other related research (8, 19, compare with 5). Thus there is reason to believe that

Americans are coming to rely for political information more and more on a medium which gives them less and less.

Proposition 4. *Not only is the political content of television generally uninvolving, but the medium itself, in the structure of its interaction with the user, requires a relatively low level of participation in the reception of information.*

This assertion is really the crux of my argument and follows directly from the research of Krugman (10, 11, 12, 13), Anast (1), and others. These scholars argue that television differs from the previously dominant print media with regard to the structure of interaction between user and medium and, more particularly, with regard to the amount of effort which the user must put forth to receive the message. Television is seen as providing a direct, highly structured, and more complete presentation which holds the consumer within tight bounds with respect to interpreting the message, while print is seen as relatively indirect, unstructured, and incomplete, *requiring* of the consumer the free flow of fantasy and artistic interpretation.

Although research in this area has not, for the moment, been extended to include political learning from television in particular, to the extent that such learning is substantively as well as sensorily uninvolving, it should prove subject to the same processes as other low involvement learning. Thus political consultant Tony Schwartz noted in his book *The Responsive Chord:* "In communicating at electronic speed, we no longer direct information into an audience *but try to invoke stored information out of it in a patterned way*" (emphasis added). In effect, then, not only does television require a relatively low level of active psychological participation by the consumer, but it is being used in ways which reinforce this effect.

Proposition 5. *As the flow of complex political information declines apace with the increasing reliance on television as a source of political information, first the perceived need, and later the ability, to perform sophisticated intellectual operations on such information, as well as an appreciation for the complexity of politics itself, will also decline.*

The result will be a continuing qualitative reduction of the intellectual content of political discourse among the mass of American citizens which may enable an elite which preserves the requisite knowledge, skills, and resources more effectively to manipulate the polity. At this point, of course, we enter much more directly into the realm of speculation, but the trend of events does seem to point in the direction indicated. Certainly many people do retain both a sense of history and an ability to reason and to communicate effectively, but many others seem to be losing (or rather, not acquiring) such skills. This suggests the development of an increasingly fundamental cleavage in American society between the intellectual haves and the intellectual have-nots, a cleavage which as has long been recognized (17), is reinforced by media use patterns in ways which seem to grow more salient as the years pass.

There are, of course, many who would hold that the end state of this gradual evolutionary process, a bipolar political commonality which we might term a "telepolitical" culture, is not in itself an undesirable end, and who would be pleased to find themselves in the vanguard of an emerging political elite. Indeed, the temptation to let things take their course is a powerful one, the more so because it requires no decisive action whatsoever, but merely an endorsement of the status quo and, importantly, an acceptance of the widely shared norm that all technological advancement is in some larger sense "progress" and that to resist new technologies is to limit the human potential.

Just as such arguments have proven historically misleading with regard to the physical environment, however, they may prove equally so with regard to the political environment as well. For notwithstanding the argument that nonparticipating masses contribute greatly to the nation's political stability and to the endurance of its political culture (4), the fact of the matter is that the principal function of democracy in the United States is to provide a symbolic source of legitimacy for the political system by offering structured, and to some extent meaningful, opportunities for political involvement (6, 7). But telepolitics, while it may facilitate the maintenance of a quiescent political mass, does at the same time prevent large numbers of people from acquiring the substantive understanding and the non-vicarious experiences which lie at the heart of the American democratic concept. Politics may (has) become for the many a remote world of non-substantive symbols and for the few a process of dramatization and information control (2, 3, 14).

In the interests of averting such a denouement, or at least further progress toward it, I would like to suggest several types of public policy, most quite limited in scope and quite feasible, toward which political action arising from the concerns expressed here might be directed.

These proposals could be considered the core of a so-called national information policy the goal of which would be to preserve the breadth and *depth* of the intellectual abilities of the American people to deal at a relatively sophisticated level with political (or other) concerns.

What is proposed here under the rubric of an information policy, I should hasten to add at the outset, is not a call for censorship of the substantive content of mass communication. Clearly, such censorship would have the effect of stifling that very redevelopment of critical ability which one might hope to engender. Rather, what is suggested here is less a form of censorship, than it is a censorship of form, a purposeful reorientation of the communication patterns of our society in ways which will support continued intellectual development. With that in mind, I offer the following proposals:

Proposal 1. *Encourage the use of print media.* This may be accomplished by making books, newspapers and magazines less expensive and more readily available. Specific policies might include subsidization of print media by restoring reduced postal rates for newspapers and magazines, the elimination of all taxes on paper products used for printing, the development of tax incentives to encourage expansion of and reinvestment in production facilities, increased spending on library facilities and purchases, and the opening of new branch libraries and bookmobiles.

Proposal 2. *Discourage the use of television.* This may be accomplished by making television more expensive and less readily available. Specific policies might include encouraging the spread of pay television, which may be expected to reduce overall home use because of increased costs, imposing restrictions on the political uses of new cable systems, restricting television broadcasting to certain (limited) hours, levying an excise tax on all new television sets sold in the United States, and levying an annual television use tax similar to that used in Great Britain.

Proposal 3. *Broaden the intellectual content of television.* Here I would offer two proposals, both aimed at increasing the substantive depth of the information which is communicated on television. The first is to revise the First Amendment to specifically include television journalists under the freedom of the press provisions and thereby to remove a source of ambiguity and restraint; the second is to pressure the Federal Communications Commission to require of its licensees a greater proportion of explanatory content in their public affairs programming. These moves would at once both encourage and require some improvement in the quality of the televised information to which citizens are exposed, though in each instance the inherent limitations of the medium itself would set clear limits to the potential efficacy of the proposed policy.

Proposal 4. *Provide social reinforcement for the use of print media.* Here the process might be less formal, with options ranging from reducing the reliance on television for formal education and educating the public to the value of print to developing special programs which directly tie television to print media content. One obvious direction here would be to increase the funding of such quasi-governmental programs as the Smithsonian Institution's Reading Is Fundamental (RIF), which encourages a wider distribution of print-related skills.

While the prospect of a formal national information policy may at first appear to threaten rather than to advance individual liberties and may be seen as an undue extension of governmental prerogatives, one must realize that a *de facto* information policy already exists. The present configuration of postal rates, taxes, regulatory structure, expenditure priorities, and laissez-faire attitudes is in effect a national information policy, albeit one whose elements and effects have never been considered as a unit. Thus what is proposed here is not the opening of a new Pandora's box of policy initiatives, but merely a conscious rethinking and a consequent reordering of our priorities. Intellectual skills are as much a national resource as are fossil fuels or virgin lands, and they are equally deserving (and needful) of careful conservation.

REFERENCES

1. Anast, Philip. "Personality Determinants of Mass Media Preferences." *Journalism Quarterly* 43. Winter 1966, pp. 729-732.

2. Anastaplo, George. "Self-Government and the Mass Media: A Practical Man's Guide." In Harry M. Clor (Ed.) *The Mass Media and Modern Democracy.* Chicago: Rand-McNally, 1974, pp. 161-232.
3. Boorstin, Daniel J. *The Image: A Guide to Pseudo-Events in America.* New York: Harper and Row, 1964.
4. Campbell, Angus, Philip E. Converse, Warren E. Miller, and Donald E. Stokes. *The American Voter.* New York: John Wiley, 1960.
5. Dominick, Joseph R., Alan Wurtzel, and Guy Lometti. "Television Journalism vs. Show Business: A Content Analysis of Eyewitness News." *Journalism Quarterly* 52, Summer, 1975, pp. 213-218.
6. Edelman, Murray. *The Symbolic Uses of Politics.* Urbana: University of Illinois Press, 1964.
7. Edelman, Murray. *Politics as Symbolic Action: Mass Arousal and Quiescence.* Chicago: Markham, 1971.
8. Epstein, Edward Jay. *News From Nowhere.* New York: Random House, 1973.
9. Freedman, Jonathan L. "Involvement, Discrepancy, and Change." *Journal of Abnormal and Social Psychology* 69, September, 1964, pp. 290-295.
10. Krugman, Herbert E. "The Impact of Television Advertising: Learning Without Involvement." *Public Opinion Quarterly* 29, Fall, 1965, pp. 349-356.
11. Krugman, Herbert E. "The Measurement of Advertising Involvement." *Public Opinion Quarterly* 30, Winter, 1966, pp. 583-596.
12. Krugman, Herbert E. "Brain Wave Measures of Media Involvement." *Journal of Advertising Research* 11, February, 1971, pp. 3-10.
13. Krugman, Herbert E., and Eugene L. Hartley. "Passive Learning from Television," *Public Opinion Quarterly* 34, Summer, 1970, pp. 184-190.
14. Lang, Kurt, and Gladys Engel Lang. *Politics and Television.* Chicago: Quadrangle, 1968.
15. Nimmo, Dan. *The Political Persuaders: The Techniques of Modern Election Campaigns.* Englewood Cliffs, N.J.: Prentice-Hall, 1970.
16. Roper Organization. "Trends in Public Attitudes Toward Television and Other Mass Media 1959-1974." Report issued April, 1975.
17. Schramm, Wilbur, Jack Lyle, and Edwin B. Parker. *Television in the Lives of Our Children.* Stanford: Stanford University Press, 1961.
18. Sherif, Carolyn W., Muzafer Sherif, and Roger E. Nebergall. *Attitude and Attitude Change: The Social Judgment-Involvement Approach.* Philadelphia: W. B. Saunders, 1965.
19. Sigal, Leon V. *Reporters and Officials: The Organization and Politics of Newsmaking.* Lexington, Mass., D. C. Heath, 1973.
20. Verba, Sidney, and Norman H. Nie. *Participation in America: Political Democracy and Social Equality.* New York: Harper and Row, 1972.

Section Three

INFLUENCING ELECTION OUTCOMES

In no area of public life have media effects been taken more seriously by politicians and studied more intensively by social scientists than in the area of elections. Political campaign organizations spend large chunks of their time, effort, and money to attract favorable news media attention to candidates at the top levels of electoral office. When their candidates lose, the tone of media coverage, or the lack of adequate media coverage, frequently is blamed. Because vigorous, information-rich electoral contests are so essential to the democratic process, scholars regularly have put the activities of involved parties, including the media, under the microscope to discover the factors influencing election outcomes.

The readings in this section deal with the images that media create for political candidates. Selections depict the difficulties campaign staffs and newspeople encounter in covering elections. They also record what types of coverage spell victory or defeat for political contenders. Thomas Patterson, in the first essay, discusses the consequences of being identified as a winner or loser during the early stages of the campaign. He notes the major role the media play in determining the scores in the electoral sweepstakes. Dan Nimmo and James E. Combs, rather than discussing specific images created by the media, analyze the dramatic setting of the electoral contest. It is this dramatic element that attracts media audiences to election coverage. Candidates create theatrical visions of a pre- and post-election world and play the kinds of characters that they imagine will win the election. Ritualistic sparring during presidential debates is one of many pseudo-events staged for the benefit of media coverage.

There is an old saying that "There is many a slip 'twixt the cup and the lip." It is one thing for politicians to try to create a particular image and another for that image to be conveyed to newspeople and, through them, to the voting public. How do candidates make sure that they receive appropriate media coverage? To find answers Christopher Arterton interviewed campaign managers and press secretaries during the 1976 presidential contest. He chronicles how campaign staffs work to gain attention and publicity from the media so that candidates will attract financial support, sustain the morale of their campaign volunteers, and, ultimately, win elections.

Timothy Crouse and David H. Ostroff round out the picture from another angle. Crouse traveled on the campaign bus during the 1972 presidential race. He vividly describes the ordeals of newspeople who accompany candidates on their campaign odysseys. Crouse also maps out the contributions made by different types of journalists. His essay highlights the unsung, yet crucial role of wire service reporters. Compared with Crouse, Ostroff sets himself a narrower task. He studied television crews as a participant-observer while they covered a gubernatorial contest. Yet, the major problem he discerned—the efforts by newspeople to avoid becoming pawns of the candidates—concerns newspeople of all types and at all levels.

The final selection by William C. Adams appraises the effect that various aspects of media coverage have on election outcomes. Adams demonstrates that media influence is a multifaceted phenomenon, which cannot be studied adequately unless it is dissected into its component parts. The selection presented here outlines the factors that must be taken into account, makes predictions about their impact, and then tests their accuracy in five presidential election campaigns.

13. VIEWS OF WINNERS AND LOSERS

Thomas E. Patterson

Editor's Note. In a book that became an instant classic, Patterson talks about creating winner and loser images, particularly during the primaries when they are most important. Early in the campaign the winner image can create a bandwagon effect. Money, volunteers, and votes are attracted to candidates who bear the winner label. In this way media prophecies about who will win and who will lose become self-fulfilling.

Patterson's study was based on a massive collection of two types of data: media content and voters' beliefs and attitudes. Media data came from content analysis of election news in television, newspaper, and news magazine sources that voters used in Erie, Pennsylvania, and Los Angeles, California, during the 1976 presidential campaign. Audience data were obtained through multiple, lengthy interviews with panels of up to 1,236 voters conducted in Erie and Los Angeles. The voters were interviewed five times during 1976 so that evolving attitudes could be chronicled.

Thomas E. Patterson is a professor of political science at Syracuse University. His extensive research concerning mass media effects during the 1972 and 1976 presidential elections was made possible by major grants from private and public foundations. The selection is from *The Mass Media Election*, New York: Praeger, 1980. Several tables have been omitted.

The dominant theme of presidential election news coverage is one of winning and losing. The returns, projections, and delegate counts of the primaries and the frequent polling and game context of the general election make the candidates' prospects for victory a persistent subject of news coverage throughout the campaign. The outcomes of the races are of considerable interest to the voters as well; in 1976 this was the most frequently discussed political subject during the primaries and continued to be a large part of political conversation during the general election.

The voters' opinions about the candidates' chances are heavily dependent on information received from the news media. To decide where a candidate

From *The Mass Media Election: How Americans Choose Their President* by Thomas E. Patterson. Copyright © 1980 Praeger Publishers. Reprinted and abridged by permission of Praeger Publishers.

stands on the issues, voters might rely on what they know of the candidate's partisanship, but for knowledge of the candidates' competitive positions, they must depend for the most part on news about primary outcomes, poll results, and so on. Indeed, in 1976 people's perceptions of the candidates' chances for nomination and election followed closely what the news coverage indicated those chances to be. When press accounts indicated uncertainty about likely winners and losers, the judgments of the electorate mirrored that uncertainty. When the news spoke of an almost certain winner, the voters expressed the same optimism for that candidate....

Winning and Losing: Two Examples

... When the Ford-Reagan race changed direction midway through the primaries, voters revised their perceptions greatly. On April 27 Ford wrapped up his eighth first-place finish in Pennsylvania, the state of the ninth primary. Only Reagan's win in North Carolina on March 23 prevented Ford's sweep of the early primaries. But Reagan then retaliated with a winning streak of his own, winning in Texas on May 1 and in both Indiana and Georgia on May 4, then winning in Nebraska but losing in West Virginia on May 11.

The interviews conducted between April 28 and May 18 indicate that people's estimates of the two candidates' chances were highly sensitive to these developments.... People interviewed in the three days immediately following Pennsylvania's primary regarded Ford as an almost certain nominee and saw Reagan's chances as slim. As the days passed and Reagan's victories accumulated, however, there was a significant change in these estimates. Reagan's prospects were thought to have improved somewhat following his win in Texas, to have improved dramatically after his double victory in Indiana and Georgia, and then to have leveled off after he split Nebraska and West Virginia with Ford. Meanwhile people's estimates of Ford's chances slipped gradually before stabilizing near the end. Over the intervening period, voters felt that Ford's advantage over Reagan had declined by about 60 percent. In their minds Reagan still trailed Ford, but by a much narrower margin than before.

Close attention to the news during this period sharpened people's reactions and judgments. First, those with heavier news exposure reacted more quickly to the changing situation. In early May, for example, nearly every voter thought that Reagan was gaining ground on Ford, but those who followed television or the newspaper regularly came to this conclusion two to three days sooner than most nonregulars. Also, the reactions of close followers of the news were stronger. Collectively, those having attended carefully believed that Reagan had closed Ford's lead by 65 percent, nonregulars felt the gap between the candidates had shrunk by 55 percent.

The impact of new information on public judgment is even more evident in a competitive situation of another kind—the presidential debates. After each debate, the news focused on analysis of its outcome. The journalistic consensus after the second debate was that Ford had lost because he had mishandled the question of Eastern Europe. Although a number of hours passed before this message reached the voters, its effect was dramatic, for while respondents who were interviewed within 12 hours of the second debate felt that Ford had won, most of those interviewed later felt Carter had won. The passing of time required for the news to reach the public brought with it a virtual reversal of opinion (figures are percents):

	Time Elapsed Between Interview and Second Debate:	
Which Candidate They Felt Won the Debate	*12 Hours or Less*	*12 to 48 Hours*
Ford	53	29
Undecided	12	13
Carter	35	58
Total	100	100

The change was clearly due to news exposure, for in their evaluation of the debate only 10 percent of the people interviewed early mentioned Ford's statement on Eastern Europe. On their own, voters failed to see in his remark the significance that the press would later attach to it. Yet over 60 percent of those interviewed late discussed his Eastern Europe statement, most indicating that they, like the press, saw it as a major error causing him to lose the second debate.

In this situation close attention to the news again intensified people's reactions. About 50 percent of nonregular news users interviewed late believed that Carter had won the debate, but nearly 65 percent of news regulars interviewed felt he had won. News regulars also were a third more likely to cite Ford's statement on Eastern Europe as the reason for his defeat.

The Making of a Bandwagon

Information about the candidates' chances can result in a bandwagon— the situation where large numbers of voters choose to back the candidate who is ahead. For a bandwagon to occur, however, two conditions must be met: first, voters must be largely unfettered by other influences; second, they must be convinced that the leading candidate is almost certain to win.

A case in point is the 1976 Democratic nominating contest. When the Democratic primaries began, most rank-and-file Democrats had few constraints on their thinking. They were concerned about the nation's unemployment level and still troubled by Watergate, but this discontent was directed at the Republican party. Unlike Vietnam in 1968 and 1972, no issue dominated their thoughts about the party's primaries. Excepting Wallace, most Democrats had no strong feelings one way or the other about their party's active candidates. Only one in five of the Democratic respondents clearly preferred one of these candidates before the primaries started. Another one in five preferred either Humphrey or Kennedy, who were not actively seeking nomination. Nearly three in five Democrats said they had no preference.

Lacking any firm notion of what or whom they wanted, many Democrats were influenced by the news coverage and outcomes of the early primaries. When a voter is firmly committed to a particular candidate or viewpoint, this attitude provides a defense against change. The commitment leads voters to see events and personalities selectively, in the way they want to see them, thus resulting in the reinforcement of existing attitudes. When voters' attitudes are weak, their perceptual defenses also are weak. When this occurs, as Herbert Krugman, Muzafer Sherif, and others have noted, voters are likely to accept incoming information in a rather direct way, thus developing a conception of the situation consistent with this information. Their perspective becomes that of the communicator, a change that directs their attention toward certain ways of acting and away from other modes of behavior. Their perception of the situation may even point toward a single option, one that they find entirely satisfactory because they had no strong initial preference. They then act upon this choice and, in doing so, form attitudes consistent with their choice. Voters, in short, have been persuaded through perceptual change rather than attitude change. Their perceptions were altered first, and then appropriate attitudes were developed.[1]

This was the process of decision for many Democratic voters during the 1976 primaries. They had no strong commitments before the campaign began, but developed perceptions of the race that led them to accept Carter and reject his opponents. In their minds the central concern became the candidates' electoral success and, once the race was seen in this way, they embraced the winner and rejected the losers. Except for Udall, the candidates who were labeled as losers by the press lost favor with the voters. . . . Jackson, Bayh, Wallace, Shriver, and Harris were regarded much less favorably after they failed to run strongly in the early primaries. This cannot be explained by the fact that Democrats had come to know and dislike these candidates' politics, for they acquired very little information of this kind during the primaries. . . . The only impression that most voters gained of any of these candidates was that they were not doing well in the primaries.

The response of Democrats to Carter was only somewhat less dependent on his performance during the early primaries. The first impression that most Democrats had of Carter was that he was doing extremely well in places like Iowa and New Hampshire, an accomplishment that evoked some surprise and a certain amount of admiration. As they heard more about him, most of them also regarded him as an acceptable nominee. This reaction was not based on the feeling that in Carter they had discovered their ideal candidate, for they knew very little about his politics or abilities. But he seemed like a sensible and personable individual and, since he had won the acceptance of voters elsewhere, he must have his good points. These were persuasive perceptions. The rush to Carter's side was not because large numbers of Democratic voters wanted to be in the winner's camp; that type of bandwagon effect was not operating during the early Democratic primaries. Rather, Carter's approval by other voters, his apparent command of the nominating race, and his lack of liabilities made him the natural choice of an electorate attuned to the race and devoid of strong preferences. The following responses, obtained during the April interviews when people were asked why they favored Carter, are typical of those given by about 75 percent of his backers at the time. Their thoughts reveal the importance of their perceptions of the race and of Carter, and indicate clearly that their attitudes toward him were still in the process of formation:

> He is the person a majority of the public is backing. He seems to be a nice man.
> He seems to be forthright, a good man. The voters like him and he is way ahead.
> I respect him. He doesn't have a machine behind him and yet is going to be nominated.
> I guess we haven't heard as many bad things about him as the others. He's popular, too.
> I know that he's doing good. He seems down to earth. He seems honest and sincere. He has a nice smile.
> He appeals to many people.
> I guess I like him best because I hear more about him.
> He seems to be honest. I don't necessarily really favor him, but I think he's going to be the one.
> I don't see anyone else with a chance. He's a fresh and engaging personality. Not committed to Washington, either.
> He must be doing the right thing. He's in popular demand.

A more systematic view of Democrats' reactions to their party's candidates is gained by looking at how their feelings changed from one interview to the next. . . . Democrats' opinions about a candidate tended to align with their perceptions of his chances. If they regarded a candidate as having a good chance, they usually had acquired more favorable feelings toward him by the time of the next interview. On the other hand, less favorable thoughts usually followed the perception that a candidate did not have much of a chance. . . .

. . . [F]rom the evidence available it is certain that most Democrats reached a conclusion about a candidate's prospects before developing a firm opinion about him. Considering the uncertainty that the Democratic respondents expressed in the interviews completed just before the first primary, and the fact that the large majority did not even know Carter at the time, it is inconceivable that great numbers of them selected Carter before hearing about his success in the opening primaries. Thus this dual change reflects mostly the pull of their judgments about the candidates' chances on their feelings toward the candidates.

Interestingly, frequent followers of the news were slightly more likely than infrequent users to judge the candidates on the basis of performance. . . . The opposite might have been predicted, since more attentive citizens generally have stronger political convictions, ones that might retard bandwagon effects. Nevertheless, heavier exposure to the newspaper and television was related to the tendency to respond favorably to winners and unfavorably to losers. Perhaps frequent users' heavier exposure to the news media's conception of the Democratic race impressed it more thoroughly on them.

An alternative explanation for why heavy media users were more responsive to winners and losers relates to the uncertainties surrounding the Democratic race—uncertainties about the identity of the candidates, about their prospects, and about their politics. Jacques Ellul posits that conditions of uncertainty make attentive citizens particularly vulnerable to mass persuasion. According to Ellul, attentive citizens feel a greater need to understand situations, and thus feel a greater compulsion to resolve uncertainty when it exists. Because the events they wish to understand are beyond their direct observation, however, they are susceptible to the media's interpretations of reality. The assessment that prevails in the press becomes their perception. Informed citizens, in fact, are often seen to be those who are able, early in the course of an uncertain event, to articulate the media's conception of it. To be sure, there are people who are deviationists, individuals who ignore the common response because of their superior understanding or strong personalities. He suggests, however, that only a very small percentage of citizens can receive information about an event and then draw unique and perceptive inferences about it. The ordinary response of the attentive citizen is to accept the communicator's definition of the situation. The inattentive citizen, in contrast, may not care or know enough to try to understand the situation, thus being somewhat less likely to adopt the media's interpretation.[2]

Obstacles to Bandwagons

Unlike Democrats, Republicans were largely unaffected by the outcomes of their party's primaries. About 75 percent of the Republican respondents had chosen between Ford and Reagan before the campaign began, some selecting their candidate because they liked or disliked Ford's handling of the presidency, others choosing one of the two men because of a conservative or moderate preference. Moreover, the large majority of these Republicans stayed with their candidate; in June 80 percent preferred the same candidate they had preferred in February. Reasonably sure about which candidate they wanted and why, their commitments shielded them from bandwagon effects. Indeed, persuaded Republicans tended to react selectively to exposure to the candidates. Their candidate gained stature while his opponent lost it, shown clearly by a comparison of the Erie and Los Angeles respondents. Before New Hampshire's opening primary in February, Erie Republicans were generally pro-Ford and Los Angeles Republicans were primarily pro-Reagan. As the primaries progressed . . . Republican opinion of Ford became more favorable in Los Angeles and more critical in Erie. Meanwhile Reagan drew opposite reactions: he was viewed more favorably by Los Angeles Republicans, less favorably by those in Erie. Within each location, moreover, pro-Reagan and pro-Ford voters responded selectively to the two candidates.

Among rank-and-file Republicans, then, the candidates' successes were generally unimportant to public response. Indeed, another pattern was evident—Republicans tended to think highly of their preferred candidate's chances. There is in fact a general tendency for voters to be optimistic about the prospects for the candidate they favor. People like to think that others will develop equally high opinions of their favorite contender; consequently, they overrate his prospects. Throughout the 1976 race, each candidate's supporters rated his chances more highly than did other voters, but the degree of exaggeration varied. People were especially positive when the indicators were soft or conflicting, as they were before the first primaries, when without a solid basis for assessing how the contests would go, voters were reasonably hopeful about their candidates' chances. It is true that Ford's backers were more confident than Reagan's and Democrats backing Jackson, Carter, and Humphrey were more optimistic than those behind other candidates, but each side held on to the possibility of victory.

Carter's success in the primaries, however, quickly dampened the hopes of opposing Democrats. Halfway through the primaries, regardless of whom they favored, Democratic voters saw Carter as the likely winner. Only Brown's supporters felt their candidate still had a reasonable chance. . . . Carter's showing had simply overwhelmed the ability of opposing voters to rationalize.

Republicans were less strongly affected by developments. After Ford's victory in Pennsylvania extended his domination of the early primaries, most of Reagan's supporters believed that Ford had the advantage. They were not convinced, however, that the race was virtually over, but felt that Reagan still had time to turn things around, an optimism apparently justified by the winning streak Reagan began in early May. His wins did more than simply persuade his supporters that his chances had improved; many felt that he had edged ahead of Ford. They were less optimistic than Ford's supporters that their candidate would prevail, but they felt he could prevail. Each side continued to feel confident through the remaining primaries—an outlook made possible by the reality of a close race. Almost certainly this impeded any bandwagon effect—most Republicans already believed their side had a good chance.

All of this helps to explain why the Republican and Democratic races, despite similar appearances at the outset, took such different routes. Ford and Carter each began the primaries with a series of victories, but only Carter's success produced a bandwagon. Once he had control of the headlines, there was little to stem the flow of Democrats to his side. To be sure, some people voted against Carter because he was winning. Jackson in Pennsylvania and Brown in California gained some votes because people saw them not as their first choice, but as capable of stopping Carter, thus enabling another candidate, such as Humphrey, to gain nomination. Voters of this type, however, were easily outnumbered by those attracted to Carter because of his success.

The Republican vote was decidedly more stable. Despite the appearance from early losses that his voters were deserting him, Reagan actually retained the large majority of his supporters throughout the early primaries, and won handily when the campaign finally reached the states dominated by conservative Republicans. Had Ford maintained his streak through the early weeks of May, Reagan supporters might have given up hope and reconciled themselves to accepting Ford as their candidate (as they did after the Republican convention). Or had a national crisis occurred, Ford might have been able to rally enough of Reagan's weaker supporters to generate a bandwagon. Or had Reagan committed a major blunder, his support might have evaporated. As things were, however, the strength of his candidacy and the commitment of his followers provided them with an effective shield from persuasion by the outcome of the early primaries.

By the same process, bandwagon effects are limited in nature during a general election. Although a third of the respondents delayed or changed their preferences during the general election, they did not gravitate toward the candidate they felt was leading. Indeed, Carter, who after the summer conventions was thought by most respondents to be ahead, lost votes during the general election. If anything, the fact that Carter appeared likely to win the presidency led voters to examine his candidacy more critically than they previously had. For the most part, changes during the general election reflected people's party, issue, and leadership preferences, influences that rather easily overrode their perceptions of the candidates' chances. Regardless of what they thought about the candidates' prospects, for example, Democrats developed increasingly negative opinions of Ford, and Republicans grew increasingly critical of Carter.

In the general election, people apparently find it easier to believe that their side can win—poll results seem to have less impact on their thinking than primary outcomes and delegate counts. When Carter led by two to one in postconvention polls, Ford's supporters felt Carter was more likely to win, but they hardly conceded him the advantage that opposing Democrats had granted him halfway through the primaries. Shortly before the general election day, when the polls had Carter narrowly in the lead, Ford backers rated Ford's chances as slightly better than Carter's, while Carter backers felt the victory would be a Democratic one. Not surprisingly, then, when a voter was faced with the possibility that his preferred candidate would lose the general election, he was more likely to change his belief about the likely winner than he was to switch candidates.

NOTES

1. Herbert Krugman, "The Impact of Televised Advertising," *Public Opinion Quarterly*, Fall 1965, pp. 349-65; Carolyn W. Sherif, Muzafer Sherif, and Roger E. Nebergall, *Attitude and Attitude Change* (Philadelphia: W. C. Saunders, 1965), chap. 1; Muzafer Sherif and Carl Hovland, *Social Judgment* (New Haven, Conn.: Yale University Press, 1961).
2. Jacques Ellul, *Propaganda*. New York: Vintage Books, 1965, pp. 112-16.

14. A MAN FOR ALL SEASONS
THE MEDIATED WORLD OF ELECTION CAMPAIGNS

Dan Nimmo and James E. Combs

Editor's Note. Dan Nimmo and James E. Combs contend that, like the men in Plato's cave, most people experience the political world only indirectly. They rely on the media to create shadow images of reality. Aware that the audience's interest needs to be aroused, the media cast political tales as stylized, familiar dramas. The audience incorporates these media-created scenarios and stereotyped characters into their personal or group fantasies about the nature of the political world. These fantasies then become the realities to which people respond with political action. The candidates, like the voting public, indulge in their own fantasies and try to act them out. Nimmo and Combs describe how candidates typically perform when they enact their parts. Jimmy Carter used the "anti-Washington outsider" role to capture public approval. Ronald Reagan played the "prudent leader" who would bring back old values and past glories. For the perceptive reader who has a ring-side seat at electoral performances, the authors' description should be a case of déjà vu.

Dan Nimmo is a professor of political science and journalism at the University of Tennessee. James E. Combs is an associate professor of political science at Valparaiso University. Both authors have written extensively about the psychological dimensions of mass media impact and the dramatic aspects of politics. The selection is from *Mediated Political Realities,* New York: Longman, 1983.

It is a five-minute biographical film, one that many Americans viewed on their TVs early in the 1980 presidential campaign. It opens with Ronald Reagan accepting his party's nomination. A flashback takes the viewer to pictures of the candidate's youth in "America's heartland, small-town Illinois," to Hollywood where Ronald Reagan attracted audiences because he was "so clearly one of them," to his World War II military record, to Reagan's work as a "dedicated union man," and, then, to his success as California's governor after taking over "a state in crisis." The overall message: "Governor Reagan dealt with California's problems. He will do as much for the nation."

There was nothing particularly unusual about the Reagan TV ad. Candidates for public office routinely employ a variety of spot advertising, minidocumentaries, lengthy biographical sketches, televised town meetings, call-in radio shows, and other electronic devices to campaign. Other propaganda pops up in brochures, newspaper advertising, billboards, yard signs, lapel buttons, bumper stickers, even—would you believe?—on toilet paper. Considerable time, money, and artistic talent is expended on convincing voters that each candidate is a man or woman for all seasons, capable of anything the times, situation, and constituents demand. . . .

Campaign Propaganda as Fantastic Art

. . . Candidates, of course, are in a position to act out their fantasies. They dramatize their fantasies by creating rhetorical visions. These visions appear over and over again in each candidate's propaganda. Each speech, brochure, position paper, slogan, TV and radio advertisement, and so on is a carefully crafted effort to portray the candidate's rhetorical vision. Such crafting is an artistic enterprise. Hence, campaign propaganda can be regarded as an example of fantastic art, that is, the use of artistic devices to promote a candidate's rhetorical vision of his presidency. If successful, the candidate's fantasy chains out to become the news media's and the voters' fantasy as well.

Campaign propaganda aims at mediating two closely related, overlapping fantasies. First, propaganda constructs fantasies about the candidate, his qualities, qualifications, program, and destiny. Second, propaganda mediates realities about the nature of the world, the array of forces, dangers, threats, and enemies that must be confronted and vanquished. The linkage of the two fantasies is essential, that is, the destiny of the candidate becomes the destiny of the political world.

An entire industry now exists to construct such fantasies, craft appropriate propagandistic artifacts for them, and espouse each candidate's rhetorical vision. This industry of "propartists" [1] consists of specialists with a variety of skills. There are, for instance, organizers, fund raisers, pollsters, TV producers, filmmakers, advertisers, public relations personnel, press secretaries, hairstylists, and all manner of other consultants. The industry has developed an aesthetic style consistent with the artistry of modern advertising. Two devices in that artistry are particularly key mechanisms, positioning the candidate and fashioning the image.

In commercial advertising *positioning* places a product at a particular point or with a particular stance as a means of distinguishing it from competing products that, in substance, are strikingly similar to the product being huckstered. The attempt is to carve out a share of the market. But it is not the unique traits or qualities inherent in the product that are stressed. Rather, advertisers mold a picture of the product as distinct because of the people who buy or consume it. Consider beers. Many are indistinguishable in taste, but TV ads alert us that Miller Lite is favored by former athletes, Schlitz is the cool and tough brew of macho James Coburn, and Natural Light is the favorite of discerning women. Now consider candidates, specifically Jimmy Carter in 1976. Remember the precampaign scenario of the news media: the 1976 Democratic nomination fight would boil down to liberals buying Morris Udall, conservatives purchasing Henry Jackson. Jimmy Carter's pollster, Pat Caddell, advised against Carter's positioning himself on the liberal/conservative continuum. Caddell noted that his polls indicated a large portion of Americans were disenchanted with government and with the failure of politicians, liberal or conservative, to solve problems. He advised Carter to position himself as the anti-Washington candidate. Carter did, carved out a whole new market, and ended up with the nomination.[2]

Positioning puts a candidate in a place to run *from* in the campaign. *Image making* is what the candidate runs *as*. The progress is not one-way. Voters' impressions of candidates' qualities derive only in part from campaign propaganda; how voters contrast the candidate's fantasies with their own makes a difference. A household cleanser or trash bag may position itself to carve out a market segment, but if "Big Wally" or the "Man from Glad" does not conform to what the pop song calls "dreams of the everyday housewife," the desired image may not follow. Fashioning image themes that strike responsive chords requires skill, resources, and luck. In 1980, with varying degrees of success, the process gave us George Bush jogging while he waved and talked, to remind voters he was not like the older Reagan; John B. Anderson telling us that he was a "candidate with ideas," to mark himself off from the Republican pack; and Jimmy Carter dramatizing himself as "moral" and "a good family man," to denote he was no Kennedy.

Following Ronald Reagan's successful 1980 campaign against Jimmy Carter, his key advisers revealed the scenario they had conceived to bring a Reagan victory.[3] Their account reveals considerable concern with both positioning and image making. In a memo entitled "Seven Conditions of Victory" the advisers speak explicitly of positioning Reagan to win support among Independents, supporters of John B. Anderson, disaffected Democrats, urban ethnics, and Hispanics. Such positioning was achieved not by emphasizing any new issues but by hammering away at inflation, unemployment, economic growth, and the ills of the federal government—all fantasy themes carefully crafted by the Reagan campaigners. Insofar as image was concerned, the focus was on leadership. In June of 1979 Reagan's pollsters conducted a nationwide survey in which they "tested six scenarios for the future." These scenarios ranged from a future wherein "less is better" to "America can do." The "can do" scenario emerged as the one Americans believed in, emphasizing that America could be strong again if it but selected good leaders. Thus, the presidential myth, once again verified, became the touchstone of image making for the Reagan forces. Postelection polls confirmed that of voters who ranked strong leadership high among attributes a president should have, two out of every three bought the Reagan fantasy and voted for him.

The No Theater of Campaign Debates

Capitalizing on enduring aspects of the presidential election's seasonal ritual, such as on the presidential myth, is a key task for each candidate's staff of prop artists. In recent presidential elections a new dimension has been added to the ritual, namely, debates between presidential candidates. These take a variety of forms. In three elections they have consisted of one or more debates between the contenders of the two major parties—in 1960 between Richard Nixon and John Kennedy, in 1976 between Gerald Ford and Jimmy Carter, and in 1980 between Ronald Reagan and Jimmy Carter. In 1980 Ronald Reagan also debated independent candidate John B. Anderson. During the prenomination acts of the election melodrama, there have also been forums in which candidates seeking their party's nomination have come together to respond to questions from a panel of interrogators.

A key rationale for these debates is to give voters an opportunity to size up the candidates, their qualities, and their positions on issues and, thus, make a more informed choice than if they had to rely solely on news-mediated or candidate-mediated fare. Watching candidates go at one another ("let's you and him fight"), however, has become a mediating ritual in its own right, one providing yet another means of fantasy creation and chaining. In fact, presidential debates provide an ideal forum for candidates to espouse their rhetorical visions.

For one thing, presidential debates are scarcely spontaneous, unre-hearsed confrontations. Instead, they are what Daniel J. Boorstin calls pseudo-events.[4] In fact, debates join most other campaign events in that respect. A pseudo-event is one that is planned for the immediate purpose of being reported, yet what actually happens is never clear, even though the event itself was intended to have a self-fulfilling character. In sum, a pseudo-event is a media event. Consider the planning of presidential debates. Considerable thought goes into deciding whether to challenge an opposing candidate to debate or whether to accept a challenge. Thus, a predebate between candidates' advisers takes place in the news media over whether to debate at all. Once that is resolved, elaborate negotiations between candidates' advisers work out details of attire, rostrum sizes, makeup, lighting and camera angles for TV, the format of the debate, who will participate, location, time, and so on. Indeed, as little as possible is left to spontaneity.

Nor are presidential debates debates. The common understanding of a debate is a conflict or argument over a clearly defined proposition. Each side speaks to that proposition for an alloted time, has an opportunity to rebut and interrogate the opposition, and sums up its position. Presidential debates never involve clearly defined propositions for argument. At best, the point at issue is vague. It boils down to "there should be a change." The ins should be replaced by the outs. In each presidential debate thus far that implicit proposition has favored the challenger—Kennedy challenging the Eisen-hower-Nixon administration in 1960, Carter challenging the Ford adminis-tration in 1976, Reagan challenging Carter in 1980. Nor is there an exchange over the implicit proposition. Instead, the basic format has consisted, with variations, of questions asked of each candidate by a panel of journalists, each candidate responding or counterresponding, but rarely confronting one another. Although follow-up questions by panelists or follow-up comments by the candidates have been worked into the debate format, the candidates are able to sidestep them. What comes from the candidates' lips are "grooved responses." Grooved refers to what one would get if a phonograph needle were placed in a recording groove, that is, a pat, predictable response generally borrowed from the candidate's standard speech made throughout the campaign. In sum, the grooved response is a rerun of the candidate's rhetorical vision.

The alleged debates are not always informative either. When they end it is not always clear just what happened. The thirst to determine immediately "what happened" is, however, considerable. The quenching takes several forms. First, there is the question, Who won? Within minutes after the debate (sometimes even during it) pollsters man their phones in efforts to conduct surveys of who people think won or lost. It may be that most people do not know, but once told that a nationwide poll said that candidate *A* won, people buy that fantasy. As later polls are taken, the candidate early surveys labeled the victor [is likely to increase his] victory margin. So important a part of the process of presidential debates have postdebate polls become that one TV network, ABC, added a new wrinkle in 1980. Following the Reagan-Carter debate, Ted Koppel, ABC correspondent, invited viewers to dial special telephone numbers (at a "small cost") to register their verdicts of winner and loser. Koppel admitted the survey was "not scientific," but was "random" (which it was not because random means everyone having an equal chance of being counted, whereas the procedure instead was one of self-selection). ABC was widely criticized for the stunt because it violated both scientific and journalistic standards for conducting and reporting systematic opinion surveys. Be that as it may, the ABC survey stands as one of the best examples of instant fantasy chaining on record.

Along with the "Who won?" question arises the issue question. Debate postmortems, however, dwell less on points of substantive differences between the candidates than on gaffes. . . . [A] gaffe is inconsistent with the rhetorical vision of the candidate making it. When President Ford in a 1976 debate said, and later reaffirmed, that, "There is no Soviet domination of Eastern Europe and there never will be under a Ford administration," he scarcely evoked the image of an informed leader. Yet, precisely because such gaffes are unexpected, unrehearsed, ungrooved, they make news. Being remarks that lie outside what is expected of the ritual, they seem to contradict the very myth that spawns the ritualistic campaigning itself, namely, the presidential myth. The candidate not comporting himself according to the rituals of that myth is in deep trouble. For, as with any pseudo-event, the end is supposed to be self-fulfilling, that is, to demonstrate that it does make a difference who is president. The mediated reality is that a gaffe serves to underscore such a difference.

One other aspect of the debate ritual requires emphasis. The presidential debates are media events, solely TV events. Recall the first debate in 1976 between Ford and Carter. As Carter commenced his final rejoinder of the debate, the TV audio went off. For twenty-eight minutes, it remained off. There was no debate. Ford remained riveted at the podium, Carter remained at the podium, sitting briefly. When the trouble was corrected, the debate renewed. The lesson was clear: no media, no debate. A study of the 1980 presidential debates by Berquist and Golden emphasizes the role played by the news media in their staging. The authors argue persuasively that in 1980 media personnel led the call for televised debates between candidates. Then, once there were debates, media accounts of them (especially criticism of candidates' performances and of formats) shaped how viewers perceived the debates. Specifically, media criticism concluded that issues of substance were less important than matters of delivery, appearance, and style and that debate formats favored the candidates' rather than the public's interest.

One version of Asian ritualistic theater is called No theater. It is so ritualistic, so repetitive, that there is no room for improvisation, character development, or plot change in even the slightest form. Presidential debates are the No theater of the mediated reality of presidential elections. . . .

NOTES

1. See Gary Yanker, *Prop Art* (New York: Darien House, 1972).
2. Nicholas von Hoffman, "The President's Analyst," *Inquiry* (May 29, 1978): 6-8.
3. Richard Wirthlin, Vincent Breglio, and Richard Beal, "Campaign Chronicle," *Public Opinion,* 4 (February/March 1981): 43-49.
4. Daniel J. Boorstin, *The Image: A Guide to Pseudo-Events in America* (New York: Harper & Row, 1964). (Colophon Books)

15. CAMPAIGN ORGANIZATIONS CONFRONT THE MEDIA-POLITICAL ENVIRONMENT

F. Christopher Arterton

Editor's Note. Arterton describes how the desire to attract appropriate media coverge shapes campaign plans during a presidential contest. Campaign managers deem it essential to dominate the perceptual environment that leads to news production. Therefore, they exercise a tight rein over their candidate's activities and time schedules. Four case studies provide illustrations. Arterton's analysis is based on interviews with campaign managers and press secretaries representing all the major 1976 presidential contenders.

The author raises important questions about the merits of the primary elections system. As currently structured, it allows the victor of the battle for media coverage to stake out a strong claim for the spoils of election victory. The media, by happenstance, become the handicappers of the presidential race. Arterton questions whether it is sound to entrust such a serious responsibility to an institution that is not designed to make well-considered political decisions.

F. Christopher Arterton received his Ph.D. from Massachusetts Institute of Technology. He teaches political science at Yale University. Arterton is no stranger to the world of political maneuvering, having served as policy maker for various action groups connected with the Democratic party. The selection is from *Race for the Presidency,* ed., James David Barber, Englewood Cliffs, N.J.: Prentice Hall, 1978.

Campaigning in the Media

... Those who manage presidential campaigns uniformly believe that interpretations placed upon campaign events are frequently more important than the events themselves. In other words, the political contest is shaped primarily by the perceptual environment within which campaigns compete. Particularly in the early nomination stages, perceptions outweigh reality in terms of their political impact. Since journalists communicate these perceptions to voters and party activists and since part of the reporter's job is

Reprinted with permission from The American Assembly from James David Barber, ed., *Race for the Presidency: The Media and the Nominating Process,* pp. 8-19. Copyright © 1978 by The American Assembly.

creating these interpretations, campaigners believe that journalists can and do affect whether their campaign is viewed as succeeding or failing, and that this perception in turn will determine their ability to mobilize political resources in the future: endorsements, volunteers, money, and hence, votes.

Both journalists and campaigners speak of the importance of "momentum," a vague conception that the campaign is expanding, gaining new supporters, and meeting (or, if possible, overachieving) its goals. In other words, in presidential nominations, because of the sequential nature of the process, the perceptual environment established by campaign reporting is seen as the meaningful substitute for political reality.

Reporters and political strategists, not surprisingly, often differ as to the nature of the race and the importance of a particular event to the general process. A passage from Jules Witcover's book *Marathon: The Pursuit of the Presidency, 1972-1976* in which he reacts to a frequently heard complaint illustrates the point:

> One unhappy Udall worker later stated in the *Washington Post* that the candidates themselves and the issues were lost in the efforts to draw press attention, and in the reporters' determination to draw significance from an insignificant exercise. "The reality of a presidential campaign," he wrote in a woeful misunderstanding of the dynamics of the system, "is the delegate count, but no significant number of delegates will be selected until March. . . ." The fact is that the reality in the early going of a presidential campaign is *not* the delegate count at all. The reality at the beginning stage is the psychological impact of the results—the perception by press, public, and contending politicians of what has happened.

Establishing "the psychological impact of the results—the perception by press, public, and contending politicians," however, is an exceedingly difficult judgment.

Consider, for example, a front page article in the *New York Times,* dated January 12, 1976, written by chief political correspondent R. W. Apple:

> A kind of rough standing among the candidates has suddenly started to emerge in the minds of political professionals around the country. . . . In the group from which the nominee is believed most likely to be selected are Senator Henry M. Jackson of Washington, Senator Birch Bayh of Indiana, former Gov. Jimmy Carter of Georgia and Senator Hubert Humphrey of Minnesota.
>
> In the second, candidates given a conceivable chance of being nominated, are former Ambassador Sargent Shriver, former Senator Fred R. Harris of Oklahoma and Morris K. Udall of Arizona. Some professionals think Mr. Udall belongs in the first category, but not many.
>
> In the third group, those most unlikely to be the nominee, are Senator Lloyd Bentsen of Texas, Gov. Milton Shapp of Pennsylvania, former Gov. Terry Sanford of North Carolina, Senator Frank Church of Idaho, Gov. George C. Wallace of Alabama and Senator Robert C. Byrd of West Virginia.
>
> Such early calculations are highly speculative. . . .

The illustration is not offered in order to criticize Apple's judgment—in fact as subsequent events revealed, his only error was in overrating Bayh's chances—but rather to point out that the criteria for asserting an emerging consensus among political professionals are not readily apparent. Apple refers to visits to twelve states and conversations with hundreds of politicians and activists as the basis for his article.

From the point of view of campaign operatives, this kind of rating has monumental consequences for their nomination prospects in two spheres: first, by facilitating or hampering their efforts to attract political support, and, second, by dictating the amount of news coverage they will subsequently receive. A subtle, reciprocal influence results from the pivotal role ascribed to campaign reporting by those who manage candidate organizations. On the one hand, beyond simply viewing the media as a convenient conduit to the electorate, campaign strategists are [led] to attempting to influence the political judgments of the journalists themselves. Accordingly, the attitudes, beliefs, and behavior of the journalist corps become a milieu for political competition between presidential campaigns. On the other hand, campaigners accommodate their political strategies to the expected nature of campaign reporting. . . .

Media Impact on Presidential Campaign Politics

The assertion that journalists exert an influence over the conduct of presidential campaigning does not imply that they intend such an impact or even that they could prevent the effects if they so desired. Whereas campaigns are quite open in their attempt to persuade journalists, the reverse influence relationship can be quite elusive. Anticipating the reactions of journalists, campaign decision-makers set their strategic plans and their daily behavior with a view toward how the press will report campaign events. The most direct influence of the media upon the campaign process derives primarily from the fact that campaign reporting is fairly predictable, and campaigners are able to design their activities taking these continuities into account.

On a superficial level, the building of campaign behavior around media considerations involves actions such as scheduling the campaign day so that events to be covered take place before deadlines; allowing a break in the schedule for filing stories; providing typewriters and telephones to facilitate the reporters' work; building into one's campaign organization a capacity to handle reporters' baggage and make their hotel and airline reservations; passing out schedules, advance texts of the candidate's major speeches, and other news releases containing reportable information; arranging private interviews with the candidate, family members, and staff personnel; and so on. In terms of organizational resources and candidate time, interactions with journalists comprise a substantial commitment of campaign effort. Much of what a presidential candidate organization actually does is related to its relations with the press, particularly those journalists who are assigned to travel with the candidate.

To a degree, this allocation is quite reasonable. For example, in his book *Political Campaign Management,* Arnold Steinberg argues that the value of the marginal advertising dollar must be weighed against the value of expending that dollar on staff work necessary for generating news coverage.

> Because visuals generate news coverage worth at least as much and probably more than commercials of equivalent time duration, the salaries of staff and related expenses to generate visuals must be measured by attaching a monetary worth to visual events.

He then goes on to estimate that the increased credibility that results from a news format makes that coverage worth at least one and a half times as much as the equivalent advertising time.

Beyond the mechanics of obtaining coverage, which, as noted above, may be taken as a rather trivial impact of news reporting on campaign behavior, campaigners frequently respond directly to criticism emanating from the corps of journalists. To present but a single prominent example, after Jimmy Carter was questioned by a reporter about his lack of a self-deprecating humor, for several days he worked humorous remarks about himself into his public appearances.

The influence of campaign journalism is felt on its most profound level, however, in the formulation of political strategies around media considerations. To the extent that they have control over the activities of their organizations, campaign managers plan with a view toward media interpretations as one facet of practically everything undertaken by the campaign. Major campaign decisions are rarely, however, based *solely* upon expected news reporting; media strategy and political strategy are intertwined as part of the same process. While few pure illustrations can be found in which campaign strategy was molded strictly by media considerations, the following case studies are instances in which the participants reported to us the supremacy of predicted news reporting in determining the campaign decisions. These examples extend to every arena in which campaigns must make strategic decisions: campaign organization, fund raising, the timing of decisions, scheduling, and the selection of key primary states.

Case 1: Sanford's "License to Practice"

... Like a number of others, Terry Sanford, the former Governor of North Carolina, decided to concentrate his efforts on a few early primaries (New Hampshire, Massachusetts, and North Carolina) and to rely upon his contacts in North Carolina to provide his financial base. Other funds were to be collected by building a financial arm into the primary organizations in states where he would make an effort. Thus, initial money would be raised only in three or four states and later the effort could be extended to the twenty states needed to qualify for federal matching funds.

By the summer of 1975, however, Sanford found his strategy running headlong into a perception among journalists that "qualification" constituted an important test of which candidates should be taken seriously. Since during the preprimary period, the amount of news space devoted to the coming presidential race is quite limited, judgments as to the newsworthiness of events of candidates can be quite consequential as to a candidate's ability to attract news coverage and, thereby, gain exposure to political activists and voters.

The Sanford staff and those of several other candidates had difficulty in obtaining coverage in the absence of meeting the qualifications for federal matching money. They reported being told specifically they would not be covered until they had qualified. As discussed by his press secretary, Paul Clancey, on July 7, 1975:

> That's definitely where the press corps has been known to influence the actions of the campaign, because we [or rather] Sanford maintained for a long time that he was not going to waste his energies on getting up political matching funds, and yet, it has become about the only game in town. . . . He had a major statement on defense spending last week and Udall got all the play because he could qualify in twenty states.

Jim Hightower, Harris' campaign manager, noted similar pressure upon his campaign, July 8, 1975:

> The press had decided that's the way they're going to certify who a candidate is, if you raise a hundred thousand dollars, which is ludicrous, number one, but it is a game they're playing. And not only are they trying to do it, but I think they've succeeded; I think we've got to go raise our $100,000 now.

John Gabusi, Udall's campaign manager, in an August 8, 1975 interview supported their view:

> The media start looking for the most simple benchmarks they can. For instance, they've all hopped on the idea that qualifying for matching funds means something more significant than in reality it may be. I mean, it really doesn't make any difference to our campaign or to Birch Bayh if they qualify on December 31st or July 1st because they still get the same amount of money on January 1, whatever it is. But, in the minds of the media, they have found a simple measuring tool that says "ah-ha, that makes them more significant because they can do it earlier."

The attention by news organizations to whether candidates had qualified or not took place despite the widespread recognition among campaigners that the test was meaningless as a real indicator of political strength. The sarcasm of Hightower's comment above was echoed by Sanford's campaign manager, Jean Westwood:

> Everyone thinks that once you've got $100,000, you're viable. Well how far does $100,000 go in a national campaign? And you receive no matching money until the 1st of January no matter how much you raise.

Despite this interpretation of the political realities confronting the campaign, Governor Sanford decided he had to conform to those standards which would facilitate access to news coverage. At his press conference on

July 2, 1975, describing qualifications as a "license to practice," he committed his organization to raising the necessary funds within one month, much to the surprise of his finance people. Raising money in twenty states instead of three or four necessitated an entirely different organizational structure, diverting resources away from the states in which he planned to make his early efforts. Staff members would have to be sent into nonessential states to set up "fund raisers" and Sanford's schedule would require him to spend less time in New Hampshire, Massachusetts, and North Carolina. . . .

Case 2: Udall and the Iowa Caucuses

From their initial decision-making in early 1975 to November of that year, the Udall campaign planned to make their first solid effort in the New Hampshire primary under the assumption that, as in years past, the print and broadcast media would devote a great deal of attention to the build-up and results of that first primary. Campaigning in New Hampshire, Udall would attract considerable press coverage; winning New Hampshire (followed, hopefully, by a win in Massachusetts) would catapult him into the front runner status. It was a familiar route: "Our strategy," explained Stewart Udall, the candidate's brother, in a July 8 interview, "has to be a McGovern/Jack Kennedy strategy in the key states, which are New Hampshire, Massachusetts, and Wisconsin." Other interviews confirmed the same strategy; while Udall did have the beginning of an organization in Iowa, which was to hold precinct caucuses on January 19, the first major test was planned for New Hampshire.

Beginning on October 27, however, the national political reporters began to devote so much attention to the upcoming Iowa caucuses that it soon became apparent that the first big splash of the 1976 race would occur there, rather than in New Hampshire. R. W. Apple's piece in the October 27th *New York Times* not only put the spotlight for the first time on Carter's growing strength, but it also signaled the fact that the Iowa caucuses would be an important event from the perspective of news reporting organizations.

The significance of Apple's piece was enhanced by the clairvoyance of his reporting in 1972, interpreting the caucus results in Iowa as demonstrating unexpected McGovern strength. As in 1972, Iowa could be the first opportunity to observe which candidates were "emerging from the pack." According to Witcover in *Marathon:*

> The media's seizing upon Iowa, though it chose only 47 of 3,008 delegates
> to the Democratic National Convention, was both understandable and
> defensible . . . in 1976, if there were going to be early signals, the fourth es-
> tate was going to be on the scene *en masse* to catch them.

All the attention caused the Udall campaign to reconsider its decision to stay out of Iowa. As frequently happens, the decision caused a split within the campaign. The efforts of key participants to explain their positions after the fact provide a unique opportunity to observe the importance of predicted media coverage in major political decisions. The campaign political director argued for making a major, albeit eleventh hour, effort in Iowa. His position was reinforced by a memo (quoted in *Marathon*) prepared by a key advisor after an exploratory trip into the state. The important passage of that memo read:

> Iowa justifies the expense. It will be covered like the first primary always has been in the national press. If we can emerge as the clear liberal choice in Iowa, the payoffs in New Hampshire will be enormous.

Despite the argument by others in the campaign that it was by then too late to make a successful effort in Iowa, the political director's side finally won with the additional argument that even if they did not win Iowa, at least their presence there would keep the (liberal) front runner from emerging in the headlines until New Hampshire. The Udall campaign committed about $80,000 and, an even more precious resource, ten days of the candidate's time to the Iowa effort.

While it can never be ascertained whether this decision to switch resources away from the New Hampshire effort resulted in a poorer showing there, it certainly did not improve their New Hampshire campaign. With hindsight, Udall staffers admitted the preeminence of the media considerations in their mistaken venture:

> Iowa was regrettable in that we had not inclination or desire to devote resources and time and money to Iowa. But it became such a media event that I think some of our staff people—national staff and Iowa staff— panicked in the face of it, and we rushed in headlong. (Press secretary Robert Neumann). . . .

Their discovery that the media planned to cover the Iowa caucuses as extensively as they would the early primaries led Udall's advisors to conclude that they could not let the other candidates (principally Bayh and Carter) get the jump on them either in sheer amount of coverage or in favorable perceptions of political progress communicated by the media to New Hampshire voters. Needless to say, by any standard this was a major campaign decision.

Case 3: Reagan and Schweiker

. . . In the 1976 Republican race . . . the estimates made by the networks and the *New York Times* . . . were widely accepted as valid statements of the progress of the race. In the middle of July, for example, the PFC [President Ford Committee] claimed to have the needed number of delegates, while the media counts showed Ford not yet there, but closing in on the nomination.

Obviously the Reagan campaign was in a difficult position. To counter their deteriorating situation, John Sears arranged for Reagan to announce that Senator Richard Schweiker would be his choice for the vice presidential nomination. That announcement raised the possibility of broadened Reagan coalition, and meant, at a minimum, that delegates would have to be repolled to record any switches. As it turned out, the day of the Schweiker announcement, CBS News had been preparing a story for broadcast *that night,* projecting Ford the nominee on the basis of their delegate polls. Clearly the proposal of Schweiker as a running mate was a response to the political situation; but the timing of the announcement was related to necessity to forestall exactly such an occurrence in which one of the news reporting organizations would declare Ford the nominee. If that happened, the race would be over:

> We realized that something like that was going to happen fairly soon. There you have a clear situation where we had to try a defense; because if that had ever been broadcast over CBS one night, we would have had much less support than we ultimately had. (John Sears)

Case 4: The Rose Garden Strategy

An incumbent President has a built-in advantage of being newsworthy in everything he does. The Presidency provides a forum from which the occupant can attempt to proselytize voters without giving the appearance of campaigning. The incumbent does not have to struggle to make the news; on the contrary, he has the luxury of deciding what kind of news he wants to make.

During the nomination campaign, Ford's advisors noticed a relationship between his national poll and ratings and the degree to which he was making news *as a candidate:*

> When he went out on the stump, his inexperience as a campaigner showed up. Throughout a day of five or six speeches, he would tend to get more strident and more partisan and harder on the attack, and when people began to see him this way on the evening news every night, his national approval ratings tapered off. Then, when he'd stay in the White House for three or four months, he'd come back a little bit in the national polling. (Robert Teeter, pollster for Ford)

A strategy book prepared for the general election campaign by Stuart Spencer and Robert Teeter recommended that Ford remain in the White House and make the news through presidential business.... According to Teeter:

> ... [T]his was the basis for the campaign strategy in the general election, the Rose Garden strategy. The President simply did better in communicating with the voters when he was perceived as President, not as a candidate for President. (*Campaign for President: The Managers Look at 76,* by Jonathan Moore and Janet Fraser)

While the briefing book emphasized the special role of television, roughly the same argument can be made for print reporting. Given a choice between making the front page of most newspapers by kissing a cowgirl, as happened during the Texas primary, versus greeting a foreign head of state at the White House, it is natural to see why Ford's advisors would lean toward the latter.

Normally, the candidate's time is one of the most precious resources available to a campaign. While Ford's advisors were persuading him not to campaign, their counterparts in the Carter organization were meticulously allocating his campaign days to key states according to an elaborate point system. Yet the Ford campaign decided to dispense with half the available days, because of the impact of campaign reporting.

An important difference exists between the first two case studies examined above and the latter two. The Reagan decision to select a running mate before the convention and the Ford plan to avoid campaign reporting were dictated simply by the fact that presidential campaigns are covered so extensively and intensively by the news media. On the other hand, the earlier campaign decisions are grounded in journalists' assumptions about the presidential race which determine campaign coverage both in substance and in allocation patterns. In the Sanford case, the assumption that qualification for federal matching funds was a reasonable criterion for separating serious from nonserious candidates imposed that standard upon the campaign. For Udall, the decision by many news reporting organizations to cover the Iowa caucuses in depth provided the stimulus for reevaluating the political strategy. The decision to allocate coverage to Iowa, of course, assumes that the Iowa results would be a valid indicator of progress in the national nomination race. The fact that it was the only barometer, or the first, does not, however, make it valid. . . .

16. ON THE BUS

Timothy Crouse

Editor's Note. In *The Boys on the Bus,* Timothy Crouse presents a firsthand, insider's irreverent view of how the press covered the 1972 presidential campaign, which, for that matter, could have been almost any other recent presidential campaign contest. The book became an instant hit. Not only was it full of entertaining gossip and funny stories from the campaign trail, but it also was an excellent piece of reporting, telling how it was and is.

The selection presented here explains why wire service reporters—men and women little known to the general public—are tremendously influential in shaping the news about elections. It also provides a glimpse of a major and troublesome phenomenon—pack journalism—which Crouse discusses at length in the book. The term refers to the journalistic practice of playing follow-the-leader when it comes to news selection and interpretation. The result is carbon copy news throughout the nation, in place of a diversity of approaches, and a failure to cover important stories that have escaped the news leaders' attention.

Timothy Crouse, a journalist and regular contributor to *Rolling Stone* and *Esquire* magazines, became "one of the boys" on the press bus during the 1972 presidential campaign. His astute observations, told in a lively style, have made his book a staple on the reading lists of media scholars. The selection is from *The Boys on the Bus,* New York: Random House, 1973.

... If you live in New York or Los Angeles, you have probably never heard of Walter Mears and Carl Leubsdorf, who were covering McGovern for the Associated Press, or Steve Gerstel, who covered him for the United Press International. But if your home is Sheboygan or Aspen, and you read the local papers, they are probably the only political journalists you know. There are about 1,700 newspapers in the U.S., and every one of them has an AP machine or UPI machine or both whirling and clattering and ringing in some corner of the city room, coughing up stories all through the day. Most of these papers do not have their own political reporters, and they depend on the wire-service men for all of their national political coverage. Even at

---

newspapers that have large political staffs, the wire-service story almost always arrives first.

So the wire services are influential beyond calculation. Even at the best newspapers, the editor always gauges his own reporters' stories against the expectations that the wire stories have aroused. The only trouble is that wire stories are usually bland, dry, and overly cautious. There is an inverse proportion between the number of persons a reporter reaches and the amount he can say. The larger the audience, the more inoffensive and inconclusive the article must be. Many of the wire men are repositories of information they can never convey. Pye Chamberlain, a young UPI radio reporter with an untamable wiry moustache, emerged over drinks as an expert on the Dark Side of Congress. He could tell you about a prominent Senator's battle to overcome his addiction to speed, or about Humphrey's habit of popping twenty-five One-A-Day Vitamins with a shot of bourbon when he needed some fast energy. But Pye couldn't tell his audience.

In 1972, the Dean of the political wire-service reporters was Walter Mears of the AP, youngish man with sharp pale green eyes who smoked cigarillos and had a nervous habit of picking his teeth with a matchbook cover. With his clean-cut brown hair and his conservative sports clothes he could pass for a successful golf pro, or maybe a baseball player. He started his career with the AP in 1955 covering auto accidents in Boston, and he worked his way up the hard way, by getting his stories in fast and his facts straight every time. He didn't go in for the New Journalism. "The problem with a lot of the new guys is they don't get the formula stuff drilled into them," he told me as he scanned the morning paper in Miami Beach. "I'm an old fart. If you don't learn how to write an eight-car fatal on Route 128, you're gonna be in big trouble."

About ten years ago, Mears' house in Washington burned down. His wife and children died in the fire. As therapy, Mears began to put in slavish eighteen-hour days for the AP. In a job where sheer industry counts above all else, Mears worked harder than any other two reporters, and he got to the top.

"At what he does, Mears is the best in the goddam world," said a colleague who writes very non-AP features. "He can get out a coherent story with the right point on top in a minute and thirty seconds, left-handed. It's like a parlor trick, but that's what he wants to do and he does it. In the end, Walter Mears can only be tested on one thing, and that is whether he has the right lead. He almost always does. He watches some goddam event for a half hour and he understands the most important thing that happened—that happened in public, I mean. He's just like a TV camera, he doesn't see things any special way. But he's probably one of the most influential political reporters in the world, just because his stuff reaches more people than anyone else's."

Mears' way with a lead made him a leader of the pack. Covering the second California debate between McGovern and Humphrey on May 30, Mears worked with about thirty other reporters in a large, warehouse-like press room that NBC had furnished with tables, typewriters, paper and phones. The debate was broadcast live from an adjacent studio, where most of the press watched it. For the reporters who didn't have to file immediately, it was something of a social event. But Mears sat tensely in the front of the press room, puffing at a Tiparillo and staring up at a gigantic monitor like man waiting for a horse race to begin. As soon as the program started, he began typing like a madman, "taking transcript" in shorthand form and inserting descriptive phrases every four or five lines: HUMPHREY STARTED IN A LOW KEY, or MCGOV LOOKS A BIT STRAINED.

The entire room was erupting with clattering typewriters, but Mears stood out as the resident dervish. His cigar slowed him down, so he threw it away. It was hot, but he had no time to take off his blue jacket. After the first three minutes, he turned to the phone at his elbow and called the AP bureau in L.A. "He's phoning in a lead based on the first statements so they can send out a bulletin," explained Carl Leubsdorf, the No. 2 AP man, who was sitting behind Mears and taking back-up notes. After a minute on the phone Mears went back to typing and didn't stop for a solid hour. At the end of the debate he jumped up, picked up the phone, looked hard at Leubsdorf, and mumbled, "How can they stop? They didn't come to a lead yet."

Two other reporters, one from New York, another from Chicago, headed toward Mears shouting, "Lead? Lead?" Marty Nolan [the Boston *Globe's* national political reporter] came at him from another direction. "Walter, Walter, what's our lead?" he said.

Mears was wildly scanning his transcript. "I did a Wallace lead the first time," he said. (McGovern and Humphrey had agreed near the start of the show that neither of them would accept George Wallace as a Vice President.) "I'll have to do it again." There were solid, technical reasons for Mears' computer-speed decision to go with the Wallace lead: it meant he could get both Humphrey and McGovern into the first paragraph, both stating a position that they hadn't flatly declared before then. But nobody asked for explanations.

"Yeah," said Nolan, turning back to his Royal. "Wallace. I guess that's it."

Meanwhile, in an adjacent building, *The New York Times* team had been working around a long oak desk in an NBC conference room. The *Times* had an editor from the Washington Bureau, Robert Phelps, and three rotating reporters watching the debate in the conference room and writing the story; a secretary phoned it in from an office down the hall. The *Times* team filed a lead saying that Humphrey had apologized for having called McGovern a "fool" earlier in the campaign. Soon after they filed the story, an editor phoned from New York. The AP had gone with a Wallace lead he said. Why hadn't they?

Marty Nolan eventually decided against the Wallace lead, but NBC and CBS went with it on their news shows. So did many of the men in the room. They wanted to avoid "call-backs"—phone calls from their editors asking them why they had deviated from the AP or UPI. If the editors were going to run a story that differed from the story in the nation's 1,700 other newspapers, they wanted a good reason for it. Most reporters dreaded call-backs. Thus the pack followed the wire-service men whenever possible. Nobody made a secret of running with the wires; it was an accepted practice. At an event later in the campaign, a New York *Daily News* reporter looked over the shoulder of Norm Kempster, a UPI man, and read his copy.

"Stick with that lead, Norm," said the man from the *News*. "You'll save us a lot of trouble."

"Don't worry,' said Norm. "I don't think you'll have any trouble from mine." . . .

17. A PARTICIPANT-OBSERVER STUDY OF TV CAMPAIGN COVERAGE

David H. Ostroff

Editor's Note. This brief analysis of the 1978 Ohio gubernatorial campaign points to some of the differences in media coverage between state and national campaigns. One major difference is the amount of coverage. Presidential campaigns are covered fully, trivia and all. In fact many observers contend that coverage is excessive. By comparison local campaigns are barely covered at all. While there are variations, it is generally true that information made available to voters during local campaigns is inadequate for making intelligent election choices.

David Ostroff illuminates the tensions generated by reporters' fears of being manipulated and used by the candidates. But measures taken by reporters to forestall exploitation may be remedies worse than the disease. The Ohio gubernatorial election illustrates this point. Of course, as Ostroff notes, some reporters may be quite willing to be exploited by a favored candidate. When that happens, stories put out by the candidate's publicity team will find ready echoes in reporters' published accounts.

David H. Ostroff is on the speech communication faculty at Bowling Green State University. This article is based on his doctoral dissertation, which he wrote at Ohio State University. The selection is from *Journalism Quarterly*, 57 (1980): 415-419.

The viewer of television network news generally receives a continuous report about presidential election campaigns. Each night's newscasts include descriptions, and usually film or videotape, of the candidates' activities of the day, no matter how trivial or similar to previous activities....

... [T]here is no evidence that local television news coverage of nonpresidential campaigns is comparable. This study represents an effort to explore systematically the question of how local television news organizations go about the task of covering local campaigns, particularly a gubernatorial campaign. It seeks to determine what information viewers in one area, Columbus, Ohio, received about the campaign from television, and why the news organizations behaved as they did....

Reprinted from the Autumn 1980 issue of *Journalism Quarterly*, by permission.

Methodology

This study focuses upon the news coverage of the 1978 Ohio election campaigns by the three commercial television stations in Columbus. Particular attention was devoted to the campaign activities of the Democratic gubernatorial candidate, Lt. Gov. Richard C. Celeste. Celeste was defeated by the incumbent governor, Republican James A. Rhodes.[1]

The primary method of data collection was participant-observation, "a manner of conducting a scientific investigation wherein the observer maintains a face-to-face involvement with the members of a particular social setting for purposes of scientific inquiry."[2] The researcher attended campaign activities independently, and with Columbus television news crews; closely observed the activities and practices within the newsroom of one of the stations prior to, during, and after the campaign period; and conducted interviews with members of the campaign staffs of the two major gubernatorial candidates, and with the news directors, producers, reporters and photographers of the three stations.

Case studies were made of news organization behavior surrounding particular gubernatorial campaign events. The researcher attended the events and conducted interviews with important participants from the news organizations and campaign organizations. Videotapes and/or scripts of the news stories presented on the respective news programs enabled the researcher to compare the news stories with his own impressions of the event and the treatments of the event by the different television news organizations, and to seek the reactions and comments of participants. In cases where one or more stations decided not to cover an event, reasons for such decisions were probed.

Finally, to provide a context for the observations, the researcher briefly enumerated and classified all of the campaign news stories presented by the three stations in the early evening and 11 p.m. weeknight newscasts during the period from Oct. 2 to election day.[3] The bases for these data were the scripts of the newscasts kept on file by the stations.

Results

Amount of Coverage. Judged by the amount of air time and the number of stories devoted to all candidates and issues during the 1978 campaign by the Columbus stations, television did not provide a large quantity of information (see Table 17-1). The amount of time devoted to election activities by the television stations is further qualified by the fact many of the stories presented in the 11 p.m. newscasts were repeats—often abridged—from the newscasts of the early evening.[4]

Many local races or issues were of interest only to portions of the audience. However, as Table 17-2 indicates, even stories about the governor's race received relatively little air time. In the case of WTVN and WBNS, a large proportion of the time can be attributed to a single story. Each station produced [a] "campaign report" about the governor's race, which summarized the personalities and major issues of the campaign. WTVN's

Table 17-1   Total Stories and Time Devoted to Campaign Activities

Station	Number of Stories	Minutes
WTVN		
5:30	26	30:00
11	26	36:10
WCMH		
6	39	33:02
11	26	18:37
WBNS		
6	34	45:35
7	23	42:55
11	18	12:45

story lasted two minutes and 55 seconds, and was shown in both the 5:30 p.m. and 11 p.m. newscasts; WBNS presented its three minute and 20 second "campaign report" in only one newscast.

Celeste conducted a more active personal campaign than did Rhodes, especially in the Columbus area; this probably explains why the Democrat received greater air time than did his opponent. Rhodes' campaign staff felt confident he would carry the Columbus area, so the governor concentrated his personal efforts in other sections of the state.

Of course, as an incumbent Rhodes might have been expected to use his office to "make news." However, the Columbus television news personnel

Table 17-2   Time and Stories Devoted to the Governor's Campaign

Station	Number of Stories		Minutes
WTVN			
5:30	Rhodes	3	1:45
	Celeste	5	3:05
	Others	1	:20
11	Rhodes	2	2:28
	Celeste	3	4:27
WCMH			
6	Rhodes	10	4:00
	Celeste	8	3:52
11	Rhodes	6	1:50
	Celeste	8	4:12
WBNS			
6	Rhodes	5	4:15
	Celeste	6	6:00
7	Rhodes	1	1:30
	Celeste	5	6:05
11	Rhodes	5	4:00
	Celeste	6	3:05

The Rhodes and Celeste totals include that candidate's proportion of the time devoted to him in the "campaign report" stories presented by WTVN and WBNS.

Table 17-3 Time and Stories Devoted to Rhodes' Official Duties

Station	* Number of Stories	Minutes
WTVN		
5:30	5	2:35
11	1	:15
WCMH		
6	2	:30
11	4	:58
WBNS		
6	1	:50
7	0	—
11	1	:45

indicated they tried to exercise care to avoid covering the Governor's "official activities" which seemed to have been undertaken primarily to score campaign points. As Table 17-3 indicates, the total time devoted to stories about Rhodes' official duties was just over five minutes.[5]

Campaign News Gathering and Reporting. Counting and classifying news stories does not provide a complete picture of how the television news organizations reported the campaigns. Observation and interviews provided further information.

The data point to some differences between the behavior of the local television news organizations and that which has been reported about the networks' coverage of presidential campaigns. The most striking was the selectivity of coverage provided by the Columbus stations, a behavior the news persons attributed to a sensitivity to being "used" by political candidates.

The news persons believed that while they had a responsibility to inform their viewers about the campaigns, most of the candidates' activities were designed to achieve campaign goals, rather than to enlighten the public. One reporter who regularly covered the gubernatorial campaign sometimes expressed distaste at being assigned to some events; she said if the candidates wanted to "advertise" themselves, "let them buy the time."

Interviews with news and campaign personnel provided an impression of a highly competitive "struggle" for the advantage in determining the content of political campaign news stories. The executive producer of one television news organization commented about publications describing manipulation of the news media by candidates: "I don't believe the candidates are as successful as they once were. After all, we've read those books, too."

Illustrating the efforts by the news organizations to maintain, or regain, control over the campaign news content, one station's coverage of the campaign consisted primarily of two to three minute summaries, or "campaign reports." Only one "campaign report" was presented about each of the major state and local races, and about the two statewide ballot issues.

The "campaign reports" were presented in WTVN's 5:30 p.m. newscast, and repeated at 11 p.m. Only the reporter's voice was used in the audio portion; according to the news director the candidates did not explain their own issue positions because such interviews "take up too much air time, but provide little useful information." Thus, the television news organization felt it was better able to use the medium to explain matters to the audience than would the candidates.[6]

In some instances the news organizations made concerted efforts to avoid being "manipulated." An illustration is provided by news organization behavior in response to a "Get Out the Vote" rally sponsored by a Columbus black political organization. The television reporters concentrated their attention, and their stories, on the "guest of honor," U.N. Ambassador Andrew Young; the television reporters ignored gubernatorial candidate Richard Celeste, who spoke to the rally, and other candidates who attended. As one television reporter explained, even before the start of the rally, "We're just here to cover Andrew Young. We won't mention the candidates; we're not going to play into their hands."

In another instance, a local candidate scheduled a news conference at which he would be endorsed by a national political figure visiting Columbus. In assigning a reporter to cover the news conference, a news executive at one station told him to concentrate his questions on the political aspirations of the national newsmaker. The story which was eventually prepared about the news conference did not mention the local candidate, who was, indeed, endorsed by the visiting politician.

Contributing to the selectivity exercised by the news organizations was the fact that their personnel gathered most of the stories used in the newscasts; with a limited number of crews available assignment editors and producers were careful in choosing the stories to which reporters would be assigned.[7] Unlike the networks, the Columbus television news organizations could not, or would not, afford the luxury of permanently assigning reporters to election coverage in general, or to individual races or candidates. Thus, most of the stories telecast about the campaign took place in the Columbus area.

The primary reason the Columbus news organizations gave for using stories gathered by their own personnel, rather than by the wire services, was a desire to include film or videotape accompaniment to the stories.[8] However, contrary to the literature, "exciting" visual media events did not guarantee coverage of campaign activities; similarly, the absence of visual material did not preclude the presentation of campaign stories on the Columbus television news programs.

Of course, the news crews attempted to find visual material to illustrate their stories. However, editors and producers gave greater weight to the importance of the information contained in a story when determining whether or not to use it in a newscast. An example is provided by the news organizations' behavior in covering a news conference conducted jointly by Richard Celeste and the Democratic candidate for secretary of state.

The theme of the news conference was the need for "new" blood in Ohio's statewide offices. The Democratic candidates pointed out their opponents had first sought statewide office in the 1950s, and noted the many changes in the world since that time. As a visual backdrop to the news conference the campaign organizations constructed a large billboard using electronically reproduced newspaper headlines from the 1950s to the present. Although the reproductions were not dark enough to provide usable television pictures, two of the Columbus stations telecast stories about the news conference. The third station sent a reporter, but she decided not to prepare a story: in her judgment neither candidate "said anything newsworthy."

One type of "media event" was almost guaranteed to attract the Columbus television news crews: the appearance by a bona fide national newsmaker at a campaign activity. Both major political parties made use of such people to attract television coverage to campaigns. For example, a Democratic rally featuring Rosalyn Carter received extensive air time on all three stations; an appearance by Gerald Ford at a Republican fundraiser received similar attention by the television news organizations. However, while some local candidates received television news exposure because of these appearances, the news organizations often ignored the local candidates entirely.

Discussion

This study provides evidence of differences between the news coverage of nonpresidential campaigns by local television stations, and network coverage of presidential campaigns. The most striking differences were the selectivity of coverage by the stations, and the cautious, almost cynical, attitude of the television news personnel towards the "news value" of most campaign activities.

These attitudes are probably a reaction to the reputed success of "media events" conducted in recent years. A successful media event implies that the news organizations are being manipulated, and have lost their control over the content of written and broadcast news stories. During the 1978 campaign the Columbus television news organizations were apparently acting in ways designed to regain control.

For the electorate and the candidates, however, the selective, relatively sparse coverage provided by local television news organizations has potentially negative consequences. The local candidates may be unable to gain access to the electorate, much of which, we are told, looks to television as its most important source of news. Therefore, the candidate may be increasingly forced to purchase access to the voter via advertising, direct mail, and similar means.

On a more positive note, the evidence presented here suggests television news organizations may be seeking to cover campaign activities which contain elements of substance, rather than simply containing "balloons and parades." The unanswered question about this behavior is whether campaign organizations will accede to this "requirement," and provide more useful information to the public, or whether they will increase their access to the television news audience through more imaginative "packaging" of their campaign activities.

NOTES

1. Although the Democrats maintained control of both houses of the legislature, and swept the other statewide offices, Rhodes received 1,393,627 votes to 1,345,151 votes for Celeste; three minor party candidates polled a total of 90,390 votes. Rhodes campaigned on his ability to bring new industry and jobs to the state; and on Celeste's supposed lack of administrative experience. Celeste's campaign was built around three issues: the need for more jobs in Ohio; the need for lower utility rates; and the need to shift educational financing from local property taxes to state sources such as income and sales taxes. This last issue dominated the campaign.
2. J. M. Johnson, *Doing Field Research* (New York: Free Press, 1975) pp. ix-x.
3. WTVN presented 30-minute programs at 5:30 p.m. and 11 p.m.; WCMH at 6 p.m. and 11 p.m.; and WBNS at 6 p.m., 7 p.m., and 11 p.m.
4. Repeating stories is not necessarily a negative practice. It allows viewers who might have missed the earlier newscast to be exposed to the information; further, the viewer seeing a story a second time might be more likely to learn the information because of the repeated exposure.
5. Not all of the "official duty" stories were necessarily favorable to Rhodes' campaign. For example, on the Friday before the election state employees received a letter with their paychecks describing likely pay increases under a new Rhodes administration. All three Columbus stations telecast stories about complaints from the employees' union that the letters represented an illegal campaign activity on the part of the governor.
6. The reports, in fact, seemed to be an effective use of television for "instructional" purposes. In addition to the narration and normal videotaped visual accompaniment, visual reinforcement for the reporter's comments was provided in the form of information about the particular race printed on the screen; the information was inserted electronically with a device called a "vidifont."
7. The smallest news organization had five crews available during weekdays, the largest about a dozen. Fewer crews were available at nights and on weekends.
8. The executive producer of one news organization said he always tried to have film or videotape. "After all," he explained, "we call our program '*Action* News.'"

18. MEDIA POWER IN PRESIDENTIAL ELECTIONS: AN EXPLORATORY ANALYSIS, 1960-1980

William C. Adams

Editor's Note. William C. Adams's examination of the impact of media coverage on elections is exceptional in a number of ways. While most scholars concentrate on one election, he takes a long-range look, focusing on media coverage of five presidential elections from 1960 to 1980. And instead of lumping all aspects of media effects together as is usual, he examines seven separate elements of media content that may influence voting decisions. He then assesses whether the Democratic or Republican contender was most likely to benefit from print and electronic media coverage. Adams's approach permits him to make interesting predictions about the probable voting patterns of various population groups.

The main lessons from this analysis are that the influence of the media varies depending on the combination of elements and that election coverage affects Democratic, Republican, and Independent voters differently. Given these complexities, scholars are remiss when they discuss "media impact" as if it were a single phenomenon, affecting all voters equally. If Adams's findings are accepted, future research on the media's impact on elections will have to adopt far more complex designs than those currently in use.

William C. Adams is a political scientist whose prolific research and writing has concentrated on the impact of televised political images on public policy. Adams is a professor at George Washington University. The selection is from *The President and the Public,* ed. Doris A. Graber, Philadelphia: Institute for the Study of Human Issues, 1982.

To pursue the relationship between the media and voting, this study assumes five tasks:
1. to distinguish ... between "media effects" and "medium effects"
2. to propose seven elements of media content that merit examination in media-voting research
3. to estimate which candidate benefited on each of the seven criteria on television in contrast to newspapers in recent presidential elections

4. to identify the voters most likely to be influenced by variations in media content
5. to determine if . . . recent elections produced voting patterns consistent with the estimates of media content differences.

Media Effects and Medium Effects

The study of media effects is frequently bedeviled by a confusion between the joint impact of all media and the relative impact of a particular medium. Many studies ostensibly studying "media effects" are actually studying what will be termed here "medium effects," that is, the relative effects of television, newspapers, and other news sources.

The distinction is crucial for two reasons. First, as a practical matter it is difficult to analyze the effects of combined media use versus non-use. Researchers are rarely able to isolate the joint effects of all American media. . . .

The second reason the distinction is important is that the absence of medium effects does not necessarily mean the absence of media effects. If messages are similar across all media, there may be no unique medium effects, even though the media may be jointly exerting a powerful pull on public opinion.

Equating unique power with shared power can distort the entire subject of media impacts. If a study finds that people who rely on television do not have a significantly different outlook on a campaign than people who rely on newspapers, the study has evidence only that unique "medium effects" are absent. Such data do not address whether both media might have together edged the electorate toward one side or the other.

An illustration of the importance of the distinction concerns the media's coverage of the presidential campaign of John Anderson. One of the pivotal political decisions of 1980 was the way editors and producers opted to treat John Anderson's third-party candidacy. The key issue was where Anderson went on the agenda, and hence the amount of status, legitimacy, and credibility to be conferred by the media. Should the media's picture of the campaign have been a triptych, elevating Anderson to create a "big three?" Or should Anderson have been reduced to the size of Oliphant's penguin and allowed to voice only brief, caustic asides?

If Anderson were denied attention uniformly across all media, the impact of that lack of visibility would not be easily discerned with survey data. The media analyst would be left to speculate on the extent to which additional media attention would have helped Anderson's efforts. If, however, television were to grant the maverick campaign more serious coverage than newspapers, it might be possible to demonstrate that people who relied on television viewed Anderson differently and perhaps voted differently from those who relied on newspapers. With one medium providing him prominence and another relegating him to spoiler status, researchers might find a strong "medium effect."

*To the extent that American media are pervasive, it is difficult to show
aggregate media effects. To the extent that American media contents are
homogeneous, it is hard to show unique medium effects. Only when significant
differences in campaign-relevant content occur should it be possible to find
medium effects associated with those content differences.*

Much scholarly and popular commentary has stressed the unique impact
of television on politics. In the relative terms of "medium effects," however, the issue is actually how television differs from other media—
how television's messages and their effects contrast with the messages and
effects of other media. The question might as well be "What is the relative
impact of newspapers?" To have medium effects on presidential voting,
distinctions in messages must be substantial enough to produce different
candidate evaluations and different voting choices. The discussion which
follows proposes seven aspects of media content that may affect message
meaning.

Seven Elements of Media Content

The seven elements that should be considered in any attempt to assess
differences in media messages are (1) themes, (2) agenda, (3) treatment,
(4) endorsements, (5) advertisements, (6) persona, and (7) entertainment.

Themes

Transcending any particular news story or coverage of a single day's
events are generalized approaches, or themes, that characterize television
news as opposed to newspaper news. Three patterns are especially noteworthy. Compared to newspapers, network television is more devoted to news
about the national government, to news about the president, and to news that
is "negative.". . .

These three television themes add up to trouble for the incumbent in the
Oval Office. Without necessarily explicitly blaming the party in power, the
implicit linkage builds up night after night: government power and societal
problems are all at the national level; the president is the pinnacle of national
leadership and power; yet grave problems, foreign and domestic, persist
and swell with hopelessly ineffectual responses from the citadel in Washington. The president and his epigones are everywhere on the evening news, yet
every problem that wanes appears to be replaced by two that wax. The
merger of these three themes suggests that the unrelenting approach of
television news, relative to that of newspapers, is likely to favor the party out
of power.

Agenda

One of the earliest findings of election studies was that voters attributed
strengths and weaknesses to each major party in different issue areas.
Accordingly, certain issues usually help Democrats, showing them off to
advantage, while others tend to help Republicans. . . .

That certain issues benefit a particular party takes on added import in light of research showing the media's role in setting the issue agenda for the voting public.[1] Sustained media coverage of a particular set of issues is likely to increase the salience of those issues and then to redound to the advantage of the candidate and party perceived as better able to confront those issues. Similarly, an issue that has failed to surface in the media would be difficult for a candidate to convert into a campaign issue for voters unless they had been primed for its significance.

Returning to the matter of medium effects, rather than media effects generally, it is the difference in the television and newspaper agendas that is important. If television news, for example, emphasizes foreign policy crises more than newspapers in a year when Republicans are widely believed to be superior for keeping peace and strength, television's news agenda is relatively more advantageous for the GOP. If newspapers stress the economy more than television news does, in a year when Democrats are seen as the party of prosperity, the newspaper agenda puts the public spotlight on a subject that helps the Democrats.

Treatment

A number of studies have sought to measure the degree to which news sources give one candidate or party more favorable coverage.... [T]he concern is again differences in media messages and whether a candidate is portrayed more favorably in a particular news medium, whatever the reasons.... Treatment of the candidates may well be an especially vital element, although it would be a mistake to assume that the public will absorb without question a medium's interpretation of events or ... ignore the six other content factors outlined in this chapter.

Endorsements

The discussion of the first three factors—themes, agenda, and treatment—has underscored the need to estimate which candidate was relatively benefited by which medium's coverage. With each of the four remaining elements, however, one medium has a virtual monopoly. The "relative advantage" for a candidate in each of these areas depends almost totally on one medium.

The factor of "endorsements" illustrates this point. If the nation's newspapers overwhelmingly endorse a Republican, then the Democratic candidate is relatively benefited by television—a medium in which the Republican candidate is not dominating endorsements—because television network news never endorses a presidential candidate.

Endorsements constitute another distinct kind of mass media message, the only one beside campaign advertisements with the avowed purpose of persuading the voter to favor one candidate over another. Whatever subtle slants might be perceived from news themes, agenda, and candidate treatment, the endorsement is unambiguous.

John Robinson,[2] Michael Hooper,[3] and Steven Coombs[4] have found that newspaper endorsements do help candidates to a small but significant degree. While candidates might ordinarily prefer to have the working press sympathetic to their cause rather than having the editorial support of publishers, endorsements are apparently not without an impact.

Advertisements

Newspapers may have a special mechanism for influencing elections with endorsements, but television prevails as the medium for potential political influence through the factors of "advertising," "persona," and "entertainment."

Since 1960, campaign advertising budgets have gone almost entirely to broadcasting and not to print media. The ratio is usually over 10 to 1, and a large share of the small newspaper advertising budget goes to promoting television shows about the candidates. Consequently, dominating television advertising is essentially the same as dominating advertising about the campaign. According to the logic of this analysis, if Republicans hold a 2 to 1 advantage in television advertising, then Republicans are helped by television—at least in terms of exposure to their commercials—and Democrats are relatively better off with the basically nonexistent advertising content of newspapers.

Assessment of this element is complicated by the matter of advertisement quality. Once a threshold of exposure is attained, advertisement quality may be more important than quantity. One candidate's commercials, though not run as frequently, may be more persuasive and compelling. Any examination of this element should consider the effectiveness of advertisements instead of assuming that quality is a constant or assuming that quantity alone determines impact.

Persona

One school of thought has long argued that television's power derives from its status as the sole audiovisual news medium. Viewers find television credible and trustworthy, say sociologists Kurt and Gladys Lang, because of a sense that they are there and are seeing the story firsthand. In the case of watching candidates on television, viewers may flatter themselves that they can discern something about the character, intellect, and personality— perhaps even the competence—of the nominees. They may less consciously respond to the personal chemistry of a candidate as it is transmitted over the air.

John Kennedy's television image became the classic illustration of the power of persona. Richard Nixon's pallor during the opening presidential debate in 1960 was so damaging in contrast to Kennedy's vigorous appearance that television viewers thought him less articulate than people who heard the first debate over radio. Candidate persona in the fullest, richest, and most vivid sense can be conveyed only through television. . . .

Entertainment

Around 1960, "Westerns" held sway over prime-time. Half the top ten programs in 1959 were Westerns—"Gunsmoke," "Rifleman," "Have Gun, Will Travel," "Frontier Justice," and "Wyatt Earp." In that setting it seemed fitting and stirring for the new president to call his program "The New Frontier." . . .

Recent research and speculation have begun to assess the nature of political messages that filter into prime-time entertainment. . . . [T]he political implications of television entertainment in an amalgam with the nightly news are unclear. Nonetheless, this factor did appear to have sufficient potential as an important element in the overall package of media messages that it merited identification as an additional element in this list.

The dramatic barrage of police, detective, law-and-order, and crime shows might have accrued to the benefit of the party perceived as "tougher" on crime—the Republican party—starting with the emergence of "the social issue" in the 1964 election. . . .

Medium Advantages in Recent Elections

If the arguments advanced above are accurate, these seven factors constitute the most politically important elements of media messages likely to influence the outcome of a presidential campaign. To the degree that the messages received from television and newspaper diverge, there may be medium effects with one candidate having a competitive advantage among voters who rely primarily on television and the other candidate aided relatively more by newspapers.

Based on available data and the considered opinions of political analysts, it should be possible to estimate the nature of medium advantages on most of these seven criteria for presidential candidates in recent elections. Table 18-1

Table 18-1   Candidate Estimated to Be Relatively Benefited by Television, in Contrast to Newspapers, 1960-1976*

	1960	1964	1968	1976
Themes	JFK	BMG	RMN/GW	JEC
Agenda	JFK	(LBJ)	RMN/GW	—
Treatment	?	?	?	?
Endorsements	JFK	BMG	GW/HHH	JEC
Advertisements	JFK	—	RMN	—
Persona	JFK	BMG	RMN	JEC
Entertainment	?	BMG	RMN	GRF
Overall	JFK	BMG	RMN/GW	JEC

*BMG	= Barry M. Goldwater	JEC	= James E. Carter
GRF	= Gerald R. Ford	JFK	= John F. Kennedy
GW	= George Wallace	LBJ	= Lyndon B. Johnson
HHH	= Hubert H. Humphrey	RMN	= Richard M. Nixon

summarizes these assessments in terms of the candidate relatively benefited by television in contrast to newspapers, although the table and the discussion that follows could as easily have been put in terms of the newspaper-advantaged candidates.

In each of these elections, the news themes of negativism, the presidency, and national news are adjudged to give a consistent thematic advantage on television to the party out of power. Aside from the factor of entertainment, the relative advantage of coverage on other factors seems to vary from election to election with no consistent partisan pattern. . . .

Medium Differences and Voting Behavior

. . . [R]eliance on television rather than print media should have been associated with voting for Kennedy in 1960, Goldwater in 1964, Nixon and Wallace in 1968, and Carter in 1976. That association should be strongest among voters with more education and among voters who are Independents, and, to a lesser degree, among those who are Democrats. Merging all these factors suggests that medium effects would have been greatest for educated Independents who relied on television and thus should have voted disproportionately for Kennedy in 1960. Their counterparts who relied more on newspapers should have voted comparatively more for Nixon.

A straightforward test of these hypotheses can be performed using Michigan Survey Research Center national election data. In the 1960, 1964, 1968, and 1976 surveys, respondents were asked on which news source they relied primarily for national campaign news. In 1972 a relative media reliance question was not asked. That election has therefore been omitted from this analysis. The basic statistical task is to cross-tabulate media reliance with reported voting behavior, controlling for education and party identification.

The findings, summarized in Table 18-2, offer partial support for the research hypotheses, along with some inconsistencies. *In each election a sizable group of voters who relied on television for news voted significantly differently than their partisan and educational cohorts who relied more on print media. In every instance the direction of the television-reliant voters was that predicted by the analysis of media differences in terms of themes, agenda, treatment, persona, advertisement, endorsements, and entertainment. In contrast to newspaper reliance, television reliance was, for at least one segment of the electorate, associated with a greater likelihood of voting for Kennedy in 1960, for Goldwater in 1964, for Nixon and Wallace in 1968, and for Carter in 1976.*

In each of these elections, better-educated voters reacted differently from the less-educated. This supports the notion that such voters are more likely to acquire campaign-relevant information from the mass media and to have more capacity to respond to and be sensitive to differences in those media messages. In only one case was there a group of less-educated voters for whom media reliance was associated significantly with voting behavior. This happened with less-educated Republicans in 1976.

Table 18-2 Differences in Democratic Voting Strength

1960	Independents (with high education):			
	Television-reliant		53.4%	Kennedy
	Newspaper-reliant and others		34.9%	Kennedy
		Difference	18.5%	
	Democrats (with high education):			
	Television-reliant		83.7%	Kennedy
	Newspaper-reliant and others		68.9%	Kennedy
		Difference	14.8%	
1964	Democrats (with high education):			
	Television-reliant		82.3%	Johnson
	Newspaper-reliant and others		91.3%	Johnson
		Difference	9.0%	
1968	Independents (with high education):			
	Television-reliant		24.5%	Humphrey
	Newspaper-reliant and others		32.5%	Humphrey
		Difference	8.0%	
1976	Republicans (with high education):			
	Television-reliant		17.1%	Carter
	Newspaper-reliant and others		5.8%	Carter
		Difference	11.3%	
	Republicans (with low education):			
	Television-reliant		25.3%	Carter
	Newspaper-reliant and others		4.8%	Carter
		Difference	20.5%	

Note: Only figures with a statistically significant relationship between primary news sources and reported voting behavior are reported.

The full pattern occurred precisely as predicted, however, only in 1960 and 1968. In 1960 educated Independents who relied on television gave Kennedy a solid majority of their votes (53%), while only about one-third (35%) of those relying on print supported him. This difference of 18 percent between media groups of educated Independents was followed by a difference of 15 percent among educated Democrats. Educated Democrats who relied on television went strongly for Kennedy (84%), but those who primarily used print news sources were less likely to favor him (69%). After the election, Kennedy referred to television and commented, "We wouldn't have had a prayer without that gadget." [5] He was right.

In 1968 educated Independents again stand out as the group most "vulnerable" to campaign-message differences between media. Only one-quarter of those who relied on television voted for Humphrey, compared to one-third of those who relied on newspapers.

In two of these four elections, television's messages were estimated to have favored the Democrats; in two elections they favored the GOP. Voting behavior and media reliance of at least one segment of the electorate duplicated those directions. That the association alternately helped both the Democrats and their opponents strongly indicates that the findings are not an artifact of television-reliant voters inherently being more pro-Democratic for socioeconomic or psychological reasons not entirely controlled for by party and education.

The findings also confirm that media message differences do not have an even impact on the electorate. Message differences appear to have been sufficiently subtle, and perceptual screens sufficiently powerful, that message differences have not been associated with differing voting behavior for most segments of the electorate. . . .

Just which voters are most likely to be influenced must be qualified in light of the results of the 1976 and 1964 elections. In 1964 educated Democrats rather than educated Independents had the more significant relationship between media reliance and reported voting behavior. The 1976 events are even more unexpected. First, 1976 was the only year in which there was a statistically significant difference among a less-educated group. Second, the media-voting associations show up among Republicans and not at all among Independents and Democrats. Republicans were supposed to have been most resistant to distinctions in media messages.

A revised interpretation can be offered. The particular appeals of the candidates and media coverage seem to interact so that in some instances the partisans are more influenced by differences in media information than are Independents. The precise pattern seems to be election-specific. It continues to appear that the impact is more likely to surface among voters with more education, although 1976 suggests that even those with less education are not immune to varying their voting in line with media input.

In each of these elections, television reliance was associated with support for the party out of power. One factor was that television's news themes favor the "outs," but that slant also happens to coincide with the relative advantage television was usually giving the "outs" in terms of agenda, persona, advertising, endorsements, and entertainment. Together the cumulative impact parallels Michael Robinson's findings of associations between television viewing and dissatisfaction with the status quo, mistrust of government, and cynicism—all reactions likely to help the "outs." [6]

Both in 1964 and in 1976, partisans who relied on television defected from the incumbent president of their own party far more than partisans who primarily used other news sources. In 1964 television-reliant educated Democrats were more likely to be unhappy with Lyndon Johnson and to prefer the challenger. In 1976 television-reliant Republicans (whatever their education) were more likely to be displeased with Gerald Ford and to defect to his challenger. In both elections only among the incumbent's own party was television reliance associated with disaffection toward the incumbent. One possible inference is that television provided a vehicle for the appeals of the challenger to reach successfully some partisans who were amenable to those appeals. A second inference is that television news may have intensified dissatisfaction with the incumbent for partisans in a way that selective reading of newspapers did not. . . .

The 1980 Election

Who was likely to profit more from television than from newspapers—Jimmy Carter or Ronald Reagan? In terms of "themes," Reagan acquired television's usual out-party advantage which Carter had enjoyed four years earlier. But the rest of the key elements reveal a mixed list. . . .

Summing up the separate factors for the earlier campaigns was easy, because in each campaign it was estimated that one particular candidate benefited from television, compared to newspapers, on most of the factors. In this instance, the pattern is more complicated. It gives Reagan a television advantage on three of the seven factors: themes, treatment, and persona. Carter appeared to have the television advantage on two elements (endorsements and entertainment). Two variables—agenda and advertisements—were a draw.

Without a system for weighting the relative importance of these factors, the simple 3:2:2 score suggests that, unlike the previous elections, in 1980 neither candidate had a marked net advantage from television as opposed to newspaper messages. If, on balance, the messages from each medium were relatively indistinguishable, there is no reason to expect that voters who relied primarily on one medium would be influenced to vote any differently from voters relying largely on the other medium.

The results shown by survey data from the Michigan Survey Research Center are interesting. There was no significant relationship between media reliance and voting for Democrats, Independents, or Republicans, controlling for education. . . .

Television may not have a unique election impact if the sum of its messages differs little from the messages of newspapers. But the case is otherwise when television's outputs are consistently more favorable to one of the candidates than those of the newspapers. In that event, the distinct messages of television do appear to be capable of influencing voting among susceptible audience segments.

NOTES

1. E.g., Maxwell E. McCombs and Donald L. Shaw, "The Agenda-setting Function of Mass Media," *Public Opinion Quarterly* 36 (Summer 1972): 176-87; Ray Funkhouser, "The Issues of the Sixties: An Exploratory Study of the Dynamics of Public Opinion," *Public Opinion Quarterly* 37 (Spring 1973): 62-75; Donald L. Shaw and Maxwell E. McCombs, *The Emergence of American Political Issues: The Agenda-setting Function of the Press* (St. Paul: West, 1977); and Phillip Palmgreen and Peter Clarke, "Agenda-setting with Local and National Issues," *Communication Research* 4 (October 1977): 435-52.
2. John P. Robinson, "Perceived Media Bias and the 1968 Vote: Can the Media Affect Behavior after All?" *Journalism Quarterly* 49 (Summer 1972): 239-46; and "The Press as King-Maker," *Journalism Quarterly* 51 (Winter 1974): 587-94.
3. Michael Hooper, "Party and Newspaper Endorsements as Predictors of Voter Choice," *Journalism Quarterly* 46 (Summer 1969): 302-5.

4. Steven L. Coombs, "The Electoral Impact of Newspaper Editorials," paper read at the Annual Meeting of the Midwest Political Science Association, April 21, 1979, Chicago.
5. Eric Barnouw, *Tube of Plenty* (New York: Oxford University Press, 1975), p. 277.
6. Michael J. Robinson, "Public Affairs Television and the Growth of Political Malaise," *American Political Science Review* 70 (June 1976): 409-32.

Section Four

AFFECTING POLITICAL ACTORS
AND THE BALANCE OF POWER

All politics involves actors. This section differs from earlier ones, therefore, only in its more concentrated focus on the effect that the mass media have on the political fates of various types of participants. The section begins with a look at the presidency, which is the office most in the media limelight. It then turns to coverage of Congress and its members. The contrast between media impact on senators and representatives and media impact on the president puts the distinctiveness of these political actors into sharper focus. The section concludes with two selections that show how media coverage affects two types of interest groups: ordinary people at the fringes of the power structure, and ordinary people who defy the mores of the established culture.

The first article presents a typical news conference in which the president confronts newspeople in what is close to an adversary procedure. The president tries but fails to control the questioning. The news conference transcript is followed by a report based on a systematic analysis of media coverage of presidents over a 25-year period. Michael Baruch Grossman and Martha Joynt Kumar delineate how impressions about presidents are created by the media. They explain why these impressions are so politically potent even though newspeople do not intend to influence the course of politics.

What happens when a president is under serious attack? Do newspeople close in for the kill like a wolf pack stalking wounded prey? Gladys Engel Lang and Kurt Lang reach surprising conclusions after examining the role played by the mass media in the resolution of the Watergate scandal. Their study also sheds light on the media's role in defining public opinion for policy makers.

Next, Michael J. Robinson illuminates the story of media treatment of Congress from several perspectives, including occasional comparisons to the presidency. He notes that different types of media—in-house, campaign, general-national, and general-local—vary in their treatment of Congress and in their impact on the political scene. He points out that publicity that may hurt a political institution may, at the same time, help its officeholders or vice versa.

A major aspect of media impact on political actors is the redistribution of power that occurs in the wake of publicity. Senator Fulbright, for instance, has claimed that "Television has done as much to expand the powers of the president as would a constitutional amendment formally abolishing the co-equality of the three branches of government." Even within an institution, command of media attention can be translated into increments and decrements of power. Mary Russell, a congressional reporter, looks at this phenomenon at the level of congressional committees.

From people in formal positions of power, the discussion turns to citizens who band together to seek governmental remedies for shared problems, or who strive to gain favorable public attention for their chosen causes. Edie Goldenberg's essay discusses how groups who lack money and expertise try with varying degrees of success to attract the media attention they need. In the final selection, Todd Gitlin explores the services and disservices performed by the media for social protest movements that advocate radical political change. He uses Students for a Democratic Society, a New Left student movement, as an example.

19. PRESIDENT REAGAN'S NEWS CONFERENCE JAN. 14, 1983

Editor's Note. We begin our look at coverage of the presidency with the transcript of a typical news conference, an event that takes place a dozen times or more in an average year. Presidents enjoy as well as dread news conferences. If they perform well, or if they are masters of repartee, a news conference can enhance their image, their standing in public opinion polls, and their effectiveness. If they perform poorly, or if they misstate an important fact or make an unfortunate slip of the tongue, the results can be disastrous.

To prepare for news conferences, presidents receive briefing papers about all current problems that are likely to surface. After they have digested this information, there usually is a dress rehearsal in which aides quiz the president, mimicking the inquisitorial style of news reporters. The president also receives a seating chart, complete with pictures, so that he can call on those reporters he considers friendly. But all these preparations are never enough. With reporters ready with hundreds of questions, and the time for answers measured in seconds, presidential misstatements are almost unavoidable.

The January 14, 1983 news conference, reported here from the *New York Times* transcript, illustrates several common practices: the president's use of an opening statement in the vain hope of guiding the discussion; the reporters' sharp and at times antagonistic questioning; the concern that publicity generated by the news conference will hurt policy making. Headings have been added by the editor.

Opening Statement

Ladies and gentlemen, I have a statement here. But before I begin, I just want to explain the subject of this. There has been such disarray approaching chaos in the press corps with regard to the subject of arms control that I thought before you unraveled into complete disorder that maybe we should straighten out the entire subject.

So, before taking your questions, I'll express a thought or two which are a matter of deep conviction for me with regard to arms control. These concern what we must do before we can expect to be successful and then what principles ought to guide us in our negotiating strategy.

First, it seems to me that the two factors that are essential to success in arms control are leverage and determination. With respect to leverage, it's clear that when I arrived in office there was virtually no hope that we could expect the Soviets to bargain seriously for real reductions.

After all, they had all the marbles. We hadn't designed a new missile in 15 years. We hadn't built a new submarine in the same period although they'd built more than 60. Our bombers were older than the pilots who flew them.

Today that's no longer the case. Working with the Congress, we have in the past two years succeeded in getting authorization for a complete modernization of the triad of strategic forces with the exception of the MX, which still requires Congressional action this spring.

My point is that now we're in a position to get somewhere and I'm determined that we shall.

The other quality I mentioned was determination. Recently I've made a few management changes so that we'll have a streamlined team in place through which we can reach decisions promptly and get results in the Geneva talks.

I want to say something else about my strategy toward arms control. It seems to me that if you look back over the history of the past 15 years of talks, certain things emerge. Frankly, some things have worked and others have not.

Let me be specific. Some people have argued that we ought to try unilateral disarmament, that we should cut our own systems without getting anything from them in return in the hope that our example will lead the Soviets to cut theirs.

That approach has been tried on a number of occasions. For example, President Carter decided to cut the B-1 bomber perhaps in the expectation that the Soviets would cut back on their bomber programs. It didn't work. Instead of cutting back, the Soviets went steadily ahead with the Backfire and another advanced bomber.

On the other hand, some things have worked. Most of you recall that in the late '60s President Johnson tried very hard to engage the Soviets in talks on antiballistic missile systems. At the time, we had no deployment planned, in short no leverage. The Soviets refused to talk. But then the United States decided to go ahead with an ABM plan, and you know the rest: When it became clear that we would go ahead with the deployment, the Soviets came to the table and we got a treaty that still endures today.

The lesson is that they will bargain when they have an incentive. And today that incentive exists, and I'm convinced that we can make real progress. It is with this thought in mind that I had an in-depth meeting yesterday on arms control with some of my arms control advisers.

Next week I'll be meeting with Ambassador Ed Rowny and Paul Nitze. We're ready, and I'm convinced that, confident that with determination we can succeed. Keeping in mind our commitment to the security of Europe and to peace and in order to insure the closest possible coordination with our European allies on arms reductions and deterrents, I've asked Vice President Bush to go to Europe for talks with my European counterparts.

And while he's there, the Vice President will meet with the Pope, Prime Minister Thatcher, Chancellor Kohl, President Mitterrand, Prime Minister Fanfani, Prime Minister Martens, and Prime Minister Lubbers as well as with our negotiating teams in Geneva.

And let there be no doubt we're ready. We'll consider every serious proposal, and we have the determination to succeed in this, the most important undertaking of our generation. Now, any of you have questions on this subject, I think we should dispose of those first.

Questions and Answers

Summit Meeting

Q: Mr. President, do you think that it would be good to have a summit meeting with Andropov first to try to nail down what they're really proposing now, what all these new proposals mean and are you ready for such a summit?

A: No, I think that since the talks are supposed to begin early in February, the first week of February, and General Rowny and Ed Nitze are prepared to go there, I think that that takes place first, and we see then what that might lead to and if there's a need for such a meeting. Questions on the same subject?

Disarray in White House

Q: Well, sir, I have a question on one of the things that you mentioned, the subject of disarray, if I may. There is a perception, Mr. President, that the disarray is here in the White House, that you have been out of touch, that you have had to be dragged back by your staff and friends on Capitol Hill to make realistic decisions in the budget. There was even a newspaper column saying that your Presidency is failing. Would you address yourself to this perception?

A: Yes, that's why I came in to point out to you accurately where the disarray lies. It's in those stories that seem to be going around because they are not based on fact. And I would suggest that sometimes in the—you get some unnamed source information—that any of us in the White House would be willing to help you out by giving you an answer as to whether that information is correct or not.

Q: Specifically, on the business of your staff, the story that your staff and your friends such as Senator Laxalt have had to sort of drag you back from an economic meeting plan that was failing—was it your decision to make these terms that we hear about toward new taxes or perhaps a different approach to cutting the budget in the defense matters?

A: Maybe the problem is that what we're doing is a little bit new to Washington. I said from the very beginning that we had a cabinet-type government as I'd had in Sacramento. That we had a Cabinet that was chosen for their ability and their knowledge and not because they controlled delegates at a convention or something. And that I would seek advice and every kind of viewpoint in arriving at decisions, we've been doing that. And it's been working very well. And it is true that I asked and want to hear differing viewpoints on things. But then I make the decisions, and this has been working very well, and we've had a very heavy agenda for the last few weeks. We've been working long hours on a number of things that are before us here, and as I say, we had a very serious and a long meeting yesterday on this particular subject. But now we're getting too far away from the general subject.

Weapons Policy

Q: By the time your first term is over [inaudible] but do you really think that by the time your first term is up that we will have an arms reduction treaty with the Soviet Union?

A: I think it would be unwise for anyone, knowing the history of some 19 attempts by this country to bring about arms reduction and control with the Soviet Union in the past, to make a prediction or put a time limit of any kind on this. I will say this: We will stay at a table negotiating as long as there is any chance at all of securing arms reduction because it is the most important problem facing this generation.

Q: Sir, could you comment on stories that have circulated in recent days that sometime after the general elections you might explore alternatives to your zero [inaudible]?

A: No, and here you're getting dangerously into an area that can't be opened to discussion, which is the tactics of negotiating and the strategy of negotiating. If you discuss that openly, then there is no strategy and you have—you've tied your hands with regard to attaining anything.

Q: Mr. President, you mentioned in your opening statement the MX missile. During the campaign you ran for office, you repeatedly ridiculed former President Carter for his failed efforts to get an MX basing plan and get the program going. How has your experience been any different than his and how could you say that your efforts have been any more successful than his?

A: Well, now, if you'll forgive me, my criticism mainly was I was in great disagreement with his plan, not a failure to get it. I just did not believe, and from the counsel and advice that it was—that I sought and was able to get, I did not believe that such a plan was practical or that it would in any way result in more security for the weapons system.

Leaked News on the Economy

Q: Mr. President, a lot of the criticism which you referred to earlier when we talked about disarray has centered around the fact that perhaps you've overpromised the recovery of the economy. And much of what's been written in recent days has centered on that when they talked of disarray, and you seem to have changed your positions by being described in articles as willing to think about taxes in the out years if they're needed to bring down the deficit. All of that has contributed to this. Do you think that's unfair?

A: I have and will continue to say that there are still decisions to be made. We've made great progress on, with regard to the budget plan. I do not believe that philosophically I have changed at all. But I'm not prepared to discuss that, and we now have left this other subject and we should get back to it. I am—

Q: I was coming back to this one, sir.

A: No, I think that, again, this has been very inaccurate—things that are only options being presented and in which there has been no decision, and, as I say, I've asked for the widest range of options. And then I suddenly see them announced as rumor that I have made a decision or that I have decided on this or I'm willing to go this way or not. That is where, as I say, the leaks have been very inaccurate and I would—I just don't think you should place so much confidence in them.

Q: Sir, may I follow that for a second? Since the policy on leaks was announced on Monday, the Secretary of Treasury put on record, or on background, virtually all of the tax measures that are being considered for the new budget, the Secretary of Defense said on television that there would be a military and civilian pay freeze—the details are open—and the Associate Attorney General revealed, on the record, your decision to veto the crime and one of the wilderness bills. All in all, sir, it's been a very good week for leaks and for reporters. Does this really serve any purpose?

A: The difference is that you were able to identify every one of those people. They didn't come and appear in your newscast or in print as an "unidentified high White House source."

Q: But that's where the perception of you seeming to change your stand, where part of it comes from.

A: Well, I haven't seen the exact words of some of those statements, but I would suggest that maybe they were trying to explain away the misstatements or the assumptions that had been made.

Defense Spending Cuts

Q: Mr. Secretary—oh, Mr. President—

A: Gee, I thought for a minute I'd lost my job!

Q: In addition to the Secretaries, Secretary Regan, Secretary Weinberger, others have spoken publicly. The Joint Chiefs of Staff spoke publicly about your defense cuts and said that they would have preferred the cuts to be in weapons systems, not in pay and personnel; that you actually hurt readiness. Doesn't this contribute to the appearance that you have backed down on your defense buildup and on your commitment not to hurt the readiness?

A: No. There has been, as the Secretary admitted, that there might be some slight stretching out of our readiness preparations, but we have already achieved great gains in those. So, it isn't as if we were starting from scratch from that. But our preference was not to delay or set back the weapons buildups that we need in order to close the window of vulnerability. And at the same time may I say, that we think with our arms control talks we are creating a window of opportunity here.

But, no, we haven't retreated from our position on that. I myself would have preferred to not have to make cuts. We're facing reality with what we're going to present in a budget to the Congress and what we believe can meet our problems and would be acceptable to Congress.

Financing Social Security

Q: Mr. President, we've been told our time with you is limited. On Social Security, your chief of staff has said on the record now you would consider moving up the payroll tax increases in Social Security, the ones that have already been passed and would come into effect down the road. What will you do if the Social Security Commission, by tomorrow, does not give you any recommendations?

A: The—well, we'll see if they're going to. If they're going to plan on a few more days before they come to such a decision, then we'll give them those few more days, or whatever time this takes. We must resolve this problem. The—I know that some of the dispute centers on the subject of whether increased tax revenues should be the answer to the some 30 years' imbalance of Social Security, or whether it should be made with cutting some costs in other areas. And that's where they're in disagreement. I'm not going to make a choice on this until I see what the entire thing is that they recommend.

There have been references to this as "my commission, the Presidential Commission." Let me call to your attention again that I announced that it would be bipartisan and that there were three of us that would appoint. I appointed representatives, the majority leader of the Senate appointed some, the Speaker of the House appointed some. So it is a commission appointed by both sides and both the Legislature and the Executive branch.

Q: But if there is no recommendation to you, don't you have to move ahead with a plan of your own in Congress this year?

A: Yes. Then, we will have to face them once again. But again, my aim in all of this has been to treat with this problem honestly and not return to the political furor that was created when we tried to bring this subject up more than a year ago. And when it was chosen, or some chose to make it, a political football for political results and frightened the life out of a great many senior citizens with the thought that this, on which they're so dependent, was going to be taken away from them, no one that I know in this Government has any intention of taking away the checks that these people are getting. I've said it over and over again, but somehow it does not get as much attention as the lies that have been told by those who want to portray us as somehow out to destroy Social Security.

Q: Thank you, Mr. President.

A: Helen, thank you very much. [Helen Thomas works for United Press International.—ed.]

Personalities

Q: Does Paul Nitze have your confidence? [Nitze served as U.S. delegate to U.S.—U.S.S.R. disarmament talks.—ed.]

A: Yes, yes.

Q: You don't agree that your Presidency is failing, do you?

A: No, and I look at the record, and as a matter of fact I got out some of your printings, at least some of your group's this morning, about campaign promises that I'd made. And this was printed before I took office. And we have either succeeded in keeping them or have made an effort to keep them and still been frustrated by the majority party in the House. But we've made a solid effort to get every one of these things.

But I would like to just leave you now, and no more time for no more questions. But I just would like to get your minds back to this, because I think this is so important that our allies should not be, from the things that they read, be concerned about whether we're lacking in determination, over whether we are indeed in disarray. We are not. There is complete—

Q: Mr. President, are the Russians—

[Unidentified voice]: Please, we've got to stop. When Helen says "thank you," that's it.

Q: But Helen's the one who then asked another question.

[Unidentified voice]: She said, "Thank you."

Q: Why did you fire Mr. Rostow, Mr. President? [Rostow served as Director of the U.S. Arms Control and Disarmament Agency.—ed.]

[Unidentified voice]: Sandra, please!

A: Sandra, that's all been explained away, and it's in here in the statement, that we're simply streamlining the management.

Q: Come back here and see us soon!

A: Yes, I enjoy this here. I guess I can't get all of you in the Oval Office.

20. THE REFRACTING LENS

Michael Baruch Grossman and Martha Joynt Kumar

Editor's Note. All presidents have complained, often bitterly, that media coverage is unfavorable and unfair to them, and that it hampers their effectiveness as political leaders. This scientific content analysis of news stories about presidents, from 1953 to 1978 in the *New York Times* and *Time* magazine and from 1968 to 1978 in the CBS evening news, contradicts the impression that coverage is preponderantly hostile. On balance in all administrations that were covered, all three media sources presented a great many more favorable than unfavorable stories.

The analysis also reveals how crucial the nature of media coverage is for the president's prestige, power, and success. The emphasis given to news stories may force presidents to direct their energies to publicized problems in ways not of their choosing. News interpretations may influence the timing and direction of their decisions, as well as shape the images that friends and foes form of the chief executive. News stories also serve as communications channels through which the disjointed parts of the governmental system communicate with each other. Perhaps it should be a matter of concern that such important functions rest on the shoulders of a comparatively small group of women and men. Many of them are unknown and beyond public scrutiny. Moreover, most disclaim any responsibility for the impact that their reports have on the presidency and on the country.

Michael Baruch Grossman and Martha Joynt Kumar teach political science at Towson State University. They share an interest in scientific exploration of media coverage of political institutions. In addition to maintaining close contact with the press corps, both have written for newspapers and magazines. This selection is from *Portraying the President: The White House and the News Media*, Baltimore: Johns Hopkins University Press, 1981.

News organizations provide the mechanism through which influentials in the Washington community as well as important constituencies throughout the nation take their assessment of the President. News about the White House influences the actions of organized interests both within and without government. Congressmen, bureaucrats, and lobbyists base their decisions to grant or withhold support for the President on perceptions gleaned from the media. National concerns as well as the immediate objectives of these important political actors are at stake. White House news has a major impact on the politically inactive segments of the public included in its general audience. Reality as refracted through the lens of the news media is for most people their only glimpse of what is going on at the White House. It provides them with a basis to judge the person who occupies the Oval Office and suggests the activities that may be needed to secure an individual or a general interest. What the media present to their audience has important consequences for the public as well as for the President, and for political institutions as well as for the individuals and groups who are actors on the national stage. . . .

. . . [N]ews organizations have become actors of considerable significance in the American political system. They play a number of important public roles, including influencing the selection and removal of those who hold office, determining the public perception of the importance of many issues, and interpreting the significance of a leader's activities. Nonetheless, news organizations are neither traditional political actors nor a fourth branch of government. They do not have clearly defined objectives, as do interest groups, and they do not seek power in the sense of winning and holding office, as do most politicians. Most media organizations do not seek to determine electoral or policy outcomes, with the exception of a few matters about which their owners and managers care deeply, or about which a few columnists, editors, and elite reporters do have opinions.

What might be said of news organizations is that they strive to become the arbiters of the political system. They legitimize and delegitimize individuals, points of view of issues, and even institutions such as the presidency itself. News enterprises act as if they set the ethical norms for candidates and the criteria by which policies are to be evaluated. In sum, these organizations attempt to establish the criteria of rectitude for political operations in the United States. It is no wonder that all the other actors, including the President, resent them. . . .

Those who work at the White House believe the President's reputation in the Washington community and his public prestige throughout the nation are the key determinants of his influence. Richard Neustadt, who introduced this notion of the basis of presidential power to the public, described the Washington community as an entity that based its judgments on impressions received through multiple conduits of information, including the news media.[1] The contemporary White House looks to its relations with the media as the most important factor determining its reputation and prestige. Officials have a good sense of several important elements of the relationship. Unlike reporters, who often minimize their institutional (although not their personal) roles, White House officials consider news organizations to be important political actors. In both interviews and conversations, officials described to us their relations with news organizations in analytical terms that would indicate that they think about these relations and discuss them among staff members. . . .

The way in which reporters frame their stories about the President to a large extent reflects the opinions of influentials in the Washington community. For example, the evaluation made by many journalists that Jimmy Carter revealed himself to be a bumbler and an incompetent may have been a congressional creation that was moved through the media to the public. Dennis Farney described the process by which this impression was created: "Carter came in as an outsider, and frightened and perplexed members of Congress. . . . He came in as a tough bastard who was going to stop dams. Then he went to a supplicant's position. He started complimenting Congress in the most unconvincing ways. So they talked to journalists and were judging him by the way that other Presidents behaved. It dawned on members that this guy could be had." [2]

Because reporters were influenced by their friends on the Hill, they tended to emphasize Carter's words and deeds that showed him alternately as too demanding or too surrendering. They chose for their articles those items that showed Carter to be ill at ease in Washington, as well as those that showed that he was unable to mobilize support behind coherent programs either in the capital or among the people. If an event involved a change of a decision, the emphasis they placed on the change in their story suggested that the President displayed qualities of indecisiveness.

This picture of Carter represented the prevalent view in Washington. At times and in particular stories it was unfair. The story was not, however, a total fabrication. In general terms it reflected the reality that the outsider Jimmy Carter had much on-the-job training to get through before he could gain control of his office. It reflected the reality that in many important areas Carter had difficulty establishing his priorities, that he had difficulty establishing priorities among areas, and that where he had clearly established certain policies as important priorities, he had not succeeded in convincing others to follow his lead. But if the story was a reflection of the reality, it also contributed to the reality of the story. Carter's reputation, as shaped and hardened by the media, contributed to his difficulties in getting control of his office.

Just as news organizations mirror, form, and reinforce the opinions of influentials, they reflect and shape the public perception of the President as a leader. The trends in opinion that indicate the level of support for the President affect the way the media covers him. Stories tend to be supportive of a president for whom things are going well. They accelerate the decline of a man who is perceived to be not up to the job. . . .

The judgments of journalists are influenced not only by others in the Washington establishment and by the national consensus, but also by other journalists. When greater numbers of unfavorable stories about the President appear, news organizations will probably produce more stories viewed from an unfavorable perspective until the trend changes. During the summer of 1978 the percentage of unfavorable stories about the Carter presidency climbed to nearly 25 percent in the three sources of news examined . . . , a trend that appeared among most news organizations. Unfavorable stories produced a momentum for continuing unfavorable stories. . . .

One way to examine the role news organizations play in presidential politics is to consider what might happen in the absence of their independent activities. The Vietnam War presents a revealing illustration. President Johnson wanted the media to present stories about Vietnam that supported his version of the war. At first a few stories indicated that their authors did not share the President's assumptions. Most of what appeared in the media pictured events as perceived by reporters and editors who did not disagree in any essential way with the official version. Eventually, however, news organizations ran more stories on developments in Vietnam that were based on a different perspective, stories that the White House thought were harmful and distorted. President Nixon wanted to keep news of American involvement in Cambodia away from the public, but the bombings and invasions were continuing subjects in the media, which remained beyond the President's control. News stories did not stop the invasion, however, nor does the evidence indicate that the media can be judged to be an antiwar group. In fact, Presidents Johnson and Nixon continued to receive a large share of favorable stories about their leadership during this period.

What the press did was to focus on news issues involving the conduct of the war—subjects that made it difficult to portray the leadership in a positive manner. In the end, the picture of the war's futility spread to the public and then to official Washington. When it was clear that he could no longer define the war for public opinion, President Johnson withdrew from politics. The war was covered, but not the way the President wanted. President Nixon was forced to accept a legislative restriction on a president's ability to move militarily in Southeast Asia or in "other Vietnams" throughout the world. This act by Congress was their response to the cross pressures of White House demands that [Congress] continue to support [the President's] Vietnam policies and the wishes of a large segment of public opinion that was war-weary. Congress yielded to the public. The role of the media was indirect but still of great importance. "The press, not Congress, told the truth of Vietnam," James Reston observed. "And made it part of the conscience of the country." [3] The news stories about Johnson and Nixon's conduct of the Vietnam War were framed by the judgments that some journalists made about presidential behavior. These judgments became the basis on which a large segment of the public evaluated the two presidents' conduct of the war. . . .

There are a number of political roles that most journalists admit they play: they identify problems that the White House has to deal with; they make interpretations that, especially when accompanied by leaked information, can influence the decisions that are made; they stimulate investigations; they change timetables; they contribute to a separate information channel in Washington that carries some important matters. Finally, their most direct political role involves their relationship with the White House.

News organizations identify problems that require specific governmental or political actions by the White House. Events frequently become problems for the President because they are reported in the media. The unbuttoned remarks of a high official who hadn't realized that he was on the record create problems for the White House, as does an encounter with a legal problem by a member of the staff. This latter situation can be particularly embarrassing because it may lead to the media's reporting previous occasions when the same event had occurred but when the law had not been involved. Sometimes the questions reporters ask at the briefing identify problems the administration can expect to face. Most frequently the press is an actor forcing a response from the White House because the matters raised in news stories would not have surfaced through bureaucratic channels. . . .

When stories appear in an influential news source interpreting an event in a manner unfavorable to the President, many White House officials respond with steps to defend the President's image. They are particularly alarmed when stories stress political complications, because they fear that the prediction of problems may become a self-fulfilling prophecy. Thus a story about a vote against a legislative proposal that is interpreted to mean that the President is in trouble in Congress may soften the President's support in Congress among his marginal followers there. They are especially concerned with obtaining a positive interpretation during a political campaign because they (and journalists) believe that an image of success creates its reality. The most damaging result occurs when a story interpreting a controversial decision is accompanied by leaked information. When that happens, as was the case during the Kennedy administration's Skybolt missile crisis, officials have to react quickly to stave off embarrassment. "It [the story] led to some rather hasty decisions," Walt Rostow recalled.[4]

News organizations also influence outcomes by stimulating investigations. Although the media have no legal power to investigate wrongdoing and cannot require that reporters be given information, press reports may create a demand for a government investigation. Once the investigation is underway, news organizations present reports that affect the reputations of those conducting the investigation and those who are the subject of its scrutiny. Sometimes government officials will leak information to the press that they hope will stimulate an investigation that they could not get by going through channels.

What appears in the press can change the White House timetable, particularly on questions involving appointments or dismissals. In 1975 President Ford and his advisers decided to make cabinet changes in a dramatic way in order to put his stamp on the administration he inherited from Richard Nixon. When the press released the story, it had the opposite effect. "It gave the public the appearance that it was a disorderly process," a Ford official explained. "It took several weeks to really get that behind us."[5]

In another political role, the media operate an internal network that provides information to Washington insiders. At one time they passed on personal information of importance about the health or personal activities of prominent political figures. The importance of this network declined during the 1970s because news organizations began publishing hearsay information about people and activities that was previously off limits. Nevertheless, reporters still provide as well as pick up information from their sources. Reporters may inform officials of what they believe to be the story about their counterparts in other organizations, although they are not ready for that story to appear in the media. Some officials want to befriend reporters so they can "cultivate their sources."

Finally, the relationship between news organizations and the White House is itself a form of political activity. Efforts by the White House to shape what appears in the media is a recognition by the President's assistants that it is a basic relationship affecting his reputation, his policies, and the quality of support he receives from the public and influentials in Washington. . . . [J]ournalists are not innocent participants in this relationship, although they do chafe at both institutional and conscious manipulation by the White House. They don't like to be channeled, and, of course, they are outraged when they are deceived. Most of the time, however, they are partners, even when they are being used by the White House. . . .

NOTES*

1. Richard E. Neustadt, *Presidential Power: The Politics of Leadership from F.D.R. to Carter* (New York: John Wiley & Sons, 1980).
2. Interview with Dennis Farney (Washington, D.C.: MJK, June 25, 1979).
3. Interview with James Reston (Washington, D.C.: MBG & MJK, January 28, 1977).
4. Interview with Walt Rostow, July 9, 1976.
5. Background interview, Ford administration official (Washington, D.C.: MJK & MBG, December, 1976).

[* The initials MJK (Martha Joynt Kumar) and MBG (Michael Baruch Grossman) identify the interviewers.]

21. THE MEDIA AND WATERGATE

Gladys Engel Lang and Kurt Lang

Editor's Note. This selection further illustrates how and why political leaders vie for media coverage during power struggles. Gladys and Kurt Lang assess the extent to which news stories affected the course of political events during the Watergate scandal that led to President Nixon's resignation. They conclude that despite voluminous news stories, media influence was only peripheral to the final outcome. Their analysis is important because it indicates the limitations, as well as the potency, of media coverage. However, even peripheral media involvement can be crucial. Would the Watergate affair have been the same without news coverage?

The selection is also important because it highlights how the media are used as a battleground in the fight to win public opinion support. The Langs call attention to the major role played by news stories in forming public opinion and in gauging and interpreting what the public thinks. These interpretations influence the conduct of politics because decision makers usually accept the media's assessment.

Gladys Engel Lang and Kurt Lang have collaborated in numerous path-breaking studies of mass media images and their effects on public opinion. Both are professors of sociology at the State University of New York at Stony Brook. The selection is from *The Battle for Public Opinion: The President, the Press, and the Polls during Watergate,* New York: Columbia University Press, 1983.

... What was the effect of the media on the creation, the course, and the resolution of Watergate? The answer is not as obvious as it may appear. Despite the heroic efforts of some journalists, Watergate had no visible effect on the 1972 Presidential election. Yet six months later, even before the televised Senate Watergate hearings, the nation's attention had become riveted on the issue, and for more than a year thereafter, until Richard Nixon's dramatic exit, Watergate dominated the headlines and the network news. . . .

Richard Nixon himself believed that public opinion was the critical factor in what he called the "overriding of my landslide mandate." For him, the struggle to stay in office, especially after the firing of Special Watergate Prosecutor Archibald Cox, when impeachment first became a real possibility,

---

was a "race for public support." He called it his "last campaign," only this time it was not for political office but for his political life.[1]

As the President saw it, the main danger of being impeached resided in the public's becoming conditioned to the idea that he was going to be impeached. This was a good enough reason for Nixon's strategists to keep a close watch on all indicators of public sentiment—letters, telegrams, telephone calls, editorials, television commentaries, press reports, and, especially, what the polls showed. At the same time, the President developed a media strategy specifically and directly aimed at winning the battle of the polls. The media were the principal battlefields on which the major confrontations took place. Television, because of how it was used by all sides, played a most active role in the conflict.

Many observers of Watergate agree that it was Nixon's defeat in the battle for public opinion that forced him to retreat at crucial points when he failed to rally support for his stand to limit the scope of any probe into the Watergate break-in. Ultimately, it left him no alternative but to bow out. In this view, the way public opinion made itself felt exemplified "democracy at work," a favorite cliché of the news media. Ford lent it official sanction in his inaugural address when he told the nation, "Here the people rule." The view in the Nixon camp was less benign. Public opinion was seen as an ever-present danger. Stirred up by the media, deliberately manipulated by his enemies, and tracked by pollsters, public opinion was to become the hostile force that ultimately *drove* Nixon from office.

Not everyone believing that public opinion influenced the resolution of Watergate agrees that it hastened the end. In fact, an argument can be made that public opinion had exactly the opposite effect, that it slowed the process and prolonged the crisis. Some members of Congress, reluctant to move against the President unless assured that they had a majority solidly behind them, felt restrained by public opinion. Polls that continued to show most people opposed to Nixon's removal from office failed to provide this reassurance, though these same polls also showed large majorities believing that the President was somehow involved in a "serious" scandal and not just caught up in the usual politics. Critics of opinion research have gone so far as to argue, some most vociferously, that during most of Watergate the major polls, whether by inadvertence or design, exaggerated the extent of opposition to impeachment. Consequently, the media were slow to register the groundswell for impeachment.

A third group of political analysts regards this emphasis on public opinion as totally misplaced and the Nixon strategy as misdirected. To them the battle for public opinion was only a sideshow. The media, in treating the issue as a political struggle for public support, diverted attention from the one crucial element in the downfall of Richard Nixon: the accumulation of incriminating evidence. If Watergate was a political contest, as it obviously was, the stakes consisted of information. Those pressing the case on legal grounds had to be mindful of public reaction but only insofar as people had to have confidence in the fairness and objectivity of the process by which the President was being judged.

Clearly the nation had experienced a dramatic shift in public opinion during the more than two years of controversy, which began with a break-in and ended with Nixon's resignation. What could account for such a reversal? The first place to look for an explanation is in the behavior of the media. TV, radio, and print are essential to the formation of public opinion in the modern nation in two ways. They disseminate information that allows members of the public to form opinions and, just as important, they convey to politicians and to others an image of what public opinion is, thus giving it a force it would not otherwise have. . . .

Watergate had broken into public consciousness only after the coverage had created a sense of crisis. This is not to say that the Watergate issue was something that the electronic and print media had created out of whole cloth. The coverage, which had stirred interest in Watergate, was dictated by events but the media themselves had become part of the field of action. Political figures with a stake in the outcome were using whatever publicity they could attract to advance their own goals and interests, thereby providing grist for the media and adding to the number of Watergate-relevant events there to be covered. As a result, the coverage reached saturation levels with Watergate on the front page and on the evening news day after day after day as well as on early morning, late evening, and Sunday public affairs programs. But the headlines alone would not have sufficed to make a serious issue out of a problem so removed from most people's daily concerns. Continuity was necessary to rivet attention to new facts as they emerged. The process is circular. Media exposure and public attention generate responses at the elite level that produce still more news in a cycle of mutual reinforcement that continues until politicians and public tire of an issue or another issue moves into the center of the political stage.

. . . On matters of concern to people, because they fall within their direct experience, as is the case with various bread-and-butter, sickness-and-health, life-and-death issues, the media clearly lack power to suppress concern. But they can do more than stimulate interest. By directing attention to these concerns, they provide a context that influences *how* people will think about these matters—where they believe the fault lies and whether anything (and what) should be done. Publicity given to essentially private concerns transforms them into public concerns. Whether or not it increases the problem for those affected, it does increase morale and legitimates the will to protest.

With regard to high-threshold issues like Watergate, the media play an even more essential role. Had it not been for the news reports about Watergate, hardly anyone would have known about campaign finance violations, "dirty tricks," illegal surveillance by persons connected with the White House, and the lot. Media attention was necessary before Watergate could be considered a problem. Yet, in publicizing a high-threshold issue like Watergate, the media do more than direct attention to a problem; they influence how people will think about it. They supply the context that, by making the problem politically relevant, gives people reasons for taking sides and converts the problem into a serious political issue. In this sense the public agenda is not so much set by the media as built up through a cycle of media activity that transforms an elite issue into a public controversy.

None of this should be read to mean that the media, all on their own, dictate the public agenda. They cannot "teach" the public what the issues are. They certainly do not operate in total autonomy from the political system. The gradual saturation of news content with Watergate depended on political developments in which the press itself was only one of several movers. Agenda building—a more apt term than agenda setting—is a collective process in which media, government, and the citizenry reciprocally influence one another in at least some respects.

Let us . . . sketch out how the news media affect this agenda-building process.

First, they highlight some events or activities. They make them stand out from among the myriads of other contemporaneous events and activities that could equally have been selected out for publicity. Making something the center of interest affects how much people will think and talk about it. This much is only common sense.

But, second, being in the news is not enough to guarantee attention to an issue. The amount and kind of coverage required varies from issue to issue. Different kinds of issues require different amounts and kinds of coverage to gain attention. Where news focuses on a familiar concern likely to affect almost everyone, this almost guarantees instant attention. In the case of a high-threshold issue like Watergate, which also surfaced at the wrong time, it takes saturation coverage to achieve this result. Specifically, recognition by the "cosmopolitan" media was not enough. Only after the more locally oriented press had become saturated with news of Watergate developments did it emerge as an issue that would remain on the political and public agenda for nearly 16 months.

Third, the events and activities in the focus of attention still have to be framed, to be given a field of meanings within which they can be understood. They must come to stand for something, identify some problem, link up with some concern. The first exposé of the political fund used to finance the unit responsible for the break-in was publicized during a Presidential campaign. It was reported and interpreted within the context of that continuing contest. The Democrats' effort to change this context by interpreting Watergate as a symptom of widespread political corruption within the Administration was not very successful. Watergate remained, at least for a while, a partisan issue. The context had first to be changed.

Fourth, the language the media use to track events also affects the meaning imputed to them. Metaphors such as "Watergate caper" and "bugging incident," which belittled the issue, disappeared that spring under an avalanche of signs of a high-level political scandal. The press, along with politicians, adopted less deprecatory codewords. "Watergate" or "Watergate scandal" came to denote the various questionable activities now being disclosed. The words stood for nothing specific, yet for anything that could possibly happen.

Fifth, the media link the activities or events that have become the focus of attention to secondary symbols whose location on the political landscape is easily recognized. They also weave discrete events into a continuing political story, so that the lines of division on the issue as it develops tend to coincide with the cleavage between the organized political parties or between other sharply defined groups. . . . When Watergate first surfaced during the 1972 campaign, it was defined primarily as a partisan clash between Democrats and Republicans. By Spring 1973 opinion still divided along political lines, but a realignment was under way as the issue changed and sides began to shape up around the "need to get the facts out," over the public "right to know" vs. "executive privilege," and on the question of confidence in the integrity of the government.

Finally, there are the prestige and standing of the spokesmen who articulate these concerns and demands. Their effectiveness stems in good part from their ability to command media attention. Democratic politicians like Larry O'Brien and George McGovern had been lonely voices in the wilderness when, during the campaign, they pressed for a full investigation. Their demands, though publicized, were neither much heard nor much heeded. They were known as people with an axe to grind. But as the controversy escalated, the publicity given Judge Sirica's admonishment that the full truth had not been told led prestigious Republicans to call for explanations, and their various attempts to get at the facts put pressure on the White House. The bystander public was being wooed. . . .

. . . Based on the evidence, we reject the paranoid version of Watergate propagated by the White House that the crisis was manufactured by a hostile press which finally drove Nixon from office. But we also reject the populist view that Nixon was forced to resign because he lost his battle for public opinion. The moving force behind the effort to get to the bottom of Watergate came neither from the media nor public opinion but from political insiders. The conflict pitted the White House against those who, for whatever reason, wanted full disclosure of the facts behind the illegal attempt to plant wiretaps in the national headquarters of the Democratic Party. . . .

The press was prime mover in the controversy only in its early phase, when the Woodward and Bernstein tandem first linked the Watergate burglars to the Nixon campaign committee and, during the campaign, uncovered other stories that hinted at the politically explosive potential of the "bugging" incident. But with Nixon's decisive electoral victory, the press came close to abandoning Watergate. Then, as the issue revived and conflict over the scope of the investigation intensified, the press mainly lived off information insiders were happy to furnish it. . . .

Had the news media, by their coverage of Watergate, directly persuaded the public of the seriousness of White House misdeeds, of Nixon's complicity, of a threat to basic values, and that impeachment might be warranted? Not directly, but by their reporting and their comments, by the way they highlighted some events, by the context within which they framed these events, by the language they used to track developments, by linking news they reported to symbols familiar to the audience, and by the persons they singled out (or who offered themselves) as spokesmen in the controversy, the media certainly influenced the way the public—and politicians as well—thought about and defined the underlying issue.

That so many of the struggles between Nixon and his opponents should have had such wide publicity, and even been played out on television, accounts for the impression that the news media and an aroused public opinion forced the downfall of Richard Nixon. Certainly, the way both parties used the media to enlist support inevitably enlarged the arena of conflict. An attentive public formed and people began to align themselves. But beyond that it is difficult to demonstrate, in the narrowly scientific way that has become the researcher's norm, that watching or listening to a particular Watergate speech, press conference, or televised testimony was what directly changed people's opinion. Many media effects remain elusive and can be understood only as the outcome of a cumulative process. Thus we have pointed to evidence that minor, incremental, and sometimes subtle changes sooner or later contributed to major shifts. For example, the most important effect of the televised Senate Watergate hearings was a "sleeper," not immediately noticeable. By subtly changing the issue, the televised hearings prepared the ground for the outburst that so instantaneously followed the firing of the Special Watergate Prosecutor. Similarly, it was the high regard in which the major spokesmen against impeachment were held as the result of the televised Judiciary Committee proceedings that made their subsequent defection so persuasive.

The charge that the Watergate coverage was unfair or somehow "distorted" remains basically unsubstantiated. Nixon was hardly at the mercy of the media. The same publicity that was effectively utilized by his opponents was available to Nixon whenever he chose to make use of it. And Watergate did yield the headlines to other news on several occasions—not only during the Middle East crisis in October 1973 but later when, shortly before the impeachment debate, Nixon traveled abroad in what he called his "search for peace." As President, it was easy for Nixon to command attention; as leader of his party, he was apt to be treated gingerly by Republican editors until his intransigence overtried their loyalties. There is no question that the media thrive on scandal, and they did thrive during Watergate; but by the yardstick of reporting during the impeachment and trial of Andrew Johnson or during the Dreyfus case, they more than adhered to the norms of journalistic objectivity.

The main contribution of the media to moving opinion along was their extensive and full coverage of critical events. The visibility of the controversy helped more than anything to legitimate the process by which Nixon was ousted. . . . Because the deliberations of the House Judiciary Committee were televised, they were cast into the mold of an adversary proceeding, with most arguments couched in legal rather than political language. The decision was depicted as compelled by the evidence, with members—regardless of personal conviction—accepting the majority decision. They saw themselves, as they had told the nation, as representatives of the impersonal authority embodied in the Constitution, the highest law of the land. . . .

Still another question is how much the public was reacting to the substance of the Watergate disclosures or to Nixon himself. After all, other Presidents had been guilty of acts whose constitutionality was questionable or of behavior that fell short of the expected high standards of personal or political propriety. Yet these others somehow managed to avoid Nixon's fate. They somehow managed to keep up appearances either by sacrificing subordinates, who took the blame, or making sure that nothing beyond unsubstantiated rumor ever got out. Why should Nixon have failed with a similar strategy, one that he had previously employed with striking success? For one thing Nixon by his behavior throughout his political career had made enemies within the working press. As President, however, he commanded deference and respect and was treated with caution. Yet, once insiders put him on the defensive, these reporters were astounded at how far Nixon had evidently been willing to go to assure his reelection and to punish his "enemies." Thereafter they were ready to resurrect the image of the "old Nixon" and were less willing to declare sensitive areas out-of-bounds. Nixon was to harm himself further with the press by a pretense of openness. When pressed on Watergate, he repeatedly assured his questioners that he would cooperate to clear up the scandal, yet always with a proviso that allowed him to renege at a later date. As a result, Nixon was to appear less and less ingenuous even to his own followers. It was not the abuse of power, revealed in the Senate hearings, as much [as] his obstruction of the legal process that in the last analysis cost him the most support. The constituency that in the early months backed him on Watergate became increasingly impatient to have the issue resolved. This included many people who were still confident that the evidence would show that Nixon had done nothing worse than had other Presidents.

In this climate the opposition to Nixon gradually gained strength. It became difficult to defend Nixon on any but the narrowly legal grounds staked out by Republicans on the Judiciary Committee. What must be reemphasized, however, is that the coalition favoring impeachment stood together on the weakest possible foundation. For many, impeachment served only as a negative rallying point for whatever they believed was wrong with the country. Watergate was as much a symptom as a cause of the general disenchantment with politics and political institutions that anticipated the controversy. How alienated many citizens had become from the process is clearly documented by the inability of the system to translate the division over Vietnam, deep as it was, into an electoral choice between an anti-war and a pro-war candidate.

Be all this as it may, there could have been no real public opinion on Watergate without the media. They alone could have called into being the mass audience of "bystanders" whose opinion had to be taken into account. It was likewise the media which, by reporting and even sponsoring polls, presented the cast of political actors in Watergate with a measure of public response to their every move. Nevertheless, the public never was an active participant in the campaign against Nixon. It did not direct the course of events, except when the reaction to Cox's dismissal signaled those in power that the time had come to do something. The impression of public support made it easier to move against Nixon simply because the bystander public withheld the vote of confidence the President had so eagerly sought in order to defeat impeachment politically. Only in this sense, and this sense alone, was Nixon "driven" from office by his loss of public support.

NOTES

1. Richard M. Nixon, *RN: The Memoirs of Richard Nixon* (New York: Grosset and Dunlap, 1978), pp. 971, 972.

22. THREE FACES OF CONGRESSIONAL MEDIA

Michael J. Robinson

Editor's Note. Michael J. Robinson spotlights the changes that modern media coverage have brought about in Congress. He provides fascinating details about the manner in which Congress is covered by a variety of media. Each medium differs in impact compared to the others, and even compared to itself at different times. Accurate assessments of the overall effects of all media in combination remain elusive because there are no adequate weighting criteria. Therefore, it is uncertain how heavily each medium counts in the total situation.

On balance Robinson concludes that media coverage has several major effects. It produces telegenic candidates, safe House incumbents, vulnerable senators, and a Congress that lacks the public's confidence. By contrast, respect for the presidency as an institution remains high, in the wake of deferential news treatment. However, incumbent presidents generally receive rougher media treatment than do incumbent members of Congress. If Robinson is correct in his assessments, the media have indeed altered the face of American politics.

Michael J. Robinson, a political scientist trained at the University of Michigan, has devoted much of his career to the study of the media's impact on American politics. He teaches at Catholic University. He also directs the Media Analysis Project at George Washington University. The selection is from *The New Congress,* edited by Thomas E. Mann and Norman J. Ornstein, Washington, D.C.: American Enterprise Institute for Public Policy Research, 1981. Several tables have been omitted.

Ask anybody on Capitol Hill about the most basic change in the relationship between Congress and the media since 1960 and the response is practically catechistic—the media have become harder, tougher, more cynical. Committee chairmen, senior Republicans, press secretaries, aides in the press galleries and media studios at the Capitol, and members of the Washington press corps express what amounts to a consensus: the biggest change in the relationship between Congress and the media is that the press has grown more hostile to Congress.

Having conducted almost fifty personal interviews and collected some sixty questionnaires from representatives, staff, and reporters between 1977 and 1980, I found that only one person in fifteen thought this toughening was not the major development.[1] One official in the House of Representatives, who has worked personally with congressional correspondents for almost thirty years, put it this way: "The biggest change has been readily discernible—the greater emphasis on the investigative approach. Years ago there was an occasional exposé, but the last six to eight years there has been a shift toward the Watergate approach."

Press secretaries seem particularly sensitive to the change in attitudes. One former reporter, who has now served almost twenty years as press secretary to a senior House Democrat, expressed his frustration with the "new journalism" he sees in and around the Capitol. The press, he says, has become "bloodthirsty." It has "developed a sickly preoccupation with the negative aspects of governmental operations, the presidency, the Congress, the administrative agencies." The media "think we're all crooks and it only remains for them to prove it." This man speaks for many of the staff who work directly with the press corps in Congress. . . .

Despite the prevailing view, this essay argues: that the mass media, in toto, have *not* hurt the membership electorally, especially in the House; that even the news media have *not* been of a piece in their relationship with Congress; that many of the major changes brought by the media to Congress have been brought *not* by a "new journalism" but by the campaign media or by practices associated with "old journalism"; that change has *not* been fundamental and continuity has *not* disappeared.

Combining these points with what I shall present later, . . . I offer these conclusions concerning the changing relationship between the in-house, campaign, and news media and the Congress over the last twenty years:

1. The in-house media in Congress have changed as fully as the news media since 1960, and they have tended to negate much of the effect that the new, hardened Washington press corps has had on incumbents.

2. The campaign media around Congress have grown at least as fast as the news media in Congress, and under most circumstances they still tend to benefit incumbents, especially in the House.

3. The new toughness of the national press corps is not much in evidence in the local press. In some respects, the local media may have actually become "softer" than they were in 1960.

4. The discrepancy between the "soft" local press and the "tough" national news media has grown wider since 1960, and this widening gap goes a long way toward explaining why people hate Congress but love their congressman.

5. The "media-mix" that has developed in Congress since 1960 helps explain both the increase in safety of House incumbents and the concomitant decline in the safety of incumbents in the Senate.

6. The greatest effect of the new media-mix on Congress as an institution has been to attract a new kind of congressman.

7. The new media-mix has continued the evolutionary process, begun with radio, through which the executive branch grows increasingly more important than Congress as a policy-making institution.

8. *The media, taken together, have not done much to damage the members of Congress* but have damaged the institution of Congress—at least a little.

This last point may be the most important of all. In fact, I believe that the membership has learned to cope very effectively with the modern congressional media—even if the institution and the leadership have not. So, while it may be true that the mass media have proved somewhat detrimental to the institution, their three faces have not looked unkindly on the members per se. The overall pattern is one of change much in keeping with David Mayhew's notions about Congress. One finds, as Mayhew might have guessed, resourceful members who have restricted the impact of the media and adapted beautifully to their new forms, but a disunified institution far less able to restrict or adapt to those very same forms.

To understand all of this, however, one must remember that the congressional media are a mixture of the national, local, and regional press, an in-house press, and an ever-growing campaign media. Any analysis that stresses only the so-called new journalism oversimplifies the changing relationship between Congress and the mass media. One must emphasize the pluralism of congressional media if one takes into account all the major dimensions of modern, mass, political communication.

"In-House" Media—Unambiguous Advantages

... The ability to communicate more often with more constituents directly through the mail has been one of the most important changes in the in-house media. In fact, much of the technology adorning the new congressional office either produces mail or can be used to facilitate mail. Mail—in its volume alone, which has increased over 300 percent—represents a revolutionary change in in-house communications over the last two decades.[2] Currently, the average American receives two pieces of mail every year from Congress.

The increase in congressional mail can be explained in part by population growth, in part by an increasing national politicization. But the major explanation is the coming of modern computer technology to Congress. In 1960 nobody had a computerized mail system. As of 1979 almost every Senate office and, according to *Congressional Quarterly*, 300 House offices have computerized mailing facilities.[3] Younger members increasingly consider computerized mail a political necessity. The House itself found in a study conducted in 1977 that the freshman class was almost twice as likely to employ computerized correspondence as senior members.[4] One can expect "managed mail" to increase rapidly as the seniors leave.

But the new in-house correspondence systems mean more than a greater quantity of mail, and more than efficient mail. The new system can also mean "targeted" mail. Most mail from members is computerized, and most of it is sent in direct response to a constituent inquiry or problem. But more and more "personalized" mail is unsolicited and is sent to types of individuals who might be pleased by what it says: this is "targeted" mail, one of the big new phenomena on Capitol Hill.

The system is simple enough. A member buys or builds a list of his constituents, which is fed into the member's own computer disc space and cross-referenced by any number of characteristics. (Some cross-referencings are illegal, such as reference by party or amount of campaign contribution.) Later his office can run mail through the referencing system and target it according to any of those characteristics. If the member wants to send letters to all Blackfoot Indians who have written to him on ERA and who live on a particular street or block, he can do it without much effort....

. . . As early as 1956 the Senate and House began operating separate in-house recording studios for members and leaders. The studios in both houses have always been used for the same purposes—to provide members with convenient, cheap, and sympathetic programming that can be mailed home to broadcasters and used on local channels as news or public affairs presentations. . . . My interviews . . . indicate that members are using the studios more and more, especially the younger members....

. . . The radio and TV studios are only part of the congressional in-house press. For over 120 years the House and Senate have maintained a network of auxiliary offices which aid the press as it covers the membership day to day. It all began in 1857 when the Senate and then the House opened their own Press Galleries. Following the establishment of the first two Press Galleries in the nineteenth century, Congress responded with five more in the twentieth—a Radio and Television Gallery and a Periodical Gallery for each house and a Photographers' Gallery for both, all of which existed by 1960. The staffs in all seven galleries work in a rather strange environment, servants of the media as well as of the Congress. While the correspondents are paid by their respective news organizations, the gallery employees are paid by the House or Senate. The galleries are there to help both the press and the Congress....

Thus, in terms of in-house media, *Congress has expanded and adapted most in the areas that help members directly. It has done less in the areas that are general and institutional in emphasis.* Congress has adjusted to developments in the media . . . selectively, and "personally," with special concern for the electoral life of its individual members.

There is one final dimension, perhaps more important than the rest, which suggests how much the in-house media have grown in the last twenty years. . . . [P]ress secretaries labeled as such were few in number in the Senate and practically nonexistent in the House when Congress entered the 1960s. Because definitions change and press secretaries are often called something other than "press secretary," it is almost impossible to quantify precisely the growth of the congressional press secretariat, but the information that does exist indicates that that growth has been striking. . . .

The growth in the congressional press secretariat suggests again that the media-mix in Congress has not been so bad for the members. They hire press people, after all, to praise them, not to harm them. It is not possible to say which side started the escalation in personnel, the press or the Congress. But in either case the growth of the new journalism has probably been countered, or its effects at least diluted, by the growth in the press secretariat....

... Nothing stands more visibly for change in the relationship between Congress and the media than the national televising of House floor proceedings. But along with change has been a commitment to continuity—House TV is another case study in how Congress has adapted to the media by looking out for number one, the membership....

... [A]ll equipment and all personnel in the system are part of the House of Representatives. Control of the system is in the hands of the Speaker, who exercises that control through a Speaker's advisory Committee on Broadcasting and an advisory team working in the House Recording Studio.

In keeping with the tradition of adapting the media to their own needs, the members and the leadership have provided for themselves quite well. H. Res. 866 provides for in-house technicians with stationary cameras (nobody can be pictured falling asleep or inadvertently acting uncongressional under this system), blackened screens during roll-call votes (members cannot be caught changing their votes at the last moment, or even voting at all for that matter), and ready access to videotape files (members can, if they wish, send "news" clips to the stations back home at very low cost). Added to all that is continuous live coverage of all proceedings, broadcast by over 850 cable TV systems across the nation on C-SPAN (Cable Satellite Public Affairs Network).[5] ...

Two factors confounding attempts to evaluate the impact on the public have been the lack of information on the size of the audience watching House proceedings on television and the lack of network (or station) utilization of the tapes themselves. The major audience for television would, of course, be the network audience—now estimated to be above 55 million viewers nightly. But the networks have tended not to use the tapes of floor proceedings, in part because they objected to the House's decision to keep control of the cameras and in part because the networks still regard the House as less newsworthy than the Senate.

The only other news audience comes through C-SPAN, the 850 cable systems which tie directly into the Capitol telecasts. The potential audience for C-SPAN is, at present, 18 million viewers, but nobody knows who watches, or how often. The fact that the networks and C-SPAN only provide for a limited coverage or a small audience is a major reason for assuming that House TV has caused little public response....

The Campaign Media: Potential Problems for Incumbents

Campaign media are those that candidates use to get elected. The major difference between campaign media and in-house media is who pays: Congress pays for in-house media out of general office accounts; candidates pay for campaign media out of private campaign funds. Since 1960 three basic changes have occurred in the relationship between Congress and its campaign media: (1) candidates now use the media more, (2) they use them more effectively, and (3) challengers find in the campaign media a new opportunity, but one still qualified by the old reality of incumbent advantage. . . .

While comparable and detailed figures on media expenditures are not available for the last twenty years, we know from the work of Edie Goldenberg and Michael Traugott that by 1978 congressional candidates were spending well over half (56 percent) of their total campaign budgets on all the mass media combined.[6] These authors estimate that in the six years between 1972 and 1978 the amount spent on broadcasting alone in House elections tripled.[7] . . .

. . . By spending so much more than ever before, congressional candidates have both created and understood a new electoral environment. The increasing use of the media is both cause and reflection of the growing impact of campaign dollars on electoral returns. . . .

. . . [A]s voters continue to grow less loyal to party and candidates continue to spend more money to attract votes, the campaign media become more influential. . . .

. . . [T]he campaign media remain for most members of Congress a *potential* threat. A serious attack that relies on campaign media *can* fatally damage an incumbent. But most often no such challenge materializes. For one thing, most challengers cannot compete in dollars and cents. . . . At least in the House, a case can be made for arguing: that the campaign media have not much redefined congressional electoral politics; that television advertising is still too expensive and too inefficient for most House campaigns, where TV dollars are largely wasted reaching people who live outside the district; that incumbents still make more use of the media than their challengers; and that, at best, the campaign media have made House campaigns a wee bit less certain than before. . . .

The News Media:
Cynicism and Symbiosis in the Two Worlds of [the] Press

The news media are what most of us think of as *the* media. But even the news media are less than monolithic in their relations with Congress. Television news differs from print, print differs from radio, radio differs from TV; and in each medium, local coverage differs from national. In terms of impact these differences are crucial.

. . . The intuition that the news media are increasingly hostile to Congress fits best the reality of the *national* press. The evidence abounds. . . .

My own content analysis of network news coverage of Congress leads me to believe that this approach is not confined to the national print media. Back in 1976, after the Supreme Court in *Buckley* v. *Valeo* gave Congress thirty days to reconstitute the Federal Elections Commission or witness its demise,

David Brinkley commented to an audience of 15 million, "It is widely believed in Washington that it would take Congress thirty days to make instant coffee." [8] The complete results of my analysis of network coverage of Congress suggest much the same thing—the national press is fairly tough on Congress. ABC, CBS, and NBC ran 263 "Congress stories" in January and February of 1976, according to my analysis, and among them I found not a single item that placed Congress or its members in a positive light. I did find 36 stories (14 percent) that tended to present Congress or its members in a negative light. [9] The fact that Congress received no good press on the evening news for a period spanning five weeks in 1976 suggests that the national press do not find much about Congress to their liking. . . .

. . . In December 1969, Senator Daniel Brewster (Democrat, Maryland) was indicted in federal court on charges that included illegally accepting money for what amounted to legislative favors—bribery. Nine years later, Congressman Daniel Flood (Democrat, Pennsylvania) was indicted on federal charges of much the same sort. Though the two cases are not identical, it seems reasonable to compare the coverage given them in the press and to take that coverage as evidence of how the behavior of the press had changed.

Using the Vanderbilt *Television News Index and Abstracts,* I counted the stories that network television broadcast on the Brewster and Flood cases, including all network stories heard on the evening news in the year of the indictment or the year following—1969 and 1970 for Brewster, 1978 and 1979 for Flood.

. . . According to the *Index,* Flood was referred to in fifty-nine different news stories, while Brewster was mentioned in eight. More incredible, Flood was the principal news focus or a secondary news focus for 4,320 seconds of network time, while stories about Brewster amounted to only 170 seconds. Flood-related stories received twenty-five times as much network news attention as did Brewster-related items, even though Brewster was a senator and Flood "only" a representative.

Some of this difference is accounted for by the fact that Brewster stood alone in his scandal, while Flood had the misfortune of being implicated in a much broader scandal—along with then Congressman Joshua Eilberg and then U.S. Attorney David Marston. Marston in particular increased the newsworthiness of the Flood case because Marston was a Republican in a Democratic administration and was eventually fired by President Carter for reasons having more to do with "old politics" than incompetence. But these extraneous factors cannot easily account for all of the difference. The Flood coverage, so much more extensive than anything even dreamed of in the Brewster case, serves to corroborate the idea that the national press had changed during the 1970s—had become more "cannibal" in its congressional reporting.

The networks' treatment of other scandals, too, is consistent with the view that the national press has changed—has grown more likely to practice investigative journalism and hard-nosed objectivity. In fact, this has been *especially* true of network journalism. . . . Conceding that the national press has become increasingly hard-bitten is easy. Making a similar case for local press coverage of Congress is much more difficult. History, logic, and the evidence all indicate that the local media have not really been overcome by the Watergate syndrome, so conspicuous in the national media. . . .

Ben Bagdikian offered similar conclusions in 1974 in "Partners in Propaganda":

> Most members still do not have to answer pertinent questions for the voters back home, and most continue to propagandize their constituents . . . with the cooperation of the local news media. This process started a long time ago, but the price of an immobilized government has now come due.[10]

At least as late as 1974, critics of the press were still complaining about what one might best call a *symbiotic* relationship between the local media and incumbents in Congress—symbiotic not only because each "partner" profited from the continued relationship, but also because each clearly understood the other's mission and needs. . . .

What may be the best evidence for believing that the local press is not Woodstein—let alone Evans and Novak—comes from the Center for Political Studies (CPS) at the University of Michigan. For the last two congressional elections Arthur Miller and his associates have been doing content analysis of local press coverage, of both Congress and congressional campaigns. Their data suggest that the local press—the press generally—do not treat incumbents negatively, even during the last weeks of a campaign. Indeed, the press tends to treat incumbents positively, at least slightly so. Using a sample of 216 newspapers, CPS found that in the last phase of the 1978 congressional campaign the average congressman received a score of 1.9 for his coverage in the local press, on a scale ranging from 1.0 (totally positive) through 3.0 (totally negative).[11] Incumbents fare well, getting positive attention, and lots of it. Incumbents receive twice the coverage their challengers get and, according to Miller's data, more positive coverage than challengers or Congress as an institution or the government generally.[12] The differences are small, but they always favor incumbents. . . .

. . . One of the less conspicuous changes affecting press coverage of Congress has been the steady increase in the size of the Capitol Hill press corps. . . . Without doubt the greatest growth has come in radio . . . an increase of 175 percent in the number of both radio and TV correspondents admitted to the congressional press corps in a sixteen-year period. During the period, the number of print journalists increased by "only" 37 percent. The rate of increase for electronic news people has been precisely five times greater than for print, and the overwhelming majority of the new media people are in radio.

Radio and electronic news coverage of Congress has rendered the Capitol Hill press corps more regional—hence, more local—in its behavior. This localizing of news through "regional" coverage of Congress has probably meant that the news about members comes out much "softer" than would have been the case without the explosion in radio. For two reasons, regional radio has probably worked to dilute the impact of the new journalism in Congress. First, regional electronic news people are, by definition, more local in outlook than the national press and, therefore, more dependent on access to members. Regional radio and local television people bring their local concerns with them to Congress, and they need to establish good relations with the new members who share those concerns. Second, the electronic media *generally* treat Congress "better" than the print media. . . .

. . . The local and national press are two separate worlds, and since 1960 they have grown more distinct. Why is this so, and what are the implications?

First, a qualification. The differences between the national and local press should not be exaggerated. The nationals do not often go out of their way to be tough when toughness is unwarranted; our analysis of congressional news in 1976 showed that eight out of ten stories on network news were *not* negative.[13] . . .

Moreover, locals can be tough when they have to be. Milton Hollstein describes, for example, the treatment Congressman Allan Howe received at the hands of the Salt Lake City media. The press, he said, served as "pillory" when Howe was caught with a decoy prostitute, and its "excessive," "gratuitous," "knee-jerk," and "questionable" coverage of the incident "made it impossible for [Howe] to be reelected" to Congress, even before the reported facts had been corroborated.[14]

Nonetheless, the basic differences in local and national coverage need some explanation. Most of those who have offered explanations have emphasized the variations between the local and national press in size and beat. A few others have dwelled on the economic self-interest of the local press; the theory holds that publishers urge editors to persuade journalists to treat the local congressman kindly in the hope that he may, at some point, vote for or amend legislation that will profit the newspaper. Another form of economic determinism has been used to explain the pleasant relationship between local broadcasters and congressmen. The theory here is that a contented congressman might go to bat for an FCC-licensed broadcaster if there were a licensing challenge. Both of these economic theories hinge on the owners' seeking to maximize their economic self-interest. The journalists are secondary.

But social psychology probably has as much to do with the relationship between the media and Congress as economics does, and the correspondents' behavior probably matters more than the interests of their capitalist publishers. At least half a dozen studies all make it clear that symbiosis emerges from a network of friendships and "mutual dependencies" between journalists and newsmakers. . . . But the representatives of local media are drawn in closer to the sources than the national press; mutual dependency is a larger ingredient in their friendships with the newsmakers. . . .

. . . [S]ize—especially the size of the networks—gives the national press a real advantage in dealing with members. The local media are still imprisoned by their smallness and weakness. . . . Nationals for the most part focus on the institution, not on individual members. . . . Focusing on institutions makes it easier to be tough. One does not have any particular pair of eyes to avoid when one attacks Congress. This is one reason why, as we have seen, Congress received more negative coverage than positive in 1978 but congressional *candidates* got more positive coverage than negative.

Add to all this the very real tendency for the national media to recruit the tougher journalists coming out of the local press and you get a fairly complete explanation for the hardness of the Washington press corps and the softness of the local news. The nationals look hard at the institution. The locals exchange glances with their representatives. This pattern holds unless the local member gets into trouble: then all the press—national, regional, local— glares. Such is the nature of the press in Congress.

Consequences

Now that we have considered the changes in the in-house, campaign, and news media as each relates to Congress, we must ask, So what? What has the new media-mix done to or for Congress? Let us consider this question along three dimensions: attitudinal, electoral, and institutional.

... Because the national news media have grown apart from the local media, and because the local media have probably been expanding more rapidly than the rest, the news media help explain a most interesting paradox in American public opinion—nationwide contempt for Congress and district-wide esteem for its members. The two types of media covering it coincide with the two sides of Congress's image. . . .

Of course, there are other interpretations of the paradox of opinion in Congress. Some authorities on Congress contend that members actually do a good job as representatives but that the institution actually fails to do its job as a legislature. Others ... contend that members work the bureaucracy so effectively in the interests of their constituents that constituents learn to respect them but not the institution. Both of these interpretations seem ultimately too literal. Constituents simply do not deal enough with their congressmen to produce the paradox of congressional public image. Only the media are broad enough in reach and scope to account for the bulk of opinion toward Congress or its members. CPS congressional election studies in the 1970s indicate that 52 percent of all citizens read about their member in the newspapers; 14 percent had met the member personally. Fewer than one person in six ever deals with a member directly, even using a very loose definition of "direct" contact.[15]

Knowing what we do about local coverage, we may plausibly assume that the local press accounts for much of the favorable image that members enjoy. . . . [D]istricts with more negative press about Congress, the institution, hold more negative news of Congress—districts with more positive press go significantly in the other direction. The national media, which reach everyone with their critical coverage of the institution, and the local media, which reach constituents and accommodate members, *together* serve as the single best explanation for the paradox of public opinion toward Congress.

... The fact that the nationals relinquish to the locals the job of covering individual congressmen has direct implications for the members' safety at election time. Locals keep their readers relatively happy with their representatives by giving incumbents lots of coverage, most of it favorable. The result is safer incumbency. And when one factors in the growth of the in-house media, which inevitably serve to protect incumbents, the result is ever greater safety for those holding office—precisely the pattern that has prevailed among House membership since 1960. . . .

. . . House members control much of their own press—much more than presidents, governors, or senators. Members control their press because they (1) make greater and more sophisticated use of in-house media, (2) attract, by and large, more money than challengers in ad campaigns, (3) maintain a closer relationship with the local press than senators, and (4) attract much less coverage from the nationals so long as they stay unindicted. House members have grown increasingly safe electorally as they have gained greater control of all the media at their disposal. . . .

The Senate media-mix is very different. Senators' relationships with the local media are less intimate because senators deal with whole states, not with one or two papers as House members do. If propinquity explains cordiality, senators lose out because they simply cannot be as close to their press—or their constituents—as members of the House. The senator also attracts better financed challengers, who can buy TV time and who can use their resources more efficiently than practically any House member. The campaign media can hurt senators more because their challengers are more likely to be able to afford them. But most important, senators attract national coverage—a must for any potential presidential contender, but a potential disaster for an incumbent who comes out looking bad on the evening news. . . . Somewhat ironically, powerful senators are less able to control their images than "invisible" House members. In the Senate campaign of 1980, thirteen of twenty-nine incumbents went down to defeat, which approaches a 50 percent attrition rate. In 1980, as in the recent past, the House incumbents were four times safer than the Senate incumbents.

. . . Obviously, not everything has changed. Some of the most important aspects of the relationship between the mass media in Congress continue much as they were in 1960. One of these is the news media's preoccupation with the presidency. Although the data are inconclusive, it seems that Congress as an institution is still very subordinate to the executive in news attention and news manipulation.[16] The print media have been inching back toward a more equitable balance between presidency and Congress, but television has stayed with the executive. . . .

The presidential hegemony that is still felt in the press means a public that "thinks presidential" and relies on presidents to get us through, make things happen, control public policy. This is not simply a quantitative advantage that the presidency enjoys. The media have consistently treated the executive less negatively than the Congress. For reasons that follow rather closely those which explain the easier coverage given the membership than Congress per se, the executive generally gets better press than the legislative branch. Even in 1974—the year of Nixon's resignation—the press treated Congress more negatively than the president: according to the Center for Political Studies at Michigan, the president received coverage that was 39 percent negative, but the Congress was saddled with negative press amounting to 42 percent of the total.[17]

The results of this continued assault on Congress have proven to be substantial. Whether the explanation is "reality" or "the media," Congress has not had a better public image than the president since 1960, except in some of the Watergate years. In fact, even in September 1979, when Jimmy Carter's public approval rating on the Associated Press/NBC poll plunged to 19 percent—the lowest level of public approval assigned to his or *any* presidency, ever—the Congress still did worse: the Congress stood at 13 percent—six points, or 30 percent, below Carter. Both the quality and quantity of national press coverage of Congress has hurt Congress in its competitive relations with the presidency. After Watergate, after Vietnam, after all of it, the media still help render us a "presidential nation"—while making us less "congressional."

There is perhaps a major lesson in all this concerning the media, our political institutions, and their respective roles. *The media,* by focusing so fully on the office of president and then inevitably on the inadequacies of any person holding the job, *may be producing an office that is more powerful but at the same time may be weakening the political power of each individual president.* On the other hand, *the media,* by treating Congress poorly but its incumbents relatively well, *may be strengthening incumbents but weakening their institution....*

...[T]he most important institutional change to have occurred as a result of the new media-mix in Congress has been with the membership. The new media-mix, in and out of Congress, has manufactured a new kind of candidate, a new kind of nominee, and a new kind of incumbent. This is not simply a matter of looks or hair style, although clearly they are part of the change. It comes down to a question of style or legislative personality—what James David Barber might call "legislative character."

We have already seen evidence of how different the new generation in Congress is in its attitude toward the media. Compared with the class of 1958, the class of 1978 was three times more likely to make heavy use of the congressional recording studio, three times more likely to regard the House TV system as "very useful," three times more likely to have relied "a lot" on TV in the last election. Over 60 percent of the class of 1978 said "yes" when asked if they had used paid media consultants in their first successful campaign for Congress. Nobody in the class of 1958 answering my survey had used a media consultant to get elected the first time. Almost beyond doubt the media culture of the membership has changed.

Although these figures pertain to campaign style more than legislative character, one may infer that the increasingly greater reliance on the media for nomination, election, status in the Congress, and reelection is one sign of a new congressional character—one more dynamic, egocentric, immoderate, and, perhaps, intemperate. The evidence here is speculative and thin. But interviews and recent studies indicate that the media, intentionally or unintentionally, have recruited, maintained, and promoted a new legislative temperament.

One media consultant who . . . started helping Republicans with their media campaigns in the late 1960s and has recently directed a major Republican presidential campaign believes that the media (plus the decision in *Buckley* v. *Valeo,* the case outlawing limits on a congressional candidate's spending) have changed the type of congressional candidate and officeholder.

> You look through . . . and you get the guys with the blow-dried hair who read the script well. That's not the kind of guy who'd been elected to Congress or Senate ten years ago. You've got a guy who is not concerned about issues; who isn't concerned about the mechanics of government; who doesn't attend committee meetings; who avoids taking positions at any opportunity and who yet is a master at getting his face in the newspapers and on television and all that. You get the modern media candidate which is, in a lot of ways, Senator [name], who has no objective right to be elected to public office.

The same consultant sees a new style of legislator:

> You get a lot of young guys particularly who do two things, sort of the typical young congressman these days. He gets elected, he hires a bunch of pros to run his office, sets up a sophisticated constituent contact operation through the mails and through other things and an actuality service and all that kind of thing. Then he goes out and showboats to get more press so that he gets reelected and is considered for higher office. Those become of much more importance to him than the functioning as a national legislator or part of a branch of government. . . .

. . . In the final analysis the changes in congressional media over the last twenty years have produced mixed blessings and not just a few ironies—for Congress, for its members, and for us.

For the House membership the changes have meant greater safety but, at the same time, greater anxiety about getting reelected. . . .

For the senators, changes in the media-mix have meant less safety but, at the same time, greater opportunity for achieving national prominence. Network news coverage of the Senate can make an investigating senator a household word in a matter of days. Some senators have become nationally prominent through television almost overnight.

On both sides of the Capitol the changes in the media have given younger members and maverick members more political visibility—and consequently greater power—than ever before. But at the same time, modern news media have also meant that all the members of Congress work in an institution that has ever increasing image problems. In a final irony the modern media in Congress mean that although more policy information is directly available to members than ever before, the members themselves spend no more time with that information than they ever did. Public relations, after all, has become more and more demanding on the members' time. Policy can be more efficiently handled by staff or subcommittee.

The media generally benefit public people, not public institutions. For the most part the new media-mix has rendered Congress no less safe, but a little less serviceable—the members no less important, but the Congress a little less viable. The major impact of the modern media on Congress has not been the result of post-Watergate journalism but the inevitable consequence of focusing more public attention on elected officials, all of whom owe their jobs to local constituents. The media have made congressmen somewhat more anxious, somewhat more adept at media manipulation, and somewhat more responsive to local interests. But this merely shows us that Congress and its membership have a highly democratic base. What the new media have done to Congress is what one would expect when the level of information concerning an essentially democratic institution increases—greater responsiveness to the locals and greater concern about saving oneself. In all that, there is obviously good news, and bad.

NOTES

1. Unless otherwise noted, the quotations in this chapter are from these interviews.
2. Figures supplied by the Senate Appropriations Committee.
3. Irwin B. Arieff, "Computers and Direct Mail Are Being Married on the Hill to Keep Incumbents in Office," *Congressional Quarterly, Weekly Report,* July 21, 1979, p. 1451.
4. Dianne O'shetski, "Analysis of Survey on Computer Support Provided to Member Offices, As of April 1977," House Administration Committee Report, August 1977, p. 10.
5. For a thorough discussion of the history and politics of House TV, see Donald Hirsch, "Televising the Chamber of the House of Representatives: The Politics of Mass Communication in a Democratic Institution," thesis, Oxford University, 1979.
6. Edie Goldenberg and Michael Traugott, "Resource Allocation and Broadcast Expenditures in Congressional Campaigns" (paper presented at the annual meeting of the American Political Science Association, Washington, D.C., September 1979), p. 7.
7. Ibid., p. 6.
8. David Brinkley, NBC "Nightly News," February 3, 1976.
9. Michael J. Robinson and Kevin R. Appel, "Network News Coverage of Congress," *Political Science Quarterly* (Fall 1979), p. 412.
10. Ben Bagdikian, "Congress and the Media: Partners in Propaganda," in Robert O. Blanchard, *Congress and the News Media* (New York: Hastings House, 1974), p. 298, reprinted from the *Columbia Journalism Review* (January/February 1974).
11. Arthur Miller, "The Institutional Focus of Political Distrust" (paper prepared for the American Political Science Association, Washington, D.C., September 1979), p. 39. . . .
12. Miller, "Institutional Focus," p. 39.
13. Robinson and Appel, "Network News."
14. Milton Hollstein, "Congressman Howe in the Salt Lake City Media: A Case Study of the Press as Pillory," *Journalism Quarterly,* vol. 54, no. 3 (Autumn 1977), p. 454.
15. Miller, "Institutional Focus," p. 37.
16. My own research shows practically no change in the level of presidential news on network evening news (all networks) between 1969 and 1977. In 1969 I found on

network news 3,516 stories featuring the president and 2,339 featuring the House or Senate or Congress. In 1977 I found 3,556 stories featuring the president and 2,080 featuring Congress—an even greater advantage for the president than in 1969. Susan Miller, using 1974—the year when impeachment proceedings were instituted against Nixon—reached very different results, with Congress getting slightly more print coverage than the president. See "News Coverage of Congress: The Search for the Ultimate Spokesman," *Journalism Quarterly,* vol. 54, no. 3 (Autumn 1977), p. 461.

17. Arthur Miller, Edie Goldenberg, and Lutz Erbring, "Type-Set Politics: The Impact of Newspapers on Public Confidence," *American Political Science Review,* vol. 73 (June 1979), p. 71.

23. THE PRESS AND THE COMMITTEE SYSTEM

Mary Russell

Editor's Note. The author, then a reporter for the *Washington Post*, explains how media attention affects the distribution of power within and among congressional committees. As is true generally of governmental relations with the media, a complicated symbiotic relationship is involved with substantial ambivalence on both sides. Committees need the press to gain publicity that advances their objectives. At the same time they fear that news stories will fail to benefit the committee and its members or that they actually may be harmful. The press depends on congressional committees to satisfy its insatiable need for fresh and exciting news. But newspeople fear that they may be turned unwittingly into committee tools. While these mutual suspicions and tensions are troublesome, they are preferable to the alternative: committees and media forming an unholy alliance to create stories that benefit members of the alliance individually at the expense of the public interest.

Mary Russell gained her insights about the relationship between the media and Congress from the vantage point of a practicing journalist. Her years with the *Washington Post* gave her extensive experience in covering Congress. The selection is from "The Press and the Committee System," *Annals of the American Academy of Political and Social Science*, No. 411 (1974): 114-119.

———————

Begin with the basic premise that committees rely on the press to inform the public about their proceedings and decisions. Add to that the hope of committee members and staffs that their words and actions will be reported in a favorable light, thus, possibly furthering careers or, in rare instances such as those of the Kefauver [C]ommittee and the Watergate Committee, making the members' names a household word. Begin with the premise that reporters must rely on committee staffs and members for information. Add to that the fact that newsmen can feel a certain responsibility to exercise a critical function in their coverage. Add, also, the fact that newsmen—as do congressmen—have ambitions and exist in a competitive world in which they are rewarded for scooping their colleagues or uncovering the big story. A

Reprinted from "The Press and the Committee System" by Mary Russell in volume 411 of *The Annals of The American Academy of Political and Social Science.* Copyright © 1974, by the American Academy of Political and Social Science.

complicated relationship between committees and the press emerges; it is full of pitfalls, dangers and opportunities for abuse—a form of love-hate relationship around which principles and egos swirl.

Media reports can be an important source of information to a committee and may even lead to a congressional inquiry. Watergate is the most recent and obvious example, although there are a number of others. Similarly, a committee investigation or hearing can develop issues or uncover scandals, causing the press to rely on the committee as a source of information. Obviously, the committee is one of the most important sources of information about the form and status of legislation under consideration. These situations can lead to a kind of unholy alliance between the press and the committee and its staff, one which can work to the advantage of both or to the detriment of both.

The Unholy Alliance

The advantages of this alliance are obvious: issues and situations which otherwise might not be brought to light are publicized, and needed action may be taken through mutual cooperation. The public is informed, the press fulfills its function and Congress has a forum for its proceedings and its individual members. The disadvantages of the system are somewhat less obvious. A newsman eager to get a story may be less critical than he should be towards the committee he is covering. He may become coopted by the committee point of view in his eagerness to remain on the good side of the members or staff. He may be used to float an idea, or he may become the type of reporter Warren Weaver, Jr., of the *New York Times* describes in his book, *Both Your Houses;* he describes members of the press who are so assimilated into the congressional scene that they become adjuncts rather than critical observers.

Weaver calls this phenomenon "institutional reporting." He claims that the Congress, itself, cooperates in the institutionalization of reporters by providing them with handouts, galleries from which to work, access to congressional leaders on a daily basis and a host of committee reports, bills and digests. They occasionally allow, in Weaver's words, "acolytes of the Establishment" to peek inside, or even to gain full admission to, the inner circle. "Protecting in print a source of important information through anonymity is one thing," Weaver says, "but withholding important information because it involves a valued source is another." [1]

The most serious result of this phenomenon is that the public never hears the bad news, nor does it get a picture of that which is wrong with the system. "There is rarely even any inference in this that there might be a better way to make laws than the closed rule and the filibuster, that an appropriation bill is five months past deadline, that a committee chairman is gently sliding from seniority into senility." [2]

While reporters can become coopted by Congress, Congress, just as surely, can become coopted by the press. The possibility of headlines may seduce committees into dealing with the sensational rather than slogging through more important, but less sensational, hearings or oversight matters. For example, when the Kefauver crime committee showed Frank Costello's hands as he mumbled over and over, "I refuse to answer on the grounds that it might incriminate me," they produced good drama; however, the legislation which resulted from the hearings failed to make very much of a dent in the activities of the Mafia or organized crime. Without implying criticism of the consumer movement, it provides one of today's opportunities for headlines. It is easier to find a dangerous drug and to hold hearings which emphasize its alarming consequences through the dramatic tales of the victims than it is to look carefully at the Food and Drug Administration in order to determine whether it is doing its job and, if not, what needs to be done about it. Alan L. Otten, in his article in the *Wall Street Journal,* notes that thorough studies of the shortcomings of an agency or program frequently do not pay: "Truly productive oversight can be dull, time-consuming, thankless work, disregarded by colleagues, press and public alike." [3]

Defining News

The problem can be partly attributed to the very definition of news. Although journalism students often spend a whole semester on this definition, a practical guideline might be that the importance of a news item is relative to: (1) the importance of people involved, (2) the effect it will have or (3) the magnitude of what happened. When applied to Congress, the definition means that a Judiciary Committee hearing on prison reform during which Jimmy Hoffa testifies will attract more media attention than will a hearing on the marking up of the farm bill—in spite of the fact that Hoffa's testimony will not greatly affect the outcome of the bill, while the farm bill will have an impact on more people in a much more basic way by affecting the amount of food produced and the price consumers will pay for it.

Thus, the press may by-pass certain committees no matter how valuable their work. Also, they may by-pass committees handling certain subjects, if those subjects are obscure, abstract or complicated—that is, too hard to explain in a single column of type. In a September column of the *Washington Star* William Safire referred to subjects which editors call MEGOS. These subjects are important, but so heavy, dull and abstract to the reader that an editor says of a story about them: "My Eyes Glaze Over." [4]

David Broder, a *Washington Post* political columnist, pointed out that few stories were written about Senator Henry Jackson's Land Use Bill passed by the Senate, despite the potential impact of such a bill on the whole nation. The bill—which amounts to the first attempt the nation has made to get a handle on the way it will grow and to order land use according to some reasonable plan—has been touted by Jackson as "the most important bill" before Congress. As Broder said:

> At the very least, I am now persuaded that the issue with which Jackson has been struggling for three years is as important to the future of this country as Watergate. And it is a matter of some chagrin that, except for the

excellent coverage of the *Christian Science Monitor's* Robert Cahn, those of us in journalism have let it go largely unreported.[5]

Probably, one of the reasons that this is true is that theoretical long range planning has only a minimum amount of the proverbial "who, what, when, where or why" which makes for action or sex appeal in a story; thus, the bill made reporters' "eyes glaze over." Bad or sensational news, such as scandals, kickbacks, junkets, cost overruns or such charges as those made during the Joe McCarthy era, tend to be looked on as more newsworthy than calm, long range planning for the future.

How Congress operates—its procedures, rules and internal set-up—often falls into the dull category. . . . Understanding such matters might well lead to a public reaction against the way Congress works; yet, on the other hand, the general public's lack of familiarity with how Congress operates may account, in part, for the low esteem in which it is currently held. . . .

Congress bears some responsibility for the lack of knowledge, since Congress exhibits an understandable ambivalence about press coverage. Members of Congress would prefer the press to know only that which they want to disclose. In many cases, the wheeling-dealing, the trade-offs, the manipulation of the process or the candid explanation of a bill's passage or demise are matters which congressmen would prefer not to have reported. This, of course, is precisely what most enterprising reporters would like to know. . . .

The Open Hearing Question

Rules which permit committees to close their doors to the public and the press have come under attack in recent years. Reforms by the House Democratic Caucus . . . have gone a long way towards opening committee sessions to the press. Now, a majority of a committee must vote to close a session to the press and public; furthermore, the vote must be taken in open session before the meeting begins. Even mark-up sessions—during which the real work of deciding what will or will not be in a bill takes place—are theoretically open in the House. Still, some committees—notably Appropriations and Ways and Means—have voted to close their doors on important occasions; Ways and Means recently decided to close its doors while marking up the Trade Bill. The Senate rules call for a majority vote to open the doors for mark-up and some other sessions.

There are many rationales for keeping the press and public out, for example: (1) senators and congressmen will not speak freely while considering the mark-up of bills if the doors are open; (2) deals formerly made in committee rooms behind closed doors will still be made, but simply pushed further back from public view; (3) sensitive matters affecting national security are discussed, which the press and public should not hear.

In the minds of most members of the press, not one of these considerations—except, possibly, that of national security—overrides the consideration that a Congress elected by the public to represent the people should be willing to perform its work in public. That can happen only if all sessions, including House-Senate conferences to iron out differences in the versions of bills, are open to the public and press. . . .

Criticizing Congress

If Congress resists letting the public find out what it does not want the public to know, what happens when a reporter goes on a search for just this kind of information? The press, exercising its legitimate role of criticism, does this in many ways. It looks at sweetheart relationships between committees and their special interests—between large cotton interest and the members of the Agriculture Committee, for instance; it looks at bills and how much money is spent, for what and whether congressmen are putting through pet projects; it looks at the effectiveness of committee chairmen and the way they run the committee; it looks at inaction on bills or failure to conduct oversight hearings. In all of these instances, the relationship between the reporter, the committee and the staff changes drastically.

Once the possibility that a reporter might be coopted or used by members of the staff no longer exists, it is likely that he will be cut off from information he cannot obtain in a public session. In such a situation the partisanship of Congress often plays into his hands. A minority member or minority staffer may be willing to leak the information to him; a disgruntled majority member or staffer might do the same. In conferences it is sometimes possible to play the Senate members off against the House members.

However, none of this is quite as easy as it sounds. Staffers are naturally fearful that they may lose their jobs if they are found out. Committee members often feel more loyalty to their colleagues and the committee than they do to the press. Even if they think the press can help them prevail on an issue, they must take into consideration the fact that they are likely to need the committee's help on a different issue.

Outside sources, lobbyists and the executive branch can then become helpful. Yet, this normally leads to stories attributed to unnamed sources—a practice even newsmen deplore, since they feel their credibility goes down in proportion to the number of unnamed sources in a story. If it is necessary to protect a source, or if there is no other way to print a story, reporters will use the device. Since members of Congress often prefer the veil of anonymity when discussing anything controversial, the practice is increasing. Only agreement throughout the press corps not to use anything "off the record" could stop it; if only one paper or reporter adopts such a rule, they are merely cutting themselves off from stories. In fact, competition for news makes any such agreement unlikely.

Critical stories are less likely to be written by reporters who must come back and cover the beat or the committee again, since losing sources could cost stories. Some would say the answer is to rotate Hill coverage or to start independent investigative reporting teams, beholden to no one and not likely to have to return to those sources. Others would say that, in a negative way, the system imposes honesty on both press and the committee, a committee member who lies to a reporter risks being dropped as a source—for a story not absolutely accurate is not worth the risk to a beat reporter, while nothing will stop that reporter from printing a story he is sure is true.

Mutual Interdependence

In the end, then, the committee system and the press contribute to one another's good points and failings through their mutual interdependence. Some reforms of the committee system could be mutually beneficial. More openness in committee hearings would obviously contribute to better reporting. More and better oversight hearings would lead to more and better reporting of them. Placing more time, money and attention on the coverage of Congress would probably lead to a better Congress and a better informed public. Willingness to concentrate on those issues which are dull but important might spur Congress to do the same. Basically, the relationship between committee members and the press is based on human values of trust, fairness and responsibility. These values can be built into the system to an extent; however, ultimately, they rest with the individual.

NOTES

1. Warren Weaver, Jr., *Both Your Houses* (New York: Praeger, 1972), p. 12.
2. Ibid., p. 12.
3. Alan L. Otten, "Politics and People," *Wall Street Journal,* 6 September 1973, p. 14.
4. William Safire, "The Mego News Era," *Washington Star,* 6 September 1973, p. A15.
5. David Broder, "Land Use Bill: 'Important as Watergate,' " *Washington Post,* 1 August 1973.

24. PREREQUISITES FOR ACCESS TO THE PRESS

Edie Goldenberg

Editor's Note. It is comparatively easy to become aware of media influence on the fate of powerful public figures. It is much more difficult to assess media influence on the lives of the many ordinary citizens who aspire to media attention in hopes of persuading the government to attend to their needs. Edie Goldenberg's unique study provides insights. She examined the tactics used by four citizens' groups in Massachusetts to attract newspaper coverage to the problems of welfare mothers, senior citizens, low-income tenants, and people deprived of fair treatment by the courts. The groups were the Massachusetts Welfare Rights Organization, the Legislative Council for Older Americans, the Cape Cod and Islands Tenants' Association, and The People First organization.

Such groups are considered "resource-poor" because they lack the kinds of assets that make it comparatively easy to gain media attention. Such assets include prominent or official status, location in an area regularly covered by a newspaper, access to information that is of interest to reporters, money for effective public relations efforts, numerical strength, high determination, and credibility—so that others feel that the group can perform in accordance with its claims.

In the selection presented here, the author delineates some of the problems faced by all resource-poor groups in gaining access to the media. She explains what kinds of publicity groups need and want and what they must do to get it. There are valuable lessons here for the many groups who face similar predicaments.

Edie Goldenberg received her PhD. in political science from Stanford University. She is a professor of political science at the University of Michigan where she also holds an appointment in the Institute for Public Policy Studies. The selection is from *Making the Papers*, Lexington, Mass.: Lexington Books, D. C. Heath & Co., 1975.

At various times, all four resource-poor groups wanted to gain visibility for their organizations, their efforts, and their goals. In order to gain visibility widely throughout the state, groups depended primarily on the mass media. Group leaders could reach selected publics through their appearances at conferences, conventions, hearings, meetings and through their individual door-knocking efforts, but in order to reach wide audiences relatively efficiently, they were dependent on media coverage.

Therefore, the media became intermediate targets for all four groups as leaders tried to attain certain intermediate objectives: (1) to establish their groups' identities as legitimate spokesmen for particular clienteles, and to establish themselves as leaders and demonstrate their capacity to get things done; (2) to project certain images and avoid others; (3) to convey specific information and withhold other information; and (4) to identify their enemies or targets publicly and place responsibility with them for the present unsatisfactory situation.

Establishing Group Identity

Establishing the group identity as the voice of a particular clientele was a more serious problem for all group leaders in the beginning of the organizing stage than later. Group leaders wanted credit for their actions. They wanted their group's name mentioned. They wanted to be contacted for reactions to events and announcements of relevance to their membership. They wanted newspaper people to show up for their news events and press conferences and to respond to their press releases and calls for coverage. . . .

. . . They wanted to be quoted in the newspaper because it helped establish their leadership credentials within the group and without. One said the following about his press attention:

> . . . I get lots of feedback from it. . . . I have been quoted in hearings. And I always hear from people who see it and get excited about it. People can identify with me since I speak about their problems with experience and take a "we" attitude, not a "they" attitude toward them.

Another talked about some effects of press attention for him:

> . . . the press reminds workers that they're doing something important. They can send articles home to Mom and some of them who are students sent articles to their thesis advisors. Cutting out articles is extremely important. Every organizer I know in Massachusetts cuts out every article and keeps a scrap book. You show them to your friends. . . . The leader was defined by the press and accepted by the outside—to be the leader doesn't necessarily require followers. . . . My wife would watch me on TV and buy the papers and read about me and she was impressed that I could make things happen. . . .

Projecting Certain Images and Avoiding Others

Projecting desired group images was a continuing problem and a goal of all four groups. Group leaders wanted their groups to appear strong and in command of sufficient resources to look potentially successful. Furthermore, they wanted to show their groups as growing organizations that would only be stronger in the future. This was desirable both for community organizing purposes and for bargaining purposes with their targets. . . .

Leaders also wanted their groups to appear successful and morally superior to their opposition—with justice on their side. Most importantly, they wanted to avoid characterizations as lazy, greedy, or cheating. They wanted the situation to which they objected and its perpetrators to appear immoral or deviant, while group actions and proposals appeared as positive as possible.

Group leaders did not want their groups to appear internally divided and disorganized. In order to prevent such characterizations, they tended to avoid the press more when there were conflicts over goals and to approach the press when there was goal agreement. . . .

A resource-poor group must be concerned with four different audiences that may require quite different messages—and even contradictory messages—to win their support and cooperation: (1) group members and potential members, (2) third parties and group supporters, (3) the mass media, and (4) governmental targets.[1] Where group images are concerned, there may be problems in projecting the desired images to the desired audiences. Where there are conflicts between the images desirable for one audience and those desirable for another, group leaders can opt for one set of images based on the immediate importance of a particular audience and try to pacify other audiences through other channels or put it off until later.

. . . [T]he metropolitan press is not a finely tuned instrument for projecting group images to specific audiences. It does not allow groups to reach narrowly specified audiences or to switch the group's overall image back and forth from militance to nonmilitance at will. Further, the press is an independent audience itself that sometimes requires, or at least favors, types of images at variance with those favorable to other group audiences. . . .

The information that group leaders wanted to convey through the press involved explanations of the issues—poverty, aging, discriminatory justice, housing—and of stated group goals presented as sympathetically as possible. . . . Furthermore, because these groups lacked most political resources, sometimes even to the point of not being able to communicate with members and supporters through mailings or by telephone, leaders wanted information of their group's activities and of relevant legislation and hearings conveyed through the press. This provided a bulletin board function to their membership that obviously worked most effectively for groups with constituents who read the newspapers. . . .

Just as there was information that resource-poor group leaders wanted conveyed through the press, there was also information that they did not want publicized. Any information that caused internal group friction, reduced group resources, or directly threatened goals was to be suppressed as much as possible. For example . . . a great deal of press attention to an organizer can cause friction within the group. One jealously guarded reward for participation and leadership in resource-poor groups is publicity, and leaders resented each other for monopolizing it. Besides, the press plays a part in defining who the leaders of a group are. Therefore, leaders who want to retain their leadership positions also want to be identified as leaders and group spokesmen in the press. Another way in which press content can cause internal friction is in publicizing ideas or goals of some members that are repugnant to others. . . .

All four groups' leaders worked to identify and "freeze" their targets even if oversimplifications and misrepresentations were necessary in order to do so. Saul Alinsky has written about the importance of doing so:

> In conflict tactics there are certain rules that the organizer should always regard as universalities. One is that the opposition must be singled out as the target and "frozen." By this I mean that in a complex, interrelated, urban society, it becomes increasingly difficult to single out who is to blame for any particular evil. There is a constant, and somewhat legitimate, passing of the buck. In these times . . . the problem that threatens to loom more and more is that of identifying the enemy. Obviously there is no point to tactics unless one has a target upon which to center the attacks. . . . The forces for change must . . . pin that target down securely.[2]

Thus, resource-poor groups use the media to establish the group's and leader's identities, to project certain images, to convey information, and to identify group enemies and targets. Certain aspects of the groups' goals are particularly relevant to the decision by group leaders to seek access to the metropolitan press. Specifically, when group leaders are trying to increase such resources as credibility, visibility, money (from outside sources), "moral superiority," and personal reputation, and when group leaders are trying to reach audiences that are large, distant, or geographically dispersed and that are thought to read the press, then the tendency is to seek access to the press. Furthermore, when group goals are widely shared within the group, leaders are more likely to seek press access and exposure than when different and contradictory goals are held by different factions within the group.

Gaining Access to the Press

Whether or not groups gain access to the press . . . depends in part on group goals. Some goals in and of themselves are more newsworthy than others; certain goals recommend particular types of approaches to the press that are more likely to gain attention than others. . . . The more a group's political goals deviate from prevailing social norms, the more likely the group is to gain access to the press, other things being equal. . . .

Related to this is the point that certain group images are more newsworthy than others, and those that are most newsworthy are not necessarily those most desired by group leaders and members. If group leaders are willing to charge their target with moral deviance, this may be newsworthy. However, if the leaders are concerned with making group members appear as moral as anyone else, then it may not be considered newsworthy. The kinds of characterizations—greedy, cheating, radical, immoral—that group members want to avoid are the very types of information that produce interesting stories, assuming that the newspapers can protect themselves from violation of the libel laws. When group goals suggest presenting group members as "crazy, rioting, sitting-in, demonstrating, black ladies," or as outside radical agitators, groups are much more likely to gain press attention than when goals suggest toning down these images and stressing instead images of reasonableness and normalcy.

The more people who are affected by the group's goals, the more likely the group is to achieve access to the press. . . . There is a significant push in the press to present situations affecting many people by focusing on one specific example. This allows reporters to deal in personalities rather than in statistics—a widely shared preference—but it usually requires some reference to the size of the group affected by similar situations. It also allows reporters to simplify otherwise complex situations by focusing on one individual's situation as typical rather than trying to describe the general situation with all of its variations and implications.

When group goals represent variations on a theme receiving attention in the press at the time, chances for gaining access are improved. . . . The more technical the goals of a group, the more difficult it is to achieve access. . . . Finally, the more specific the group's goals, the more likely leaders are to gain access to the press. As long as goals involve readily verifiable facts and observable events or demands, press attention is relatively easily gained. It is more difficult, however, when interpretation is required. For example, newspapers have been generally unwilling to encourage stories that deal with underlying problems or issues rather than merely with new events. . . .

Seeking Access to the Press

. . . The first step in seeking access to the press is to decide to do so. Most of the members of a group (organizers aside) have never had experience with the press before and know no one who has. They have no well-developed ideas about how politics works, and whatever ideas they have usually do not include the press as an important intervening political actor and target. This may explain why, in those cases where resource-poor groups did exist before outside organizers appeared on the scene, there was virtually no interaction with the press. . . .

If contacting the press occurs to group members, then in deciding whether or not to do it, they are often stymied by feelings of low self-esteem expressed in terms similar to "why should they [the press] be interested in us?" Implied here is more than a realistic assessment of the group's low level of resources; it is also implied that the group is not interesting to anyone other than members, and that it is unimportant in the larger scheme of things. Until group members overcome these initial doubts concerning what they have to offer the press, they rarely contact reporters or make serious efforts to seek access or influence over media personnel. . . .

In addition to thinking of contacting the press as a possible strategy and feeling worthy of press attention, it is also essential that resource-poor group members feel capable of approaching the press successfully. They usually lack knowledge of how the press operates, and they rarely have the money (or are willing to use the money) to hire someone with such knowledge. If they do not know how to contact the papers and they do not expect to succeed in gaining press attention and coverage, then they are unlikely to make any press-related efforts at all. In all four groups studied here, it was necessary for someone with experience in dealing with the press to call in the press and demonstrate to group members that reporters would in fact show up and write stories about them. . . .

Before group leaders decide to seek access to the press . . . they must . . . expect to benefit from the kind of attention and coverage they anticipate. . . . If groups are in fact small or severely divided, leaders may prefer to avoid the press rather than to project undesirable images. This is particularly so if leaders know they cannot mask group weaknesses by falsifying figures. . . .

There are several ways a resource-poor group can become newsworthy and attract the attention of the metropolitan newspapers. First, a group may become newsworthy by virtue of its association with other newsworthy institutions, events, or people. Groups may emerge at institutions that are regularly covered by newspaper beat reporters and interact with reporters there. . . . Or groups may associate with people of high status who are judged newsworthy but who are not regularly covered by beat reporters. . . .

Second, groups may become newsworthy because of some action they engage in, which in and of itself is judged newsworthy. These actions can be dramatic protests or rallies—where there are many people in attendance or where some disruption or threat of disruption occurs—or they may be less dramatic news events. For example, all four of the groups studied here engaged in early protest activities—rallies, marches, and sit-ins. In most cases, the groups initiated the press contact by calling reporters or newsrooms to alert them to the planned activity. . . .

A third way in which groups can become newsworthy is by gaining credibility as legitimate spokesmen for a particular clientele or as a potential threat to established interests. Resource-poor groups can establish their credibility without already having previously interacted with the metropolitan press either through stories in alternative media or through the credibility that specific group leaders or members bring with them from their earlier activities. . . .

Access and news coverage do not usually occur without some personal interaction between resource-poor source and newspaper reporter. Continuing access requires continuing interaction. If the interactions become regularized, then access is usually facilitated. With regularized interactions, sources and reporters enter a bargaining relationship in which each actor extends efforts to interact with the other. A skillful source can build a relationship similar to that which often exists between resource-rich source and beat reporter, in which the reporter depends on the source for news and, as a result, the reporter is willing to listen to and act on behalf of the source's interests. Without regularized interactions, the main burden of interacting with newspaper reporters falls on the source. Newsworthiness must be shown over and over again. The reporter does not become dependent on the source for news. Instead, the source may become dependent on the reporter for attention—so dependent that news management is impossible. . . .

Implications

Whether one is heartened by the ability of resource-poor groups to gain access to the press at all and even occasionally to regularize interactions with press personnel or one is discouraged by the difficulties resource-poor groups face in regularizing interactions depends somewhat on one's expectations in the first place. . . . The problem is that leaders . . . are so resource-poor—especially in terms of experience, information, and money (with which experience and information can be acquired)—that they fail to take advantage of the media even when media people might be receptive. This prevents them from reaching policy makers through the media and also from using the media to raise further resources.

. . . [R]esource-poor group leaders can be heard from time to time when they take certain initiatives. However, it is much more difficult for them to achieve access than it is for others with greater resource bases. There is a bias in the system that consistently favors some and neglects others. E. E. Schattschneider wrote that "all forms of political organization have a bias in favor of the exploitation of some kinds of conflict and the suppression of others because *organization is the mobilization of bias.*" [3] This is no less true of the subsystem composed of the metropolitan press and its sources.

The trouble for resource-poor groups is first their tendency not to seek access to the press and second the high costs of gaining access and their inability to sustain access over time by regularizing interactions. To argue that the "opportunity" to be heard exists and that these groups choose not to take advantage of it is to miss the point. What does it mean for opportunity to exist if groups so lack resources that members are unaware of access possibilities and potentials—that is, they lack the experience, information, and leadership needed to suggest access strategies? As a group resource, numbers are not enough. Of what use is the opportunity to be heard if group leaders and members are so pessimistic about the likelihood of success that they choose not to bother? One might argue that if group leaders do not choose to speak, that is no fault of our democratic system. However, if intensely felt interests go unarticulated and therefore are unnoticed and unaffected by policy makers, one important aspect of rule of, for, and by the people is weakened. One cannot assume by definition that any interest not articulated must be one that is lacking in intensity of feeling. Further, if group leaders do seek access to the press, the opportunity to be heard is a costly one for which the group itself usually must assume total responsibility. Access gained is difficult to sustain over time under these circumstances.

The opportunity to be heard becomes important once leaders emerge who bring to the group the experience, information, and confidence needed to seek press access. These may be leaders brought in from outside, or they may be indigenous leaders who pick up media skills by watching other similar groups interact with the press or by learning from experiences in which press people approach their own groups as they engage in various newsworthy activities.... [T]he media can do a great deal to reach these resource-poor groups in the early stages of organizations and to encourage their interest in the press.... With considerable newspaper initiative, many of the weaknesses of resource-poor groups can be overcome.

However, the newspaper initiatives are not generally forthcoming except in response to extraordinary situations such as the violence of the 1960s. While the victories of resource-poor groups in the press may occasionally occur, long-term discussion of significant political issues is likely to proceed with relatively little resource-poor group input. Neither the groups nor the newspapers are likely to pursue regularized interactions. Those groups most in need of press attention in order to be heard forcefully in the political arena are those least able to command attention and those least able to use effectively what few resources they do control in seeking and gaining press access.

NOTES

1. Michael Lipsky, *Protest in City Politics* (Chicago: Rand McNally, 1970), pp. 163-84.
2. Saul Alinsky, *Rules for Radicals,* pp. 130-32. Reprinted by permission of Random House. © 1971 Random House, Inc.
3. E. E. Schattschneider, *The Semisovereign People* (New York: Holt, Rinehart and Winston, 1960), p. 71.

25. MAKING PROTEST MOVEMENTS NEWSWORTHY

Todd Gitlin

Editor's Note. Todd Gitlin studied how the desire for media attention and the resulting coverage affect the evolution of protest movements and the course of political change. In the essay presented here, he analyzes the media's role in the development and demise of Students for a Democratic Society (SDS). SDS was a major New Left protest movement on American campuses in the 1960s. Gitlin bases his findings on stories from the *New York Times* and CBS news—sources deemed politically influential because they were widely used and respected by political elites. These sources also were monitored carefully by people within the protest movements.

Gitlin concludes that the New Left was forced to define itself in ways that made it newsworthy for the establishment media. In the process, it sowed the seeds of its own destruction. The major lesson for protest movements, Gitlin believes, is that they must learn to protect their identity in the face of media blandishments.

Todd Gitlin has worked as a writer and as a teacher of politics and poetry. He has been particularly interested in studying counterculture movements. His writings have appeared in the *Nation,* the *New Republic,* the *Christian Century,* and *Commonweal.* The selection is from *The Whole World Is Watching,* Berkeley, Calif.: University of California Press, 1980.

. . . In the late twentieth century, political movements feel called upon to rely on large-scale communications in order to *matter,* to say who they are and what they intend to publics they want to sway; but in the process they become "newsworthy" only by submitting to the implicit rules of newsmaking, by conforming to journalistic notions (themselves embedded in history) of what a "story" is, what an "event" is, what a "protest" is. The processed image then tends to *become* "the movement" for wider publics and institutions who have few alternative sources of information, or none at all, about it; that image has its impact on public policy, and when the movement is being opposed, what is being opposed is in large part a set of mass-mediated images. Mass media define the public significance of movement events or, by blanking them out, actively deprive them of larger significance. Media images also become implicated in a movement's self-image; media certify leaders and officially noteworthy "personalities"; indeed, they are able to convert leadership into *celebrity*, something quite different. The forms of coverage accrete into systematic framing, and this framing, much amplified, helps determine the movement's fate.

For what defines a movement as "good copy" is often flamboyance, often the presence of a media-certified celebrity-leader, and usually a certain fit with whatever frame the newsmakers have construed to be "the story" at a given time; but these qualities of the image are not what movements intend to be their projects, their identities, their goals. . . .

The year 1965 was a pivotal one in the history of SDS [Students for a Democratic Society], and in the student movement as a whole: pivotal both in reality and in the realm of publicity. SDS organized the first major national demonstration against the Vietnam war, and then failed to lead the antiwar movement that was burgeoning. Politically, SDS moved away from its social-democratic progenitors, eliminating its anti-Communist exclusion principle for members. Organizationally, SDS was tense with generational conflict as a new ideological and geographical wave began to displace the founding generation.

Also during 1965, SDS was discovered by the national media. As SDS became a famous and infamous national name and the germ of a national political force, publicity came to be a dimension of its identity, a component of its reality. By the end of that year, an SDS program that barely existed was front-page news all over the country, and SDS was being denounced by members of the Senate and by the attorney general of the United States. In 1965, SDS changed irreversibly from an organization that recruited its elites and communicated its ideas face to face, to an organization that lived in the glare of publicity and recruited both elites and members on the basis of reputations refracted in large part through the channels of mass media. The nature of that publicity changed too, over time; but the spotlight remained, an invariant fact that for the rest of the movement's life had to be taken into account. For the next several years, the student movement faded in and faded out—even the cinematic language seems appropriate—under the globular eye of the mass media. Its actions were shaped in part by the codes of mass media operations. It conducted its activities in a social world that recognized it, liked it, and disliked it through media images, media versions of its events and rhetoric. To some extent the movement even recognized *itself* through mass-mediated images. In 1965, then, the spotlight was turned on for good. As different filters were clamped onto the floodlamp, it changed colors; the movement tried, at times, to place its own filters onto the lamp or to set up its own; but the spotlight was there to stay. . . .

. . . As movement and media discovered and acted on each other, they worked out the terms with which they would recognize and work on the other; they developed a grammar of interaction. This grammar then shaped the way the movement-media history developed over the rest of the decade, opening certain possibilities and excluding others. As the movement developed, so did the media approaches to it, so that the media's structures of cognition and interpretation never stayed entirely fixed. . . .

It bears emphasis that the media treatment of the movement and the movement approach to the media were themselves *situated,* sewn into an historical context. Movements and media are not creatures of each other; they work on each other, but, as Marx said in another connection, not in conditions of their own making. . . .

The Struggle Over Images

What was the course of the media-movement relation in 1965?

For their different reasons, the media and the movement needed each other. The media needed stories, preferring the dramatic; the movement needed publicity for recruitment, for support, and for political effect. Each could be useful to the other; each had effects, intended and unintended, on the other. As Herbert Gans has written more generally: "In any modern society in which a number of classes, ethnic and religious groups, age groups and political interests struggle among each other for control over the society's resources, there is also a struggle for the power to determine or influence the society's values, myths, symbols, and information." [1] The struggle of movement groups with reporters and media institutions was one instance of a larger and constant struggle; so was, and is, the continual jockeying in which elements of the State intervene to shape or constrict media content. The interaction not only existed in history, it *had* a history. At times, movement and media were symbiotic, at times antagonistic. We can even detect distinct, though overlapping, phases. At first the mass media disregarded the movement; then media discovered the movement; the movement cooperated with media; media presented the movement in patterned ways; the quality and slant of these patterns changed; different parts of the movement responded in different ways; elements of the State intervened to shape this coverage. These were "moments" in a single, connected process, in which movement participants, media institutions and the State—themselves internally conflicted—struggled over the terms of coverage: struggled to define the movement and the nature of political reality around it.

In the single pivotal year 1965, the media-movement relationship went through a number of transformations. For each phase, the central questions are: Who took the initiative? Why? How was each move received by the other side and countered? What conflicts developed within each side? Why did the phase end? . . .

In the struggle over the right and the power to define the public images of the movement in 1965, one can discern five essential phases:

I. Starting in 1960, and up through the late winter of 1965, SDS was not covered by major news media. For its part, SDS did not actively, forcefully, or consistently seek major media coverage. That was not the way a political organization got started. As SDS's first president and national secretary Alan Haber says about the period 1960-62: "The coverage wasn't much and I didn't feel much about it. The kind of stuff we did wasn't organizing demonstrations where we'd look and see what they said about it. . . . SDS was not media-oriented." [2] And for their part, the media were simply not interested in an organization so small and tame. SDS had 19 chapters on paper (of which 6 were real) and 610 members in October 1963; 29 chapters and almost 1,000 members in June 1964; but 80 chapters and more than 2,000 members in June 1965; and 124 chapters and 4,300 members by the end of 1965. [3]

In SDS's early days, organizers visited campuses and expounded SDS's declaration of values, its political analysis and programs. *The Port Huron Statement,* adopted by SDS at its 1962 convention, argued from the human capacity for reason to the necessity of participatory democracy: "People should make the decisions that affect their lives." The analysis centered on the failure of corporate liberalism, the bankruptcy of both the Old Left and the New Deal, the inadequacy of the welfare state, and the destructiveness and obsolescence of the Cold War; it celebrated the promise of the civil rights movement and the breakdown of the Cold War consensus; and it proclaimed the need for "local insurgency" and the special role of students as galvanizers of radical activity. SDS mimeographed and distributed dozens of its own publications and sought to move liberals and local activists toward a more radical, coherent understanding of the world. One SDS leader from that time, Richard Flacks, remembers "there was a general assumption that since we weren't part of the Establishment, we wouldn't be covered by the Establishment media." Rather, SDS gradually became a distinct voice of campus radicalism, known for ideas summed up in phrases like "participatory democracy" and "the issues are interrelated," associated with the force and presence of some of its leaders. If it was a small voice, why should it be otherwise? This was a "network of individuals.". . .

To get its ideas across to a fragmented, scattered left and to left-liberal groups, "what SDS wanted was to get written up in left oriented small circulation things," not the mass press. If anything, the prevailing attitudes toward mass media were disdain and suspicion. Celebrities were distrusted. "We weren't even in that world," as Flacks says. "Why would any of the media be interested in SDS?" [4]

For their part, the media paid little attention. SDS did not perform photogenically; it did not mobilize large numbers of people; it did not undertake flamboyant actions. It was not, in a word, newsworthy.

II. In the late winter of 1965, after the independent upwelling of the Berkeley Free Speech Movement, the media discovered SDS. A few reporters took the initiative and SDS, for its part, cooperated actively. That winter, a sympathetic reporter, Fred Powledge of the *New York Times,* on his own initiative, wrote at length and respectfully about SDS's politics and approach, heralding the emergence of a "new student left." Powledge's article, published in the *Times* of March 15, 1965, certified student radicalism as a live national issue. The SDS leadership of 1964-65 showed a growing interest in large scale student organization and in publicity, but was far from organizing actions or propounding slogans for the sake of "how they would look." Under National Secretary C. Clark Kissinger, the National Office began to send out press releases more regularly, and, especially after the steady bombing of North Vietnam started in February, members of the SDS elite began for the first time to entertain thoughts of a *mass* student movement.[5] Still, SDS did not envisage a central role for the press in the process. Indeed its own communications were scanty and improvised. The National Office published an irregular mimeographed monthly *Bulletin,* and sent newsy biweekly "Work List" mailings to key local and national activists; there were phone and mail contacts with chapters and individual members, and occasional visits by "campus travelers" and speechmakers; but SDS did not publish its own weekly newspaper until January 1966.

III. With the SDS March on Washington on April 17, 1965, student antiwar protest—and SDS activity in particular—became big news. Now reporters began to seek out SDS leaders and to cover protest events. That spring, major articles on the New Left appeared in newsmagazines (*Newsweek, Time, U.S. News & World Report*), large circulation weeklies (the *Saturday Evening Post,* the *New York Times Magazine*), and the liberal weeklies (the *Nation,* the *New Republic,* the *Reporter*); and television news produced its own survey pieces. The movement was amplified.

But which movement? The observer changed the position of the observed. The amplification was already selective: it emphasized certain themes and scanted others. Deprecatory themes began to emerge, then to recur and reverberate. The earliest framing* devices were these:

● *trivialization* (making light of movement language, dress, age, style, and goals);

● *polarization* (emphasizing *counter*demonstrations, and balancing the antiwar movement against ultra-Right and neo-Nazi groups as equivalent "extremists");

● *emphasis on internal dissension;*

● *marginalization* (showing demonstrators to be deviant or unrepresentative);

● *disparagement by numbers* (under-counting);

● *disparagement of the movement's effectiveness.*

In the fall, as parts of the antiwar movement turned to more militant tactics, new themes and devices were added to the first group:

● *reliance on statements by government officials and other authorities;*

● *emphasis on the presence of Communists;*

● *emphasis on the carrying of "Viet Cong" flags;*

● *emphasis on violence in demonstrations;*

● *delegitimizing use of quotation marks* around terms like "peace march";

---

* Gitlin (*The Whole World Is Watching,* p. 7) defines media frames as "persistent patterns of cognition, interpretation, and presentation, of selection, emphasis, and exclusion, by which symbol-handlers routinely organize discourse, whether verbal or visual."

● *considerable attention to right-wing opposition to the movement,* especially from the administration and other politicians.

Some of this framing can be attributed to traditional assumptions in news treatment: news concerns the *event,* not the underlying condition; the *person,* not the group; *conflict,* not consensus; the fact that *"advances the story,"* not the one that explains it. Some of this treatment descends from norms for the coverage of deviance in general: the archetypical news story is a crime story, and an opposition movement is ordinarily, routinely, and unthinkingly treated as a sort of crime. Some of the treatment follows from organizational and technical features of news coverage—which in turn are not ideologically neutral. Editors assign reporters to beats where news is routinely framed by officials; the stories then absorb the officials' definitions of the situation.[6] And editors and reporters also adopt and reproduce the dominant ideological assumptions prevailing in the wider society. All these practices are anchored in organizational policy, in recruitment and promotion: that is to say, in the internal structure of institutional power and decision. And when all these sources are taken into account, some of the framing will still be explained unequivocally; some must be understood as the product of specifically political transactions, cases of editorial judgment and the interventions of political elites. The proportion of a given frame that emanates from each of these sources varies from story to story; that is why stories have to be scrutinized one by one, as concretely as possible, before we can begin to compose general theories.

When we examine stories closely, we discover that there were exceptional moments of coverage within both the *Times* and CBS News. Not only was there—within the boundaries of the norms—some latitude for expressions of individual idiosyncrasy, for random perturbations within the general terms of the code; there were also larger conflicts within the news organizations about how to cover the movement, conflicts that were fought and resolved in different ways at different times. The overall effect of media coverage was blurred and contradictory; there was not a single voice. But increasingly the impression was conveyed that extremism was rampant and that the New Left was dangerous to the public good.

In short, the media were far from mirrors passively reflecting facts found in the real world. The facts reported were out there in the real world, true: out there *among others.* The media reflection was more the active, patterned remaking performed by mirrors in a fun house.

IV. As media actively engaged the movement, an adversary symbiosis developed. Within the movement, arguments emerged about how best to cope with the new situation. Some groupings within the movement stayed on the defensive; others turned to the offense. In neither case was it possible to ignore the media spotlight, or to turn it at will to the movement's own uses.

Some movement organizers responded casually, at first, to the media's attentions. Their commitment to face-to-face organization remained primary; in their view, the press would play a secondary role in transmitting news and images to uncommitted publics. They were working within a pre-spotlight organizational form; they were eager to maintain the movement's own distinct communication channels. But in the fall of 1965, media attention and right-wing attacks caught them by surprise. The strategy they improvised called for a sort of judo operation: using the weight of the adversary to bring him down. They would use the unsought media attention to amplify the antiwar message. They began to speak into the symbolic microphone.

Others, committed to an antiwar movement before all else, and operating mostly outside SDS, began to organize symbolic events deliberately to attract the media spotlight. Very small groups of draft-card burners could leap to national prominence. Three pacifists, trying to awaken a national conscience, immolated themselves and died. Some within SDS proposed attention-getting actions—later called "media events"—that would, they hoped, place the issue of the war at the focus of national politics. Galvanizing opposition, even repression, from the administration or from the political Right could be a means to that end.

V. As the spotlight kept on burning, media treatment entered into the movement's internal life. The media helped recruit into SDS new members and backers who expected to find there what they saw on television or read in the papers. The flood of new members tended to be different from the first SDS generation—less intellectual, more activist, more deeply estranged from the dominant institutions. Politically, many of them cared more about antiwar activity than about the broad-gauged, long-haul, multi-issued politics of the earlier SDS. They were only partially assimilated into the existing organization; they viewed the SDS leaders, the remnants of the founding generation, with suspicion. The newcomers overwhelmed SDS's fragile institutions, which had been created for a tiny organization, a network of so-called Old Guard elite clusters living in intense political and personal community. The fragile person-to-person net of organizational continuity was torn.

This new generation coursed into SDS in the wake of the April 1965 antiwar march, and by June 1966 they had moved into the key positions of leadership. They were known as the Prairie Power people, underscoring—and at times exaggerating—their non-Northeastern, non-elite origins. True, this generation *did* differ from the founders in many ways; the distinction cannot be laid purely and simply at the door of the media and their selectivities. For one thing, the Old Guard elite had already graduated from college, many from elite colleges at that; many had moved into Northern ghettoes as community organizers. Most of the new leaders, by contrast, were still students at state universities. Coming from more conservative regions, Texas and the Great Plains primarily, many of the new generation had become radical quickly, because even mild rebellion against right-wing authority—hair grown slightly long, language grown obscene, or the like—provoked repression. If one were to be punished for small things, it was only a small step to declaring oneself an outlaw in earnest, a communist, a revolutionary: as soon be hanged for a sheep as a goat. So, as cultural rebels, they tended to skip the stage of consciousness that marked the Old Guard generation and informed its politics: a *radical disappointment* with existing liberal institutions, liberal promises, and liberal hopes. In style, too, they declared their deep disaffection from the prevailing culture: many were shaggy in appearance, they smoked dope, they had read less, they went for broke. Even Northeastern members of the Prairie Power leadership shared the new style.

The media not only helped produce and characterize this sharp break within SDS, but they proceeded to play it up; in so doing, they magnified its importance—both to the outside world and inside the organization. When it happened that, as the former SDS National Secretary wrote in December 1965, "chapters, regional offices, and members find out what the organization is doing by reading the newspapers," [7] mass-mediated images were fixing (in the photographic sense) the terms for internal debate; they were helping define the organization's situation for it. Again, none of this happened in a vacuum. The drastic escalation in the war was at the same time pushing many people, both in and out of SDS, toward greater militancy, greater estrangement from dominant American values. The default of liberal forces isolated the whole generation of radical youth, pushing them toward the left. Larger cultural forces were nourishing the possibility of a deviant counter-culture. But the media blitz, by amplifying and speeding all these processes, prevented SDS from assimilating them. The organization tried—and failed. Thus the internal frailties that were later to undo the organization were already built in at the moment of its greatest growth and vigor. In its beginning as a mass organization was its end. . . .

. . . Again, *I am not arguing that the mass media system in general, or its particular ways of covering the New Left, were responsible for the destruction of the movement.* The movement arose in a specific social situation: it emerged from a limited professional-managerial class base, it was socially and politically isolated, and at the same time it was committed to the vast and complex political ambition of organizing the radical transformation of the entire society. Not only that, it hurled itself against an enormously destructive war. Its class narrowness, its deformities and misapprehensions, and the power of the State all weighed on its fate and threw it back on its self-contradictions. . . . The important point is that the movement paid a high price for the publicity it claimed and needed. It entered into an unequal contest with the media: although it affected coverage, the movement was always the petitioner; the movement was more vulnerable, the media more determining. But the movement was never powerless, never without choices, never without responsibility within the limits of the media-movement system as a whole.

To paraphrase Marx: media treatments shape movements, but not in conditions of their own making. . . . [T]he media impact on the New Left depended heavily on the political situation as a whole, on the institutional world that the media inhabit, and on the social and ideological nature of the movement. For covenience's sake at the outset, I can stake out my argument too schematically, and before the necessary qualifications and complications, by saying that the media pressed on SDS and antiwar activity in these ways:[8] (1) generating a membership surge and, consequently, generational and geographical strain among both rank-and-file members and leaders ... ; (2) certifying leaders and converting leadership to celebrity ... ; (3) inflating rhetoric and militancy ... ; (4) elevating a moderate alternative ... ; (5) contracting the movement's experience of time, and helping encapsulate it ... ; and finally, (6) amplifying and containing the movement's messages at the same time. . . .

Implications for Movements

... Since the sixties, opposition movements have become still more sensitive to the impact of the media on their messages and their identities. At one extreme, the Symbionese Liberation Army learned how to manage an exercise in total manipulation, commandeering the media for a moment of spurious glory. At the other, the women's liberation movement, recognizing some of the destructive and self-destructive consequences of the spotlight, has learned from the experience of the New Left and worked with *some* success to decentralize leadership and "spokespersonship," avoiding *some* (not all) of the agonies of the single-focused spotlight.[9] This is after much trial and much error. The results are uneven.

To what extent have the terms of hegemony been renegotiated? Hegemony exists in historical time, and its boundaries are adjustable as the media adjust to new social realities. *The more closely the concerns and values of social movements coincide with the concerns and values of elites in politics and in media, the more likely they are to become incorporated in the prevailing news frames.* Since the sixties, for example, consumer organizations have been elevated to the status of regular news makers; they and their concerns are reported with sympathy, sufficiently so as to inspire corporate complaints and counter-propaganda in the form of paid, issue-centered advertising. Ralph Nader and other public-interest lawyers have become respected celebrities, often interviewed for response statements, photographed in suits and ties and sitting squarely behind desks or in front of bookshelves, embodying solid expertise and mainstream reliability. They have learned to make the journalistic code work for them, while journalists have extended them the privilege of legitimacy. At times, environmentalist groups like the Sierra Club have been adept at using the media to publicize particular issues and to campaign for particular reforms. In the seventies, the prestigious media policymakers have legitimized some political values of their ecologically-minded peers in class and culture. These concerns have been institutionalized in government agencies like the Environmental Protection Agency and the Council on Environmental Quality, which now serve as legitimate news sources. The more radical wings of the environmental movement—those which challenge the raison d'être of centralized mass production and try to join the concerns of labor and environmentalists—are scanted.

Indeed, the very concept of a *movement* has been certified; an *activist,* left or right, is now a stereotyped persona accorded a right to parade quickly through the pageant of the news. Consumer activists, environmentalists, gay activists, feminists, pro- and anti-busing people, as well as anti-abortionists,

Jarvis-Gann supporters, Laetrile legalizers, angry loggers, farmers, and truck drivers—many movements which can be presented as working for (or against) concrete assimilable reforms have become regular, recognizable, even stock characters in newspapers and news broadcasts. The media spread the news that alternative opinions exist on virtually every issue. They create an impression that the society is full of political vitality, that opinions and interests contend freely—that the society, in a word, is pluralist. But in the process, they do extend the reach of movements that agree, at least for working purposes, to accept the same premise—and are willing to pay a price.

It is hard to know in advance what that price will be, hard to generalize about the susceptibilities of movements to the publicity process and its internal consequences. Of internal factors, two seem bound to increase a movement's *dependency* on the mass media: (1) the narrowness of its social base; and (2) its commitment to specific society-wide political goals. And then two other factors, when added onto the first two, seem to produce the most destructive *consequences* of media dependency: (3) the movement's turn toward revolutionary desire and rhetoric in a nonrevolutionary situation; and (4) its unacknowledged political uncertainties, especially about the legitimacy of its own leaders. Thus, in the case of the New Left: (1) It was contained within a relatively narrow social base: students and the young intelligentsia. (2) It had a specific political purpose, to end the war. These two factors in combination were decisive in forcing the movement into dependency on the media, although they did not by themselves generate destructive consequences. Proceeding into national reform politics from its narrow social base, the movement could hope to end the war only by mobilizing wider constituencies. Attempting to affect government policy in a hurry, it was forced to rely upon the mass media to broadcast the simple fact that opposition existed. And then the other factors came into play. (3) The New Left, in its revolutionary moment, allowed itself to believe it was in a revolutionary situation. . . . And at the same time, (4) the New Left's ambivalence about criteria for leadership, especially when coupled with its inability to engender a coherent political ideology and organization, left all parties damaged: leaders were vulnerable to the temptations of celebrity, while the rank and file were stranded without means of keeping their leaders accountable. On the face of it, the black movement of the sixties and seventies shared these vulnerabilities, and for the same reasons. . . .

. . . If a movement is committed to working for specific political goals but refuses to devote itself to revolutionary politics, it may avoid the most severe dependency on the media; it is more likely, too, to be able to control the content of its publicity. The United Farm Workers, for example, are entrenched within a narrow social base and are committed to specific goals; but they have an undisputed leader whose media presence is (I am told) heralded with pride rather than envy; and by avoiding revolutionism, they have been able to occupy the media spotlight without subjecting themselves to its most destructive glare.

Reformist movements, then, are less vulnerable to structural deformation in the publicity process than are revolutionary ones. Reformists can achieve media standing by getting *their* experts legitimated; the standard frames are equipped to show them—and their class—to relatively good advantage. Revolutionaries, by contrast, can achieve media standing only as deviants; they become "good copy" as they become susceptible to derogatory framing devices; and past a certain point, precisely what made them "good copy" may make them dangerous to the State and subject, directly or indirectly, to blackout. But to say that reformist movements are less vulnerable to disparagement is not to say that they are immune. They too, must confront the spotlight's tendency to convert leadership to celebrity, to highlight extravagant rhetoric (if not action), and to help induce transitional crises of generations. Likewise, the standard journalistic frames persist in marginalizing the most radical aspects of movements and setting them against the more moderate. They cover single-issue movements, but frame them in opposition to others: feminists against blacks, blacks against chicanos. *The routine frames ... endure for reformist as well as deeply oppositional movements.* Even reformist movements must work industriously to broadcast their messages without having them discounted, trivialized, fragmented, rendered incoherent. Awareness of the media's routines and frames is no guarantee that a movement will be able to achieve publicity for its analysis and program on its own terms; the frames remain powerful, processing opposition into hegemonic order. But surely ignorance of the media's codes condemns a movement to marginality. . . .

NOTES

1. Herbert Gans, "The Politics of Culture in America: A Sociological Analysis," in Denis McQuail, ed., *Sociology of Mass Communications* (Harmondsworth, England: Penguin Books, 1972), p. 373.
2. Interview, Alan Haber, December 9, 1976.
3. These figures are taken from Kirkpatrick Sale's extraordinarily accurate *SDS* (New York: Random House, 1973), pp. 119, 122, 193, 246.
4. Interview, Richard Flacks, January 9, 1977.
5. Ibid.; and telephone interview, Mike Davis, February 15, 1977.
6. See Leon V. Sigal, *Reporters and Officials: The Organization and Politics of Newsmaking* (Lexington, Mass.: D. C. Heath, 1973), p. 47 and chap. 6; Harvey Molotch and Marilyn Lester, "Accidental News: The Great Oil Spill as Local Occurrence and National Event," *American Journal of Sociology* 81 (September 1965): 235-260; and Herbert Gans, *Deciding What's News* (New York: Pantheon, 1979), chap. 4.
7. C. Clark Kissinger, quoted in Sale, *SDS*, p. 255.
8. A certain cautionary note is both banal and obligatory. It is only for analytic convenience, which requires sequence, that I construct categories and discuss them one at a time. Analytic categories are mutually exclusive where history is continuing, multi-stranded, borderless, and messy. In what follows, a distinct category for grasping and investigating a phenomenon should not be mistaken for the single factor, the isolated "variable," that is neatly produced and separately measured for effects in a controlled experiment. Moreover, the continuing consequences of media coverage . . . were already

at work in 1965, so no hard-and-fast chronological divisions are justified.

9. On relations between the feminist movement and the media, see Monica B. Morris, "Newspapers and the New Feminists: Blackout as Social Control," *Journalism Quarterly* 50 (1973): 37-42; Kate Millett, *Flying* (New York: Alfred A. Knopf, 1974); Jo Freeman, *The Politics of Women's Liberation* (New York: David McKay, 1975), pp. 111-116, 147-150, 228; and Gaye Tuchman, *Making News* (New York: The Free Press, 1978), chap. 7.

Section Five

_____

GUIDING PUBLIC POLICIES

The media affect public policies in a variety of ways. They may be a major factor in creating problems that then require public policy solutions. Or they may, through publicity, engender governmental action that might not have taken place otherwise. Alternatively, by mobilizing hostile public or interest group opinions, they may force a halt to ongoing or projected policies. This section contains examples of policy impact studies involving all of these contingencies and spanning both domestic and foreign policy domains.

In the opening selection, Robert Muccigrosso discusses the validity of charges that the media have generated or accelerated urban crime and racial rioting. He also touches on the role played by the media in the passage of civil rights legislation. The verdict is mixed about the extent of media influence in these important public policy areas. However, the evidence strongly suggests that it was and is a sizable factor. His essay also illustrates how media coverage can produce swift remedial action for problems that are more limited in scope and time, such as a school's mishandling of mentally retarded children.

But media coverage is not always forthcoming when needed. In fact, it frequently is barely in evidence, even when important and controversial matters of public policy are concerned. A. Clay Schoenfeld describes how a crucial piece of legislation, which set the course for environmental policies for decades to come, escaped media attention almost completely during its successful journey through Congress. Its passage raised questions about the claims, often made by public relations experts and political activists, that mass media publicity is an indispensable prerequisite for political success.

What happens when the public is faced with an impending environmental disaster and must rely on the media for information about emergency protective measures and for guidance in evaluating long-range policies? The problems involved in such situations are discussed by Peter M. Sandman and Mary Paden, who observed newspeople during a potentially disastrous accident at a nuclear energy plant. The incident and its aftermath raised many questions concerning the quality of public information about nuclear energy developments and their impact on the public's safety.

Usually, the media act as adversaries of officialdom who alert Americans to governmental misdeeds or governmental failures to protect the public from misdeeds by the private sector. But there are also situations when officials and journalists work together to bring about needed action. Susan Heilmann Miller tells a fascinating tale of one such collaboration. When members of Congress and journalists joined forces, they were able to spur State Department action to bring about the release of American prisoners held in Mexican jails for violating drug laws.

The selection by Micheal J. Kelly and Thomas H. Mitchell discusses highly sensitive issues about the appropriate policies on those occasions when the duty to cover the news fully and fairly clashes with security interests and plays into the hands of political outcasts. If terrorism thrives on ample media coverage, is the answer media- or government-imposed restraint of coverage? Or does publicity actually help to defeat terrorism in the long run? Kelly and Mitchell supply thoughtful answers, based on an analysis of coverage given by the *New York Times* and the *Times* of London to 158 incidents of transnational terrorism.

The final two articles deal with the media's impact on two recent foreign policy crises. David Halberstam, whose critical news reports about U.S. policies in Vietnam aroused the ire of several presidents, traces the decline of public support for the Vietnam War in the wake of adverse media coverage. In a tremendous tribute to the influence of one television personality, Halberstam credits Walter Cronkite with changing the course of foreign policy. According to Halberstam, government officials capitulated when Cronkite declared during a network broadcast that the war was unwinnable and at an end for America.

In many respects, the media's influence on the conduct of foreign policy was even more pronounced and visible during the Iranian hostage crisis than during the Vietnam War. David Altheide looks at the media's role in that crisis. Several newspeople became go-betweens who bridged the diplomatic chasm that separated U.S. and Iranian diplomats after more than 50 Americans had become hostages inside the U.S. embassy in Tehran. The focus given by television newscasts to the story, and the access to American television provided for Iranian spokesmen, sharpened and narrowed the options available to official U.S negotiators.

26. TELEVISION AND THE URBAN CRISIS

Robert Muccigrosso

Editor's Note. It has become fashionable to blame the media for most of the nation's major social ills such as civic apathy, decline in educational standards, and rising rates of crime and corruption. The review of several urban problems presented here shows that verdicts about media responsibility remain open in many cases. Even in those instances where Robert Muccigrosso directly credits or blames the media, others remain unconvinced. The selection thus serves as a chastening reminder that a diagnosis of media impact rarely will receive unanimous support from scholars and news personnel.

Robert Muccigrosso is a Columbia University-trained historian who specializes in late nineteenth and twentieth century United States intellectual and cultural history. He is a professor of history at Brooklyn College. The selection is from *Screen and Society,* ed. Frank J. Coppa, Chicago: Nelson-Hall, 1979.

While it is clearly impossible to render anything remotely approaching a detailed account of how television has tried to deal with the urban crisis, it is possible to examine certain areas in which the medium has covered, analyzed, and put forth suggestions for solving urban issues. The story is one of triumph, failure, and mixed results. Above all, it is one of the problems which have continued to defy adequate solution.

Whether or not violence is indeed a way of life for Americans, it has widely been held to be so. As a purveyor of a great (some would say inordinate) amount of violence, television has been castigated as a contributor to one of the cities' and nation's greatest problems. At the time of the assassination of Robert F. Kennedy, Morris L. Ernst, the eminent lawyer who in the 1920s successfully fought the legal battle against the censorship of James Joyce's *Ulysses,* cried out on a popular talk show (the Merv Griffin program): "We're being murdered by TV, not by the guns." [1] Even before Ernst's outcry there was putative evidence that television may have been abetting crime and violence. The murder rate had shown a downward trend in 353 of the nation's cities in the twenty years between 1937 and 1957 but had begun a steadily upward swing commencing in 1958, the year that television reached what was commonly regarded as a near-saturation figure of fifty million sets in American households.[2] When the robbers of a New York bank admitted in 1961 that they had learned their particular techniques from watching a television program entitled "The Perfect Crime," critics of the medium had further ammunition.[3]

The critics feared the effect of televised aggression on children and youths as much as on adults. . . . Responding to the growing controversy, the government in the late 1960s authorized Surgeon General Jesse L. Steinfeld to investigate for possible links between violence in the medium and aggressive behavior on the part of children. After consuming two years of work and one million tax dollars, a twelve-member Scientific Committee on Television and Social Behavior reported its findings in 1972.[4]

After citing the enormously widespread enjoyment of television by the public (ninety-six percent of American homes had one or more television sets which were turned on for an average of six hours a day), the Committee noted that there had been no significant change in the prevalence of violence between 1967 and 1969. While violence had increased in comedy and cartoon programming, it had become generally less lethal in nature, with fewer characters involved.[5] Although there were approximately eight violent scenes per hour, the Commission found no correlation between the actual percentage of violent programs and the data on violence issued by the Federal Bureau of Investigation's Uniform Crime Report in 1971.[6]

As its major finding the Surgeon General's group agreed that "the accumulated evidence . . . does not warrant the conclusion that televised violence has a uniformly adverse effect nor the conclusion that it has an adverse effect on the majority of children."[7] The evidence, as analyzed, indicated that children already in possession of hostile tendencies acted more aggressively than those whose proclivities were less hostile. The Commission raised the related question of environment as a determining factor but reached no definite conclusion: "The family, the church, the legal system, and the military, among other institutions, communicate codes, ethics, and guidelines for aggression and violence. The extent to which television reinforces or weakens these codes or guidelines is not presently known."[8] . . .

Today the problem of televised violence and its exact effects on audiences, particularly pre-adults, remains a moot point. Networks have worked to eliminate some of the worst excesses by introducing a proliferation of nonviolent programs and by relegating many violent episodes to late-hour viewing. Still, the criticism continues largely unabated. . . .

Another major problem, one by no means unrelated to that of violence, which forms an integral part of today's urban crisis concerns ethnic minorities, especially blacks, and race relations. Once again television's record has been mottled with both success and failure, and once again its overall effect has been called into question.

Precisely what meaning television had for blacks during the 1950s and the early 1960s is difficult to pinpoint. Certainly programs and commercials warmly invited blacks to share the better life of the Affluent Society. Yet when hard-core economic realities failed to change, frustration may have grown immeasurably. Did television coverage of the battles for civil rights in Little Rock, Selma, Oxford, and on the Freedom Marches serve to inspire blacks with renewed hope or only to augment a sense of racial division? Did it have relatively little consequence? Eric Sevareid, for one, felt that the momentous Civil Rights Act of 1964 could not have reached fruition without the beneficent role of television. . . . Yet another writer, also knowledgeable about the communications media, flatly declared that "the black revolution in America and its acceptance by the white majority was not a product of mass communications, but of forces more fundamental to the formation of private and public attitudes. . . . In racial matters, as elsewhere, the media merely acted as a mirror of society, not the 'molder' of its opinions, as the cliche would have us believe." [9] . . .

During the summer of 1964 New York's Harlem and Bedford-Stuyvesant, two of the nation's most notorious slum areas, were rocked by riots. Television not only duly covered these riots but also, in the opinion of one observer, directly fostered them: "During spring and early summer, almost daily interviews with 'Negro leaders' predicting a holocaust were visible on television. Many of these men were spokesmen without a following, ambitious activists eager for exposure. But their words created an air of tension and expectancy, convincing the ghetto dwellers that violence was indeed imminent. Nobody was surprised when it came." [10] The riots, for all their pain and ferocity, drew relatively little attention or concern outside of New York and brought forth only sparse criticism of the media. The next summer, however, was to witness another major urban riot, this time on the opposite coast of the country. Very soon Watts would become a household name and television would be embroiled in fierce controversy over its handling of the episode.

On August 12, 1965, Watts, a Los Angeles ghetto nearly fifty square miles in area, erupted. Within a few hours three dozen persons lay dead, more than seven hundred and fifty were injured, twenty-five hundred were arrested, and two hundred business buildings were destroyed. Later estimates placed property losses for these two hours of pandemonium in excess of forty-four million dollars.[11] . . .

Questions concerning the manner in which television covered the rioting immediately arose. Did the cameras accelerate the tempo of violence? Should the stations have reported all the events? Did they employ judicious rhetoric and should they have omitted catching and sometimes literally inflammatory phrases such as "Burn, baby, burn?" FCC Chairman E. William Henry applauded coverage by the medium.[12] Others reacted adversely. John Gregory Dunne, a regular contributor to *The New Republic,* for example, castigated the performance: "Consciously or not, electronic journalism is essentially show business, and show business demands a gimmick. With its insatiable appetite for live drama, television turned the riots into some kind of

Roman spectacle, with the police playing the lions, the Negroes the Christians. The angle, in this case, was that the Christians were winning. Not only did television exacerbate an already inflammatory situation, but also, by turning the riots into a Happening, may even have helped prolong them." [13] . . .

. . . In the summer of 1967, two years after Watts, violence broke out in fifteen American cities, most severely in Detroit and Newark. . . . [Detroit] Police Commissioner Ray Girardin, responding to the deaths of forty-three persons killed during the mayhem, angrily contended that "TV could have performed a civic duty by informing people to stay away from dangerous sections." A Newark police official hurled a similar accusation during the riots which occurred in his city that same summer. [14]

Commissioner Girardin and the Newark official were not the solitary voices crying in the wilderness against television's purported mishandling of the riots. Max Lerner denounced both the medium and his fellow countrymen, fulminating that "Americans seem to have struck a Faustian bargain with the big media, by which they have received total and instant coverage and have in turn handed themselves over the vulnerable chances of crowd psychology and of instant infection." [15] Carl T. Rowan, a black journalist and onetime State Department official, voiced the concern of moderate blacks when he complained: "The truth today is that someone who legitimately speaks for thousands of Negroes, who articulates their hopes and frustrations, can show up in most American cities and get no better than routine press coverage. But let a Negro show up who says: 'If you don't do this or that we're going to burn down this damned town.' I guarantee you he'll make front page headlines and all the TV shows." [16] Others concurred that televised appearances by radicals like Stokely Carmichael and H. Rap Brown should be minimal. [17]

Television was not bereft of defenders, however. Eric Sevareid reminded his listeners that the nation's worst race riots had taken place before the advent of either radio or television. Moreover, he cited word-of-mouth communication as the principal culprit in the present situation. [18] CBS President Richard S. Salant, while agreeing that television could and should use greater restraint in certain cases, posited a classical defense of the medium by arguing that it simply could not avoid confronting problems which fell under the rubric of news. [19] . . .

. . . President Lyndon B. Johnson . . . responded in timeworn American fashion by calling for a committee to investigate the situation. Headed by Illinois Governor Otto Kerner, the President's Commission on Civil Disorders speedily completed its study and drew three basic conclusions: (1) despite various inaccuracies and misrepresentations, the medium had honestly tried to give a balanced version of the riots, (2) it had been guilty of exaggeration, and (3) it had "failed to report adequately on the causes and consequences of civil disorders and the underlying problems of race relations." [20]

After viewing nearly a thousand sequences of the rioting as filmed by local and network stations, the Commission, avowing that it had earlier thought otherwise, opined that the industry actually had reported many more "calm" than "emotional" scenes and had concentrated on showing more moderate than militant black spokesmen. While there were isolated incidents of irresponsibility—the helicopter coverage of the Watts riot, the interference with law enforcement by cameramen in Newark, the instance of a New York newspaper photographer persuading a youth to throw a rock in order to achieve a more sensational story—reporters had behaved well.[21]

For all its positive achievements, the medium had sometimes exaggerated or misread what had actually happened. It had, according to the Commission, portrayed the disorders as instances of black-white confrontation. Since the preponderance of rioting had occurred in black areas, the Commission reasoned, with less than compelling logic, that there had been no *race* riots.[22] Further—and worse—television had failed to inculcate in both its black and white viewers any deep sense of the problems the nation faced, along with possible solutions. This failure was not accidental: television had been guilty of the same racial bias and paternalism so deeply rooted in society at large. And while the Kerner group found this situation "understandable," it also found it inexcusable "in an institution that has the mission to inform and educate the whole of our society." [23] Citing the blacks' distrust of the medium, a distrust intensified by experiencing one reality while witnessing another on television, the Commission further berated the industry for failing to give whites a true understanding of the nature of ghetto life." [24] . . .

Although television has had a mixed impact on the urban crisis with respect to violence, minorities, and race relations, there have been specific instances when its effect has been decidedly benign. During the disastrous forest and brush fires that swept through southern California destroying several suburban communities in 1964, helpful reporting and repeated urging for calm by local stations may have been instrumental in preventing widespread panic.[25] Several years later this spirit of "good neighbor" reporting had increased in tempo. Whether it was Geraldo Rivera's sympathetic interview with drug addicts conducted on the rooftops of tenement buildings in East Harlem . . . in July, 1971, or the splendid program on ecology, "The Eighth Day," presented . . . in Seattle, local television was proving itself increasingly responsive to local needs.[26] Few local programs, however, were able to equal in dramatic intensity the superb documentary Rivera compiled in early 1972 . . . on the deplorable conditions at Willowbrook State School for the mentally retarded.

Technically a school, Willowbrook, pleasantly situated on Staten Island, was in actuality a hospital for the mentally retarded. On January 5, 1972, Rivera agreed to visit the premises at the request of a friend, a physician who had been dismissed for having asked the parents of the patients to seek improved conditions. When young Rivera reached Willowbrook he was shocked to find sixty or seventy naked or nearly naked children living in Building 6 in the midst of rank filth and disease. The institution could comfortably accommodate three thousand patients; it was then housing over five thousand. Sharing the same scarce toilets and contracting one another's diseases, patients were dying at the appalling rate of three or four a week. Only twenty percent of the children, moreover, attended any classes whatsoever—this in what was ostensibly a school.[27]

Dr. Jack Hammond, who had served as director of Willowbrook since 1965, warned Rivera the following day about presenting certain televised footage and refused to permit recognizable faces to be shown. Nevertheless, [a New York television station] did offer seven minutes of Rivera's handiwork on its 6:00 P.M. news and received roughly three hundred phone calls from concerned viewers that same evening. The number of calls soared to seven hundred by the following afternoon. On the next day the station showed film clips of a Willowbrook tour conducted by Dr. Hammond. Somehow—perhaps not surprisingly—the children appeared healthy. When Rivera returned to the institution on January 10 he learned that many children had received drugs, that the food was poor, and that there were not enough attendants to care for the patients. By the next day Willowbrook had captured the city's attention. Parents rallied at the site; Assemblyman Andrew Stein offered his services; televised clips of the late Senator Robert F. Kennedy's visit to the school in 1965 served to increase popular demand for reform.[28]

Inaction now had become impossible. Willowbrook agreed to rehire three hundred employees, although the school would still remain six hundred employees short of authorized strength, a condition necessitated by severe cuts in the state's budget. Rivera, meanwhile, had gone to California to study that state's decidedly superior system for caring for the retarded. Returning to New York on January 21, the reporter took more film of Willowbrook for his upcoming special, "The Last Disgrace." Ten days later the Staten Island Chapter of the Society for the Prevention of Cruelty to Children began hearings and at the same time called for the state and national governments to investigate conditions. On February 2 Rivera's special was aired. Two and one-half million people watched, making the program the highest rated local news special in television history. Looking back upon his endeavors, Rivera noted some change for the better; wards were cleaner and most of the children were wearing clothes. He remained unimpressed, concluding that "we've got to close that goddamned place down." [29]

With a bit of reflection one can easily extend the list of useful services television provides for beleaguered denizens of the cities: warnings about impending bad weather, reports on traffic congestion, emergency appeals, programs intended to stimulate the social conscience, to enlighten the citizenry, and to impart miscellaneous information, to name a few. It even has been argued that the power of urban bosses has visibly declined thanks in no small part to the efforts of local stations. At the very least, so the argument runs, television has prevented a worse breed of politician from taking office.[30] . . .

NOTES

1. Erik Barnouw, *The Image Empire* (New York, 1970), p. 318.
2. Jerome Ellison, "Stimulant to Violence," in *Violence in the Streets,* ed. Shalom

Endleman (Chicago, 1968), pp. 110-11.
3. Harry J. Skornia, *Television and Society: An Inquest and Agenda for Improvement* (New York, 1965), p. 173.
4. Surgeon General's Scientific Advisory Committee on Television and Social Behavior, *Television and Growing Up: The Impact of Televised Violence. Report to the Surgeon General, United States Public Health Service.* Washington, D.C., 1972.
5. Ibid., pp. 2, 5.
6. Ibid., pp. 5, 77-78. The Commission did conclude, however, that there might be a connection between real airplane hijackings and bomb threats and those fictionalized by the medium.
7. Ibid., p. 11.
8. Ibid., pp. 18, 39.
9. Martin H. Seiden, *Who Controls the Mass Media? Popular Myths and Economic Realities* (New York, 1974), p. 11. Seiden, however, did credit television for giving blacks a greater role in the medium after the civil rights movement of the 1960s.
10. Neil Hickey, "A Look at TV's Coverage of Violence," in *Television: A Selection of Readings from TV Guide Magazine,* ed. Barry G. Cole (New York, 1970), p. 66.
11. William Small, *To Kill a Messenger: Television News and the Real World* (New York, 1970), p. 59.
12. William A. Wood, *Electronic Journalism* (New York, 1967), p. 55.
13. John Gregory Dunne, "The Television Riot Squad," *The New Republic,* 153 (11 September 1965): 27-28.
14. Hickey, "A Look at TV's Coverage of Violence," p. 64. A year later Girardin decided that television was maturing in its handling of dangerous situations. (pp. 75-76)
15. Ibid., p. 65.
16. Carl T. Rowan, "The Mass Media in an Age of Explosive Social Change," in *Mass Media in a Free Society,* ed. Warren K. Agee (Lawrence, Kansas, 1969), p. 46.
17. Theodore F. Koop, "Television: America's Star Reporter," in Ibid., pp. 56-57.
18. Small, *To Kill a Messenger,* p. 64.
19. Hickey, "A Look at TV's Coverage of Violence," p. 68.
20. *Report of the National Advisory Commission on Civil Disorders,* with an Introduction by Tom Wicker (New York, 1968), p. 363.
21. Ibid., pp. 363-64, 368-69, 372, 377.
22. Ibid., p. 365.
23. Ibid., p. 366.
24. Ibid., pp. 374, 383.
25. Wood, *Electronic Journalism,* pp. 86-7.
26. *Survey of Broadcast Journalism, 1970-1971,* ed. Marvin Barrett (New York, 1971), pp. 24-5.
27. Geraldo Rivera, *Willowbrook: A Report on How It [I]s and Why It Doesn't Have to Be That Way* (New York, 1972), pp. 9-27, passim.
28. Ibid., pp. 29-56, passim. On January 13, Rivera, accompanied by Congressman Mario Biaggi, visited the Letchworth Village Rehabilitation Center in Rockland County. Both found conditions worse than at Willowbrook.
29. Ibid., pp. 93, 99, 129, 142, 146-47.
30. Seiden, *Who Controls the Mass Media?* pp. 69-76, 223.

27. THE PRESS AND NEPA:
THE CASE OF THE MISSING AGENDA

A. Clay Schoenfeld

Editor's Note. The National Environmental Policy Act (NEPA) became law in 1969 without the benefit of major attention from the media. A. Clay Schoenfeld speculates that this lack of attention avoided controversy that might have delayed or prevented passage of the Act. Given its profound impact on environmental protection policies, it is unfortunate that public debate was muted because of the sparseness of media coverage.

The NEPA story also raises questions about the process by which public policy formation attracts or fails to attract media scrutiny. Should it be left to such vagaries as the mix of general news, the issues spotlighted by politicians, the particular interests of reporters, and the activities of lobby groups?

A. Clay Schoenfeld is chairman of the Center for Environmental Communications and Educational Studies at the University of Wisconsin at Madison. He has written a number of articles analyzing ecological awareness among members of the news profession. The selection is from *Journalism Quarterly,* 56 (1979): 577-585.

... This is a study of the apparent relationship—or lack of it—between press coverage and the evolution and ultimate passage of a strategic piece of federal legislation, the National Environmental Policy Act (NEPA, Public Law 91-190, 1969). . . .

NEPA is uniformly regarded by adherents, foes and scholars alike as a landmark act. With pardonable pride of sponsorship, Sen. Henry Jackson termed NEPA "one of the most significant steps ever taken in the field of conservation." [1] Fisher later praised it as "the most comprehensive legislative statement of the nation's . . . commitment to protect the environment," one which has had "a profound impact on agency decision-making." [2] Because it has energized "a staggering amount" of litigation in the courts and hence wasted resources in "processing papers," Fairfax has recently damned NEPA as "a disaster in the environmental movement." [3] Finn says "no law has done more to make the federal government sensitive to environmental values,"

Reprinted by permission from the Autumn 1979 issue of *Journalism Quarterly.*

penetrating the bureaucratic structure "like a whiplash" to force "early consideration of ecological factors in federal decision-making;" he quotes Washington observers that "no federal statute of modern times has been read by a greater proportion of federal officials," and that "not since women received the vote has the discretion of the government been so thoroughly bruised." [4] Rosenbaum has called the Act "unprecedented." [5] Before NEPA, in the eyes of ecologist Lamont Cole, "environmental management policy (had been) based on considerations of economics, engineering convenience and political expediency, but seldom on esthetic considerations and even less on sound ecological considerations." [6] NEPA proposed to change all that—and has to a significant extent. Under NEPA, says the Council on Environmental Quality, the environment is a "totality," and public officials must "perceive the totality of the environment and the interrelationships of pollutants in all media." [7] . . .

In action NEPA has led directly or indirectly to modifications, delays or halts to assorted dams, canals, power plants, roads, ski resorts, golf courses, oil leases, pipelines, jetports, insecticides, SST's; paved the way for the Environmental Quality Improvement Act of 1970 and the organization the same year of the Environmental Protection Agency; has spawned some 30 state EPA's; has reformed public participation in policy formation, particularly on the part of the Corps of Engineers and the U.S. Forest Service;[8] produced a monumental backlash and a "Save NEPA" coalition; has become the subject of a dozen books and scores of papers in learned journals; has markedly stimulated a new profession of environmental law; and has led to at least one course in environmental impact analysis in practically every college and university.[9] For good or ill, perhaps no other single piece of literature has come so to embody the letter and the spirit of the environmental movement of the 1960s and 1970s as the National Environmental Policy Act.

In passing NEPA the Congress appeared to have had five major purposes in mind: to mandate federal agencies to protect and restore environmental quality in accordance with a general national policy, to establish specific action-forcing procedures for the implementation of that policy, to create a Council on Environmental Quality in the Executive Office of the President, to foster the development of information on and indices of environmental quality, and to provide for an annual CEQ report of progress toward NEPA's goals.[10] Perhaps the most visible evidence of NEPA in action was to become the "environmental impact statements" required under Section 102(2)(C). . . .

What of the media's role a decade ago? According to a broad interpretation of the agenda-setting role of the print media,[11] the evolution of such a crucial act as NEPA might be expected to have gone something like the following:

The print media early on identify elements of news that signal the absence of "a national policy that will encourage productive and enjoyable harmony between man and his environment," as NEPA would ultimately read. By lending quantitative and qualitative salience to such issues, the media place the essence of NEPA on the public agenda. Public opinion begins to coalesce around a felt need for remedial action. Several Congressmen respond with prototype legislation. As the various bills are debated in detail in protracted committee sessions and public hearings, the media lend extensive news coverage, accompanied by "mobilizing" editorials. When the final vote on a conference-report NEPA approaches, press attention peaks.

Actually, it wasn't that way at all.

While various proposals which could be said to be antecedent to NEPA had been introduced in Congress as early as 1959, it was in 1968 that there appeared a half-dozen principal bills bearing elements of what was to become NEPA. That year as well, two important Congressional documents helped set the agenda: *Managing the Environment,*[12] and *A National Policy for the Environment.*[13] What is more, on July 17 committee aides staged what was supposed to be a big "media event," an unprecedented joint House-Senate colloquium on "a national policy for the environment," reminiscent somewhat of the famous White House Conference on Conservation in 1908, with a full panoply of cabinet officials, expert witnesses and politicians, all expounding that environmental degradation was linked to fragmented governmental decision-making.[14]

So 1968 is a fitting year in which to begin to take a look at media coverage of the NEPA concept. Finn had already surveyed the Washington dailies and the *Christian Science Monitor* in 1968-69 for evidences of NEPA coverage. We used the New York *Times* and its *Index* as the principal record. (Such a use of prepared indices "seems to be both highly efficient and reliable.")[15]

Despite an array of compelling NEPA-related news pegs, in the whole of 1968 the *Times* carried just one news article on the antecedents of NEPA. What Finn has called the "milestone" colloquium went unnoticed, even though a committee aide had "made an earnest effort" to attract press interest.[16] A Dec. 30 editorial did call for "an all-out effort to halt destruction of the environment," but it did not discuss any existing variants of what was to become NEPA.

NEPA's immediate forebears were HR 6750, introduced Feb. 17, 1969 by Congressman John Dingell, and S 1075, introduced the following day by Senator Jackson. The *Times* mentioned neither. The *Times* did report routinely the beginning of Senate hearings on S 1075 on March 4, and its subsequent passage by the Senate on July 11. It did not cover the Dingell bill, nor follow the exquisite political maneuvering that took place among Congressional committees and between Congress and the President before NEPA emerged from conference in its ultimate form on Dec. 17, to be passed by both houses Dec. 20. Even that penultimate decision went unmentioned in the *Times,* although a May 3 editorial had applauded S 1075.

How can we explain this paucity of NEPA coverage in the NYT? It was certainly not because the *Times* was not "environment-minded." One of its editorial directors, John Oakes, was known personally as a conservation leader. Its columns had been open for many years to nature writer Hal

Borland. A February 1966 editorial, "The Threatened Land," had stressed the need for more information on the environment and had recognized an early NEPA prototype bill as a promising approach.[17] The *Times* was one of the first dailies to designate an "environmental reporter"—Gladwin Hill in 1969.[18] Feature stories on the general environment and its problems had risen in the *Times* from 1 in 1965 to 158 in 1969. The paper had lent its support to Humphrey over Nixon in 1968 in part because the latter was "flawed on conservation." In 1968 and 1969, 35 *Times* editorials were indexed as "Environmental"—yet none sought to "mobilize" public action on NEPA. The *Times was* covering "the ecology beat"—and on the front page....

Whatever the reasons for the *Times* blindspot with respect to NEPA, it was representative; the *Times* was not alone in considering NEPA unnewsworthy. While several articles did appear in the Washington dailies, "they were at random, and not particularly perceptive."... Beginning in February 1969, one daily reporter did keep on top of the NEPA story—Robert Cahn, Pulitzer-prize-winning environmental reporter for the *Christian Science Monitor*. On June 4, 1969 he outlined the "several weeks of behind-the-scenes maneuvering" that led to a crucial understanding the White House would not attempt to block Senator Jackson's bill.... On Dec. 16 Cahn correctly read into NEPA the "stronger-than-expected broad controls for what may prove to be a landmark environmental package."... Cahn excepted, Finn concluded that "the media reporting of the events surrounding the enactment of PL 91-190 hardly met the responsibility of the press." [20] ...

It is interesting to speculate what would have happened if the press had in fact turned a searchlight on S 1075. Several Congressional staff members involved in NEPA's development now believe that "if Congress had really appreciated what the law would do, it would not have passed."[21] Perhaps environmental legislation with a real bite can come to flower only in the shadows. It may or may not be significant that the most sweeping environmental legislation of the 19th century, the so-called Forest Reserve Act of 1891, empowering the President to set aside what are now the National Forests, was not a discrete Congressional act at all but an obscure amendment to an omnibus land bill, added in committee and passed without hearing, debate or press coverage.[22]

How can we best explain the general lack of press attention to NEPA? Perhaps NEPA was simply hard-pressed to compete in 1968 and 1969 with the events of what historian Robert Kelly calls "the years of the whirlwind:" [23] race riots, assassinations, Vietnam, women's lib, oil spills, moon landings, flower children, the imperial presidency, urban tensions, farm revolt, Weathermen, Black Panthers, Russia, China, emerging nations, tumultuous national conventions and campaigns—it was a crowded agenda, indeed. As Funkhouser says, "It is astounding that it all took so few years to happen." [24] Neither ... party platform nor any presidential candidate made a big thing out of environmental issues in the 1968 campaign, and the press did not prompt them,[25] although a Brookings Institution observer was saying the environment would be "one of the incoming president's four inevitable preoccupations in the field of public policy." [26] As McLeod, Becker and Byrnes have noted, in an election year the agenda-setting role is a mixed bag, with politicians and the press jockeying for position.[27] In examining the environment particularly as a case study in the development of an important public policy issue, Trop and Roos say "it is most difficult to specify the direction of causality: various events ... are intermingled, making it almost impossible to untangle the causal linkages." [28] In the case of NEPA, at least, NEPA may be said to have set its own agenda in 1968, undismayed by press and presidential-candidate attention focussed elsewhere.

Unquestionably "the environment" in 1968-69 may have seemed so abstract and complex a general problem and NEPA so abstract and complex an approach that Washington reporters were simply unprepared at the time either to catch the significance of S 1075 or to untangle the fascinating symbolic and substantive minuet being performed by its Congressional supporters and their antagonists. For certain, as the government's first holistic approach to the environment, NEPA did not fit in anybody's particular "beat." NEPA probably seemed peripheral alike to agriculture, commerce, defense, education, fish and wildlife, labor, parks, science, state, public works, urban affairs and treasury reporters—although in a couple of years they would all confront its implications. In 1968-69, NEPA fell neatly between the newsroom chairs, and this fact alone may have accounted for its "invisibility." It was not until the 1970s that "the environment" really took shape as a beat speciality on its own,[29] and "the unexpected" became "routinized," as Tuchman[30] describes a newsroom phenomenon. Gradually an "ecological conscience" was to appear in at least some newsrooms.[31]

Why and how did NEPA pass Congress without the press arousing public interest? Was it in response to an effective, elite environmental lobby? It hardly seems likely. Compared to today, there was no sustained environmental lobby in Washington in 1968-69....

... More likely, what the NEPA saga suggests is that legislators can at least at times set an agenda of their own—a collective intrapersonal agenda relatively independent of media or public agendas—that Congress can indeed "respond admirably" to a quiet crisis,[32] "vigorously performing the legislative tasks ... central to lawmaking,"[33] with or without the press or public pressure.... Parenthetically, what the NEPA saga also suggests is that you don't necessarily need a big PR "media hype" to get a law passed.

NOTES

1. U.S. *Congressional Record,* 91st Congress, First Session, 1969, CXV, Part 30, 40924.
2. Joseph L. Fisher, in "Foreword" to Anderson, *NEPA in the Courts.* (Baltimore: Johns Hopkins University Press, 1973), p. v.
3. Sally K. Fairfax, "A Disaster in the Environmental Movement," *Science,* 199:743-747 (Feb. 17, 1978).
4. Terence T. Finn. *Conflict and Compromise: Congress Makes a Law,* Ph.D dissertation, Georgetown University, Ann Arbor, Michigan: University Microfilms, 1973, p. 2.

5. Walter A. Rosenbaum. *The Politics of Environmental Concern.* New York: Praeger, 1977, p. 117.
6. U.S. Congress. House. Subcommittee on Science, Research, and Development. *Hearings on H.R. 7796,* Committee Print, 1966.
7. Council on Environmental Quality, *Environmental Quality: Second Annual Report* (Washington, D.C.: Government Printing Office, 1972), p. 341.
8. Richard Liroff, "The Council on EQ." *Environmental Law Reporter,* 3:50050-50070. (August 1973).
9. Clay Schoenfeld and John Disinger, *Environmental Education in Action—II* (Columbus, Ohio: ERIC-SMEAC, 1978).
10. U.S. Congress, Senate. Committee on Interior and Insular Affairs, National Environmental Policy Act of 1969. *Senate Report No. 91-296,* 91st Congress, 1st Session, 3, 9, 10, 14 (July 9, 1969).
11. Donald Shaw and Maxwell McCombs, *The Emergence of American Political Issues: The Agenda-Setting Function of the Press* (St. Paul: West Publishing Co., 1977).
12. U.S. Congress, House. Committee on Science and Astronautics. *Managing the Environment,* 90th Congress, 2nd Session, 1968. Committee Print.
13. U.S. Congress, Senate. Committee on Interior and Insular Affairs. *A National Policy for the Environment.* 90th Congress, 2nd Session, 1968. Committee Print.
14. U.S. Senate, House. Committee on Interior and Insular Affairs, Committee on Science and Astronautics. *Joint-House-Senate Colloquium to Discuss a National Policy for the Environment.* 90th Congress, Second Session, July 17, 1968. Committee Print.
15. Maxwell McCombs and Donald L. Shaw. "A Progress Report on Agenda-Setting Research." Paper. Theory and Methodology Division, Association for Education in Journalism, San Diego, California, August 1974.
16. Finn. *op. cit.,* p. 308.
17. Senator Gaylord Nelson's Ecological Research and Surveys Bill, which Caldwell calls "a pivotal [piece] of legislation" in NEPA's history. See Lynton Caldwell. *Environment: A Challenge for Modern Society* (Garden City, N.Y.: Natural History Press, 1970), p. 201.
18. See William G. Omohundo, "Journalists Assess Environmental Future." *Environment Midwest,* June 1977, pp. 3-5.
19. Finn., *op. cit.,* p. 608.
20. Ibid., 608.
21. Liroff, *op. cit.,* p. 16. Even Senator Jackson is said not to have foreseen the potential of NEPA.
22. Samuel P. Hays, *Conservation and the Gospel of Efficiency* (Cambridge: Harvard University Press, 1959), pp. 263-264.
23. Robert Kelly, *The Shaping of the American Past,* Vol. 2 (Englewood Cliffs, New Jersey: Prentice-Hall, 1975), p. 874.
24. G. Ray Funkhouser, "Trends in Media Coverage of the Issues of the '60s," *Journalism Quarterly* 50:523-528 (Autumn 1973).
25. Studying the quantity of environmental coverage, 1962-1977, in the New York *Times* and the Chicago *Tribune,* O'Meara *(op. cit.)* found an interesting dip in the years 1964, 1968, 1972, 1976—presidential election years. Apparently the environment competes ineffectively for space on the press agenda against the drama of presidential campaigns, whatever may be the issues involved.
26. Stephen K. Bailey, "Managing the Federal Government," *Agenda for the Nation,* Gordon, ed. (Washington: Brookings Institution, 1968).
27. Jack McLeod, Lee B. Becker, and J.E. Byrnes, "Another Look at the Agenda-Setting Function of the Press," *Communication Research* 1:131-166 (1974).
28. Cecile Trop and Leslie L. Roos, Jr., "Public Opinion and the Environment," in Roos, ed., *The Politics of Ecosuicide* (New York: Holt, Rinehart, and Winston, 1971).

29. William Witt, "The Environmental Reporter on U.S. Daily Newspapers," *Journalism Quarterly*, 51:697-705 (Winter, 1974).
30. Gaye Tuchman, "Making News by Doing Work: Routinizing the Unexpected," *American Journal of Sociology*, 79:110-129 (July, 1973).
31. Clay Schoenfeld, "Ecological Conscience in the Newsroom: The Sociology of the Environmental Reporter," in press.
32. Geoffrey Wandesforde-Smith, "National Policy for Environment," in Richard A. Cooley and Geoffrey Wandesforde-Smith, eds., *Congress and the Environment* (Seattle: University of Washington Press, 1970), pp. 205-226.
33. Finn., *op. cit.,* 661. On Dec. 16, 1969 no fewer than 80 Congressmen joined in "A Call for the Environmental Decade." See U.S., *Congressional Record,* Dec. 16, 1969, H 12541.

28. AT THREE MILE ISLAND

Peter M. Sandman and Mary Paden

Editor's Note. Despite the fact that the media are private institutions, they are expected to carry out important public information functions, especially during times of crisis. The media's capacity to handle such a task was tested in 1979. A breakdown at the nuclear facility at Three Mile Island, Pennsylvania, raised the specter of a hydrogen explosion and a massive escape of nuclear radiation endangering the safety of millions of people. Because of serious criticism of the performance of the media and public information officials in the wake of the accident, President Carter created a special commission to investigate the matter.

Peter M. Sandman and Mary Paden look at the situation from the perspective of the newspeople who were at the scene. They conclude that, aside from some melodramatic stories and a few staged incidents, the media accomplished their task very well in the face of extreme difficulties in getting reliable, comprehensible information. Still, news stories left much to be desired. The public remained frightened and confused throughout the crisis. Personal and business affairs were severely disrupted in areas near the stricken plant. News stories also had lasting adverse consequences for future use of nuclear energy as a major fuel source in the United States.

Peter M. Sandman is a professor of journalism and public relations at Cook College, Rutgers University. He was a member of a team of scholars who conducted research for the President's Commission on the Accident at Three Mile Island. Mary Paden worked as a reporter for the Middletown, N.Y., *Times-Herald-Record,* one of several newspapers serving the accident region. The selection is from *Columbia Journalism Review,* July/August 1979: 43-58.

. . . [T]he excitement at Three Mile Island had come in surges. The day it all began, Wednesday, March 28, was dominated by the slowly leaking radiation, and the slowly leaking news that despite the denials of the utility, Metropolitan Edison, the accident was probably the most serious in the history of the American nuclear industry. RADIATION SPREADS 10 MILES FROM A-PLANT MISHAP SITE was the headline over Tom O'Toole's story in the next morning's *Washington Post.* Thursday the tension

---

subsided; Met Ed, the Nuclear Regulatory Commission, and Pennsylvania Governor Dick Thornburgh agreed that the crisis was past, and editors who had staffed the accident quickly and heavily began wondering if they had overreacted. Bryce Nelson's story in the *Los Angeles Times* carried a one-column head: PLANT STILL LEAKS RADIATION BUT PERIL SEEMS OVER. Friday all hell broke loose, with two more uncontrolled bursts of radiation, a recommended evacuation of preschool children and pregnant women, and a mysterious bubble that some N.R.C. officials said might be hard to remove without risking a catastrophic meltdown. Friday night, Walter Cronkite intoned that "the world has never known a day quite like today," and *The New York Times* put four Three Mile Island stories on Saturday morning's front page, under this foreboding headline: U.S. AIDES SEE A RISK OF MELTDOWN AT PENNSYLVANIA NUCLEAR PLANT; MORE RADIOACTIVE GAS IS RELEASED. By Saturday more than 300 out-of-town reporters had converged on Harrisburg.

But Saturday was quiet there. Met Ed and the N.R.C. continued to disagree over the size of the bubble and the seriousness of the accident, but the big news came out of Washington. N.R.C. Chairman Joseph Hendrie suggested that if simpler methods didn't work, a twenty-mile-radius mass evacuation might be a good idea before they really went after the bubble. The N.R.C.'s man on the scene, Harold Denton, hadn't talked to reporters since the night before, when he had wryly admitted that the bubble was a "new twist" not envisioned in the commission-approved emergency procedures. Crowded into a spare room in gubernatorial press secretary Paul Critchlow's capitol office, the N.R.C.'s public-information people had little to add besides a list of the maneuvers Denton might try to get rid of the bubble.

At 8 p.m. Saturday there were only twenty reporters in the capitol newsroom, most of them complaining to each other that Critchlow was unreachable and that his staff wouldn't say whether the lid was on for the night or not.

Except for the newcomers like us, they looked haggard. Three Mile Island was a tough assignment; some veterans said it was the toughest they'd ever had. Somehow the TV reporters managed to stay crisp, but the print people showed the strain as they slogged through one sixteen-hour day after another....

Jim Panyard, a veteran Philadelphia *Bulletin* correspondent whose seniority and centrally located desk made him unofficial newsroom host, had sent his family out of the area Thursday morning. "I work here," he said matter-of-factly. "If I left I'd lose my job." Panyard was rumpled, tired, tense, and angry. He could cover a legislative session in his sleep, but this was unlike anything he had handled before. Sources seemed to speak a foreign language, he said with a sigh. You asked them a straight question about how much radiation is escaping and they answered with mumbo-jumbo about millirems, manrems, rads, and picocuries. Once you had figured out what they were saying you discovered another source was saying something different—and without a nuclear physics degree you couldn't come up with the right follow-up question to tell who was lying. "We've been given complete misinformation and conflicting statements from the N.R.C. here, the N.R.C. in Washington, the governor's office, and the utility," Panyard said. "There is no doubt that the situation is dangerous, but how dangerous is the question. I'm concerned, and I think other reporters are too." . . .

A Technical Tale

At the beginning, at least, the vast majority of reporters had no idea what anybody was talking about. Anchorless on a sea of rads and rems and roentgens, of core vessels and containments and cooling systems, they built their stories around the discrepancies between sources, confident that the news, when they finally came to understand it, would center on the facts in dispute. What is surprising about the T.M.I. coverage that emerged is not that it was sometimes technically wrong, but that it was so often technically right.

It's Monday noon in the Middletown Borough Hall gymnasium, and [Harold] Denton and [Roger] Mattson [N.R.C. officials] are holding court before some 200 reporters who have battled for a precious spot where they can both see and hear. Denton stands on the free-throw line, half hidden behind a forest of microphones. There's no PA system yet, and transcripts are still iffy, so you have to listen hard. Curious townspeople drift in and out of the bleachers, marveling at the cameras and frowning at the cusswords. The big news is the shrinking bubble, of course, but later someone asks how the accident started. Here's Mattson's answer, praised by reporters as the clearest and most complete chronology of what had happened:

> The steps leading to the situation we're in today can roughly be character-ized as the loss of feedwater on the secondary side of the power plant; a rise in pressure on the primary side of the reactor power plant; a discharge of coolant through the pressurizer; the initiation of the backup safety injection system, the emergency core cooling system which comes on automatically on high containment pressure, or loss of coolant from the facility; the continued high pressure of the facility with the high pressure injection system actuated; then the turning off of the safety injection system for some period of time; . . . and shortly thereafter the reinitiation of the emergency core cooling system after a gas situation that develops in the reactor core, for the emergency core cooling system by itself without a loss of cooling accident was unable to keep down the temperature in the core. That was finally stabilized by reestablishing the flow of the primary coolant and by restarting the main reactor coolant pump, the one that is still running.

That's it—no wall chart, no glossary, no technical experts hanging around afterward for questions. Okay, now write a few grafs on what went wrong at the plant. Or walk across the gym to your phone, call your station, and tell your listeners how the accident happened. (When that's done, try to discover if the N.R.C. is hiding anything.)

The reporters who were given this technical assignment fell into four categories, judging by responses to questionnaires we handed out.

• About a third were frankly bewildered. They relaxed when the questioning turned momentarily nontechnical, took frantic verbatim notes when the going got rough, and stopped writing altogether when it got rougher still. They seldom asked questions, but the questions they did ask often brought the briefings back to basics: "Just how dangerous is this?" "What are the chances of an evacuation now?" These were the reporters whose recurring nightmare was that Denton would announce a meltdown in technical language and they wouldn't realize what had happened. After each news conference they gathered in small knots to compare notes, and whenever possible they checked their stories against wire copy before filing. Included in this category were most of the non-network broadcasters, reporters from small newspapers, almost everyone who covered the story alone, and almost everyone who arrived later than Saturday ("fresh meat," rotated in because of radiation anxiety.)

• Only a handful of reporters knew much about nuclear power before they reached T.M.I. They were all science and energy writers—although not all the science and energy writers qualified. At the briefings they asked highly technical questions. Between briefings they badgered the information people to call the plant for specific data, quickly collecting an audience of colleagues who wondered aloud what they wanted to know that for. Stuart Diamond of *Newsday* typified this breed. Most out-of-towners landed in Harrisburg with only the clothes on their backs and a notebook; Diamond brought along his Rolodex and reference books from past nuclear stories, and spent hours on a borrowed phone at the Harrisburg *Patriot* calling his network of expert sources.

• Nearly a quarter of the reporters had a single expert on tap—a source from an earlier story, a science writer back in the office, or a paid consultant on the scene. These reporters often read their questions at briefings, stumbling over the jargon; they couldn't ask follow-ups until they had checked with their expert to find out what the first answer meant. If the expert was nearby, the system worked. NBC, ABC, and the *Chicago Tribune* all got good mileage out of their technical consultants, but CBS probably got the most for its money. Long Island radiologist Harry Astarita arrived Friday evening to check the radiation badges of the CBS crew. Quickly dubbed "Radiation Harry," he wound up checking copy as well—and prompting reporters with questions, scotching phony stories, and correcting false analogies. He even managed an exclusive two-hour off-the-record interview with a Met Ed engineer to get the reactor schematics straight. We wanted to talk to Astarita. He could only spare us a minute, he apologized happily: "I have to make a deadline."

• The rest of the reporters made *themselves* into experts—fast. In the wee hours of Sunday morning, reporters at Lombardo's (Harrisburg's plushest bar) clustered around Ben Livingood as though he were Harold Denton himself, while Livingood drew diagrams on cocktail napkins to explain the dynamics of the hydrogen bubble. Livingood is a political reporter for the Allentown *Call-Chronicle*. "I don't know what happened," mused a colleague. "None of us knew anything about this stuff Wednesday. Ben went away for six hours, and when he came back, he knew it." On Friday, Livingood turned to a Penn state nuclear engineer for help and he continued to use him on background throughout the crisis. But, like many other reporters, Livingood himself acquired an impressive amount of nuclear expertise at T.M.I. (It helped, he says, that he "tried not to get stuck on the conflicting-sources angle.")

The science writers on the scene weren't a lot better off than aggressive political reporters like Livingood. "Unless you were a nuclear scientist," ABC energy specialist Roger Peterson later told *The New York Times,* "you didn't know what on earth was going on"—and science writers are seldom nuclear scientists. There were perhaps forty full-time science journalists at the site, about a fifth of the nation's total. Some, like the *Milwaukee Journal's* Paul Hayes, covered the story alone, while others, like *The Boston Globe's* Jerry Ackerman, were part of a team. Either way, their stories on the breaking news were almost indistinguishable from what general assignment reporters produced. They did have a head start on the backgrounders, but many editors decided that the backgrounders could be written just as well back at the office. The big advantage went to those few science writers with a personal file of expert contacts. While *Newsday's* Diamond and the few others who had covered nuclear power extensively ran up long-distance phone bills, their colleagues scrambled—often unsuccessfully—for someone knowledgeable to interview in town.

Left with the Flacks

Even biased sources were scarce. Anti-nuclear experts Ernest Sternglass and George Wald came to Harrisburg for a press conference on Thursday, and then took off again. Mobilization for Survival, a Philadelphia-based anti-nuclear group, and Three Mile Alert, a small Harrisburg affiliate, co-sponsored the Sternglass and Wald visits, but reporters who called Alert's unlisted phone number over the weekend were lugubriously informed by an answering service that everyone was gone and would stay gone until it was safe to return.

The nuclear industry wasn't afraid of radiation; it was afraid of reporters. Hundreds of industry experts crowded the nearby motels, ID tags and dosimeters clipped to their lapels. The Atomic Industrial Forum, never before at a loss for words, sat vigil with Met Ed's publicists in their suite at the posh Hershey Motor Lodge, but it gave no interviews.

Any expert at T.M.I., however biased, would have had a captive audience of hundreds. In the absence of experts, PR people ruled the roost. And charges of cover-up aside, the PR logistics were intolerably bad. Karl Abraham arrived from the N.R.C. regional office in suburban Philadelphia on Wednesday, but he had no back-up until Friday afternoon and no press facility, apart from Critchlow's office, until Sunday night. Critchlow and his deputy, Roland Page, meanwhile, were busy asking questions on behalf of the governor; they left the question-answering to the junior staff, who mostly just took messages.

Even getting through to the N.R.C. by phone was virtually impossible during the first four days. And when a reporter did reach the office, more often than not the question had to be relayed to a technical specialist, a task that took hours more. Logistics slowly began improving when the N.R.C. got its Middletown facility in operation Monday. By then the commission had emptied its regional offices and had seven of its ten PR professionals in Pennsylvania and the other three in Washington. But they were quickly overwhelmed by the sheer volume of the requests. Moreover, until Monday night, when safety engineer Robert Bernero arrived, the N.R.C. did not have a single technical expert assigned to talk to reporters at T.M.I. Tom Elsasser, an engineer who normally handles relations with state officials, had filled the vacant briefer's slot Sunday and had done his best.

Running with the Pack

Meanwhile, reporters helped each other. Viewed from the desk, T.M.I. was a hotly competitive story, and few reporters escaped a daily call from an editor asking why they had missed an angle. But viewed from the site, the story required collaboration. From the moment the Harrisburg press corps heard about the accident, explains *The Philadelphia Inquirer's* Tom Ferrick, "we all shared information. We got drawings and pieced together the sequence of events at the plant. We went out and got books on nuclear energy and compared them and discussed how a reactor works." Newspaper Enterprise Association columnist Bob Walters calls this "pack journalism at its worst." To reporters trying to get a technical story right, without ready access to the experts, it seemed like good sense.

Three Mile Island offered few alternatives to pack journalism. Reporters occasionally found a fresh color angle, or broke away from the herd with a background piece—but the main event was inside the T.M.I. reactor, and information on that event had to come from the N.R.C. or Met Ed. A few individual news organizations managed to stand out—the A.P. with its detailed play-by-plays of conflicting statements; *The Washington Post* with its unmatched contacts at N.R.C. headquarters (the *Post* covered the story more from Washington than from Pennsylvania); *The Philadelphia Inquirer* with its all-out muckraking zeal. But enterprise reporting rarely dominates a breaking story, certainly not a breaking technical story. Most hard news pieces on T.M.I. were interchangeable. And most of the reporters who wrote them collaborated like unprepared students on an unfair homework assignment: "What have you got for how big the bubble is this morning?"

When they got something wrong, they all got it wrong. Most reporters parroted misleading information about radiation exposure for days—even weeks—after the accident. At the beginning they ignored the differences between the radiation dose per hour in a plume that passes by, the cumulative dose received by a person who stays in Middletown, and the continuing radiation from a particle of Iodine-131 that is absorbed by the thyroid. Some of these errors were cleared up by the end of the week, but Met Ed's false comparison of radiation-leak dosage with X-rays lasted much longer: your whole body is not exposed to a chest or dental X-ray, a difference reporters unconsciously acknowledged by crossing their legs whenever radioactivity was discussed.

The news about radiation at Three Mile Island was generally reassuring. But somehow neither readers nor reporters were reassured. On April 9 Bill Drummond did a sensitive piece on radiation anxiety in the *Los Angeles Times,* based largely on interviews with psychologists. He could as easily have interviewed reporters. "I felt safer in Biafra than I do here," said Ray Coffey of the *Chicago Tribune.* "I'd be a lot happier if we could paint this shit purple or make it smell." . . .

29. REPORTERS AND CONGRESSMEN: LIVING IN SYMBIOSIS

Susan Heilmann Miller

Editor's Note. Conflict usually makes more exciting news than cooperation. But not always. Miller's essay presents a case study of close cooperation
between a member of Congress and reporters who worked together so that each
could achieve a major purpose. The member needed publicity for the problems
of several constituents so that pressure for congressional hearings would mount.
These hearings would then lead to action by the executive branch. The
reporters were eager for tip-offs on governmental wrongdoing so that they could
write exciting investigative stories and claim credit for engendering appropriate
remedies. Ultimately, through a combination of luck and clever planning, the
venture attracted substantial attention from television. With wide media
coverage the barrier of obscurity was broken, and this along with several other
favorable factors put the issue on the congressional agenda.

The data for the case study come from interviews conducted in 1975 with
65 reporters representing newspapers, news magazines, television, and news
services; 25 members of Congress; 97 congressional aides; and 5 other observers.
The author also monitored relevant congressional hearings, as well as media
coverage of the story in the *Washington Post,* the *Los Angeles Times,* the
Chicago Tribune, and the New Orleans *Times-Picayune.*

Susan Heilmann Miller is a Stanford Ph.D. who has applied her
journalism training by working for newspapers and journalism publications.
This essay is excerpted from her doctoral dissertation,"Congress and the News
Media." The selection is reprinted from *Journalism Monographs,* No. 53,
1978.

A good example of the extent to which cooperation [between members of
Congress and reporters] can be carried was an investigation that eventually
led to a series of hearings on the plight of ·U.S. citizens serving time in
Mexican jails.

It began with a letter that arrived in the Washington office of California
Congressman Fortney "Pete" Stark in the spring of 1974. The letter, from

---

Reprinted with permission from *Journalism Monographs* No. 53 (January 1978): Susan
Heilmann Miller, "Reporters and Congressmen: Living in Symbiosis."

the family of an American being held in a Mexican jail, told of torture and extortion, and charged that personnel at the U.S. embassy in Mexico City had been less than responsive about investigating the situation. The writers, Stark's constituents, had first approached him through his district office in Oakland, California. Then a second family was heard from.

David Julyan, at that time a special assistant to Congressman Stark, told the families he would look into the matter, and he soon found other families with similar complaints. Prisoners were expected to pay for food, showers and toilet paper, costing up to $100 per month, and there was also an initial "lodging" fee of $800 to $2,000. All prisoners had to pay, but the fees for Americans appeared to be higher. Some families had also been victimized by lawyers who promised reduced or suspended sentences and then absconded with thousands of dollars more. Some prisoners said they had been sexually abused, tortured, forced to sign confessions they didn't understand, and otherwise denied legal rights and due process as provided by Mexican law and international accords. . . .

Once Stark decided to take on the prisoners' cause, the challenge was to gather enough information to demonstrate the need for a Congressional inquiry. As a junior member of Congress, Stark didn't have chairmanship of a committee with proper jurisdiction. He would have to convince his Congressional colleagues that the topic warranted their attention. The best way to do this, in the minds of Stark and his staff, was to collaborate with an investigative reporter. Stark explained, "We've done other things that way, too. . . . You go to an investigative reporter if you think he'll put some effort into it. . . . Sometimes you play boy editor—try to guess where a story fits, and who might be interested in it."

In this case, the obvious first choice was the Washington bureau of the Los Angeles *Times*. First of all, many of the families of prisoners lived in Southern California. The *Times* has a solid national reputation for investigative reporting. The news service it provides jointly with the Washington *Post* reaches hundreds of newspapers all over the country. Hundreds of copies of the *Times* itself are flown in each day from Los Angeles for distribution to Washington officialdom. Furthermore, the Washington bureau makes a point of staying in close contact with the entire California delegation. . . .

. . . [B]ureau chief Jack Nelson was available—and interested. . . . He and Julyan struck a bargain. As Julyan explained, "I said we'd like to share the story with them if they'd agree to go big. . . . Or, if they didn't go, we wanted their word they'd not disclose anything if they decided to drop it." There was also a confidentiality clause:

> They'd not make public anything without the approval of a source who had given us something on a confidential basis, or without *our* approval if it was from somebody in prison. . . . We'd show them everything we had in our files, and they'd agree not to disclose anything without our approval.

Nelson looked at what they had, and liked it. He notified *Times* editors in Los Angeles, and they agreed to put both a reporter in Los Angeles and the

Times reporter in Mexico City on the story. Nelson pointed out that the understandings about confidentiality, as well as understandings about sharing information, were "more implied than anything else. It's understood by anyone who has, shall we say, played the game." He added, "I give a staff member something and if he can, he follows it up. And if he can help me, he will. Of course, a part of that is that anything I tell him, he won't release to another reporter." ...

Pete Stark pointed out that a big advantage of working with the Los Angeles *Times* was that the paper had a reporter based in Mexico City. "It wasn't feasible for us to go to Mexico at that time," he said, adding, "One of our big concerns at that point was: What if we're wrong? What if these people are making up this stuff? We'd look pretty silly. The information from the Los Angeles *Times* was our first independent, unbiased review, and verified that the problems were real."

Nelson added that there were advantages to the *Times* to working with Stark.

> They had a lot of information volunteered to them—because they were part of Congress—that probably wouldn't have been volunteered to us, or that we would have had to work so hard to get that it wouldn't have been worthwhile. We wouldn't have had the time or the resources to pursue the story without their information. People were less reluctant to talk to them than they would have been to talk to a reporter. On the other hand, I interviewed the head of DEA [Drug Enforcement Agency] and got information and things they had no way to get—or, they wouldn't have gotten the same reaction, because we're reporters and they aren't.

In summary, each side had certain sources, skills or assets that the other lacked. By putting their heads and their information together, the Los Angeles *Times* and Stark's staff were able to come up with a more complete picture than either could have gotten on its own.

The cooperation went even further than the sharing of information and sources. Julyan and Nelson also coordinated the timing of the release of their information. There was nothing in the press from mid-September to the first week in December. Both were working as quietly as possible until there were enough data for Congressman Stark to make public allegations about embassy insensitivity and perhaps criminal culpability to support his call for a thorough investigation, plus enough data for a six-part series in the Los Angeles *Times*. Just as the series began to appear, Stark released a copy of a letter he had sent to President Ford and Secretary of State Kissinger, outlining the situation, and suggesting a course of action. The *Times* ran a separate story about Stark's letter on the second day of the series.

Explained Julyan, "Of course they knew it was being written, and when it would be released. We wanted to feed one off the other. It was a good handle for a story for them, and it was good for us to get the publicity for our letter and for the issue." He added, "It was a natural outgrowth of the confidence and cooperation built up over that eight-week period that we plan the timing. Besides, we had so much lead time. We knew three weeks ahead when their series would run, and we had a tacit agreement to coincide." . . .

In the second article, Jack Nelson described the hesitancy of U.S. embassy officials to deal with the prisoners' charges of torture and other forms of mistreatment. He noted they evidently did not want to offend the Mexican government and observed they tended to play down or deny accusations. He also noted, "If embassy personnel have difficulty in finding out about arrests, Mexican lawyers have no such difficulty." Nelson then detailed complaints by American parents that a lawyer to whom they had paid thousands of dollars and gotten no assistance had been recommended by U.S. consular official Danny Root. Root denied the charges. U.S. counsel general Peter Peterson said that he couldn't believe that Root would have done such a thing and the parents must have misunderstood what Root was saying.

The third story, again . . . from Mexico City, carried other comments by Peterson. He denied that the U.S. government was pressuring Mexico to keep the Americans in prison. . . . The fourth story . . . was based on interviews with State Department officials in Washington. Joseph Livornese, acting director of the State Department office of special consular affairs, stated that U.S. embassies were limited in what they were able to do for Americans arrested in foreign countries. He noted that the State Department had sent a protest note to the Mexican government in July after receiving numerous reports of brutality and extortion against American prisoners. Although the note and several others had not been answered formally, Livornese pointed to fewer arrests of Americans at the Mexico City airport in recent weeks as evidence that the Mexican government was responding to the complaint. . . .

The fifth story . . . described the "appallingly similar" stories of the heavy-handed techniques Mexican prison officials used to extort money and the high-pressure techniques of Mexican attorneys, one of whom contacted families through a cousin in Los Angeles. It was headlined, "Mexican Drug Busts: The Families Also Pay." The final story . . . pointed out that although Mexico was believed to supply 60 per cent of the heroin reaching the U.S.—and that U.S. officials were praising Mexico's recently stepped up efforts to stem the influx—heroin was not much of a problem in Mexico. Ironically, the number one drug problem there was glue sniffing. The implication was that the drug arrests of Americans in Mexico were being carried out as a courtesy to the U.S.

The primary interest of the Los Angeles *Times* in working with Stark and his aides had been to gather enough information to produce a series of articles. Their daily contact ended with the running of the series.

However, for the people in Congress, the work was just beginning. A few weeks after Stark's letter and press release, some State Department personnel visited his office, talked with Julyan and agreed to launch an investigation. There were a few stories about the investigation during the first few months of 1975, but relatively little media interest in the issue and few efforts by Stark or Julyan to push it. Then, in March, Stark became dissatisfied with what he considered a lack of action—even interest. Said Julyan, "We came out of low profile. We started beating the drum—saying that State was doing a whitewash, and we didn't trust their investigation, and it should be given to the House."

Julyan drafted a resolution of inquiry—a privileged motion that calls for the gathering of information. Once referred to a Congressional committee, it must be acted on within a specified period of time. Explained Julyan, "It's very difficult to get a hearing in Congress. You've got to figure out how to get your issue to the front of the hearing list." ...

... The first of what was to be a series of hearings on U.S. citizens imprisoned in Mexico was held at the end of April. It was largely based on information that Congressman Stark and the Los Angeles *Times* had gathered, and both Stark and David Julyan were invited to testify. The committee [International Policy and Military Affairs subcommittee] also heard from numerous State Department officials.

The outcome was that the subcommittee asked Stark to select 15 test cases. It then asked the State Department to prepare an extensive report on the allegations these prisoners were making and on what the State Department could do about them. ... When the State Department reported back to the subcommittee in July, it was once again pointed out that the department's authority in a foreign country was limited and suggested that many of the charges voiced by Stark and the prisoners had been exaggerated.

This time the subcommittee was skeptical. The hearing was closed, and the written transcripts of all such hearings are edited before they are published to avoid not only security leaks and diplomatic blunders, but also minor embarrassments. ...

Even though the hearing was closed, there was a lot about it in the press. Congressmen Stark and [Dante] Fascell had an impromptu press conference afterwards, releasing a copy of Stark's testimony and others' comments. Reporters got wind of everything else from the various "principals" or their aides.

By this time press interest in the topic was beginning to mount. No more than a month later, the August 14 issue of *Rolling Stone* magazine carried an article entitled "The Black Palace and the Women of Santa Marta: Tales of Torture, Extortion and Abandonment by the U.S. Embassy from Americans Currently Imprisoned on Drug Charges in Mexico." The Black Palace and Santa Marta are two of the many men's and women's prisons where Americans are being held. ... Essentially, it was the same story that the Los Angeles *Times* had told six months earlier, even down to some of the same examples. And, like the *Times'* stories, it referred to the efforts being made by Pete Stark.

The difference was that, for reasons peculiar to journalism, this story triggered interest in the rest of the nation's news media. Some people call it agenda-setting: the ability of some media to define which topics their readers talk about and other media carry. Various media are recognized as having preeminence in particular subject areas. For international news it's the New York *Times;* for Washington news, the wire service daybooks; for national domestic issues, the Washington *Post;* and for anything that might be considered "anti-establishment" or "counter culture," the agenda-setting publication is *Rolling Stone.*[1] Thus it was that, shortly after the August 14 story appeared, Stark's office began getting phone calls from reporters....

In addition to the various newspaper stories, there was a piece on NBC News and a ten-minute spot on the "Today" show. Both were tied to the third hearing, in October, 1975. Explained Julyan, "We suggested they tie it to the hearings for a news peg. That's true of a lot of people. We'll suggest they may want to wait a day or two to tie their story to something coming up."...

The October hearing was open to the press, and the news media were there in force. Once again the State Department representatives indicated that there was a limit to what they could do, and in any case their investigation of prisoners' complaints was being hampered by the sheer number of cases. By now there were 550 Americans in Mexican jails—most of them on drug offenses....

A few days later the committee sent a letter of protest to Secretary of State Kissinger and released a copy to the media. By now, the committee had become impatient with both the U.S. government and the Mexican government and felt that media publicity was its best hope of getting changes in the treatment of Americans arrested in Mexico. Shortly after the October hearing subcommittee staffer Mike Finley explained:

> The Mexican case has gotten to a certain point where it's my opinion and I think it's also Mr. Fascell's that we need to change the attitude of the Mexican government by getting our own executive branch to say something—or by getting the American people so upset that it makes an impression on the Mexican government regardless of what the executive branch is doing. We're now trying deliberately to get publicity. Trying to spark interest with publicity. Trying to get the word to the Mexican government that the U.S. Congress is not going to forget about the issue.
>
> Here, the press has involvement, a role to play—if we can assume the press were a passive instrument, and that's not quite the case. But we realize that if they report something it can help our cause and we can use that for our ends. What can we do to get publicity? We can ask a prisoner to take off his clothes and show us his scars in front of the glowing TV lights. That's what I mean by the press having a role to play in what we do. We might get total cooperation of the executive branch and still not get anywhere with the Mexican government. But if we get people so upset that it cuts down on tourism, now *that* will make an impression. If we get Walter Cronkite saying Mexico is a lousy place, that will have an impact on the Mexican government with or without anything our government does.

He added, "We're seriously considering bringing in prisoners to testify. We may do that in January. There are different ways to use the press."

Explained Congressman Stark:

> The problem with dealing with a bureaucracy is that the people seem to be incapable of changing. They keep saying, "We've done nothing wrong....

We've done everything according to our regulations." There's no way to get them to try something different. The only thing they understand is that you can ridicule them in the media. Make them look silly. They respond then, because they don't like to be laughed at.

A few days after the October hearing, the Washington *Star* ran an extensive front-page story outlining the positions of Stark, the subcommittee, the State Department and the Mexican government. . . .

What began with a letter from two families to their Congressman eventually became an issue that dozens of Congressmen were hearing from constituents about, that a Congressional subcommittee was investigating and that the State Department was being forced to reconsider. It would later lead to efforts to arrange a prisoner exchange. When the first American prisoners returned to the U.S. in December, 1977, Congressman Stark and the news media were conspicuously present.

The news media functioned in a variety of ways to make the prisoners an issue. Stark believes that one of the most important functions in the early stages was to establish the validity of the prisoners' complaints. Said Stark, "The Los Angeles *Times* series gave us a certain legitimacy. There's always a question in Congress of raising hell, demanding an investigation, and then not having anything to back it up. . . . The press did two things: It provided information and legitimized the issue."

However, the Los Angeles *Times* series apparently played only a minor part in actually bringing about the hearings. People associated with the subcommittee insisted they would have responded regardless of whether there had been prior publicity in the press. . . . David Julyan explained, "We wanted a Congressional forum . . . and we used both the resolution of inquiry and press interest as an argument to Congressman Fascell. . . . Our argument was that it was a good issue and that the press had generated a lot of public interest. "But," said Julyan, "the press by itself wouldn't have been sufficient." Nor did the investigative reporting itself bring about any immediate response from the State Department. . . .

However, press coverage did get television into the act. Said Stark:

When the press gets the electronic media interested, two things happen. You get far broader coverage. Ten minutes on the "Today" show gets interest all over the country, and the electorate hears about the issue. Secondly, when the electronic media come to a hearing, you get all the members there. They start to demagogue and become more attentive and assertive. Witnesses from the State Department start to act and sound much more concerned. So, what happens is that TV at a hearing gets *everybody* sounding more concerned about the issue—and that gets a certain sense of importance for the issue.

Of course, TV coverage also broadened the mail, and then other Congressmen referred their complaints to us.

In other words, coverage of the issue served two different but complementary functions. It directly changed the public behavior of State Department officials. It also generated interest among the electorate. This, in turn, increased the interest of members of Congress in getting further modifications in State Department policies and routines.

Finally, coverage of both the hearings and the general topic served still another function. It put the Mexican government on notice that U.S. citizens, Congress and the State Department were pressuring for a change.... Mexican officials—like their U.S. counterparts—are conscious of their public images and anxious to avoid unfavorable publicity. Thus, the fact that the U.S. news media were now championing the prisoners' plight may have been as potent a political force as anything Congress itself could do.

NOTES

1. For a general discussion of the agenda-setting function, see Maxwell E. McCombs and Donald L. Shaw, "The Agenda-Setting Function of Mass Media," *Public Opinion Quarterly* 36:176-187 (Summer 1972). It was Bernard Cohen, *The Press and Foreign Policy* (Princeton: Princeton University Press, 1963) who first called attention to the phenomenon. Carol Weiss, "What America's Leaders Read," *Public Opinion Quarterly,* 38:1-22 (Spring 1974); Raymond Bauer, Ithiel de Sola Pool and Lewis Anthony Dexter, *American Business and Public Policy* (New York: Prentice Hall, 1963); and Clark Mollenhoff, *Washington Cover-Up* (Garden City, N.Y.: Doubleday 1962) and *Tentacles of Power* (Cleveland: World, 1965) give examples of public officials whose agendas are influenced by those of the news media. The data here tend to show that the process, as between reporters and Congressional sources, is a reciprocal one.

30. TRANSNATIONAL TERRORISM
AND THE WESTERN ELITE PRESS

Micheal J. Kelly and Thomas H. Mitchell

Editor's Note. Newspeople are acutely aware that terrorists perform as they do for the sake of publicity and that the media play into the hands of terrorists when they give prominent coverage to their acts. Beyond advertising the goals of terrorists, media coverage may also provoke copycat disturbances. But if the media fail to publish the story prominently, they neglect their duty to give appropriate coverage to newsworthy events. They may also lose out to their competitors. In addition, they can be accused of unfairly denying terrorist groups a hearing for their cause at a time when terrorists could normally expect to draw widespread attention. This dilemma is unfortunate for newspeople and for policy makers concerned about the consequences of terrorism.

The issues raised by Kelly and Mitchell are relevant for domestic terrorism, including hostage taking and airplane hijacking. The authors' finding that coverage of terrorist activities may be counterproductive for terrorist groups sheds new light on an intriguing subject.

Both authors teach political science at Canadian universities. Micheal J. Kelly is affiliated with the University of Ottawa and Thomas H. Mitchell with Carlton University. They have contributed to the report, "Collective Conflict, Violence and the Media in Canada," issued by the Ontario Royal Commission on Violence in the Communications Industry. The selection is from *Political Communication and Persuasion,* 1 (1981): 269-296. Several tables have been omitted.

... [D]espite the preoccupation of scholars with the phenomenon of terrorism, there has been relatively little research undertaken to date of a rigorous methodological nature.[1] Nowhere is this lack of empirical research more obvious than in the analysis of the role of the news media, which is perhaps the terrorists' most important weapon. Recognizing this apparent gap in the literature, this paper will attempt to combine a theoretical discussion of the relationship between transnational terrorism and the news media with an empirical examination of how the Western press has dealt with incidents of

Political Communication and Persuasion, Volume 1 Number 3, (1981) pages 269-296. Copyright © 1981 Crane, Russak & Company, Inc., New York 10017.

terrorism. First, however, it is necessary to define and clarify some of the basic concepts used in this analysis.

The most basic concept of course is that of "terrorism" itself. One of the more useful definitions of terrorism, and one which was adopted for the purpose of this study, is that developed by Thomas P. Thornton. Thornton views terrorism as a "symbolic act designed to influence political behavior by extranormal means, entailing the use or threat of violence." [2] This definition suggests that terrorism is, above all else, a form of psychological warfare whose prime purpose is to propagandize and disorient a target population by attacking certain symbols of the state and the society. Terrorism's efficiency is premised on its symbolic nature. It is a psychological rather than a military strategy. It is aimed at creating a climate of fear by carrying out violent acts in what appears to be an unpredictable and indiscriminate fashion, while attracting attention to the terrorists' grievances and goals. As has often been suggested in the literature, terrorism is the weapon of the weak.[3] Terrorism provides an opportunity for a relatively small number of activists to achieve a substantial propaganda impact, in many cases out of all proportion to the real significance of the incident.[4] Looking at the balance sheet of casualties from terrorist incidents is indicative. While, according to one study the number of deaths resulting from all incidents of transnational terrorism for the period from 1968 to 1976 was approximately 800, the homicide rate in the United States in any given year is said to approach 20,000.[5] In sheer military terms the terrorist group is in most cases a miniscule force; its tactical strength, however, derives from its ability to attract publicity for its cause. The ultimate objective of the terrorist group is to undermine the legitimacy of established governments by revealing them to be either brutally repressive or simply incapable of maintaining order and public safety.

The success of a terrorist group depends on a number of factors, including its degree of internal organization, its efficiency in carrying out operations, and perhaps most important, its ability to generate attention, recognition, and legitimacy for its cause. Because of their generally small membership and lack of political resources, terrorist groups are increasingly sensitive to the kinds of activities and tactics that are likely to be included in the nightly television news or reach the front page of the daily newspaper. The Western mass media through their attention provide the terrorist group with the credibility it might not otherwise have. As we have suggested, terrorism per se is relatively trivial in terms of casualty figures and property damage. What creates the climate of extreme anxiety known as terror is the group's ability to publicize its actions and create the impression that no one is truly safe or secure. As Walter Laqueur has suggested, "the media are the terrorist's best friend (others might suggest accomplice), the terrorist act by itself is nothing, publicity is all." [6] In a very real sense the media give terrorism the potential of being an effective strategy. Modern terrorists are keenly aware of the kinds of actions and operations that newspapers and electronic media are likely to report. The symbiotic relationship between the journalist and the terrorist is a frequently discussed and often documented phenomenon.[7]

While there are admittedly several different categories of terrorism, this study focuses on the transnational variety, which appears to be the most media-oriented. . . .

To a large extent, many previous studies of terrorism and the media have concentrated on the contagion hypothesis, rather than on the actual use of the media by terrorists. For instance, it has been argued that one of the major consequences resulting from extensive media coverage of terrorism is the exportation of violent techniques which in turn often trigger extreme actions by other individuals or groups. To paraphrase Clutterbuck, bombings beget bombings, hijackings beget hijackings, and assassinations beget assassinations.[8] As usually stated, however, the contagion hypothesis is fraught with conceptual and methodological difficulties.[9] Moreover, as communications researcher George Gerbner indicates, the contagion hypothesis has been greatly misunderstood. Gerbner argues that the most pervasive effect of broadcast violence is not the imitation of violence, but the spreading of intimidation, of the fear of victimization. Terror, he argues, can only succeed if the act is conveyed to the audience whose behavior the terrorist is seeking to influence.[10] Far from being concerned about the imitation of his method, the terrorist seeks rather to communicate his existence and his power. Therefore, it is essential to examine transnational terrorism as a form of political communication. The continuing existence of the terrorist, as well as his credibility, is based on his ability to attract and hold the attention of the news media. The fortunes of the terrorist, like those of the politician, can rise and fall at the whim of the press. The analysis that follows seeks to examine how "terrorist communications" are treated by the Western news media. While it is impossible to gauge the effect such communications have on the subject audience, we can nevertheless obtain a good indication of how effective the terrorist is in attracting publicity. . . .

Two major world newspapers were selected for content analysis: *The New York Times* and *The Times* of London.[11] Not only are these newspapers opinion leaders in their own cities but both also have wide influence on their respective continents. Therefore, an analysis of the news contents of these papers should give us a good indication of how terrorist incidents are reported in the news media in Western Europe and North America—the major audiences which a great many of the terrorists seek to reach by their actions.

The data on transnational terrorism were taken from Brian Jenkins and Janera Johnson, *International Terrorism: A Chronology 1968-1974*. This chronology contains a total of 507 incidents for the seven-year period.[12] A random sample of 158 incidents was drawn from this chronology.[13] These 158 incidents were then located in both newspapers and the coverage recorded. . . .

Terrorism and News Coverage

... [O]ur findings do indicate that terrorists were not completely unsuccessful in attracting media attention during this period. The 158 incidents of transnational terrorism surveyed generated a total 27,587 square inches of coverage. This coverage consisted of 629 articles, 277 photographs, and 26 editorials. Concerning our sample of incidents, *The New York Times* had a somewhat greater degree of coverage with 348 articles and 182 photographs. *The Times* of London carried 281 articles and 95 photographs. *The Times* of London led slightly in the volume of coverage devoting 13,846 square inches of news space to transnational terrorism, the equivalent of approximately 30 full pages. *The New York Times* in comparison had 13,741 square inches of coverage. *The Times* of London also led in the prominence given to incidents of transnational terrorism, having 134 first-page articles, including 35 headline articles. *The New York Times* had 120 first-page articles, including 25 headline articles.[14] In all, 31 percent (49) of all terrorist incidents surveyed received first-page coverage in *The Times* of London as compared to 20 percent (32) in *The New York Times*.

One of the most interesting findings was the extent to which certain acts of transnational terrorism were ignored by both newspapers. *The New York Times* overlooked, or did not consider newsworthy, 69 of the 158 incidents in the sample, a rather surprising 44 percent. Likewise, *The Times* of London ignored 68 incidents, or 43 percent. In the majority of instances, both newspapers declined to report the same incidents. The lack of coverage of certain incidents of transnational terrorism is noteworthy given the general impression that terrorist incidents almost always receive widespread publicity. This particular finding would seem to suggest the importance of focusing on the types of incidents and groups that make the news, as well as on the kind of coverage they receive.

From the outset, it was evident that each paper had a definite regional bias in its coverage of transnational terrorism. As Table 30-1 indicates, there are notable differences in regional coverage. *The New York Times* has an obvious North American and Middle East bias, although coverage of Central American terrorism was also relatively prominent. Interestingly enough, Western Europe, the major theater of transnational terrorism in this survey, was generally under-reported. Equally revealing was the lack of South American coverage. South America has some of the most highly organized and active terrorist groups in the world.[15] Moreover, the most frequent targets of such groups are American diplomatic and business personnel, and the property of large multinationals. Yet, with a few notable exceptions, these groups consistently failed to attract the attention of the Western press. *The Times* of London also had an obvious bias, focusing most of its coverage on Europe and the Middle East, although here too Central America received surprisingly prominent coverage. South American terrorism was again under-reported with barely over one-third of the incidents getting coverage. As far as the Western

Table 30-1 Coverage of Terrorism by Region

Region	Total Number Incidents	% Covered* The New York Times	% Covered* The Times
North America	21	81 (17)	48 (10)
Western Europe	47	51 (24)	68 (32)
Middle East	32	69 (22)	69 (22)
Central America	11	64 (7)	64 (7)
South America	33	42 (14)	36 (12)
Eastern Europe	3	33 (1)	100 (3)
Asia	7	43 (3)	43 (3)
Africa	4	25 (1)	50 (2)
Total Incidents	158	89	91

* All percentages rounded.

media seem to be concerned, South America is both out of sight and out of mind.

Transnational Terrorism: Tactics and Coverage

Given the generally acknowledged need of the terrorist for publicity, it is interesting to look at the kinds of techniques that the terrorist has used to capture and hold the attention of the media. What kinds of terrorist tactics were likely to get the most media coverage? To ascertain this, we broke our sample into eight general types of terrorism. . . .

The two major techniques used by transnational terrorists in our sample were bombings and hijackings. These two tactics accounted for 67 percent of all incidents of transnational terrorism. When we include kidnapping, we have accounted for over 80 percent of the sample. It is notable, however, that the ability of the various tactics to attract attention is varied. . . . [H]ijacking, kidnapping, and armed attacks were found to be the best methods for capturing the attention of the media. Bombing, on the other hand, which was by far the most popular tactic, was also the least likely to attract publicity. Fifty-nine percent of all bombings were ignored by both newspapers.

There was also significant variation in the amount of coverage given to the various types of terrorism. . . . [T]errorist murders got the most publicity, with typical coverage consisting of 9 articles and approximately 543 square inches in *The New York Times,* and 7 articles and 418 square inches in *The Times* of London. The only other terrorist tactic which received even half this amount of coverage was the "armed attack." Bombings, even when reported, received very little coverage. On the average, bombing incidents received minimal coverage in terms of both the number of articles and the volume of news space. The two tactics that generated the most coverage were notable for only one thing—the number of people killed or injured. . . .

The tactics that received the most extensive coverage did not necessarily always receive the most prominent coverage. . . . [W]hile an "armed attack" was likely to capture the headlines, no other terrorist technique was consistently able to generate this kind of coverage in either newspaper. It is also interesting that terrorist murders, the tactic that received by far the most extensive coverage, did not always receive equal consideration with respect to prominence of coverage. Twenty-three percent (5) of all terrorist murders made the headlines of *The New York Times,* whereas only fifteen percent (2) made the headlines of *The Times* of London. . . .

. . . There was a noticeable lack of effort to offer any explanation of what was happening and why. For the most part, the news coverage focused on the sensational aspects of the incident—the blood and gore, the horror of the victims, etc. . . .

In all, less than 10 percent of the coverage in either newspaper dealt in even the most superficial way with the grievances of the terrorists. When issues were discussed at all, it was usually in relation to incidents in which Palestinians were involved.[16] It would therefore seem that terrorism is not a very effective way to propagandize if one wants issues and goals to be known or understood.

In the first part of this study we made reference to the communications goals of terrorists, among which were attention, recognition, and legitimacy. Terrorism can be an effective strategy with respect to the first two goals, but the most important goal, legitimacy, upon which the ultimate success of terrorism is dependent, would seem to be seriously undermined by the kind of coverage the news media provide. The media buy only part of the terrorist's package. The terrorist's exploitation of the media turns into the media's exploitation of terrorism. The media seem only to be interested in the act of terrorism and have evidenced little concern for the underlying motivations or causes. If the psychological warfare goals of terrorism were as stated, that is to propagandize and create a climate of fear, it seems that the media help only with the latter. The terrorist is in something of a trap. The media will help him attract the attention of an audience but it will not let him transmit his message. The implications of this are disturbing. By sapping terrorism of its political content, the media turn the crusader into a psychopath.[17] This puts the terrorist in a situation where he is encouraged to continue to maim and kill without any hope of ever obtaining the political support that he needs to enact the transformation he seeks. It prolongs the agony of the victimizers as well as the victim. . . .

Our final conclusion is the one that is most disturbing. While the transnational terrorist frequently succeeds in attracting attention to himself and thus obtaining recognition of his existence, he is seldom capable of communicating his cause to the population whose attention he has attracted. Even the Palestinians were confronted with problems in articulating their causes. Although we have lumped the various Palestinian groups together for analytical purposes, the press seldom demonstrated the ability to distinguish among them, or their numerous different and frequent antagonistic objectives.

If terrorism is ultimately a battle for the hearts and minds, as the psychological warfare approach would suggest, it seems that the press is neither a totally reliable nor a totally effective weapon. . . .

NOTES

1. Notable exceptions to this are Edward Mickolus's work with the ITERATE Project (International Terrorism Attributes of Terrorist Events), the work of Dr. David Hubbard and associates at the Aberrant Behavior Center, and several research projects undertaken by the Rand Corporation under the direction of Brian Jenkins.
2. Thomas P. Thornton, "Terror as a Weapon of Political Agitation," in H. Eckstein, ed., *Internal War.* New York: Free Press, 1964, p. 73.
3. See Walter Laqueur, "The Futility of Terrorism," *Harper's,* 252 (March 1976), pp. 99-105.
4. For a discussion of the propaganda value of terrorism, see Carlos Marighella, *Minimanual of the Urban Guerrilla.* Havana, Cuba: Tricontinental, n.d.
5. United States, Central Intelligence Agency Research Study, *International and Transnational Terrorism: Diagnosis and Prognosis,* Washington, D.C., U.S. Government Printing Office, 1976, p. 23.
6. Laqueur, op. cit., p. 104.
7. See William J. Drummond and Augustine Zycher, "Arafat's Press Agents," *Harper's,* 252 (March 1976), pp. 24-30; William R. Catton, Jr., "Militants and the Media: Partners in Terrorism?" *Indiana Law Journal,* 53 (Summer 1978), pp. 703-15; Walter B. Jaehnig, "Journalists and Terrorism: Captives of the Libertarian Tradition," *Indiana Law Journal,* 53 (Summer 1978), pp. 717-44; Herbert A. Terry, "Television and Terrorism: Professionalism Not Quite the Answer," *Indiana Law Journal,* 53 (Summer 1978), pp. 745-77.
8. See Richard Clutterbuck, "Terrorism is Likely to Increase," *The Times* (London), April 10, 1975. . . .
9. See H. L. Nieburg, *Political Violence: The Behavioral Process.* New York: St. Martin's Press, 1969, p. 30; and Desmond Ellis, "Violence and the Mass Media," *Proceedings of the Workshop on Violence in Canadian Society.* Toronto: Centre of Criminology, University of Toronto, September 8-9, 1975, p. 92.
10. Cited in Walter B. Jaehnig, op. cit., pp. 723-24.
11. John C. Merrill ranks these two papers as first and fifth in the world in terms of overall quality. See John C. Merrill, *The Elite Press.* New York: Pitman Publishing, 1968, p. 45.
12. The Jenkins/Johnson chronology was compiled primarily from a review of *The New York Times,* the *Arab Record and Report,* the *Foreign Broadcast Information Service,* and a staff study prepared by the Committee on Internal Security, U.S. House of Representatives, 1973, entitled *Political Kidnapping 1968-1973,* as well as several other unofficial sources.
13. A sample of this size has a one percent tolerance limit. See H. W. Smith, *Strategies of Social Research: The Methodological Imagination.* Englewood Cliffs, New Jersey: Prentice-Hall, 1975, p. 126.
14. For the purpose of this analysis an article was considered a headline article if its placement was in the upper half of the first page. Other stories beginning below the fold on the first page, or located on any subsequent page were measured for total volume but were judged to be of lesser prominence.
15. A similar research finding was reached by Brian Jenkins in his article, "International Terrorism: Trends and Potentialities," *Journal of International Affairs,* 32 (Spring/Summer 1978), p. 119. See also Walter Laqueur, *Terrorism.* London:

Abacus, 1977, pp. 216-28.

16. Editorial coverage is difficult to gauge as we have no comparative figures. Five percent (8) of the incidents evoked editorial response from *The New York Times,* and *The Times* of London responded editorially to 8 percent (13) of the incidents. The Palestinians once again were the chief objects of editorial response.

17. Dr. Frederick Hacker offers a typology which distinguishes between "criminal" terrorists and what he calls "crazies" and "crusaders." The media treatment of terrorism would not allow one to make the distinction. See Frederick J. Hacker, *Crusaders, Criminals, Crazies: Terror and Terrorism in Our Time.* New York: Bantam, 1976.

31. TELEVISING THE VIETNAM WAR

David Halberstam

Editor's Note: The fact that most American homes had television sets made it possible for the Vietnam conflict to become a "living room" war. Many observers believe that people, including public officials, were turned against the war by vivid color scenes of death, suffering, and destruction. They also maintain that future wars cannot be fought for any length of time without encountering the same revulsion, if the public is made an eyewitness to battlefield horrors.

Be that as it may, David Halberstam, who saw the war firsthand and personally knew many leaders of government and press, presents his version of television's role in turning war hawks into doves. He describes how the early trivialization of the fighting in television newscasts gave way to displays of massive destruction, acts of brutality, and intolerable human suffering. The enemy, at first nearly invisible, emerged as a flesh and blood foe capable of winning major battles. All this took place in grisly visual detail, night after night after night. At the same time, reporters and the public were becoming increasingly disillusioned with the administration's widely publicized and unreliable victory predictions and with its constant deceptions about the nature and extent of American involvement. When Walter Cronkite finally made his celebrated announcement that the war was over for America, the groundwork for its acceptance had long ago been laid by other television newscasters.

David Halberstam is a Pulitzer Prize-winning journalist and author who has covered national and international news for a variety of papers, including the *New York Times*. His dispatches and books have provided many fresh insights into America's involvement in the Vietnam War and other crises. The selection is from *The Powers That Be*, New York: Alfred A. Knopf, 1979.

. . . Television in the beginning had trivialized both the debate and the forces involved in Vietnam. It had confirmed the legitimacy of the President, made his case seem stronger than it was, and made the opposition appear to be outcasts, frustrated, angry, and rather beyond the pale. The Fulbright*

---

* The Senate Foreign Relations Committee, headed by William Fulbright, held hearings on the conduct of the Vietnam War.

From *The Powers That Be*, by David Halberstam. Copyright © 1979 by David Halberstam. Reprinted by permission of Alfred A. Knopf, Inc.

hearings gradually changed this balance. . . . [T]hey were the beginning of a slow but massive educational process, a turning of the tide against the President's will and his awesome propaganda machinery. It was the ventilation of a serious opposition view (without it seeming to be the opposition party—most of the key members of the Fulbright committee were from the President's own party). From that time on, dissent was steadily more respectable and centrist. It was not that the opposition witnesses made such powerful cases against the war . . . it was the failure of the Administration under intense questioning to make a case *for* the war. It was not the opposition that won, it was the Administration that failed. This strengthened the frail heartbeat of the networks; they could always claim to the President, and quite rightly, that they had put on far more of his own witnesses than those of the opposition.

What the television cameras did to this particular war was to magnify, slowly but surely, its inconsistencies and brutalities. It was not a quick process; at the beginning, with the exception of an occasional devastating film clip, television was, in fact, very much on the team. It showed the government side far more than the antiwar side and there was often a pejorative tone to the voices of commentators in the early days of the antiwar protest, a certain distaste evinced. The major news shows accepted almost unquestioningly American goals and American statements. . . . In the early days much of the film seemed to center on action rather than the more substantive qualities of the war, an emphasis on what the television correspondents themselves called "bloody" or "bang-bang." There was a group of younger correspondents for CBS who felt that somehow the network was always managing to sanitize the war, that there was nervousness about using some of the harsher and bloodier footage.

If it was a consensus medium, then in the early days, the consensus was for the war, although gradually that changed. For two things happened: First, the war turned out to be very difficult and victory did not come quickly, the predictions of the great men in Washington were wrong; the other side controlled the rate of the war and they could either speed up or slow down the tempo depending on their, rather than our, needs. Thus the slowness, the cumulative sense of the war went against Washington, which had hoped for and planned a quick victory. And second, the camera caught the special quality of *this* war, magnified the impropriety and brutality of it, emphasized how awesome the American firepower was and that it was being used against civilians, that you could not separate civilian from combatant. The camera also magnified the length of the war; the beginning of the combat escalation came with the bombing in February 1965, and the Tet offensive, which sealed the doom of the American mission, came three years later, and three years was, in the television age, an infinitely longer time than it used to be. The war played in American homes and it played too long. It made the American involvement there seem endless, which it was.

But in the early days of the war television was quite respectable. No one seemed to symbolize the consensus and television's acceptance of it more than

Walter Cronkite. Later he changed as the nation changed, and he helped the nation to change faster. It was hard to tell who was leading whom; his own feelings on the war and his own responses a precise echo of American attitudes. In 1968 when Cronkite disassociated himself from the war, Lyndon Johnson knew it was all over, but in the early days Cronkite had accepted the government line and had in fact used his own credibility to amplify it. At his best he seemed to reflect the best of a kind of American tradition, essential good faith and trust; as a journalist he knew how hard to look and how hard not to look, and he had almost automatically given his trust to those who had titles and positions. . . .

He was, when he went to Saigon, what he himself termed a Kennan containment man; he did not doubt the seriousness of the corruption and the weakness of the South Vietnamese government, and he did not expect to see democracy flower, but he had been conditioned for a long time to the rhetoric of a generation, indeed he had helped push some of that rhetoric. In spite of all the dark shadows, he felt it was something we ought to do. Why bother to figure the cost, we were that rich. We might buy them some time, perhaps we could hold an umbrella long enough over the South Vietnamese so that something might grow there. A beginning. Besides, Cronkite was in essence a conventional man and this was the conventional wisdom at the time. He did not feel at ease in the early days with the people who were attacking the conventional wisdom, they were not his kind of people, and when he finally arrived in Saigon in 1965 he did not like the brashness of the younger correspondents who sat at the military briefings, tearing into the military officers.

So he gave the men who briefed him, men with several stars on their uniforms, the benefit of the doubt; he, like the rest of the country, was simply not ready to accept the idea that these same men who had fought and won the greatest war of the century did not know what they were talking about and, worse, were not to be trusted. . . .

He was also, whatever his sympathies on the war, the man who, as managing editor of the show, ultimately passed on the reporting of the younger, more alienated reporters from Vietnam, and while the CBS report from Saigon had its faults—the lack of time, the lack of a cumulative meaningful texture, an emphasis on bang-bang in film—it nonetheless distinguished itself by its coverage of Vietnam. To the American military it was known as the Communist Broadcasting Station. But CBS was better than the other two networks. . . . Though the CBS correspondents themselves often rebelled at the limits of their craft, at the brevity that forced them to trivialize, at their inability to say what they really felt and to vent their own growing anger and frustration, nonetheless television subliminally caught that even when the words were edited out, and the war as broadcast on CBS gradually came to seem both endless and hopeless.

As the sum of this kind of reporting began to mount, as the dates for victory set by the architects came and went, as the war dragged on, the country began to be affected by the hopelessness of it, and so too did Walter Cronkite

293 David Halberstam

Not the morality of it, war to him was war; but the disproportion of it, the fraud of it, increasing doubts about the credibility of the men running it. So he was changing and so was his audience and Walter Cronkite was always acutely aware of his audience and its moods; he was very good at leading and being led at the same time. The consensus was slipping and changing, time was beginning to work against Lyndon Johnson, as the President well knew, and he became even more sensitive to television. . . .

Thus as 1968 opened, even the President was on the defensive. Television was no longer an asset to him, he had done his television thing. . . . The war had played too long, the glib predictions of White House officials had been put on once and then twice too often. Now television was about to start aiding the other side. Until January 1968, Hanoi and the Vietcong had always fought in a highly specialized way, shepherding their resources, fighting always at night and in the country because they had no airpower and little artillery or technological weaponry. Always gone before dawn. Daylight was a foe, daylight meant much heavier casualties, but daylight was required to film them. All of this meant that the enemy's sheer professionalism and toughness were rarely caught on film, and that at home in America the enemy was perceived as evasive, and perhaps not entirely serious, by the time the television camera crews arrived the Vietcong had slipped away. Indeed, network reporters even had a kind of brand name or label for that type of battle and film: "The Wily VC Got Away Again."

But the Tet offensive of 1968 changed that. For the first time the other side fought in the cities and fought in the daylight, day after day, where the American military could use the full force of their great technological might— and where American cameras could film the force and resilience and toughness of the enemy. Each day the battle went on television—showing the battlefield valor of the enemy—reduced the credibility of the Washington leadership. The first casualty of the battle was the Washington propaganda machinery. Fighting like this in the cities cost Hanoi infinitely more in human terms, but it made clear to millions of Americans the toughness and durability of the North Vietnamese. Whether Hanoi was sophisticated enough in its knowledge of American television to have scheduled the battle is debatable; no one knows (although the fact that it was perfectly timed for the upcoming presidential election is clear). What is not debatable is the effect. It changed the country, it forced the beginning of the end of the American combat participation, and it changed Walter Cronkite.

For this was crucial to the press coverage of the Tet offensive. The great impact of the offensive was not on the journalists who had covered it, reporters who had long ago become pessimistic about the eventual outcome of the war and who believed that the other side was resilient and in fact was controlling the rate of the war. . . . The real impact of the Tet offensive was on the editors and many of the readers at home, people of a different generation, of World War II, who had had great difficulty in accepting that America might be on the wrong course, that the various generals in Saigon might be wrong, that the President might be both misled and misleading. The events of that month changed the way men like Walter Cronkite and Hedley Donovan and Ben Bradlee viewed the war, and that was significant, for it meant that their powerful news institutions would no longer be so cautious in reflecting the doubt and pessimism of their reporters in Saigon.

When Tet happened Cronkite decided to go to Saigon.... It was an Orwellian trip—Orwell had written of a Ministry of Truth in charge of Lying and a Ministry of Peace in charge of War—and here was Cronkite flying to Saigon, where the American military command was surrounded by defeat and calling it victory. He and ... his producer, flew out together and they had trouble landing in the country. All the airports were closed. When they finally reached Saigon there was fighting going on all around them....

... [F]or the first time the credibility gap had surfaced in front of everyone's eyes, newcomer and all; in the past someone had to search for the difference between what Saigon said and what was happening, it was somehow subsurface, but here now was this ferocious fighting and yet in Saigon, American generals, four-star commanding generals, could sit and brief very senior American correspondents—correspondents who would go on television and speak to all the American people—and say the battle was over, when it was in fact still very much in doubt. Which meant that the generals were liars or fools, and if they lied about something like this, they might as easily lie about everything else. Cronkite was shocked not so much by the ferocity of the fighting as by the fact that the men in charge of the war were not to be trusted....

So for a man who cherished his objectivity above all, Walter Cronkite did something unique. He shed it, and became a personal journalist. He had already talked it over with his superiors in New York and they all knew the risk involved, that it was likely to be a severe blow to the reputation for impartiality that he and CBS had worked so hard to build, that it was advocacy journalism and thus a very different and dangerous role. (Later, when Nixon attacked the press, Cronkite knew that he was more vulnerable because of his Tet role, that all of the press was in bad odor, including Cronkite himself, and that Nixon had exploited this.) It was not something that he wanted to do, but something he finally felt he had to do. He broadcast a half-hour news special which he insisted on writing himself, in itself unusual. He said that the war didn't work, that a few thousand more troops would not turn it around, and that we had to start thinking of getting out. These were alien and hard words for him but he did not feel he could do otherwise. He was ready for it and the country was ready for it; he moved in part because the consensus was moving, helping to shift the grain by his very act. It was an act that made him uneasy and was in some ways sure to damage him, but he believed that it had to be done....

Cronkite's reporting did change the balance; it was the first time in American history a war had been declared over by an anchorman. In Washington, Lyndon Johnson watched and told his press secretary, George Christian, that it was a turning point, that if he had lost Walter Cronkite he had lost Mr. Average Citizen. It solidified his decision not to run again....

Walter Cronkite, almost alone among major television figures, held both his respect and his affection. He believed that Walter cared about the good of the country. He had liked Walter early on, and he had never thought of him as one of those Kennedy-type media people. As the war dragged on he had not liked the CBS show, the CBS reporters were the worst, but he had exempted Walter from this. In his mind Walter had tried to remain straight and tried to report the war as it was. So when Cronkite gave his post-Tet report, this affected Lyndon Johnson in two ways. First, he realized that he had lost the center, that Walter both was the center and reached the center, and thus his own consensus was in serious jeopardy. Second, because he liked and admired Cronkite so much and thought him so fair a reporter, he found himself believing that if Walter Cronkite was reporting these things, he must know something, he was not doing this just to help his own career, the way so many other reporters were. The Cronkite reporting coincided with the effort that Clark Clifford, another trusted friend, was making to convince him to pull back, so it had an added effect. Later, after Johnson had left the presidency, Cronkite, hearing of what the President had said about him, tried on several occasions to raise the subject with him, but Johnson knew the game, and began instead several long, rather incoherent tirades against the press in general and in particular the press's sinister betrayal of the national interest. . . .

32. IRAN VS. U.S. TV NEWS:
THE HOSTAGE STORY OUT OF CONTEXT

David Altheide

Editor's Note. Based on content analysis of television newscasts during a six-month period from 1979 to 1980, Altheide concludes that the Iranian hostage story was poorly covered. The media's emphasis was on the hostage-taking event and demonstrations around the captured U.S. embassy. The reasons for the event, as seen through Iranian eyes, and the normalcy of life in Iran, aside from the embassy area, were not depicted. These distortions have been typical of U.S. television coverage of foreign events for a long time.

Less typical is the fact that television has become a forum for open diplomacy, conducted by American government officials and their foreign counterparts in front of millions of viewers. The officials' goal is mobilization of public opinion in favor of their positions.

For instance, during the hostage crisis the Iranian government had rebuffed official emissaries from the United States who had been sent to negotiate for the release of the hostages. Instead, Ayatollah Ruhollah Khomeini, the country's leader, met with American television correspondents in front of cameras to answer prescreened questions about the situation. Millions of Americans saw him and heard his arguments and proposals. Several reporters used the televised interviews to suggest policies that might resolve the crisis and to elicit Iranian counterproposals. The merits of such television diplomacy remain in dispute. The networks have been hailed as democratic saviors and condemned as dupes and traitors. The selection presented here offers Altheide's conclusions.

David Altheide is professor of sociology at Arizona State University. He has investigated and reported the ways that television news creates false realities and the reasons that lead newspeople to make such misrepresentations. This selection is from *Television Coverage of the Middle East,* ed. William C. Adams, Norwood, N.J.: Ablex, 1981. Several tables have been omitted.

Americans became interested in Iran during the fall of the Shah's government in late 1978. That interest was sustained by the subsequent rise and fall of two transitional leaders and by the Iranian revolution in 1979

---

which culminated when the Ayatollah Khomeini returned from exile and assumed control of the religious and secular affairs of the embattled country. However, Americans never entirely realized the seriousness of the situation in Iran or the stake and role of the United States in this faraway land until November 4, 1979. On that day the American embassy was occupied by dozens of Iranian "students"—later referred to as terrorists, militants, or kidnappers—who detained Americans as hostages. . . .

Television Diplomacy

Television's role went beyond merely bringing the sad faces and fears of hostage families into the homes of millions of Americans. Television also became the dominant forum for negotiation and diplomacy, largely because the Iranians, like the US government, made considerable effort to join public relations to foreign policy. As *Washington Post* correspondent Don Oberdorfer said about the media's role in Iran on the *MacNeil/Lehrer Report* (December 12, 1979):

> In some ways television is almost the essence of this crisis. . . . We have two contending parties that are trading blows by wars of words, and the primary objective on the part of those holding the hostages in the American Embassy in Tehran is to make a change in the mind of the American public about what the American government must do, with the Shah, with national policy, in all kinds of ways. They're also trying to reach out, through communications means, to the rest of the world, especially the Third World. . . . We in this country and our government have been completely tied up really for more than five weeks with this matter. There is no physical threat to fifty Americans. But it's a completely different sort of thing than the usual international crisis of armies marching or missiles on the ready and so on, and it's really all about this kind of war of opinion.

This role of television diplomacy was explicitly referred to during NBC's discussion of the interview with Corporal Gallegos [one of the hostages]. The following exchange occurred between moderator Garrick Utley and reporter Ford Rowan:

> ROWAN: Some officials say that it will be harder to find a remedy to win the hostages' release now. They say prime time TV exposure for the students' spokesmen and for their handpicked hostage may lead the students to believe that they are winning their effort to influence American public opinion and that time is on their side.
> UTLEY: Ford, as press secretary Powell intimated just a moment ago, they were not at the White House very happy to see this in prime time and yet television has been *the* [principal] means of communicating information in this whole story over the past five weeks.
> ROWAN: You are absolutely right that there has been a breakdown in traditional diplomacy. . . —the conduit [for information] has been—the news media. [People in Washington] are poring over this interview to find out any clues they can and to try to piece together the information that has come from Tehran. . . . But the criticism comes from the people who believe

that the American media ... has been manipulated by the Iranian officials and the so-called students, and that we have played into their hand and in effect sold out to them. .... They are guessing that there will be continuing efforts to manipulate the American news media and that you will see more PR from Iran and that it probably will escalate in the days ahead.

As stressed throughout this paper, television news was integrally involved with both Iranian and American diplomatic motions. And the media people clearly took this to heart, accepting this responsibility which no one had given to them. For example, just prior to the Rowan-Utley exchange, Utley had asked White House Press Secretary Jody Powell if Gallegos were trying to communicate a secret message. Powell replied (November 19, 1979):

Well, Garrick, I detected no secret message, and I think it's quite clear that, had we been able to do so, the worst thing we could do would be to say so on television.

The role of TV news in particular had already been accepted in this crisis, largely because of the growing emergence of a tie between the logic and relevance of the mass media and numerous other aspects of daily life, including foreign policy and international communication. Most reporters saw no difficulty in TV diplomacy—although others would disavow that this was in fact taking place. Indeed, the reporters who interviewed Gallegos clearly illustrate the role of the journalist as observer, information gatherer, and broadly informed communicator who could clarify and straighten out ambiguous twists on complex issues and events; in addition, reports in the present study tended to support administration practices and "viable options."

During the Gallegos interview, an NBC reporter took issue with this hostage of five weeks who suggested that perhaps the Shah was not a "good cause" for him to continue being held captive. The interviewer said: "Let me ask you one other question. If President Carter accedes to the demand that the Shah be returned, isn't that inviting similar attacks on other US embassies elsewhere in the world? Isn't that saying to the world, in effect, you want something from America, just occupy one of our embassies and take a few hostages?"

As the foregoing suggests, broadcast journalists tended to support the administration's general view and approach. In some instances, however, reporters mentioned possible tougher actions, such as a military option, before any official publicly discussed it. ABC's Sam Donaldson, for example, concluded a report on November 8, 1979, just four days after the embassy takeover, by saying:

Notwithstanding such constraint, it is understood here and ought to be understood in Iran, that, if any harm does come to the Americans, the president will not hesitate to order an appropriate American military response.

This pronouncement and the gusto with which it was offered implied that Donaldson agreed with this scenario. More importantly, it was not at all clear whether this was a White House "off the record" appraisal or the reporter's own warning. Just two days after the embassy takeover, on November 6, 1979, CBS' Marvin Kalb observed, "Resorting to force won't save lives, and sticking with diplomacy isn't getting the hostages out either." He then paraphrased what one official had said as part of his closing remarks. "This is getting to be a national humiliation, and there is no way out yet."

Conclusion

The major television networks played a central role in the definition and presentation of the history, nature, and consequences of the hostage situation in Iran. Despite network disclaimers to the contrary, there can be no question that decisions to emphasize certain events, individuals, and themes had a bearing on the character of developments in Iran. Despite the obvious manner in which international diplomacy became wedded to regular newscasts, no claim is being made that television prolonged the crisis or could have prevented it from happening. Yet, public impressions and resultant "opinion poll" messages to political leaders here and abroad were clearly important ingredients in the Iranian situation. Exactly what those effects have been awaits further research. . . .

Of critical value in this study is the clarification of the role of television news throughout the coverage of these events. For the most part, broadcast journalists were advocates, surrogate diplomats, and occasionally the "devil's advocate" for governmental initiatives and policies. . . . [O]ne seldom finds examples of independent investigation or alternative ways of interpreting events. To the contrary, network correspondents tended to be spokespersons for State Department and other governmental officials, providing what amounted to a unified "policy" of selection, interpretation, and presentation of information.

There were some instances of journalistic reflection on reporting procedures and obvious limitations. Most of these segments originated from Iran, involved dependence on Iranian officials who were not always cooperative, and often involved matters of censorship. . . . [T]welve . . . reports were presented about problems of censorship—chiefly about Iranian officials denying access to interviews, or cutting off transmitting power and other technological necessities of television broadcasting. . . . [J]ournalists seldom keep track of reports over time, especially those of colleagues. As a consequence, facts in those stories are no longer relevant to a current report. What is recalled instead is the ongoing story line or "theme," the unifying "big picture" which permits journalists to join one report to another over a period of several days, weeks, and, in this case, even months. The potential distorting influences of this practice on subsequent reports is a troublesome issue that few journalists have seriously examined (cf. Altheide, 1980).

The organization of television does impose certain limitations on what is likely to be presented and in the depth of reporting. Broadcast journalists often defend superficial but very entertaining reports by saying that they do not have the time to study, evaluate, and thoroughly understand complex events and by noting that those events are to be presented within a time frame of one or two minutes. Coverage of the Iranian situation raises serious questions about this standard defense for poor reporting. Because the episode continued for so long, reporters and network staffs had literally months to familiarize themselves with the intricacies of Iran and of past American policies and also had many dozens of hours of news stories in which to distill these matters. On the whole, this was not done. Network news is prepared according to formats; and in the case of Iran, formats were developed to further accommodate the established practices.

The ABC late evening newscast, *Crisis in Iran,* was a regularly scheduled newscast which was originally intended to be devoted mainly to Iran, but it evolved into *Nightline* on March 24 and quickly turned to other topics as well. The format of this show involved live interviews with officials, experts, and other concerned people about a variety of topics. In the case of Iran, ABC might have an Iranian official, such as Foreign Minister Sadegh Ghotzbadeh, on one telephone, with a member of the hostage's family or a US official on another telephone. The moderator, Ted Koppel, may ask each questions and they could also ask each other questions. Such a format is superior to the short and visual film reports characteristic of regular network newscasts, although even this approach tended to evolve into argumentation rather than clarification, putting the reporter on center stage, and generally presenting the administration's position. Perhaps not surprisingly, even after months of such reports, the journalists involved evidenced little detectable change, expertise, or sense of perspective, although they did appear to become more frustrated.

The Iranian situation was reduced to one story—the freeing of the hostages—rather than coverage of its background and context, of the complexities of Iran, of alternative American policies, and of contemporary parochial politics in a world dominated by superpowers. Such messages were not forthcoming in the face of counts of the number of days of captivity and more footage of angry demonstrators and emotional relatives of hostages. That was part of the story, but, as this essay has suggested, that was not the only story. . . .

REFERENCE

Altheide, David L. "Learning from Mistakes: Toward a Reflective Journalism." *Gazette: International Journal for Mass Communication Studies* 26 (2) 1980: 111-20.

Section Six

CONTROLLING MEDIA EFFECTS

The media are powerful political actors. What happens when they misuse their power? What happens when they become advocates for special interests rather than an open forum where a broad spectrum of voices are heard? In the United States, the answers are firmly linked to the First Amendment which prohibits Congress from making any "law abridging the freedom of the press." Aside from a limited degree of control by judicial decisions, the print media are free to use their power as they see fit. This includes the freedom to support or undermine governmental policies and philosophies—intentionally or unintentionally, and the freedom to grant or deny publicity to various interest groups and viewpoints.

The situation is somewhat different for the electronic media. Government regulations substantially curtail their freedom to publish despite the fact that the intent to control news content has been explicitly denied. Erwin G. Krasnow, Lawrence D. Longley, and Herbert A. Terry describe how governmental controls invariably thrust the electronic media into the thick of political controversy. Their essay includes a model that provides an exceptionally clear overview of the patterns of interaction among the various parties involved in broadcast policy making.

The extent of print media freedom becomes clear from the excerpts of *New York Times v. U.S.*, the so-called "Pentagon Papers" case. The central question in that case was whether the government may restrain the print media's right to publish news when national security is at stake. The answer given by the majority of Supreme Court judges was "no." But it was by no means an absolute no.

If media institutions are exempted from governmental controls, are they obliged to use self-control to make sure that their stories do not endanger important public interests? William J. Small, a news executive, wrestles with that troublesome issue in his discussion of media self-censorship during the Bay of Pigs invasion of Cuba by U.S.-supported forces, and in the Cuban missile crisis, which carried the United States and the Soviet Union to the brink of war. Small's essay also touches upon another form of control over news dissemination: the often successful attempts by news sources to either misrepresent or withhold vital information from the media.

Ben H. Bagdikian analyzes a different type of manipulation of news at the source—the distribution of free public relations releases to print and electronic media. These releases frequently are designed and executed beautifully and provide news in a convenient form. For financially strapped news enterprises, they provide a tempting way to fill the columns of a paper or take up slack time on radio, television, or in movie houses. News media that rely heavily on public relations releases may be selling their freedom to control news content for the proverbial mess of pottage. But since privately owned media are as beholden to making a profit as they are to serving the public and guarding press independence, it is not surprising that profit making often takes first place.

Finally, the selections by John C. Merrill and Herbert I. Schiller point to still another form of control of the news flow—the domination of the media marketplace by the sheer size and economic power of particular enterprises, such as the television networks. Concentration of market control is an internal as well as an external problem for American media. Internally, news produced by the three major networks dominates the television market. The Associated Press and United Press International are the kingpins in providing wire service news. Competition in the daily newspaper field is eroding steadily as more and more papers join forces under the aegis of newspaper chains and as the number of towns with competing papers dwindles.

On the international level, Third World nations are asking for curbs on the worldwide dissemination of news, claiming to be swamped by often useless and harmful news from the rich and powerful western media. Curbs are strongly resisted by the United States and other western nations on the grounds that they would interfere with the free flow of information. The issue boils down to whether freedom to disseminate information has degenerated into license that benefits the powerful at the expense of the weak. Both sides of the argument are presented in this section. Herbert Schiller speaks for UNESCO and the Third World while John Merrill expresses the views representative of opinions held in western nations.

33. THE POLITICS OF BROADCAST REGULATION

Erwin G. Krasnow, Lawrence D. Longley, and Herbert A. Terry

Editor's Note. The authors of this selection discuss the major factors that have shaped and continue to shape broadcast regulation and now deregulation. They take an especially close look at the ups and downs of cable industry regulation. Technological changes are occurring at a dizzying pace, but it is still "politics as usual." Despite mounting pressures to scrap the Federal Communications Act of 1934, several recent efforts have failed to win passage for a new act more suitable for modern technology and developments.

One major policy issue that has made passage of a new act difficult is the extent of electronic media regulation. The media have been regulated in the past because it was feared that a scarcity of broadcast channels would prevent vigorous competition. Technology has changed so that there is more competition now among electronic media than among daily newspapers. Still, pressures to continue regulation remain strong, on the grounds that broadcasting will not serve the mandate of "the public interest, convenience and necessity."

If regulation continues, several existing rules will need reexamination because they have proved unworkable or have had highly undesirable side effects. Due for renewed scrutiny are the equal time rule, which has hampered debates among candidates, and the fairness rule, which has stifled controversial broadcasting. Controversy over these and other rules makes it certain that the politics of broadcast regulation will continue to be exciting. The political battles yet to come will continue to provide excellent insights into the interaction of media institutions with their political environment.

Erwin G. Krasnow is a communications lawyer who serves the National Association of Broadcasters as a senior vice-president and general counsel. Lawrence D. Longley, a professor of government at Lawrence University, specializes in interest group politics. Herbert A. Terry, who has been affiliated with the National Citizens Committee on Broadcasting, supplies expertise in telecommunications, a subject he teaches at Indiana University. The selection is from *The Politics of Broadcast Regulation,* 3rd ed., New York: St. Martin's Press, 1982.

Reprinted from *The Politics of Broadcast Regulation,* 3rd Edition, by Erwin G. Krasnow, Lawrence D. Longley, and Herbert A. Terry. Copyright © 1982 by St. Martin's Press, Inc. Reprinted by permission of the publisher.

The Historical Context of Broadcast Regulation

Broadcast regulation, like broadcasting itself, has a history spanning just over a half-century. There is more constancy, both substantively and structurally, to that history than one might expect for so dynamic a field. For example, the basic statute under which the FCC currently operates, the Communications Act of 1934, is fundamentally identical to the legislative charter given to the Federal Radio Commission in 1927. The process that produced the 1927 and 1934 acts in fact displayed many features that characterize the regulatory process today. Just like today, the creation of the legislative framework involved many parties—indeed, almost the same parties as those of the 1980s. Like today, the result was compromise—compromise that continued to be susceptible to reconsideration and reinterpretation. . . .

Several aspects of the early history of broadcast regulation deserve emphasis. Five key participants emerged, themselves giving rise to a sixth, the Federal Radio Commission and its successor, the FCC. The broadcast industry was involved in the genesis of broadcast regulation. Self-regulation was attempted but proved inadequate. After that, the industry worked actively with the executive and legislative branches of government to shape what was viewed as legislation required to eliminate audio chaos. Also involved from the beginning were the courts. . . . The public was involved as well, its complaints about deteriorating radio service helping advance radio legislation on Congress's agenda by 1927.

Congress and the executive branch of government are the two remaining participant groups. . . . Disputes between the president and Congress are reflected in the "temporary" nature of the FRC and the continuing interaction today between the president and Congress whenever an FCC member is nominated and subjected to the confirmation process. When Secretary of Commerce Hoover's regulatory activities were blocked by the courts, the salvation of American broadcasting lay with Congress. When Congress *did* act to establish a regulatory agency, the agency's existence and financing were subjected to yearly congressional consideration.[1] By giving the FRC limited financial and technical resources, Congress effectively ensured the Commission's dependence on congressional good will and kept a firm grip on this "independent" regulatory agency.

A final distinctive feature of the federal government's early regulation of broadcast stations was the focus on licensing as a primary regulatory tool. . . . The strong emphasis on the FCC's licensing role results in part from the fact that Congress did not expressly give the Commission the power to regulate the rates or profits of broadcast stations.[2] It predetermined that there would be strongly fought battles over several aspects of licensing in the future: Should the "traffic cop" review such things as choices of content in making licensing decisions? What, in general, would be both the process and standards for getting licenses renewed? . . .

Taylor Branch has divided government agencies into two categories: "deliver the mail" and "Holy Grail." "Deliver the mail" agencies perform neutral, mechanical, logistical functions; they send out Social Security checks, procure supplies—or deliver the mail. "Holy Grail" agencies, on the other hand, are given the more controversial and difficult role of achieving some grand, moral, civilizing goal. The Federal Radio Commission came into being primarily to "deliver the mail"—to act as a traffic cop of the airwaves. But both the FRC and the FCC had a vague Holy Grail clause written into their charters: the requirement that they uphold the "public interest, convenience and necessity." This vague but also often useful congressional mandate is key to understanding today's conflicts over broadcast regulation. . . .

Former FCC Chairman Newton Minow has commented that, starting with the Radio Act of 1927, the phrase "public interest, convenience and necessity" has provided the battleground for broadcasting's regulatory debate.[3] Congress's reason for including such a phrase was clear: the courts, interpreting the Radio Act of 1912 as a narrow statute, had said that the secretary of commerce could not create additional rules or regulations beyond that act's terms. This left Hoover unable to control rapidly changing technologies. The public interest notion in the 1927 and 1934 acts was intended to let the regulatory agency create new rules, regulations, and standards as required to meet new conditions. Congress clearly hoped to create an act more durable than the Radio Act of 1912. That plan has been at least somewhat successful as it was not until about 1976 that Congress seriously began to consider a major change in its 1934 handiwork. . . .

The meaning of the phrase, however, is extremely elusive. Although many scholars have attempted to define the public interest in normative or empirical terms, their definitions have added little to an understanding of the real relevance of this concept to the regulatory process. One scholar, after analyzing the literature on the public interest, created a typology for varying definitions of the term, but in the end he decided not to "argue for adoption of a single definition, preferring instead to categorize ways in which the phrase may be used. Different circumstances . . . may employ different usages."[4] . . .

Besides providing flexibility to adapt to changing conditions, the concept of the public interest is important to the regulation of broadcasting in another sense. A generalized public belief even in an undefined public interest increases the likelihood that policies will be accepted as authoritative. The acceptance of a concept of the public interest may thus become an important support for the regulation of broadcasting and for the making of authoritative rules and policies toward this end.[5] For this reason the courts traditionally have given the FCC wide latitude in determining what constitutes the public interest. As the U.S. Supreme Court noted in 1981:

> Our opinions have repeatedly emphasized that the Commission's judgment regarding how the public interest is best served is entitled to substantial judicial deference. . . . The Commission's implementation of the public interest standard, when based on a rational weighing of competing policies, is not to be set aside . . . for "the weighing of policies under the public interest standard is a task that Congress has delegated to the Commission in the first instance."[6]

Judge E. Barrett Prettyman once expanded upon the reasons for such deference:

> It is also true that the Commission's view of what is best may change from time to time. Commissions themselves change, underlying philosophies differ, and experience often dictates change. Two diametrically opposite schools of thought in respect to the public welfare may both be rational; e.g., both free trade and protective tariff are rational positions. All such matters are for the Congress and the executive and their agencies. They are political in the high sense of that abused term.[7]

Despite the usefulness of the public interest concept in keeping up with changing means of communications and the general tendency of the courts to defer to the FCC's decisions, conflicts over the meaning of the public interest have been recurrent in broadcast history. On occasion, the vague statutory mandate to look out for the public interest has hampered the development of coherent public policy since Congress (or influential members of Congress) can always declare, "That is not what we meant by the public interest."[8] Few independent regulatory commissions have had to operate under such a broad grant of power with so few substantive guidelines. Rather than encouraging greater freedom of action, vagueness in delegated power may serve to limit an agency's independence and freedom to act as it sees fit. As Pendleton Herring put it, "Administrators cannot be given the responsibilities of statesmen without incurring likewise the tribulations of politicians."[9] . . .

Unresolved Regulatory Problems

. . . Disputes concerning legal prescriptions imposed by the Communications Act often have centered on recurring value conflicts—assumptions about what ought or ought not to be done. One such question is the extent to which broadcasting should pursue social as well as economic and technical goals. The emphasis on the social responsibilities of licensees rests on the view that "the air belongs to the public, not to the industry" since Congress provided in Section 301 of the Communications Act that "no . . . license shall be construed to create any right, beyond the terms, conditions, and periods of the license." In recent years, for example, the FCC has adopted rules and policies designed to make broadcasters meet social responsibilities by requiring them to implement equal employment opportunity programs for women and minorities and to provide "reasonable opportunities for the expression of opposing views on controversial issues of public importance"—the Fairness Doctrine— and to schedule television programs for children.

Some of these rules and policies require broadcasters to present, or refrain from presenting, content contrary to what they would choose to do on their own. How far the FCC may go in the direct, or indirect, regulation of content without violating either the Communications Act's own prohibition in Section 326 against censorship or the First Amendment to the U.S. Constitution remains unsettled. Section 326 of the Communications Act states:

> Nothing in this Act shall be understood or construed to give the Commission the power of censorship over the radio communications or signals transmitted by any radio station, and no regulation or condition shall be promulgated or fixed by the Commission which shall interfere with the right of free speech by means of radio communications.

However, as we noted above, in the same act Congress also directs the Commission to regulate "in the public interest, convenience and necessity." [10] Using that standard, the Commission has promulgated many rules and policies governing broadcast programming that would be regarded by the courts as unlawful censorship of the print media. Early court cases, however, determined that the FCC did not have to ignore content, that it could consider it without necessarily engaging in censorship;[11] later court cases have perpetuated the view that government supervision of broadcast content is somehow more acceptable than review of print.[12] Clearly broadcasting continues to be plagued by divergent views of how to balance freedom with achieving socially desired and responsible service, while still not engaging in censorship.

Complicating this controversy is the conflict between First Amendment provisions guaranteeing the right of broadcasters, like other media owners and operators, to be free of government control over the content of programming and First Amendment theories that have been developed exclusively for broadcasting and that hold the rights of listeners and viewers to receive information to be "paramount" over the rights of broadcasters.[13] The theory is that in the "scarce" medium of broadcasting, some affirmative government intervention concerning content may be needed to ensure that the public hears diverse ideas and viewpoints. J. Skelly Wright, a judge of the U.S. Court of Appeals, has commented:

> [In] some areas of the law it is easy to tell the good guys from the bad guys.... In the current debate over the broadcast media and the First Amendment ... each debater claims to be the real protector of the First Amendment, and the analytical problems are much more difficult than in ordinary constitutional adjudication.... The answers are not easy.[14]

These colliding statutory ground rules governing the freedom and obligations of broadcasters have been melded into one of the law's most elastic conceptions—the notion of a "public trustee." [15] The FCC views a broadcast license as a "trust," with the public as "beneficiary" and the broadcaster as "public trustee." The public trustee concept is a natural consequence of the conflicting statutory goals of private use and regulated allocation of spectrum space. Congress gave the FCC the right to choose among various candidates for commercial broadcast licenses and left it up to the Commission to find a justification for providing a fortunate few with the use of a valuable scarce resource at no cost. Legal scholar Benno Schmidt, Jr., thinks the public trustee concept was designed to dull the horns of the FCC's dilemma: to give away valuable spectrum space, with no strings attached, would pose stubborn problems of justification.

As has been noted above, however, some of the strings attached—especially those, like the FCC's Fairness Doctrine, that are content-related—are constitutionally suspect.[16] One option exercised by the FCC to reduce controversy over its activities has been to substitute "content-neutral" or "structural" policies for policies that involve direct review of content. The objective of the Fairness Doctrine, for example, is diverse and balanced expression of views on controversial issues of public importance. Under the doctrine, the FCC can order a station to present an underrepresented view, clearly not a content-neutral act. As an alternative to such content regulation the FCC can attempt to structure the broadcast marketplace so that there are many stations with different owners and assume thereby that diversity of opinion will result naturally and without direct government review. Many FCC rules and policies—for example, the regulation of station ownership patterns—have been of this type. They do not, on their surface, look normative but are in fact examples of content-neutral means of achieving social objectives. . . .

[T]here have long been two complementary and determinative features of American broadcasting: spectrum space scarcity and technological innovation. Scarcity, of course, has always been the underlying *raison d'être* for broadcast regulation. Because one person's transmission is another's interference, Congress concluded that the federal government has the duty both to select who may and who may not broadcast and to regulate the use of the electromagnetic spectrum to serve the public interest.

Scarcity has been a special problem in the case of broadcast television. Whereas an FM broadcast needs a section of the spectrum 20 times wider than an AM broadcast, a TV broadcast requires a channel 600 times wider than an AM broadcast station's signal.[17] Until 1952 the FCC's allocation policy confined television to a twelve-channel Very High Frequency (VHF) system incapable of offering even two or three stations in many cities. Broadcasters with the only television station (or with one of the two) in a market at that time were in an awkward position to be complaining about governmental regulation, given the profits they were receiving from their near monopoly. The All-Channel Receiver Bill of 1962 and many related FCC policies have been aimed at making additional television service available in many areas, with the expectation that greater diversity in programming would result eventually. Only recently have the economic support systems begun to emerge that could make this twenty-year belief of the Commission true. . . .

Scarcity seems to be much less of a problem in radio broadcasting. Broadcasters argue that there is little justification for rigid government regulation of ten or twenty competing radio stations in a market while monopoly newspapers operate freely. As scarcity decreases, they have argued, so should regulation. In the early 1980s radio broadcasters gained some government support for their argument. When the FCC decided not to regulate radio broadcasters' choice of program formats, the U.S. Supreme Court in 1981 declined "to overturn the Commission's Policy Statement, which prefers reliance on market forces to its own attempt to oversee format changes at the behest of disaffected listeners." [18] Also in 1981, the FCC decided that marketplace competition made it unnecessary for the Commission to supervise the amounts of commercials or nonentertainment programming on commercial radio stations.[19] Later, under Chairman Mark S. Fowler, appointed by President Reagan, the FCC proposed to Congress that much of the legislation supporting FCC content regulation be repealed. The Commission argued that "[t]he traditional spectrum scarcity argument which has provided the basis for support of the Fairness Doctrine [and other content regulations] has become increasingly less valid as new technologies and the proliferation of existing broadcast facilities has made the diversity of opinion available to the public via radio as pleantiful [sic] as that available via print media." [20]. . .

Whatever scarcity there is for commercial broadcasting and other private uses of radio is partly a manmade problem whose dimensions are defined by the executive branch. The FCC's jurisdiction over the radio spectrum is limited by Section 305 of the Communications Act, which exempts from the Commission's power all "radio stations belonging to and operated by the United States." The federal government through its various agencies and departments, operates a host of radio services occupying approximately one-half of the total available frequency space. With the government's total investment in telecommunications running into the hundreds of billions of dollars and its annual expenditure for equipment, research, and development of over $7 billion, the White House is reluctant to turn these frequencies over to the FCC.[21]

The classic pattern of limited broadcast facilities, which has led to government regulations, also has encouraged technological innovations to expand programming possibilities. Throughout its history the FCC has had to wrestle with new problems brought about by such technical developments as network broadcasting, FM broadcasting, VHF and UHF telecasting, color television, cable television, direct broadcast satellites (DBS), multipoint distribution services (MDS), and other new or modified systems. The making of public policy in each of these areas goes far beyond resolving technical issues. Technical issues frequently disguise what actually are economic interests vying for control of some segment of broadcasting and related markets. The politics of broadcasting are thus present in technical as well as social controversies.

. . . [T]he FCC, like other regulatory bodies, has been subjected to considerable criticism concerning its inability to cope with change—the most common charge being that it is concerned mainly with preserving the status quo and with favoring the well-established broadcast services. . . .

An agency's ability to respond to and foster technological change is largely a matter of how dependent the agency is on dominant industry factions—the "haves" as opposed to the "have nots." Throughout its history the FCC has lacked sufficient skilled personnel and funds to weigh the merits of new technology and has been forced to rely on outside advice and technical opinion. When faced with complex technical questions, the Commission often has taken the easy road of finding in favor of the "haves" over the "have nots." Frequently, the result is delay in the development of these technologies. . . . Throughout most of its history, the Commission (usually with the support of the "haves") sought to limit the growth of technology rather than use technological innovations as correctives to problems. Beginning in the late 1970s, however, the FCC has adopted policies designed to foster technological growth as a way of promoting greater competition in the marketplace and a greater diversity of services.

The ability of a regulatory commission to inhibit or to promote a technical innovation that challenges the regulated (and sometimes sheltered) industry is a measure of the vitality and strength of that agency. . . . [T]he FCC has not been highly successful at giving birth to new communications services. At times, in fact, it has almost destroyed them. These failures result, at least in part, from the highly political environment in which the FCC operates. The history of the on-again, off-again FCC regulation of cable television provides perhaps the best example of how difficult policy making becomes when traditional commercial broadcasting confronts new competitors.

The maneuverings with respect to cable television between 1968 and 1981 provide a classic illustration of the political environment in action. In 1968, after the Supreme Court affirmed the FCC's authority to regulate cable systems directly, the Commission took the textbook action: it issued a voluminous set of cable policy proposals and invited comments from broadcasters, cable operators, citizen groups, members of the general public, and other interested parties. Three years and several thousand pages of dialogue later, FCC Chairman Dean Burch sent the House and Senate Communications Subcommittees a fifty-five-page summary of the kinds of rules the Commission had tentatively concluded were necessary for the healthy development of the cable industry. Burch assured Congress that the new rules would not be made effective until several months later—March 31, 1972—in order to allow time for congressional review.

The consideration of cable rules, however, was not to be left to the discretion of the FCC and Congress. President Nixon became involved, in July 1971, by appointing a cabinet-level advisory committee on cable, headed by Dr. Clay T. Whitehead, director of the White House Office of Telecommunications Policy. . . . During the fall of 1971, Chairman Burch and Dr. Whitehead met privately with representatives of cable, broadcast, and copyright interests in an effort to reach a compromise agreement. Meanwhile, the Supreme Court was considering an appeal of a lower court ruling that the FCC had no authority to require cable systems to originate programs—a central element in the Commission's regulatory strategy.

All branches of government—legislative, executive, and judicial—were independently considering the future of cable when the FCC, in a 136-page decision in February 1972, adopted new cable rules based on a private agreement among cable operators, broadcasters, and a group of copyright owners after White House prodding. In a biting dissenting opinion, former Commissioner Nicholas Johnson, a liberal Democrat, said:

> In future years, when students of law or government wish to study the decision making process at its worst, when they look for examples of industry domination of government, when they look for Presidential interference in the operation of an agency responsible to Congress, they will look to the FCC handling of the never-ending saga of cable television as a classic case study.

Chairman Burch, a former head of the Republican National Committee, accused Johnson in a special concurring opinion of using a "scorched earth" technique to distort an act of creation into a public obscenity. Burch said that there was no conspiracy, no arm twisting, no secret deals. The cable decision, he said, was the result of months of regulatory craftsmanship of the highest order. Commissioner (later Chairman) Richard E. Wiley, quoting Edmund Burke on the need for compromise, defended the decision on the ground that the "choice realistically confronting the Commission, after all, was this particular program—or none at all." [22]

The comprehensive 1972 rules proved to have a short life. Their key feature was that while they allowed cable television to begin to grow by providing some cable system access to "imported" distant TV signals, the cable television industry was required to provide certain public interest tradeoffs in return. Among them were requirements for relatively large channel capacity systems (twenty channels), two-way potential, and provision of "access channels" for use by government, educational, and citizen groups. Two premises underlay the FCC rules. First, the Commission assumed cable television, through its ability to provide alternatives to local broadcast service, would divide the TV audience (a potentially devastating prospect for UHF), reduce revenues, and eventually cause harm to the ability of local broadcasters to serve the public interest. Second, based largely on its 1968 court victory, the FCC believed it could require a number of public interest services of cable operators if whatever was being required was at least related to broadcasting. By the late 1970s both premises had come under vigorous attack—an attack led jointly by the cable TV industry and the courts.

The first major setback for the FCC came in 1977 when the U.S. Court of Appeals for the District of Columbia Circuit overturned complex FCC rules that limited pay-cable access to movies and popular sporting events. The rules originally had been based on the idea that without such limits popular "free" programs would be "siphoned" from broadcast TV to pay-cable systems. The court, in effect, ruled that such cable rules could be justified only if the FCC had a reasonable basis for expecting that harm to broadcasters and the public would in fact happen. The court found that the FCC could not sustain that burden of proof. For good measure, it also observed that cable, unlike broadcasting, was not technologically "scarce" and suggested that for that reason too the pay-cable limits were invalid.[23] In the wake of this decision, the FCC opened an inquiry into the economic relationship between cable television and broadcasting. In 1980 the Commission used the results of that inquiry—in which it concluded it had previously overestimated the impact of cable on broadcasting—to justify repeal of other FCC cable rules designed to "protect" broadcasters.[24]

At about the same time that the "economic impact" theory for cable regulation was weakening, the Commission's "tradeoffs" in the 1972 cable rules were under attack by the cable industry. This dispute, eventually settled by the U.S. Supreme Court, led to the Commission's elimination in 1980 of its access, twenty-channel, and two-way potential requirements.[25]

By 1981 most of the 1972 compromise had unraveled. The FCC had reduced its regulation of cable television, but state and local government regulation of franchises was becoming more important. Broadcasters, who thought they lost most with the collapse of the compromise, continued to fight the trend in a few court cases,[26] but primarily they hoped that Congress could be persuaded to put some limits on cable through amendment or revision of the Communications Act of 1934 and the copyright statutes. Despite this hope, however, broadcasters had to stand in line with others who thought the Communications Act had to be amended to deal with new technologies and new economic theories. . . .

From this brief example, it is clear that the regulatory process as applied to broadcasting and related fields is laced with an ample dose of political maneuverings, including U-turns. . . .

Broadcast Regulation: An Analytic Review

Broadcast regulation, we have seen, is shaped by six primary determiners—the FCC, the industry, citizen groups, the courts, the White House, and Congress. In addition there are miscellaneous participants—the Federal Trade Commission or the Commission on Civil Rights, for example—sometimes involved in specific broadcast-related issues but whose participation in the regulatory process, while important, is less constant. . . . [T]he six primary determiners rarely can accomplish much by unilateral action. The president, for example, names members of the FCC but checks out potential appointees in advance with significant interest groups (the industry and, infrequently, citizen groups). In the end, the Senate must formally approve nominations. The determiners, in other words, interact with each other in a complex fashion. Often those interactions are as important as, or more important than, what the determiners do on their own. Any attempt to understand what goes on in broadcast regulation must explain regulation as the outcome of complex interaction patterns within a dynamic system. . . .

The politics of broadcast regulation can be seen in terms of an analytical framework or model we term the "broadcast policy-making system." Such a framework can be used both to understand the regulatory process and to suggest to scholars a conceptual orientation for work in this area.

As is the case with any model, the one we are suggesting is a simplification of reality. Yet to simplify is to streamline, to strip off surface complexities in order to show the essential elements of a system. . . .

Figure 33-1 The Broadcast Policy-Making System

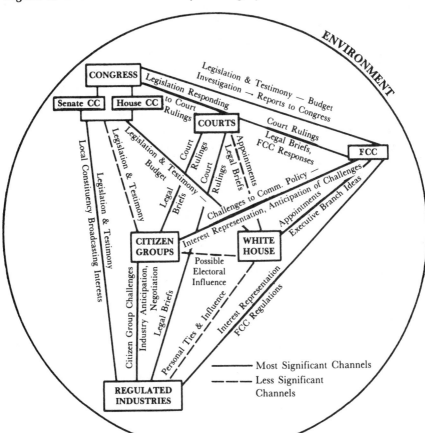

Figure 33-1 represents the broadcast policy-making system. The six recurring participants in the regulatory process ... are the authoritative decision-making agencies at the heart of the model. The figure also charts various channels of influence among these six participants. It is significant that there is no one pathway through the core of the broadcast policy-making system, and any one of the various routes necessarily involves many participants. The key to understanding the politics of broadcast regulation lies in simultaneously analyzing the individual participants and their interactions. ... Although outside pressure, or "inputs," and the internal politics of each of the decision-making bodies can raise issues and define alternatives, it is the political relationships of, and interactions among, the six key determiners that are truly crucial to broadcast regulation.

Three of the principals (the White House, the courts, and citizen groups) usually play a less immediate, sustained, and direct role than the other three (the FCC, Congress, and the regulated industries). Thus, the primary channels of influence, information, and contact are traced among these three most significant determiners as the outer triangle in Figure 33-1.

The system produces policy dynamically. Policy decisions—which might be called "outputs"—emerge from the interaction of some or all of the participants. Although the need for policy decisions may sometimes be stimulated by parties outside the system—for example, by an action of the Federal Trade Commission—in most instances, the functioning of the system itself generates the need for still more policy decisions. In other words, although some policy decisions may have long lives, many remain accepted and unchanged only briefly: one day's policy outputs in this system commonly become the inputs for the next day's policy making.

The policy outputs of this system are varied. They include "public" policies such as FCC rules and regulations, final court actions, laws enacted by Congress, and executive orders. An example of legislation would be the statutory requirement . . . that all television sets sold after a certain date have UHF as well as VHF receiving capacity; an example of an agency decision would be the FCC's desire that incumbent broadcast station licensees should have preferred status, in renewal proceedings, over challengers for their licenses. . . . Outputs may even take the form of decisions not to do something, exemplified by recent trends in "deregulation" such as the FCC decision not to supervise the number of commercials radio stations carry. . . , or its decision not to concern itself with the entertainment programming format those stations use. . . . In our model, policy outputs may even include many of the actions of the regulated industries, whose implementation of or operation under FCC rules and regulations or the Communications Act of 1934 is, in many instances, authoritative because it is unchallenged.

In most instances, such policy outputs (or authoritative decisions) bestow rewards or impose penalties on other affected interests. Reactions of those interests—or, occasionally, outside interests—stimulate the system to generate further policy output. They become, in effect, input back into the system. Some inputs are specific, such as a demand by a citizen group that a broadcast station not be permitted to change its format. Other inputs are exceedingly general, such as the mood that can be cast over an independent regulatory commission by a president or by the current public image of the agency. It is important to realize, too, that the system does more than merely respond to demands; it also molds political demands and policy preferences.

The system, of course, does not function in a vacuum. It operates in the context of an environment consisting of many factors . . . including the historical element of broadcast regulation, the basic technical and economic characteristics of broadcasting, and broad legal prescriptions. The environment outside the system also encompasses other factors, such as public attitudes toward broadcasting and government regulation and the actions of related systems—the Federal Trade Commission, for example—which may at times inspire and influence the broadcast policy-making system. It even includes actions and groups beyond the United States, for the spectrum is an international resource and U.S. broadcast networks and programs have a worldwide effect. In recent years, for example, U.S. policies toward spectrum allocation for radio and toward the location and function of communications satellites have had to be reconciled with the desires of our international neighbors. The United Nations Educational, Scientific and Cultural Organization (UNESCO) has debated policies toward a "new world information order" that, although perceived by third world nations to be important to their development, are seen by Western nations as antithetical to notions of press freedom. The major demands and supports—outputs and inputs—that determine what the system does, however, generally originate from within. . . .

One important feature of the broadcast policy-making system is that it is highly turbulent. Largely because communications is influenced by rapidly changing technology, few specific policy decisions are stable and long-lasting. The system is always responding to new or changed conditions, with consequent incessant interaction among its participants. The operation of the policy-making system in specific instances is inherently unique; each policy-making problem is likely to differ in important respects from all others. However, certain recurring patterns about the politics of broadcast regulation can be identified.[27]

1. *Participants seek conflicting goals from the process.* Pluralism and dispersion of power in policy making do not by themselves suggest that the process is inevitably a struggle for control or influence. Conceivably the participants in such a process could share certain perspectives concerning what is to be done. Such is rarely the case, however, in the broadcast policy-making process. . . . [T]he gains of one set of participants are usually made at the cost of the interests of another. The policy demands of different groups often conflict; they must usually compete for scarce rewards.

2. *Participants have limited resources insufficient to continually dominate the policy-making process.* In a pluralistic complex such as that outlined in Figure 33-1, policy-making power tends to be divided. Although the FCC frequently initiates policy proposals, it lacks the ability to implement most of them single-handedly. To prevail, it must win significant support from other participants. Similarly, none of the other five participants has hierarchical control over the policy-making process, which is simply to say that nobody dominates the process consistently. In such a system policy making results from the agreement—or at least the acquiescence—of multiple participants, not from the domination of one. Coalitions of diverse participants work together and reward those belonging to them.

3. *Participants have unequal strengths in the struggle for control or influence.* Inequality among participants can arise because one party is inherently strong, cares more, or develops its potential more effectively. In the 1970s, for example, citizen groups had considerably less strength than the Federal Communications Commission and the broadcast industry in their ability to influence policy concerning radio station format changes. Even when one federal court agreed with the views of a citizen group, another federal court—supported by the FCC and by broadcasters—prevailed.

Favorable public opinion, legal symbols, congressional allies, and the like are all potential sources of strength that participants have access to in differing degrees and that they may use with varying success on different issues.

4. *The component subgroups of participant groups do not automatically agree on policy options.* Each of the six groups we have identified consists of many subgroups: citizen groups range from liberal to conservative; the FCC is organized into bureaus representing interests that may conflict, such as cable television and broadcasting; there is not one single court but, instead, a hierarchy of courts, and it is common for a superior court to overturn the actions of an inferior court; radio broadcasters may sometimes view issues differently than television broadcasters. Thus, while it is useful to refer to the six principal participants as if each was one, it is important to recognize that each group may be unable—or find it very difficult—to agree on a common objective or course of action.

5. *The process tends toward policy progression by small or incremental steps rather than massive change.* One means of minimizing opposition to a policy initiative is to show its close relationship to existing and generally accepted policy. Frequently, earlier actions are cited to prove that the desired change is not unprecedented but only a logical continuation of past concerns and policies. One of the beauties of administrative law is that precedents usually can be found for almost any initiative. Although agencies are not as bound by precedent as are courts, they still hesitate to turn their backs on the past when it is pointed out to them. Such slow and gradual shifts in policy are not only strategic but probably inevitable, given the multiplicity of participants with conflicting goals, unequal strengths, and limited resources. Incrementalism tends to be at least a safe, if not necessarily the safest, course of action. As a result, however, the system is rarely bold or innovative and has a hard time responding to environmental pressures for massive change. . . .

6. *Legal and ideological symbols play a significant role in the process.* Throughout the evolution of policy a recurring theme of participants is the legal and ideological symbolism they may attach to a discussion of alternatives. In many instances policies are seen as threatening or protecting the "rights" of broadcasters or the "rights" of listeners and viewers, without refined and, most importantly, commonly agreed upon specification of the meaning of those concepts. Broadcast policy-making discussions can also become embroiled in arguments over stock, symbolic rhetoric such as "localism," the "public interest," "access to broadcasting," or "free broadcasting." The terms become symbols cherished by participants in and of themselves without careful thought, or they are not commonly understood, so that ideological rhetoric sometimes supersedes real issues and actions in importance.

7. *The process is usually characterized by mutual accommodation among participants.* Customarily, participants in broadcast policy making do not attempt to destroy one or more of their opponents. Rather, the process is characterized by consensual, majority-seeking activities. Mutual adjustment among participants may occur in a variety of ways, including negotiation, the creation and discharge of obligations, direct manipulation of the immediate

circumstances in which events are occurring, the use of third parties or political brokers capable of developing consensual solutions, or partial deferral to others in order to effect a compromise. To some participants, on some issues, however, accommodation is difficult if not impossible, and on these issues policy debate is intense and the perceived stakes the greatest. . . .

NOTES

1. Congress followed a similar approach with the Corporation for Public Broadcasting, which initially received funding and authorization only on an annual basis, although it eventually received some advance, multiyear support.
2. See Roger G. Noll, Merton J. Peck, and John J. McGowan, *Economic Aspects of Television Regulation* (Washington, D.C.: Brookings Institution, 1973), p. 98. Section 153(h) of the Communications Act provides that "a person engaged in radio broadcasting shall not, insofar as such a person is so engaged, be deemed a common carrier."
3. Newton N. Minow, *Equal Time: The Private Broadcaster and the Public Interest* (New York: Atheneum, 1964), p. 8.
4. Barry M. Mitnick, *The Political Economy of Regulation: Creating, Designing and Removing Regulatory Forms* (New York: Columbia University Press, 1980), pp. 278-279. See, in general, Mitnick's chapter IV, "The Concept of the Public Interest."
5. See Virginia Held, *The Public Interest and Individual Interests* (New York: Basic Books, 1970), pp. 163-202.
6. *FCC* v. *WNCN Listeners Guild,*—U.S.—, 101 S. Ct. 1266, 67 L.Ed.2d 521, 535, (1981).
7. *Pinellas Broadcasting Co.* v. *FCC*, 230 F.2d 204, 206 (D.C. Cir. 1956), *certiorari denied*, 350 U.S. 1007 (1956).
8. [An] example . . . [is] a Commission initiative to control advertising "in the public interest," which led to a stern rebuke from the House of Representatives.
9. Pendleton Herring, *Public Administration and the Public Interest* (New York: McGraw-Hill, 1936), p. 138. Vagueness, however, may also serve to protect the agency when its decisions are challenged in the courts, since the judiciary may be loath to overturn actions protected by a broad statutory mandate.
10. Congress did not uniformly use the phrase "public interest" in the Communications Act. For example, the standard of "public interest" is specified in Sections 201(b), 215(a), 221(a), 222(c)(1), 415(a)(4), 319(i) and 315; "public convenience and necessity" in Section 314(f); "interest of public convenience and necessity," Section 214(a); "public interest, convenience and necessity," Sections 307(d), 309(a), and 319(a); and "public interest, convenience or necessity," Sections 307(d), 311(b), and 311(c)(3). On September 17, 1981, the FCC recommended that Congress drop all broadcast-related mentions of "convenience" or "necessity." It called the words "superfluous. . . . To the extent the issues embodied in these terms are relevant to radio regulation, they are subsumed under Commission review of the 'public interest.' " *FCC Legislative Proposal, Track I*, September 17, 1981, p. 25 [mimeo.].
11. See *KFKB Broadcasting Association, Inc.* v. *Federal Radio Commission*, 47 F.2d 670 (D.C. Cir. 1931) and *Trinity Methodist Church, South* v. *Federal Radio Commission*, 62 F.2d 850 (D.C. Cir. 1932).
12. See *Red Lion Broadcasting Co., Inc.* v. *Federal Communications Commission*, 395 U.S. 367, 89 S.Ct. 1794, 23 L.Ed. 2d 371 (1969) and *Federal Communications Commission* v. *Pacifica Foundation*, 438 U.S. 726, 98 S.Ct. 3026, 57 L.Ed.2d 1073 (1978). In *Pacifica*, at 746, the court stated: "We have long recognized that each medium of expression presents special First Amendment problems. . . . And of all

forms of communications, it is broadcasting that has received the most limited First Amendment protection."

13. *Red Lion Broadcasting Co.* v. *FCC,* 395 U.S. 367, 390, 89 S.Ct. 1794, 23 L.Ed.2d 371 (1969). See also *CBS* v. *FCC,* ... 101 S.Ct. 2813, 69 L.Ed.2d 706 (1981).

14. Quoted in Fred W. Friendly, *The Good Guys, the Bad Buys and the First Amendment: Free Speech vs. Fairness in Broadcasting* (New York: Random House, 1975), p. ix.

15. This discussion is based on a theme developed by Benno C. Schmidt, Jr., *Freedom of the Press vs. Public Access* (New York: Praeger, 1976), pp. 157-158. ...

16. See Steven J. Simmons, *The Fairness Doctrine and the Media* (Berkeley: University of California Press, 1978). Under Chairman Fowler, the FCC recommended that Congress repeal the Fairness Doctrine. See *FCC Legislative Proposals, Track II,* September 17, 1981 [mimeo.], pp. 23-24.

17. See Clare D. McGillem and William P. McLauchlan, *Hermes Bound: The Policy and Technology of Telecommunications* (West Lafayette, Ind.: Purdue Research Foundation, 1978), pp. 27-34. See also William P. McLauchlan, "Telecommunications Policy: An Overview," *Policy Studies Journal,* VII (Winter 1978), 301-310.

18. *FCC* v. *WNCN Listeners Guild,* ... 101 S.Ct. 1266, 67 L.Ed.2d 521, 539 (1981).

19. *Deregulation of Radio,* 84 FCC 2d 968 (1981). At the same time the FCC also decided it was no longer necessary for the government to require commercial radio broadcasters to keep detailed program logs or to specify the procedure by which broadcasters decided what problems existed in their communities that should be addressed by news or public affairs programs. See also Lawrence Mosher, "The Approaching Boom on the Tube: The Regulatory Boxes No Longer Fit," *The National Journal,* February 23, 1980, pp. 304-310.

20. *FCC Legislative Proposals, Track II,* September 17, 1981 [mimeo.], p. 23.

21. Some scholars argue that scarcity is primarily the product of, rather than the justification for, regulation. See Bruce M. Owen, *Economics and Freedom of Expression: Media Structure and the First Amendment* (Cambridge, Mass.: Ballinger, 1975).

22. *Cable Television Report and Order,* 36 FCC2d 141, 324 (1972). The FCC's policy on the development of cable television has been subject to considerable criticism. ...

23. *Home Box Office, Inc.* v. *FCC,* 567 F.2d 9 (D.C. Cir. 1977), *certiorari denied,* 434 U.S. 829 (1977).

24. Cable Television Channel Capacity and Access Channel Requirements, 45 *Federal Register* 76178 (November 18, 1980).

25. See *Federal Communications Commission* v. *Midwest Video Corp.,* 440 U.S. 689, 99 S.Ct. 1465, 59 L.Ed.2d 733 (1979).

26. For example, *Malrite TV of New York* v. *FCC,* 652 F2d 1140 (2d Cir. 1981).

27. The generalizations that follow were suggested in part by Charles E. Lindblom, *The Policy-Making Process* (Englewood Cliffs, N.J.: Prentice-Hall, 1968).

34. THE PENTAGON PAPERS CASE

Editor's Note. In the "Pentagon Papers" case, the U.S. government sought an injunction to stop the *New York Times* and *Washington Post* from publishing classified documents concerning foreign policy during the Vietnam era. The papers had been surreptitiously copied by an aide working for the National Security Council at the Pentagon, just outside Washington, D.C. The government claimed that publication would do irreparable harm to the national interest, which the president, as commander in chief and primary foreign policy official, had a right to prevent.

The Supreme Court conceded that publication of the documents might cause serious harm to the nation's foreign and domestic policy. But a majority of the judges felt, nonetheless, that the press should be protected from prepublication restraints. The decision leaves the power of the president, and other government officials, to prevent publication of potentially damaging news severely circumscribed. The selection is excerpted from the five supporting and the three dissenting opinions in the Court's decision. The fact that each judge deemed it important to express his views on the case in a separate opinion is unusual. It attests to the grave importance attributed to the issues in the case. The opinion written by Justice Douglas is particularly significant because it makes a strong case for the public's "right to know."

The justices sitting in the case, in the order presented in this selection, were Justices Hugo L. Black, William O. Douglas, William J. Brennan, Jr., Potter Stewart, Byron R. White, Warren E. Burger, John M. Harlan, and Harry A. Blackmun. The selection is from 403 U.S. 713, 1971.

New York Times Co. *v.* United States

MR. JUSTICE BLACK, with whom MR. JUSTICE DOUGLAS joins, concurring. . . .

To find that the President has "inherent power" to halt the publication of news by resort to the courts would wipe out the First Amendment and destroy the fundamental liberty and security of the very people the Government hopes to make "secure." No one can read the history of the adoption of the First Amendment without being convinced beyond any doubt that it was injunctions like those sought here that Madison and his collaborators intended to outlaw in this Nation for all times.

The word "security" is a broad, vague generality whose contours should not be invoked to abrogate the fundamental law embodied in the First

Amendment. The guarding of military and diplomatic secrets at the expense of informed representative government provides no real security for our Republic. The Framers of the First Amendment, fully aware of both the need to defend a new nation and the abuses of the English and Colonial governments, sought to give this new society strength and security by providing that freedom of speech, press, religion, and assembly should not be abridged. . . .

MR. JUSTICE DOUGLAS, with whom MR. JUSTICE BLACK joins, concurring. . . .

These disclosures . . . may have a serious impact. But that is no basis for sanctioning a previous restraint on the press. . . .

The Government says that it has inherent powers to go into court and obtain an injunction to protect the national interest, which in this case is alleged to be national security.

Near v. *Minnesota,* 283 U.S. 697, repudiated that expansive doctrine in no uncertain terms.

The dominant purpose of the First Amendment was to prohibit the widespread practice of governmental suppression of embarrassing information. . . .

Secrecy in government is fundamentally anti-democratic, perpetuating bureaucratic errors. Open debate and discussion of public issues are vital to our national health. On public questions there should be "uninhibited, robust, and wide-open" debate. . . .

MR. JUSTICE BRENNAN, concurring. . . .

. . . The entire thrust of the Government's claim throughout these cases has been that publication of the material sought to be enjoined "could," or "might," or "may" prejudice the national interest in various ways. But the First Amendment tolerates absolutely no prior judicial restraints of the press predicated upon surmise or conjecture that untoward consequences may result. . . . Our cases, it is true, have indicated that there is a single, extremely narrow class of cases in which the First Amendment's ban on prior judicial restraint may be overridden. Our cases have thus far indicated that such cases may arise only when the Nation "is at war," *Schenck* v. *United States,* 249 U.S. 47, 52 (1919), during which times "[n]o one would question but that a government might prevent actual obstruction to its recruiting service or the publication of the sailing dates of transports or the number and location of troops." *Near* v. *Minnesota,* 283 U.S. 697, 716 (1931). Even if the present world situation were assumed to be tantamount to a time of war, or if the power of presently available armaments would justify even in peacetime the suppression of information that would set in motion a nuclear holocaust, in neither of these actions has the Government presented or even alleged that publication of items from or based upon the material at issue would cause the happening of an event of that nature. . . . [O]nly governmental allegation and proof that publication must inevitably, directly, and immediately cause the occurrence of an event kindred to imperiling the safety of a transport already at sea can support even the issuance of an interim restraining order. In no event may mere conclusions be sufficient: for if the Executive Branch seeks judicial aid in preventing publication, it must inevitably submit the basis upon which that aid is sought to scrutiny by the judiciary. . . .

MR. JUSTICE STEWART, with whom MR. JUSTICE WHITE joins, concurring.

In the governmental structure created by our Constitution, the Executive is endowed with enormous power in the two related areas of national defense and international relations. This power, largely unchecked by the Legislative . . . and Judicial . . . branches, has been pressed to the very hilt since the advent of the nuclear missile age. For better or for worse, the simple fact is that a President of the United States possesses vastly greater constitutional independence in these two vital areas of power than does, say, a prime minister of a country with a parliamentary form of government.

In the absence of the governmental checks and balances present in other areas of our national life, the only effective restraint upon executive policy and power in the areas of national defense and international affairs may lie in an enlightened citizenry—in an informed and critical public opinion which alone can here protect the values of democratic government. For this reason, it is perhaps here that a press that is alert, aware, and free most vitally serves the basic purpose of the First Amendment. For without an informed and free press there cannot be an enlightened people.

Yet it is elementary that the successful conduct of international diplomacy and the maintenance of an effective national defense require both confidentiality and secrecy. Other nations can hardly deal with this Nation in an atmosphere of mutual trust unless they can be assured that their confidences will be kept. And within our own executive departments, the development of considered and intelligent international policies would be impossible if those charged with their formulation could not communicate with each other freely, frankly, and in confidence. In the area of basic national defense the frequent need for absolute secrecy is, of course, self-evident.

I think there can be but one answer to this dilemma, if dilemma it be. The responsibility must be where the power is. . . . If the Constitution gives the Executive a large degree of unshared power in the conduct of foreign affairs and the maintenance of our national defense, then under the Constitution the Executive must have the largely unshared duty to determine and preserve the degree of internal security necessary to exercise that power successfully. It is an awesome responsibility, requiring judgment and wisdom of a high order. I should suppose that moral, political, and practical considerations would dictate that a very first principle of that wisdom would be an insistence upon avoiding secrecy for its own sake. For when everything is classified, then nothing is classified, and the system becomes one to be disregarded by the cynical or the careless, and to be manipulated by those intent on self-protection or self-promotion. I should suppose, in short, that the hallmark of a truly effective internal security system would be the maximum possible disclosure, recognizing that secrecy can best be preserved only when credibility is truly maintained. But be that as it may, it is clear to me that it is the constitutional duty of the Executive—as a matter of sovereign prerogative and not as a matter of law as the courts know law—through the promulgation and enforcement of executive regulations, to protect the confidentiality necessary to carry out its responsibilities in the fields of international relations and national defense. . . .

. . . [I]n the cases before us we are asked neither to construe specific regulations nor to apply specific laws. We are asked, instead, to perform a function that the Constitution gave to the Executive, not the Judiciary. We are asked, quite simply, to prevent the publication by two newspapers of material that the Executive Branch insists should not, in the national interest, be published. I am convinced that the Executive is correct with respect to some of the documents involved. But I cannot say that disclosure of any of them will surely result in direct, immediate, and irreparable damage to our Nation or its people. That being so, there can under the First Amendment be but one judicial resolution of the issues before us. I join the judgments of the Court.

MR. JUSTICE WHITE, with whom MR. JUSTICE STEWART joins, concurring.

I concur in today's judgments, but only because of the concededly extraordinary protection against prior restraints enjoyed by the press under our constitutional system. I do not say that in no circumstances would the First Amendment permit an injunction against publishing information about government plans or operations. . . . Nor, after examining the materials the Government characterizes as the most sensitive and destructive, can I deny that revelation of these documents will do substantial damage to public interests. Indeed, I am confident that their disclosure will have that result. But I nevertheless agree that the United States has not satisfied the very heavy burden that it must meet to warrant an injunction against publication in these cases. . . .

MR. CHIEF JUSTICE BURGER, dissenting. . . .

. . . In these cases, the imperative of a free and unfettered press comes into collision with another imperative, the effective functioning of a complex modern government and specifically the effective exercise of certain constitutional powers of the Executive. Only those who view the First Amendment as an absolute in all circumstances—a view I respect, but reject—can find such cases as these to be simple or easy.

These cases are not simple for another and more immediate reason. We do not know the facts of the cases. . . .

. . . [T]he frenetic haste is due in large part to the manner in which the Times proceeded from the date it obtained the purloined documents. It seems reasonably clear now that the haste precluded reasonable and deliberate judicial treatment of these cases and was not warranted. . . .

The newspapers make a derivative claim under the First Amendment; they denominate this right as the public "right to know"; by implication, the Times asserts a sole trusteeship of that right by virtue of its journalistic "scoop." The right is asserted as an absolute. Of course, the First Amendment right itself is not an absolute, as Justice Holmes so long ago pointed out in his aphorism concerning the right to shout "fire" in a crowded theater if there was no fire. There are other exceptions, some of which Chief Justice Hughes mentioned by way of example in *Near* v. *Minnesota*. There are no doubt other exceptions no one has had occasion to describe or discuss. Conceivably such exceptions may be lurking in these cases and would have been flushed had they been properly considered in the trial courts, free from unwarranted deadlines and frenetic pressures. An issue of this importance should be tried and heard in a judicial atmosphere conducive to thoughtful, reflective deliberation, especially when haste, in terms of hours, is unwarranted in light of the long period the Times, by its own choice, deferred publication. . . .

MR. JUSTICE HARLAN, with whom THE CHIEF JUSTICE and MR. JUSTICE BLACKMUN join, dissenting. . . .

. . . It is plain to me that the scope of the judicial function in passing upon the activities of the Executive Branch of the Government in the field of foreign affairs is very narrowly restricted. This view is, I think, dictated by the concept of separation of powers upon which our constitutional system rests. . . .

From this constitutional primacy in the field of foreign affairs, it seems to me that certain conclusions necessarily follow. Some of these were stated concisely by President Washington, declining the request of the House of Representatives for the papers leading up to the negotiation of the Jay Treaty:

> "The nature of foreign negotiations requires caution, and their success must often depend on secrecy; and even when brought to a conclusion a full disclosure of all the measures, demands, or eventual concessions which may have been proposed or contemplated would be extremely impolitic; for this might have a pernicious influence on future negotiations, or produce immediate inconveniences, perhaps danger and mischief, in relation to other powers." 1 J. Richardson, Messages and Papers of the Presidents 194-195 (1896).

The power to evaluate the "pernicious influence" of premature disclosure is not, however, lodged in the Executive alone. I agree that, in performance of its duty to protect the values of the First Amendment against political pressures, the judiciary must review the initial Executive determination to the point of satisfying itself that the subject matter of the dispute does lie within the proper compass of the President's foreign relations power. . . . Moreover, the judiciary may properly insist that the determination that disclosure of the subject matter would irreparably impair the national security be made by the head of the Executive Department concerned—here the Secretary of State or the Secretary of Defense—after actual personal consideration by that officer. . . .

But in my judgment the judiciary may not properly go beyond these two inquiries and redetermine for itself the probable impact of disclosure on the national security.

"[T]he very nature of executive decisions as to foreign policy is political, not judicial. Such decisions are wholly confided by our Constitution to the political departments of the government, Executive and Legislative. They are delicate, complex, and involve large elements of prophecy. They are and should be undertaken only by those directly responsible to the people whose welfare they advance or imperil. They are decisions of a kind for which the Judiciary has neither aptitude, facilities nor responsibility and which has long been held to belong in the domain of political power not subject to judicial intrusion or inquiry." *Chicago & Southern Air Lines* v. *Waterman Steamship Corp.*, 333 U.S. 103, 111 (1948) (Jackson, J.)

Even if there is some room for the judiciary to override the executive determination, it is plain that the scope of review must be exceedingly narrow. I can see no indication in the opinions of either the District Court or the Court of Appeals in the *Post* litigation that the conclusions of the Executive were given even the deference owing to an administrative agency, much less that owing to a co-equal branch of the Government operating within the field of its constitutional prerogative....

MR. JUSTICE BLACKMUN, dissenting....

I strongly urge, and sincerely hope, that these two newspapers will be fully aware of their ultimate responsibilities to the United States of America. Judge Wilkey, dissenting in the District of Columbia case, after a review of only the affidavits before his court (the basic papers had not then been made available by either party), concluded that there were a number of examples of documents that, if in the possession of the Post, and if published, "could clearly result in great harm to the nation," and he defined "harm" to mean "the death of soldiers, the destruction of alliances, the greatly increased difficulty of negotiation with our enemies, the inability of our diplomats to negotiate...."... I hope that damage has not already been done. If, however, damage has been done, and if, with the Court's action today, these newspapers proceed to publish the critical documents and there results therefrom "the death of soldiers, the destruction of alliances, the greatly increased difficulty of negotiation with our enemies, the inability of our diplomats to negotiate," to which list I might add the factors of prolongation of the war and of further delay in the freeing of United States prisoners, then the Nation's people will know where the responsibility for these sad consequences rests.

35. CRISIS NEWS MANAGEMENT
IN THE KENNEDY YEARS

William J. Small

Editor's Note. Even though the First Amendment protects the print media from practically all forms of censorship, they are not able to print all the news that is of major public interest. There are three reasons. The most intractable one is space and time limitations. The diversity of the United States with its worldwide interests and connections makes the scope of significant political happenings so vast that no paper can mention them all, let alone cover them adequately. Television and radio can do little more than present annotated headlines.

The other two reasons, which William J. Small discusses in his essay, are formal and informal censorship by news sources and self-censorship by news media. Government and other societal institutions withhold and often deliberately conceal massive amounts of information that they do not want to publicize. Government has the additional power to declare information "classified" so that access to it becomes limited even inside government. A few of these suppressed stories surface because the information is leaked to the press or due to investigative reporting. But most classified information remains hidden.

The issue of press self-censorship arises less frequently and generally involves information pertaining to national security or to the rights of persons accused of crime. But when the issue occurs, it poses serious dilemmas for newspeople and often leads to recriminations afterwards. Small, speaking with the voice of experience, discusses self-censorship issues faced by the press during the administration of John F. Kennedy.

Wiliam J. Small, a broadcaster and author, has spent much of his career as a news director. He has served CBS and NBC in various executive capacities, including a stint as chief of CBS's Washington news bureau. The selection is from *Political Power and the Press,* New York: Norton, 1972.

. . . [President John F. Kennedy] was a master of the electronic medium and knew it. He also knew what it permitted him to do to offset newspaper reaction. Said Kennedy one evening in the White House, "We couldn't survive without TV."

[Press Secretary Pierre] Salinger felt the wire services, AP and UPI, were the single most important client he had since they serviced all newspapers and broadcasters but he considered the networks "the second most powerful faction in the establishment." He started adding a network reporter to the small presidential pools and dealt privately with the three network bureau chiefs to arrange presidential appearances on television.

The combination of wire services and networks, he noted, permitted the president to communicate with "unbelievable speed to the nation and the world." In ten minutes, a presidential announcement of importance could be on the airwaves and on the teletype machines. This was especially important to have during the Cuban crisis, as Salinger himself has recalled:

> There were desperate moments during the Cuban missile crisis when communications between JFK and Khrushchev were running hours behind because of the total inadequacy of diplomatic channels. We decided to release JFK's statements directly to the networks and wire services, knowing that Moscow was monitoring our radio frequencies and news wires and would have the word hours faster. Khrushchev did the same with Radio Moscow and Tass, and the speed-up in communications may very well have been a factor in preventing escalation of the crisis. This necessity for instantaneous communication was the reason for prompt agreement, after the Cuban crisis, on installation of the hot line (teletype system) between Washington and Moscow.

Cuba, of course, both during the abortive Bay of Pigs adventure and the later missile crisis, gave the Kennedy presidency its most dramatic moments. The first was his greatest embarrassment and the other his most satisfying accomplishment. The role of the press in both confrontations involving Cuba is important.

The *Nation* on November 19, 1960 published an editorial, "Are We Training Cuban Guerrillas?" It told of a U.S. financed, "Guatemala-type" invasion, with forces being trained in Guatemala to invade Cuba. In January, the *New York Times* reported such training but said authorities explained that it was to meet any assault from Cuba, not to go into Cuba.

In April, Gilbert Harrison of the *New Republic* sent presidential aide Arthur Schlesinger, Jr. the galley proofs on an article "Our Men in Miami," which Schlesinger called "a careful, accurate, and devastating account of CIA activities among the (Cuban) refugees." Schlesinger took the article to Kennedy who expressed the hope that it could be stopped. Harrison agreed, Schlesinger wrote, in "a patriotic act which left me oddly uncomfortable."

Meanwhile Tad Szulc, the able Latin American correspondent for the *Times* was developing the same story in Florida, a story of recruiting men to engage in an "imminent" invasion of Cuba. Turner Catledge, the managing editor, called James Reston to ask advice. Reston cautioned him against pinpointing the time of the landing. Szulc recalled that the editors dropped mention of the CIA involvement as well. At the *Times,* editors Ted Bernstein and Lew Jordan protested. Never before had the front-page play in the *Times* been changed for policy reasons. They appealed to the publisher, Orvil Dryfoos. He said national security and the safety of the men going ashore were involved.

Ironically, there was a "shirttail" to the Szulc story which said some of the things that were dropped. A separate item was printed just below the end of the Szulc report telling of a CBS News report of plans for the invasion of Cuba in their final stages, ships and planes from Florida preparing for the assault.

Kennedy was reported to be furious at stories about the upcoming invasion. At one point he told Salinger, "I can't believe what I'm reading! Castro doesn't need agents over here. All he has to do is read our papers. It's all laid out for him."

The April 17, 1961 invasion was a complete failure and an extreme embarrassment for Kennedy. Officials, once the landings started, told reporters in Miami that five thousand men were involved. They hoped to encourage the Cuban people to rise up and support a large invasion force, but when the landing of a thousand (not five thousand) men ran into trouble, the same officials tried to minimize the defeat and said there was no invasion, that two hundred to four hundred men had landed simply to deliver supplies to anti-Castro guerrillas already in Cuba. James Reston wrote in the *Times,* "Both times the press was debased for the Government's purpose. Both times the Castro government and its Soviet advisers knew from their own agents in the anti-Castro refugee camps and from their own observation on the beaches that these pronouncements were false and silly. And both times the American people were the only ones to be fooled."

Newspapers attacked the White House for hiding the facts. Ambassador Adlai Stevenson, himself ignorant of the invasion plans, had gone before the United Nations to deny U.S. participation in the Bay of Pigs.

The president was criticized for his refusal to speak on the Cuban question at his first news conference afterwards ("I do not think that any useful national purpose would be served by my going further into the Cuban question this morning"). Bitterly he told Salinger, "What could I have said that would have helped the situation at all? That we took the beating of our lives? That the CIA and the Pentagon are stupid? What purpose do they think it would serve to put that on the record? We're going to straighten all this out, and soon. The publishers have to understand that we're never more than a miscalculation away from war and there are things we are doing that we just can't talk about."

On April 20, the president had an opportunity to straighten out the press when he appeared before the meeting of the American Association of Newspaper Editors. He spoke on Cuba but made no reference to press aspects of the Bay of Pigs other than to say "There are, from this, sobering lessons for us all to learn."

A week later, however, he spoke at a New York dinner of the American Newspaper Publishers Association and this time the president did go to the press issue. "Every newspaper now asks itself with respect to every story, 'Is it news?' All I suggest is that you add the question, 'Is it in the interest of national security?'"

In a harsh indictment of the press, he said: "This nation's foes have openly boasted of acquiring through our newspapers information they would otherwise hire agents to acquire through theft, bribery, or espionage; details of this nation's covert preparations to counter the enemy's covert operations have been available to every newspaper reader, friend and foe alike; the size, the strength, the location, and the nature of our forces and weapons, and our plans and strategy for their use, have all been pinpointed in the press and other news media to a degree sufficient to satisfy any foreign power; and, in at least one case, the publication of details covering a secret mechanism whereby satellites were followed required its alteration at the expense of considerable time and money."

He asked the publishers to recognize their own responsibility, to reexamine standards to see "our country's peril." Even the First Amendment, he asserted, "must yield to the public's need for national security." He then offered to cooperate in something he called "the voluntary assumption of specific new steps or machinery" to do this.

The audience took that to be a call for some form of self-censorship. The St. Louis *Post-Dispatch* warned that this could "make the press an official arm in totalitarian countries." The Indianapolis *Star* said Kennedy was trying to intimidate the press. The Los Angeles *Times* said it was a Kennedy "smarting with chagrin" who angrily sought to make a scapegoat of the press. Noting that the press had accepted the administration denials prior to the invasion, the *Times* said instead of a president chiding the press, "it should have been twitted for having its leg pulled."

A group of editors and publishers arranged to meet with the president to see what he had in mind. They met for over an hour, the president saying he didn't want to restrict the publishing of news but stressing the critical period of history of the moment. Kennedy's staff had listed a series of allegedly harmful disclosures that had appeared in print.

The president asked the editors if they did not agree that it was a period of extreme peril to the nation. He was surprised to get the blunt answer: "No." They said they saw no need for censorship short of a declared national emergency. Kennedy said he had no intention of making such a declaration. The meeting ended with the puzzled committee agreeing to think about it, unclear as to what Kennedy had in mind and convinced that the president himself had only a vague notion of what he wanted.

Clifton Daniel, the managing editor of the New York *Times*, revealed details of the *Times'* involvement in the Bay of Pigs when he spoke in June, 1966 to the World Press Institute meeting in St. Paul. Daniel says that Kennedy turned to Turner Catledge at the White House meeting and, in an aside, said, "If you had printed more about the operation you would have saved us from a colossal mistake." A year later, the president told the *Times* publisher Orvil Dryfoos much the same: "I wish you had run everything on Cuba."

Daniel himself agreed. In his St. Paul speech, he said, "My own view is that the Bay of Pigs operation might well have been cancelled and the country would have been saved enormous embarrassment if the *New York Times* and other newspapers had been more diligent in the performance of their duty." He reported however that James Reston did *not* agree: "If I had to do it over, I would do exactly what we did at the time. It is ridiculous to think that publishing the fact that the invasion was imminent would have avoided the disaster. I am quite sure the operation would have gone forward. The thing had been cranked up too far. The CIA would have had to disarm the anti-Castro forces physically. Jack Kennedy was in no mood to do anything like that."

But five years earlier, on the day after the editors met Kennedy to discuss the lessons of press coverage of the Bay of Pigs, Reston had written in a different vein. "The trouble with the press during the Cuban crisis," he said then, "was not that it said too much but that it said too little. It knew what was going on ahead of the landing."

A year after Daniel's detailed account of the *Times* and the Cuban crisis, Senator Robert F. Kennedy spoke before ASNE [American Society of Newspaper Editors] and said, "Clearly, publication of U.S. battle plans in time of war would irresponsibly imperil success and endanger lives. On the other hand, President Kennedy once said that wider press discussion of plans to invade Cuba—known to many reporters and patriotically withheld—might have avoided the Bay of Pigs. . . . In looking back over crises from Berlin and the Bay of Pigs to the Gulf of Tonkin, or even over the past fifteen years, I can think of few examples where disclosure of large policy considerations damaged the country, and many instances where public discussion and debate led to more thoughtful and informed decisions."

President Kennedy faced an even more serious crisis on Cuba when, late in 1962, it was discovered that the Soviets were placing missiles on the island. There, too, the press was involved but this time the president took direct and personal action to preclude what he considered premature disclosure.

The election campaign in the fall of 1962 was full of charges that the Soviets were moving missiles with atomic capability into sites on the island of Cuba. The president's chief national security advisor, McGeorge Bundy publicly denied this just one week before it became public, stating, "I know there is no present evidence and I think there is no present likelihood that the Cubans and the Cuban government and the Soviet government would in combination attempt to install a major offensive capability." At the time he said it, the White House was already examining aerial photos of the installations under construction. John F. Kennedy was to return from a campaign appearance in Chicago, allegedly to nurse a bad cold as the last weekend of Cuba crisis planning began. On Monday he went on television and told the American people about it.

Earlier, however, James Reston had talked to Bundy about the matter and it was clear from Reston's questioning that he knew what was up. Bundy told Kennedy and the president telephoned Reston. He told him of his plans to go on television Monday night and said publication in advance would result in a Khrushchev ultimatum before the president could personally report to the people. Reston said he understood and would recommend that the *Times* hold up publication but he also recommended that Kennedy talk to the publisher. He did. Dryfoos then put the issue up to Reston and his staff. The story was withheld. At the time of the publisher's death, the president wrote Mrs. Dryfoos that "this decision of his made far more effective our later actions and therefore contributed greatly to our national safety."

Some say that the Bay of Pigs marked the end of Kennedy's very brief honeymoon with the press. Others say it lasted longer. In either case, his administration gave rise to the phrase "news management" and both Cuban affairs were very much a part of that. . . .

36. JOURNALIST MEETS PROPAGANDIST

Ben H. Bagdikian

Editor's Note. The independence and power of newspeople rest largely in their freedom to select news for publication and feature it as they choose. The many individuals and institutions in and out of government who want and need media publicity try to influence these media choices. One of the prominent new professions that has emerged to help publicity seekers reach their goals is public relations. Representatives of the major interests in the public and the private sectors all have public relations staffs charged with gaining entry to the media.

These staffs rely heavily on print and electronic news releases. In this essay Ben H. Bagdikian alerts the reader to the widespread use and abuse of news peddled by public relations staffs on behalf of a variety of commercial and governmental clients. Bagdikian points out how readily their releases are accepted into mass media news channels. His article was first published in 1963. Since then, the names in the public relations game have changed and so have a few of the tactics. But as the French say, plus ça change, plus c'est la même chose. The basic game has not changed at all. Media channels continue to be flooded with stories planted by the agents of special interest groups.

Ben H. Bagdikian has worked as a reporter, foreign correspondent, and editor for various newspapers, including the *Washington Post*. He also has been a prolific, widely published critic of media performance. He is the dean of the Graduate School of Journalism at the University of California, Berkeley. The selection is from *Columbia Journalism Review* 2 (Fall 1963): 29-35.

...One day in November, 1952 ... the *Miami Herald* ran a story without credit and therefore seemingly its own:

"Somehow dahlias, daisies, pine trees and 65-degree weather aren't the picture most people visualize when they think of a tropical country like the Dominican Republic. Yet this is just what...."

Two weeks later *The Hartford Courant* ran, also seemingly on its own:

"Somehow dahlias, daisies, pine trees and 65-degree weather aren't the picture...."

This, of course, was tourism puffery (which, even so, bears significant political benefits for the country involved) taken unaltered from a foreign government handout. For some reason editors regard this, along with women's-page, financial-page and entertainment-page puffery, ethically sound and no disservice to the reader.

A couple of years after the dahlias and daisies appeared to sprout indigenously (in many more papers than just those of Miami and Hartford) there appeared an editorial, seemingly locally written, in the late *Montpelier Evening Argus:*

"Dona Maria Martinez Trujillo, wife of Generalissimo Rafael L. Trujillo, the fabulous four-time president of the Dominican Republic, has written a book. . . ."

This laudatory editorial, word-for-word, was printed also in Zanesville, Ohio, and in other papers from Calais, Maine, to Deming, New Mexico. All appeared to be local editors' opinions of an obscure book.

A year after that the *New Bedford Standard-Times* ran an editorial, seeming to be locally written.

"Today the Dominican Republic . . . is a bulwark of strength against Communism and has been widely cited as one of the cleanest, healthiest, happiest countries on the globe. Guiding spirit of this fabulous transformation is Generalissimo Trujillo who worked tirelessly. . . ."

At about the same time a small weekly in Mooresville, North Carolina, ran an editorial called, "What a Great and Good Ruler Can Accomplish for a Country," and it began with what seemed the Mooresville editor's analysis:

"Today the Dominican Republic . . . is a bulwark of strength against Communism and has been widely cited as one of the cleanest, healthiest, happiest. . . ."

The innocuous dahlias and daisies were gifts from Trujillo's New York agent, the late Harry Klemfuss. The editorial on the book of Mrs. Trujillo, wife of the fabulous four-time president, was also compliments of Mr. Klemfuss through the services of a syndicate called U.S. Press Association, Inc., which received $125 from Klemfuss to send out the editorial to its list of 1,300 dailies and weeklies (who get a batch of editorials free every week). The "cleanest, healthiest, happiest country" editorial came via the same route with the help of $125 of Trujillo's money. The Montpelier paper had two other editorials on its page with the one urging purchase of Mrs. Trujillo's book. One editorial told readers to use reflectorized tape on their car bumpers to prevent accidents; the other told how American baby foods had produced good in the world. These last two were also with the compliments of U.S. Press Association (which had been paid $125 each by manufacturers, respectively, of reflectorized tape and of American baby foods). . . .

If one looked further into the activities of Trujillo's publicity agent, one finds that on September 13, 1955, the *New Orleans Item* carried an interview in New Orleans with Klemfuss in which the paid agent of Trujillo praised Trujillo as a leading fighter against communism in the Western Hemisphere. The story was written, but not signed, by a reporter for the *Item,* Roland Von

Kurnatowski, who, according to Klemfuss records and his own admission, was paid more than $500 by Klemfuss to place this and other pro-Trujillo stories in the *Item*. Kurnatowski was the *Item's* Latin American editor. He says the paper knew and approved of his relations with Klemfuss and Trujillo.

If, further, one inspected the Klemfuss file in the Foreign Agents Registration Section of the Department of Justice he would find that in 1958 there were two provocative entries about Trujillo expenditures in the United States: "August, 1958 . . . United Press reporting assignment, $75," and "June 20, INS Special Services Division, $226.20." And thereby hangs a tale.

Senator Fulbright drew out part of this tale [during hearings by the Senate Foreign Relations Committee in 1963.] Hearst's International News Service, before its purchase by United Press, turned over its reporters to commercial clients who paid a fee. The reporters would ask news sources questions the private client ordered and put together a report. For additional fees, INS put the client's material on its news wire—or at least the records of the Trujillo regime indicate that INS did this for him at $2,000 a month and offered to continue to send Trujillo material as news to its wire-service customers under the byline of an INS editor.

This arrangement paralleled another Trujillo news alliance in this country. On February 5, 1959, an agent of Trujillo handed $750,000 in cash to Alexander L. Guterma, president of the Mutual Broadcasting System, in return for which Guterma agreed to have Mutual broadcast to the American people every day a minimum of 14 minutes of "news" desired by Trujillo. Guterma ultimately went to jail and Mutual stopped the agreement. INS never made so large a haul, so far as the record shows, but it did offer for sale both its reporters and space on its "news" tickers. . . .

Public-relations firms play a substantial role in the world of news, as both they and news organizations are forever reiterating. It is perfectly obvious that the job of collecting the day's news must include public-relations offerings. But this is legitimate, so far as significant news and obligation to the reader is concerned, only if the press is knowing, discriminating, and ruthless in its selection of such material.

What happens when the newsgatherer is under contract to serve Stan the PR man when he has cash in hand at the same time that he is under moral obligation to be ruthless with Stan the PR Man when he appears with press release in hand? Or more realistically, when Stan the PR Man's client is involved, along with many less articulate parties in a news situation?

The traditional defense of a double standard has been that when the newsgatherer puts on his news hat he then proceeds to bite the hand that feeds him. . . . One is reminded that when some old pals from the past showed up at the White House to rake in some patronage, a newly installed President walked in and announced:

"Gentlemen, Chet Arthur of New York and Chester A. Arthur, President of the United States, are two different persons. Good day." . . .

Hamilton Wright, an expert in [public relations], says a "documentary" or short subject may cost his foreign client $10,000 to $50,000 to produce. He then sells this to a major film distributor for $1. The film distributor in turn sells it for profit to movie houses for varying rentals. Or the PR firm, or a foreign government directly, may pay a distributing outfit a flat fee, on the order of $2.50 to $12.50 per placement, to get the PR film run on local television stations. The odds are overwhelming that any slack-time, and perhaps a prime-time, "documentary" seen on local television was made and paid for by someone looking for free publicity or public indoctrination. In most cases, there is no indication who made the film. The relationship between the men who decide what will be seen by the public and the PR firms who want them to peddle the stuff is extraordinarily congenial. . . .

The status of Nationalist China and the offshore islands is a delicate one and on occasion has threatened the peace. Charles Baily, short-subject sales manager for Warner Brothers, planning what to tell the film audience about the issue, wrote to Wright, who was getting about $300,000 a year from the Nationalist Chinese government to push its line: "You know what we can use and I will leave it to your judgment."

This congeniality between axe-grinders and "news" executives extended to feature syndicates. Louis Messolonghetis, of King Features Syndicate, was entertained by Mexico. To assure Mexico that the vacation had paid off, Wright sent them tearsheets of an eight-column newspaper feature page on Mexico sent out by King Features. Courtland Smith, an editor of Central Press Association, a branch of King Features, himself sent proofs to Mexico "to show how we have made good use of Hamilton Wright's photos on half a dozen occasions during recent weeks. These particular pages were included in our service to nearly 100 daily papers throughout the United States. The feature story went to more than 200."

The next day Smith wrote to Wright: "Dear Ham, We had a terrific week in Mexico. . . . The suite at the Hilton was lavish. . . . You told me the government would pick up the full tab, so we signed for everything." On another occasion Smith told Wright that to accommodate a request by the Nationalist China PR man Smith would eliminate the signs that the material originated as PR for a foreign government and would substitute "the large KSF slug you said might be helpful."

These executives are gatekeepers of American news. PR men who know the field know that they are far more important than the editors of individual newspapers, not only because they can dump their material into news channels wholesale, which they do, but also because the material usually reaches the individual newspaper, magazine, or station with the slug of the distributing organization—implying that it is the result of their own initiative and reporting. As Hamilton Wright told his client, Nationalist China:

"This material will be released direct to the following syndicates who service 95 percent of all the newspapers in the U.S.A. These syndicates 'sell' their services to the largest and smallest newspapers, supplying them with pictures (wirephotos), Sunday features, articles on every subject, rotogravure layouts, etc. We have worked with these editors for more than 35 years. They know us—we know them. In 75 percent of the releases, neither the editor of the newspaper—nor the newspaper reader—HAS ANY KNOWLEDGE WHERE THE MATERIAL ORIGINATED. Only the editor of the syndicate knows."

The upper-case letters are Mr. Wright's.

The elder Mr. Wright is prone to exaggerate. For example, he claimed that every foot of newsreel film from Nationalist China and the offshore islands seen anywhere in the United States, movie houses or television, for a period of five crucial years, was straight PR processed by him. He is not strictly accurate on this. Not *every* bit was his, only most of it.

PR-in-the-news cannot be dismissed as merely a self-serving fantasy created by public relations men, intent on promoting themselves with unearned credit. There is much of this, to be sure, and PR clients are notoriously gullible to the meaningless scrapbook and inflated claims of influence. But the impact of press agentry in the news is all too real. There is too much evidence of effective tainting of the wellsprings and conduits of news. The largely anonymous men who control the syndicate and wire service copy desks and the central wirephoto machines determine at a single decision what millions will see and hear. Whether they are properly trained and selected for this responsibility—and many of them are less discriminating than editors on individual papers who must work with what these gatekeepers send them—is one issue. But there seems little doubt that these gatekeepers preside over an operation in which an appalling amount of press agentry sneaks in the back door of American journalism and marches untouched out the front door as "news."

Some clandestine PR operations put local editors at a severe disadvantage. The Fulbright Committee determined that the PR firm of Selvage & Lee, under a contract with Portuguese interests to spend up to $500,000 a year to push the line that Portuguese administration of the African Colonies of Angola and Mozambique is enlightened and happy, created a dummy "Portuguese-American" committee in Boston and then used it as a lobbying and pressure group. When Senator Gore of Tennessee made a speech asking that American guns not be used in killing Africans, the Washington office of Selvage & Lee composed a letter-to-the-editor implying that the Senator was arguing against anti-Communism in Africa and stating explicitly that this was the letter of an American citizen group. It sent the letter to Boston to have it mailed to 162 newspapers in districts where Senator Gore runs for election. It also ran a letter campaign against Philip Potter of the Baltimore *Sun*. Against this type of operation editors can exercise only normal skepticism and rules of relevancy.

But it is not all so blind nor unwitting. The National Editorial Association, NEA (not to be confused with the syndicate, Newspaper Enterprise Association, no relation) represents 6,200 smaller papers in the country, including 500 dailies. In January, 1963, they sent a junket of more than fifty newspaper editors through Africa, where Selvage & Lee paid for the trip through Angola. Attached to the trip and identified as representing the "South Sioux City (Nebraska) Star," was Paul Wagner, who was of great help to his fellow newspapermen in deciding what to see and what it meant. He provided them with fact sheets and stories about conditions in Angola. Wagner was in fact the publisher of the small Nebraska paper until 1951. But he is now an account executive for Selvage & Lee and is a paid propagandist for the Portuguese interests in Angola.

After that, Selvage & Lee purchased at something under $2,500 a two-page spread of NEA's publication, *Publisher's Auxiliary,* to run rhapsodic pieces in news type by NEA editors and by Wagner himself, all of them on the wonders of life and times in Angola (but nothing from the few editors on the junket who caught on to the PR operation and objected).

This is not a freak combination of what purports to be a serious editorial association of newspapers and direct PR insertion into the news. *Publishers' Auxiliary* regularly runs a service for PR firms, corporations, utility industries, and others, whereby a mat will be sent to any of the 14,000 papers receiving the publication who asks for it, this mat being a PR plug for the product or publicity line of the firm that pays *Publishers' Auxiliary.* This is nothing clandestine. It is free to the newspaper; it plugs something any editor of normal intelligence can detect; and two previous handlers get paid to send it out. As an executive for Selvage & Lee said of the editors who get such material and print it:

"The people who print it . . . they know that they are getting it free. . . . They are not so naive."

It may be time for the executives of great news organizations to reconsider the role of public relations in the news. Public relations is useful but it has taken over some editorial functions. That it would try to do this is inevitable and it must be said that public-relations men are far clearer in their objectives than are editors and publishers. The PR men are bound to further the interests of their clients and they, at least are doing what they are getting paid to do. They don't have the responsibility of editors and news executives, who arrogate to themselves a crucial and exalted position in American democracy and who insist they exist and are paid primarily to protect the reader's interests in a fair presentation of the significant news.

PR is not going to disappear. But one first step in keeping it under control might be an intense course for newspapermen and editors on the way PR actually works. This would include not just the sociological treatises on publicity but some of the backdoor minuets glimpsed briefly in the Fulbright hearings.

The news editor today is lighting manager of a stage from which the audience hears innumerable wild sounds and the thump of falling bodies. To illuminate this multifarious action intelligibly is difficult at best. It is so difficult that the lighting manager is often bedeviled by a peculiar habit on the news stage: some of the actors carry their own spotlights. These actors, like good PR men, turn their own light on themselves when they look good, often at considerable expense to themselves and with many asides to the audience on how much light they contribute to this shadowy world. There are times, however, when these actors are up to some villainy or else their suspenders have just broken, at which point they prudently turn off their light or shine it at someone else. Thus, at the most crucial points in the news drama, the function of PR and of the press may be diametrically opposed: The PR men are paid to prevent exposure of the client when he is in significant error or disability; the press is paid to do precisely the opposite. This is so obvious that some of the press has forgotten it. . . .

. . . [N]ot so long ago many news organizations were complaining bitterly, and sometimes justifiably, that their own government was managing the news. And yet large news organizations, central in our system of information, not only did not seem to mind but actively assisted (and profited financially) when news to the American people was managed by foreign governments and private special pleaders.

37A. A GROWING CONTROVERSY: THE "FREE FLOW" OF NEWS AMONG NATIONS

John C. Merrill

Editor's Note. In 1977 the UNESCO-sponsored "McBride Commission," named after its chairman Sean McBride, began to investigate ways to create a New World Information Order that would mitigate world communication problems. One of the major issues of controversy and concern was media imperialism. This issue raised questions about the right of nations to regulate news flow within their own borders and as a prerequisite, to exclude news from other nations. Also of concern was the countries' responsibility for the quality of their journalists' news product and for the consequences of news dissemination.

More than two years later the McBride Commission issued a final report containing 82 recommendations. Many of these were widely accepted by the world community. Others aroused fierce controversy. The United States objected particularly to provisions that seemed, to it, to impair the free flow of information and the right of the press to be free from government controls.

In the selections presented here, John C. Merrill presents his views about the merits of complaints by Third World countries that led to proposals to restrain American and other western media. On balance he finds most of the charges ill-considered. Herbert I. Schiller, a well-known critic of media imperialism, looks at the same situation from a Third World and socialist perspective. He comes to the opposite conclusion. The arguments presented on either side of the case demonstrate the wide gap that splits the world's nations when it comes to questions of news media control.

John C. Merrill is director of the School of Journalism at Louisiana State University. He has served as correspondent for a number of European newspapers and television stations. His lectures have taken him to all parts of the world.

Herbert I. Schiller is professor of communications at the University of California, San Diego. He is a prolific author who also has lectured widely abroad. The selections are from *Crisis in International News,* edited by Jim Richstad and Michael H. Anderson, New York: Columbia University Press, 1981.

In this day when news flow is said not to be what it should be, there is at least one kind of information flowing freely: denunciation of Western journalism for alleged inadequate and biased reporting and news dissemination as relates to the so-called Third World—the "developing" or "nonaligned" countries. Largely propelled by Unesco conferences on the subject, proliferating throughout the world in recent years, a barrage of Third World criticism of Western news practices pounds upon the ear and has become a major theme in communications literature.[1]

Among the main targets are the big international news agencies of the West—the U.S.'s Associated Press and United Press International, Britain's Reuters, and France's Agence France-Presse. Quite simply, it seems, the Third World is greatly disturbed over what it sees as the unenlightened, biased, and inadequate journalistic theory and practice of the capitalistic Western nations—especially the United States. Hardly a day goes by that some editor or political leader in the Third World does not take a public swing at Western journalism for its "injustices" in the area of news coverage; and, it might be added, this criticism flows rather freely into the media journals and general press of the West.

The Fundamental Issue

What is the main problem? Actually, the Third World has a whole list of complaints against the Western press but at present the main target seems to be what is referred to as the "free flow" of news across national boundaries. According to Third World spokesmen, the Western news agencies—especially the AP and UPI—are disrupting this free flow of news, are distorting the realities of the developing countries, and are basically presenting negative images of the Third World. This is the basic criticism, although there are many others.

The leaders of these developing countries, ... both political and journalistic, recognize the great importance of mass communication, the potency of international information dissemination, and the impact of national images on the conduct of foreign relations. They are, justifiably, sensitive to the kind of press treatment they receive. And, by and large, they feel they do not fare well in the Western press—especially in stories from the big news agencies.

Individually, and through the international forum of Unesco, these Third World countries are mounting an escalating campaign against Western journalism.[2] They seek to eliminate the impediments they see blocking the free flow of information throughout the world. In other words, they want to see news flow as freely *from* the Third World to the Western countries as it flows from the West *to* the Third World. The big Western news agencies, they say, have a virtual monopoly on news dissemination and fail to provide the world with a realistic picture of what is really happening in the Third World. Too biased, they say. Too heavy on negative news—poverty, illiteracy, riots, revolutions, volcano eruptions, antics of national leaders, kidnappings, etc. They ask: What about the *good* things that are going on—bridge building, highway construction, new schools, and the like? Why is it that the AP and UPI, and to a lesser degree Reuters and Agence France-Presse, so grossly neglect these aspects of the Third World?

Basic Conceptual Differences

Having talked with journalists in some twenty Third World countries in the past several years, I have concluded that what they really mean by free flow of news is a "balanced flow." Western journalists mean something else by free flow. In other words, Western newsmen put the emphasis on the *free* and the Third World journalists stress the *flow*—with the main part of this flow relating to a desired *balance* or *equality* in the news that moves among nations and parts of the world.

This difference in concept is important, but it is not often stressed in discussions and debates. Western journalists, for example, have found many (most?) of the Third World nations to be highly restrictive and secretive societies whose leaders go to great lengths to keep correspondents (and not only *foreign* ones) at arms length. Sources in these countries are hard to reach; meetings are closed; leaders are secretive and touchy, and the record shows that in recent years foreign journalists have been threatened often with expulsion—and many have been expelled for reporting what in the West would be the most obvious kinds of news events. The Western journalists say that if there is a problem with news flow it largely rests with the controlled systems in which they are trying to report. How can Western journalists permit the news flow to be *free* when the Third World nations themselves do not have free societies with press systems which are free? In other words, a *free* flow of news must include the flow within countries themselves and not simply the flow between and among nations. It is the situation *within* countries that most often affects news flow, say the Western journalists trying to report the Third World.

Third World critics, of course, reject this Western perspective, and they shift the emphasis from the internal restrictive problems of the nations to the Western news agencies and foreign correspondents. So we are constantly told that Western reporters in the Third World are either biased or uninformed (or both), that they are too few, that they are too bound by traditional Western news values, that they are blinded to Third World developmental concerns, and that they are too warped in their reporting by extreme anticommunism and by suspicions that the Third World generally is not really "nonaligned."

What the Third World Wants

So, briefly, what the Third World seems to want from Western journalism is this: (1) a kind of "balanced" flow of news in and out of the Third World; (2) more thorough, incisive, and unbiased news coverage of their countries on a continuing basis, and (3) more emphasis on "good" or positive news of the Third World, including what has come to be called "development" news.

Western journalists readily admit that there is some truth in the indictments of the Western press. Certainly there *is* an unevenness in news flow among nations—but, say Western journalists, this is also true of news flow *within* individual countries. And, certainly, much international coverage can be said to contain bias—but, *all* reporting can be so indicted. Also, what the Third World means by development news is really not considered particularly newsworthy by Western standards—or, it may be said, that the Western concept of news would include *all* news in the concept of development of the nation—not just that dealing with obvious construction, educational innovations, scientific achievements, and the like.

To Western journalists it is naive to expect the world to have a balanced flow of news. News simply does not flow evenly—for example, there is not as much news flowing from South America to Europe as from Europe to South America, or as much flowing from the northern Mexican town of Saltillo to Mexico City as the other way around. Who can talk of a "balance of news flow" in the real world? We do not have any balance in news flow even within a single country, so certainly we cannot expect to have it in the whole world. . . .

Flow of news is related to supply, consumers, and producers. News, like oil, flows mainly from where the supply is greatest; also it flows from where there are more workers "drilling" for it; and finally, it flows mainly to places where consumers seem to demand it. If, for instance, the Third World begins to be a producer of a news product desired by the West, then and only then will the news flow tend to become more balanced. At present this is not the case: the West is simply not interested in the more routine news of the Third World. . . . (It might be noted here that several researchers have found that one Third World country is not interested in development news of another Third World country.)

Also, it should be said that the Third World nations can help the flow imbalance by not relying so heavily on the Western agencies; they can do more to develop their own news organizations; they can cooperate in Third World news pools to a greater extent; and, if they really feel so antagonistic toward Western news agencies, they can stop using the agency material altogether.

The Third World also wants Western journalism to be "unbiased" and to present news on a "continuing" basis, eliminating the "piecemeal," sporadic nature of news coverage. This, of course, is a worthy goal for any journalism, but it is unrealistic in practice. And, certainly the existence of such news does not indicate any Western prejudice against the Third World. News is *always* piecemeal and biased as to reality, and is so because of *somebody's* perspective. A journalist—in *any* society—selects what will be news and fashions it according to his value system; this works within the United States and it works with news agency correspondents who report news internationally. Since journalistic decisions are strained through the journalist's subjectivity, it is safe to say that all news is biased in some way—unfaithful to reality and manipulated by journalistic judgment. It is unreasonable for the Third World nations—or any nations—to expect otherwise. There is certainly no proof that Western journalism maliciously and with premeditation biases news stories against Third World countries. . . .

Then, there is the indictment of Western news agencies for not presenting enough positive or "good" news of the Third World. First, what do the critics mean when they talk of not "enough" news of the Third World? How much is enough, and who is to decide this quantity? As long as the Western agencies are operating in a free-enterprise system and are doing the collecting and transmitting, they are the ones who will make these decisions. It is not reasonable for anyone to think otherwise.

It may well be true that much (or even *most*) of the news emanating from the Third World has a "negative" character, but this can also be said (and *is* said) of news flowing within Western countries themselves. Certainly, the news agencies do not seem to play favorites in this respect. . . .

And What About Third World Editors?

Third World editors who are critical of the West for the above practices themselves have basically the same values and do the same things. In selecting and printing stories, they generally agree with the Western concept of news (if they exercise any real freedom of editorial determination), for it is easy to see in their papers reflections of the same negative and sensational news—generally about *other* (usually Western) countries, of course. . . .

Of course, the editors may complain that through the years they have been "brainwashed" by the Western concept of news (or have studied journalism in the West); this, perhaps is to some extent true, but it seems clear that at least part of the blame lies with those who allow themselves to be brainwashed. And, certainly, no foreign journalist is coerced into studying journalism in the West.

However reluctant the editors in the Third World are to face it, they bear some responsibility. For example, the Western agencies send many stories about Third World countries. Surely, many Third World editors get more such stories than are used. In fact, the editors admit that few of these are used. Why? There are two general answers: (1) the stories are not written to suit the editors, and (2) the readers are simply not interested in such stories from other Third World countries. So, it seems that Third World editors themselves do not really have a dedication to presenting other Third World news in their papers. . . .

This whole matter of news flow is a tough one. Undoubtedly it will be one of the world's basic journalistic issues for a long time. For as long as countries go their different ideological ways, these differences will be reflected in their journalistic philosophies and systems.

NOTES

1. The terms "West" and "Western journalism" are used in this article to refer to the capitalistic industrialized nations of Western Europe and North America (and Japan); the journalism of this group of nations is contrasted to that of the Third World (developing, nonaligned, new) nations, some of which are certainly in the West. The West in this article is also contrasted with Communist nations such as the U.S.S.R., China, and Cuba, although the last-named is geographically part of the West.
2. It is indeed strange that the Third World and Unesco have little or no criticism for the journalism of the Communist world; evidently the news flow to and from these countries is satisfactory—balanced and free.

37B.* GENESIS OF THE FREE FLOW
OF INFORMATION PRINCIPLES

Herbert I. Schiller

... New communications technology—computers, space satellites, television—combined with a powerful and expanding corporate business system, assisted the push of the United States into the center of the world economy.

Without public pronouncements, private, American-made media products and U.S. informational networks blanketed the world. Especially prominent were films produced more and more frequently outside the country,[1] the exportation of commercial television programs,[2] and international distribution of North American magazines and other periodicals. *Reader's Digest, Time, Newsweek, Playboy,* and Walt Disney Corporation productions reached millions of viewers and readers outside the United States. Moreover, foreign book-publishing firms disappeared into U.S. "leisure time" conglomerates. Along with these more or less conventional media penetrations, a variety of additional informational activities accompanied the global surge of private American capital. Foremost, perhaps, was the extension of the opinion poll and consumer survey, now undertaken all over the world, often under the auspices of American-owned research companies.[3]

Largely as a reaction to the flood of American cultural material and the usurpation of national media systems that were required to disseminate it, a new mood with respect to the doctrine of free flow of information became observable in the international community in the late 1960s and early 1970s. Besides the free-flow view, one began to see frequent references to cultural sovereignty, cultural privacy, cultural autonomy, and even admissions of the possibility of cultural imperialism.[4]

Another factor that perhaps is contributing to the shift of emphasis, outside the United States, away from the *quantity* to the *consequences* of free flow of information is the changed nature of the international community itself. Since 1945, more than ninety new national entities, most of them still in an early stage of economic development, have emerged to take their places in

---

* See Chapter 37A Editor's Note, p. 338.

Reprinted from *Crisis in International News*, edited by Jim Richstad and Michael H. Anderson by permission of Columbia University Press. Copyright © 1981 by Columbia University Press.

the community of nations. A paramount concern of these states is to safeguard their national and cultural sovereignty. Then, too, the results of two decades of *de facto* free flow of information have not gone unremarked. It is difficult, in fact, to escape the global spread of U.S. cultural styles featured in the mass media of films, television programs, pop records, and slick magazines. Their influence prompts sentiments such as that expressed by the Prime Minister of Guyana: "A nation whose mass media are dominated from the outside is not a nation." [5]. . .

Finally, the possibility of direct satellite broadcasting from space into home sets without the mediation of nationally controlled ground stations, whether or not likely in the immediate future, has created a sense of urgency concerning the question of cultural sovereignty. This has been especially observable in the United Nations.

The Working Group on Direct Broadcast Satellites was established in 1969 "to consider mainly the technical feasibility of direct broadcasting from satellites." [6] It has met more or less regularly since that time, extending its range from the technical aspects to the social, legal, and political implications of direct satellite broadcasting.

Moreover, Unesco, the strongest advocate of the free-flow doctrine at one time, has veered noticeably away from its formerly unquestioning support. In its "Declaration of Guiding Principles on the Use of Satellite Broadcasting for the Free Flow of Information," adopted in October 1972, Unesco acknowledged that "it is necessary that States, taking into account the principle of freedom of information, reach or promote prior agreements concerning direct satellite broadcasting to the population of countries other than the country of origin of the transmission." [7] The U.N. General Assembly supported this view in November 1972, by a vote of 102 to 1—the United States casting the single dissenting vote.

Reactions in the private communications sector in the United States were predictably hostile and self-serving. Frank Stanton, one of the most influential American media controllers in the era of U.S. informational hegemony, wrote: "the rights of Americans to speak to whomever they please, when they please are [being] bartered away." [8] His chief objection to the Unesco document, he claimed, was that censorship was being imposed by provisions that permitted each nation to reach prior agreement with transmitting nations concerning the character of the broadcasts.

Stanton, along with a good part of the media's managers (including the prestigious *New York Times*), finds the right of nations to control the character of the messages transmitted into their territories both dangerous and a gross violation of the U.S. Constitution's provision concerning freedom of speech: "The rights which form the framework of our Constitution, the principles asserted in the Universal Declaration of Human Rights, the basic principle of the free movement of ideas, are thus ignored." [9]

Along with the hubris displayed in regarding the U.S. Constitution applicable to, and binding law for, the entire international community is a second, even more questionable, consideration. Stanton and those in agreement with him matter-of-factly assume that the United States' constitutional guarantee of freedom of speech to the *individual* is applicable to the multinational corporations and media conglomerates whose interests they so strongly espouse. Yet more than a generation ago, Earl L. Vance[10] asked, "Is freedom of the press to be conceived as a *personal* right appertaining to all citizens, as undoubtedly the Founding Fathers conceived it; or as a *property* right appertaining to the ownership of newspapers and other publications, as we have come to think of it largely today?"

Stanton et al. extend the *property*-right concept of freedom of speech to all the advanced electronic forms of communication and expect universal acquiescence in their interpretation. But the national power behind this view is no longer as absolute or as fearsome as it was in 1945. . . .

To be sure, the United States and its closest allies (and competitors) still emphasize the free-flow doctrine as the basis for peace and international security. The Helsinki Conference on Security and Cooperation in Europe, begun in mid-1973 and concluded in July 1975, made this very clear. In its preliminary consultations, the conference was instructed to "prepare proposals to facilitate the freer and wider dissemination of information of all kinds." [11] And it was this issue to which the Western delegates gave their greatest attention, seeking to make all other decisions contingent on a resolution of the free-flow question acceptable to themselves. . . .

But despite the insistence of most of the political and economic leaders of Western, industrialized, market economies on the continued importance of an unalloyed free-flow doctrine, alternate formulations are appearing. One was contained in the speech of Finland's president Urho Kekkonen, before a communications symposium in May 1973. Kekkonen, in a comprehensive review of the fundamental premises of international communications, singled out the free-flow doctrine for his scrutiny:

> When the Declaration of Human Rights was drawn up after the Second World War, the Nineteenth Century liberal view of the world in the spirit of the ideas of Adam Smith and John Stuart Mill was the guideline. Freedom of action and enterprise—laissez-faire—was made the supreme value in the world of business and ideology, irrespective of at whose expense success in this world was achieved. The State gave everyone the possibility to function, but did not carry the responsibility for the consequences. So the freedom of the strong led to success and the weak went under in spite of this so-called liberty. This was the result regardless of which of them advocated a more just policy for society and mankind.

Kekkonen applied this general perspective to international communication and the free-flow doctrine. He noted:

> At an international level are to be found the ideals of free communication and their actual distorted execution for the rich on the one hand and the poor on the other. Globally, the flow of information between States—not least the material pumped out by television—is to a very great extent a one-way, unbalanced traffic, and in no way possesses the depth and range which the principles of freedom of speech require.

These observations led Kekkonen to inquire: "Could it be that the prophets who preach unhindered communication are not concerned with equality between nations, but are on the side of the stronger and the wealthier?" He remarked also that international organizations were in fact moving away from their original advocacy of the free-flow doctrine:

> My observations would indicate that the United Nations and ... Unesco have in the last few years reduced their declarations on behalf of an abstract freedom of speech. Instead, they have moved in the direction of planing down the lack of balance in international communications.

From all this, Kekkonen concluded: "a mere liberalistic freedom of communication is not in everyday reality a neutral idea, but a way in which an enterprise with many resources at its disposal has greater opportunities than weaker brethren to make its own hegemony accepted." [12]

Kekkonen's analysis is, in fact, the general conclusion, however long overdue, that is beginning to emerge with respect to *all* international and domestic relationships—not just those concerned with communications. When there is an uneven distribution of power among individuals or groups *within* nations or *among* nations, a free hand—freedom to continue doing what led to the existing condition—serves to strengthen the already powerful and weaken further the already frail. Evidence of this abounds in all aspects of modern life—in race, sex, and occupational and international relationships. Freedoms that are formally impressive may be substantively oppressive when they reinforce prevailing inequalities while claiming to provide generalized opportunity for all.

Not surprisingly, individuals, groups, and nations increasingly are seeking means to limit the freedom to maintain inequality. Measures aimed at regulating "the free flow of information" are best understood from this perspective.

NOTES

1. Thomas Guback. *The International Film Industry* (Bloomington, Ind.: Indiana University Press, 1969).
2. Kaarle Nordenstreng and Tapio Varis, *Television Traffic—A One-Way Street?* Reports and Papers on Mass Communication, no. 70 (Paris: Unesco, 1974).
3. Herbert I. Schiller. *The Mind Managers* (Boston: Beacon Press, 1973).
4. Ibid.
5. *Intermedia* (1973), 3:1.
6. *Report of the Working Group on Direct Broadcast Satellites of the Work of Its Fourth Session,* A/AC. 105/117 (New York: United Nations, 22 June 1973), annex 1, p. 1.
7. Unesco Declaration of Guiding Principles on the Use of Satellite Broadcasting for the Free Flow of Information, Spread of Education and Greater Cultural Exchange, document A/AC. 105/109, 1972 (mimeographed).
8. Frank Stanton, "Will They Stop Our Satellites?" *New York Times,* October 22, 1972, pp. 23, 39.
9. Ibid.
10. Earl L. Vance, "Freedom of the Press for Whom?" *Virginia Quarterly Review,* (Summer, 1945), 21:340-54.

11. *Final Recommendations of the Helsinki Consultations* (Helsinki: Government of Finland, 1973), p. 15.
12. Urho Kekkonen, "The Free Flow of Information: Towards a Reconsideration of National and International Communication Policies," address before Symposium on the International Flow of Television Programs, University of Tampere, Tampere, Finland, May 21, 1973.